Come Back in September

Come Back in September

——— A LITERARY EDUCATION ON ———
WEST SIXTY-SEVENTH STREET, MANHATTAN

Darryl Pinckney

Farrar, Straus and Giroux

New York

Farrar, Straus and Giroux
120 Broadway, New York 10271

Printed in the United States of America
First edition, 2022

Grateful acknowledgment is made for permission to
reprint the following material:
Lines from "But sometimes everything I write," "Dunbarton,"
"Man and Wife," and "Waking Early Sunday Morning" from
Collected Poems by Robert Lowell. Copyright © 2003 by
Harriet Lowell and Sheridan Lowell. Reprinted by
permission of Farrar, Straus and Giroux.
"Christ, / May I die at night" (unpublished version) by
Robert Lowell. Copyright © 2022 by Harriet Lowell and
Sheridan Lowell. Printed by permission of Farrar, Straus
and Giroux on behalf of the Robert Lowell Estate.

Library of Congress Cataloging-in-Publication Data
Names: Pinckney, Darryl, 1953– author.
Title: Come back in September : a literary education on West
Sixty-seventh Street, Manhattan / Darryl Pinckney.
Description: First edition. | New York : Farrar, Straus and Giroux, 2022.
Identifiers: LCCN 2022023644 | ISBN 9780374126650 (hardcover)
Subjects: LCSH: Pinckney, Darryl, 1953– | Pinckney, Darryl, 1953-–
Friends and associates. | Hardwick, Elizabeth. | Epstein, Barbara,
1928–2006. | Authors, American—20th century—Biography. | New York
(N.Y.)—Intellectual life—20th century. | New York (N.Y.)—Biography.
Classification: LCC PS3566.I516 Z46 2022 | DDC 818/.5403 [B]—
dc23/eng/20220720
LC record available at https://lccn.loc.gov/2022023644

Our books may be purchased in bulk for promotional, educational,
or business use. Please contact your local bookseller or the Macmillan
Corporate and Premium Sales Department at 1-800-221-7945, extension
5442, or by email at MacmillanSpecialMarkets@macmillan.com.

www.fsgbooks.com
www.twitter.com/fsgbooks • www.facebook.com/fsgbooks

1 3 5 7 9 10 8 6 4 2

In memory of Barbara Epstein

I'm here on the edge of metamorphosis.

—Aimé Césaire

—— Part 1 ——

I made Elizabeth Hardwick laugh when I applied late to get into her creative writing class at Barnard College in the autumn of 1973. Not only could I, a black guy from Columbia across the street, rattle off a couple of middle-period Sylvia Plath poems when she asked me what I was reading—Blacklakeblackboattwoblack cutpaperpeople—I told her that my roommate said we would kidnap her daughter, Harriet, if she didn't let me into the class. His sister was her daughter's best friend. I'd met her at a party of his Dalton School friends. I was in.

> *Where do the black trees go that drink here?*
> *Their shadows must cover Canada.*

I walked her to the subway at 116th Street and Broadway. Plath had come around once for her husband's class when they lived in Boston. Professor Hardwick remembered her as almost docile, nothing like the poems that would make her famous.

Professor Hardwick was fresh and put together. Her soft appearance made the tough things she said even funnier. In her walk, she rocked gently, from side to side. She was on the job, in a short black leather coat and green print scarf, carrying a stiff leather satchel with short handles just wide enough for a certain number of student manuscripts. I hadn't yet seen her bound up from a chair and break free, flinging over her silk shoulder a silver evening bag on its chain, saying to an astonished table of graduate students and free spirits who'd just agreed among themselves that poetry was everywhere,

—I'm sure you're very nice, but I can't bear that kind of talk.

And then dancing away from their party because she'd rather be at home looking forward to Saturday night delivery of the Sunday *New York Times*.

At our first official teacher-student conference in dingy Barnard Hall, I made Professor Hardwick laugh again, because I recited the last paragraph of Lillian Hellman's memoir *An Unfinished Woman*:

> Although I do have a passing sadness for the self-made foolishness that was, is, and will be . . .

—That fraud, Professor Hardwick said. She tried to do everything but have me killed.

Six years earlier there had been a Mike Nichols revival of Hellman's play *The Little Foxes* at Lincoln Center, and she, Hardwick, had reviewed it for *The New York Review of Books*, calling it awkward, didactic, and full of cliché. She didn't believe in the South as an idea, she said.

—Her use of black people, she said. You would die.

Agrarianism was a bore. Had I read Allen Tate? A poet I'd never heard of.

—You don't need him. Faulkner?

The Bear.

—You do need him. But don't ever do that again.

—Excuse me?

—Read Lillian. People were cutting me on the street. She got people to write letters. She told them, I'm not used to being attacked by someone who has been a guest in my house. I made up my mind that I didn't care if I never went to another dinner party at Lillian's. Dashiell Hammett was always trying to get away from her, for Patricia Neal.

I was discovering so much: Rimbaud, Frank O'Hara, Baldwin's essays, Gertrude Stein's autobiography. Every day, from hour to hour, there was something new, a name to put on my list of names to reckon with. One afternoon I walked by an open door and a guy with long blond hair was at his upright, preparing to play. The music had poignance and a couple of other people also paused. My mother loved the piano, but I had never heard of Erik Satie. Friends and professors had a lot to tell me.

Soon I would commit to memory passages from 'Writing a Novel,' the opening chapter of a novel that Professor Hardwick was writing, *The Cost of Living*. The opening had recently been published in the tenth-anniversary issue of *The New York Review of Books*.

I first learned of Harriet's father, Robert Lowell, from his introduction to Plath's *Ariel*. And I'd read his latest collection, *The Dolphin*.

I can't in my memory figure out how it happened. It happened so fast. I quoted from that first chapter of her novel *The Cost of Living*, a letter that the first-person narrator begins after suggesting that the reader

> Think of yourself as if you were in Apollinaire's poem:
>
> *Here you are in Marseille, surrounded by watermelons.*
> *Here you are in Coblenz at the Hotel du Géant.*
> *Here you are in Rome sitting under a Japanese medlar tree.*
> *Here you are in Amsterdam . . .*
>
> Dearest M: Here I am in Boston, on Marlborough Street,
> number 239. I am looking out on a snow storm. It fell
> like a great armistice, bringing all struggles to an end.

It is a beautiful moment. She didn't want to hear herself quoted, but she couldn't help remembering the pleasure of a technical problem, the transition, solved, just like that.

—I found that and I knew it would work. Nothing is worse than a transition.

The letters to M were written as part of something for *Vogue*, she explained. She had suddenly asked for them back, the letters addressed to M, even though she didn't know what she wanted to save them for.

It happened so fast. My going from that letter and saying how good she was at letters to pointing to another example, a letter of hers quoted in a poem in *The Dolphin*:

> *You can't carry your talent with you like a suitcase.*
> *Don't you dare mail us the love your life denies.*

I stopped talking. She reached for her purse. I was saying something as I got up and she said into the tissue that I was to stay. No, I was sorry. So very sorry. I to this day do not know why I did that, how I could have done that, been so unthinking and carried away. Her tears had appeared and then were gone.

—I didn't write that, she said. Cal used my letters. I don't think that's so good.

She meant those lines.

What I trust of my memory of that conference stops here. I don't remember how much more she went on to tell me that afternoon about *The Dolphin*, or even if she did say anything more about it then. I sort of think not.

She never held my impertinence against me, my blunder about that book of poems. What happened to the letters she wrote to Lowell when he left and then divorced her was a question that gnawed at her down through the many years in which I knew her, the injustice of having words supposed to be from her letters fitted into those gone-husband's sonnets. *The Dolphin* had come out in July, yet I was unaware of what a trial its publication had been, and still was, for her. Harriet and her friends hadn't spoken of it around me.

We'd ventured into an education of sympathies. I'd become Hardwick's student when I got into her class, but that afternoon

I signed up for the journey and understood that I should listen in a whole new way. 'You cannot learn unless you fall in love with the source of learning,' Alfred North Whitehead said. Yes, another classic I would find, this one in Hardwick's shelves not entirely empty of Lowell's books in the stylish old apartment where she and Harriet had learned to live without him on West Sixty-seventh Street, just a couple of doors in from Central Park.

I NEVER HEARD Elizabeth Hardwick say, 'I took a walk in the park.' What she wanted when she went out were shops, sidewalks, traffic, to be among strangers on Main Street, the small-town girl's dream. Yet she liked to remember the sound of the great anti–Vietnam War rallies booming down West Sixty-seventh Street from Central Park. Sometimes she sat in her dining room window and listened, she said, not really expecting the noise to become intelligible, but able to feel in the echo excited youth's will to resist death.

(She wrote about it somewhere. Where? I'm forgetting what I've read. Maybe that is why I want to write this now.)

Professor Hardwick was full of admiration for the way Hannah Arendt could footnote from memory passages of Aristotle that she cited in *Between Past and Future*.

(Have I the right ancient? The right Arendt title?

—Yes, but it was always the same passage she quoted no matter what she was writing, Isaiah Berlin would say.)

Professor Hardwick praised Nadezhda Mandelstam for committing to memory her husband's endangered and dangerous poetry.

Explain Frances Yates to me, I might have asked. But not of Professor Hardwick. Frances A. Yates, English historian, a pure scholar whom the subject of magic ran away with, and hero to Barbara Epstein, co-editor of *The New York Review of Books*. They were friends, Elizabeth Hardwick and Barbara Epstein, close friends. They were also neighbors on West Sixty-seventh Street. Barbara lived a few doors west, toward Columbus Avenue. Their apartments were even of the same design, built at the turn of the twentieth century as studio dwellings for artists, in brick buildings of reasonable size with limestone fronts at street level.

Fourteen floors and three apartments per floor. You stepped across the threshold into a tiny entrance, beyond which lay a two-story room, the atelier itself, converted into the living room. The front door looked across some distance to a fireplace. An enormous segmented window that reached almost to the ceiling took up the central wall, the north wall, admitting the artist's light. The dining room and kitchen were darkly off this one huge room. Facing south, the stairs started close by the front door and led first to a balcony that overlooked the main room and then to bedrooms beyond.

—It's like a stage set, Professor Hardwick once said. There's nothing else.

She meant that the living room was imposing, but the rooms in the rest of the apartment were modest in scale.

(Explain Frances Yates to me. What is actually between those columns she said the Romans made visual in their minds when they were learning orations? But I don't remember asking Barbara the question, either.

I live with a poet, a former classicist.

—It's Cicero, James Fenton said. Imagine the rooms of a house and make a tour of that house in your mind and attach your arguments to objects in the rooms as you go. The book by Frances Yates is called *The Art of Memory*. We have it, he, my poet, said. You can look it up.

I must be willing to get up from my unsuitable swivel chair and look at some books if I am going to try to describe the spell cast by these unrepeatable women. I don't want to make up things. Unless the writer has to, I am on the verge of pretending Elizabeth Hardwick said. Not if it's supposed to be true, I am as willing to have Barbara Epstein say.)

I'm sure I walked the fifty blocks from Morningside Heights to

West Sixty-seventh Street, the first time I went to Professor Hard-wick's house on my own, without the class. She held our last class of the semester in her big living room with the deep red velvet sofa and gilded mirrors and grandfather clock with a yellow moon as its face. That large, not exactly beautiful painting of a dark horse on a red bridge over the entrance to the dining room was by Harriet's godfather, Frank Parker, her father's prep school classmate. My fellow aspirants included Daphne Merkin and Tama Janowitz. Professor Hardwick told us that there were really only two reasons to write: desperation or revenge. She told us that if we couldn't take rejection, if we couldn't be told no, then we could not be writers. The tone she took with us in class was just to get us ready, we assumed.

—I'd rather shoot myself than read that again.

That writing could not be taught was clear from the way she shrugged her shoulder and lifted her beautiful eyes after this or that student effort.

—I don't know why it is we can read Dostoevsky and then go back and write like idiots.

But a passion for reading could be shared, week after week. The only way to learn to write was to read. She brought in Boris Pasternak's *Safe Conduct*, translated by Beatrice Scott. She said she hated to do something so pre-Gutenberg and then proceeded to read to us in a voice that was surprisingly high, loud, and suddenly very Southern:

> The beginning of April surprised Moscow in the white stupor of returning winter. On the seventh it began to thaw for the second time, and on the fourteenth when Mayakovsky shot himself, not everyone had become accustomed to the novelty of spring.

When she got to Pasternak's line about 'the black velvet of the talent' in Mayakovsky, she threw herself back in her chair, light brownish layers of hair answering. Either we got it or we didn't, but it was clear from the way she struck her breastbone that, for her, to get it was the gift of life.

We had a good time in that class. I tried to get some of us together one more time for a Suicide Party on the eleventh anniversary of Plath's death, complete with séance. Professor Hardwick said she agreed with Virginia Woolf about the importance of reading poetry before you began working. She had stressed in class how freeing of the mind it could be to read poetry before you wrote prose. Something that had nothing to do with what you were about to do but that somehow opened up the possibilities of language in your head. Then, suddenly, in the middle of the spring semester, shortly after Luc Sante (as Lucy Sante was then, long before she transitioned) and I had taken over *The Columbia Review*, the moribund campus literary magazine, Professor Hardwick summoned me for dinner on West Sixty-seventh Street.

I knew what it was about. I walked across College Walk to Broadway—Amsterdam Avenue did not hold the same interest—and then down to Seventy-second Street. I had to be told every time I went by the Dakota that that dark, forbidding building was where they'd shot the film *Rosemary's Baby*. I headed down Central Park West, home to some of the most famous liberals in the city, to West Sixty-seventh Street. No. 1 meant the black doors of an apartment building, the Hotel des Artistes, a very glamorous address. Professor Hardwick was next door, the entrance of her building a neo-Gothic embellishment of spires. You entered the street doors and as you waited for the doorman to answer the bell to the inner doors up a few steps, you could see three painted panels in the gray stone of the narrow lobby. I can't remember what they depict.

—Burne-Jones, Professor Hardwick said she once heard someone on the street say of them. It made her laugh. She said,

—I thought, Come again?

I was late. Harriet made coffee and retired. I knew what this conference was about. I had on lots of sweaters and so did Professor

Hardwick. She wore as usual her necklace of large amber pieces that she toyed with when she talked to you on the red sofa. Until her fist came down into the cushion. Though our class with her had ended, I'd asked her to read my manuscript of poems. Unfortunately, I can remember even now what title I gave the manuscript and what the poems were like. Harriet was upstairs. Professor Hardwick went stanza by stanza. She scolded, winced, and deplored.

She said, among other things, —You're the worst poet I've ever read. You mustn't write poetry anymore.

I didn't destroy the manuscript. Not right away. And I didn't heed her warning. Not right away. Alas, I would have some new poems that I wanted to lob in the path of a superbly indifferent guy by way of the campus literary magazine. Those poems had not been included in the special edition of said manuscript that I'd given to my mother for Christmas. My mother duly put that gift away in some unknown place. After my parents died, I realized how much I'd longed for them to die so I could find and burn that only existing copy of . . .

She showed me the notations Lowell made in his copy of the first English edition of *Ariel*.

—He didn't know what she meant.

Apparently, to judge from the marks, he was quite taken and surprised. It had appeared out of the blue, she said, from England.

(*Ariel* was published in 1965.)

—We couldn't get over it.

Professor Hardwick let me stay and stay. She made dinner that night, the night she told me that I wrote too much poetry and maybe I should try not writing any. It was a Saturday, not Sunday. Dinner on Sunday became our regular appointment and my mother stopped phoning to thank her for feeding me. But this was a Saturday. I was having Scotch with ice that night. What could I have been thinking? I never drank Scotch.

A Winslow cousin of Lowell's, Devereux Meade, who lived in

the building, joined us. Devie was a graduate student. The Elizabethans. Sir Thomas Wyatt told me that love in Kenneth Koch's Poetry and Form class was no different from love at the Tudor court. I'm sure I was completely drunk. I can hear myself screaming along:

And softly said, 'Dear heart, how like you this?'

We were in the dining room. A very dark chandelier of carved wood hung down low over the table. Crimson wallpaper and white trim. Everything in the dining room was dark, the sideboard, the chairs, the end tables, the glass cabinets. These were old Mrs. Lowell's things, the plates, the china, the silver.

I would come sit at that dining room table of reddish wood for years, decades. She was not a good cook. Recipes, from friends, turned oily or shrank as she spooned juice, with slow shakes of her head that conveyed her doubts, over whatever was drying out in the baking dish. But she had unlimited amounts of Mouton Cadet, red and white, from a secret connection.

O Rose.

Devie, the graduate-student cousin, got Jonathan Swift and Ben Jonson down from the shelves. She spread a book flat in her left hand and let out smoke and waved her cigarette and touched the neck of her blouse or the edges of her sweater as she delighted in the beauty of this line or the subtlety of that meaning, intoning in her soft, sparkling voice.

Go, go, go, seek some other where; importune me no more

Professor Hardwick fetched her Greatest Hits, as she called Marlowe, Chaucer, and Donne, while Devie followed, turning pages.

I was insisting on 'To His Coy Mistress' one moment, then 'Ode to a Nightingale' the next, whatever came into my head, like a party piece. Professor Hardwick said she didn't understand Keats, laughed, caught Harriet by her hand, and kissed it.

—Isn't this fun?

The bookshelves on either side of her living room soared. Ladders attached to the top rail rolled from the poetry section that started low on one end above the phonograph table to the thick volumes of *The Rise of the Dutch Republic* that Lowell had left behind high up on the other end. Opposite was all fiction. Harriet cleared plates.

—Isn't she dear? God has been so good to me.

Professor Hardwick had had a tender reaction to my appreciation of Randall Jarrell the previous semester. Even Luc Sante was impressed by his essay on Walt Whitman. She said Jarrell's friends suspected that the troubled poet and critic deliberately put himself in the path of the car that killed him down in Chapel Hill in 1965.

> *Let Randall rest, whom your self-torturing*
> *cannot restore one instant's good to, rest . . .*

So on to another one of her recommendations I'd got from the library though she of course had it in her shelves: Which was she in Philip Rahv's scheme of high vs. popular literature, Paleface or Redskin? Stunned by Rahv's news that Henry James and Whitman could not abide with each other, that they, closet case and bear, represented irreconcilable traditions, I meant to stick to the high road when talking about Philip Rahv, engaged critic and editor of *Partisan Review* when Elizabeth Hardwick was starting out as a writer in the 1940s. But it was she who stepped off into the personal, sighing over how unhappy he'd been in his last years.

—Poor Philip.

—*Dying is an art.*

Professor Hardwick slammed her glass on the table.

—I hate that line. Dying is not an art.

It all seems to belong to this one night, denouncing Plath and showing, at my insistence, photographs of Cal, —Mr. Lowell, as I said like some darky or family retainer. Across from the red sofa, against the wall between the entrance to the dining room and a narrow passage that led to the kitchen, on top of a broad wooden desk, a Cartier-Bresson of a young Harriet on her father's shoulders.

—He's gorgeous, Harriet.

We weren't drunk; we were enchanted, and I was swaying in the door and trying to say

Mothers of America let your children go to the movies!

as my good night.

The New York School was all tone and John Ashbery was the undisputed master of it, Professor Hardwick said, but she liked Frank O'Hara for his speed and sharpness. We'd forgot to ring for the elevator.

Allen Ginsberg with his harmonium, chanting for peace at the Sundial on campus, let you know that you were in the right place. Over here is where Jack Kerouac smiled. Every week your idols were reading downtown in the East Village at the St. Mark's Poetry Project. Most of David Shapiro's class would turn up. As a professor, Shapiro was scarcely older than his students. His photograph appeared in *Life* magazine in 1968 showing him smoking a cigar in the president's chair during the student takeover at Columbia. (Lucy told me not long ago that the pose copied a scene from Eisenstein.) Shapiro invited us everywhere and showed us everything. I told John Ashbery I was born in Boston on Pinckney Street. (I could put that in a self-forgiving context: Drunk as Hart Crane about to jump overboard, I . . .)

We chose 'Prufrock' over *The Waste Land*. Why? And although Ginsberg would give a public reading with Lowell (I heard the literary critic Morris Dickstein say that reading the Beats got Lowell to relax his verse), there was no question that Thomas Stearns Eliot and Robert Traill Spence Lowell were the establishment and they, gay and straight sons of Wallace Stevens, William Carlos Williams, and French literature, not the classics, were free. But I'd finally read

The Armies of the Night. Robert Lowell was the nation's conscience, our poet laureate, the successor to Robert Frost. He had been on the cover of *Time* magazine. I'd also by this time gone through *Life Studies*, the volume that unreadable books on American poetry said had inaugurated the confessional school. I kept to myself my guilty feeling about his poem 'Man and Wife.' I shouldn't be eavesdropping; I shouldn't find in his example so much permission to be a mess.

> *. . . still all air and nerve:*
> *you were in your twenties, and I,*
> *once hand on glass*
> *and heart in mouth,*
> *outdrank the Rahvs in the heat*
> *of Greenwich Village, fainting at your feet—*
> *too boiled and shy*
> *and poker-faced to make a pass,*
> *while the shrill verve*
> *of your invective scorched the traditional South.*

WHEN I SAW her again, Professor Hardwick had rolled down to Rio, was writing about Lévi-Strauss, and Thomas Pynchon had been denied the Pulitzer Prize by the Pulitzer's board, though *Gravity's Rainbow* was the choice of the critics' jury, of which she had been one. She was not in the mood to find it ironic that both she and Nixon had attacked the Pulitzer's board.

(*Gravity's Rainbow* was a book I wanted to be seen with, but I took my time before I opened it.

—What are you waiting for. It's funny.

She was immediately curious about what found its way into her hands. Even a bad book told her something. She stuck with most everything to the end, for hours, though a few books she was relieved to have an excuse not to finish. She stayed away from academic criticism, theory, analytical philosophy.)

I'd seen Barbara Epstein for the second time, this time in the chaotic offices of *The New York Review of Books*. They were on the fourteenth (thirteenth?) floor in the faintly ratty Fisk Building, on the corner of West Fifty-seventh Street and Broadway. A girl I'd become friends with when she was Professor Hardwick's lodger worked there in the charged silence. One evening a petite figure, Barbara Epstein, crossed the main room to her office. She advanced chin-first. She wore black pants. She carried papers and was chewing gum. She'd quit smoking, it was whispered. One story had Robert Silvers setting fire to the hair of an editorial assistant who happened to lean over his desk just as he moved forward in his chair with his burning brown Sherman.

And *Seduction and Betrayal: Women and Literature* had been published, Professor Hardwick's first book in more than a decade. The dedication:

To my friend Barbara Epstein, with love

It would take me a while to understand this collection as an act of self-rescue. Divorce, a prism that rayed her understanding of being a woman, a state she and Barbara would talk from probably more than they talked about.

When I came over to say goodbye for the summer, Professor Hardwick and Harriet were dressed for a dinner Jason Epstein was giving for them.

—An old fox in the book publishing business, said in the dry voice Professor Hardwick used when she wanted you to know that she was quoting someone. She'd lower her head and raise her eyes at you to signal mischief.

He was her editor. He had a letter from Mary McCarthy about *Seduction and Betrayal* that Professor Hardwick was proud of. She was wearing her favorite pair of shoes, bought in Rome years before, burgundy suede heels with large rhinestone butterflies on the toes.

I'd brought as a present an album of late Billie Holiday recordings. On 'My Man,' Professor Hardwick grimaced and clutched her head. Then she was stricken with a pain in her chest.

—Like sandpaper or a bruise, she described it.

She was in such pain but refused to call a doctor or lie down.

—Why can't you lie down?

—I don't know why. I just can't. I can't explain it.

Hannah Arendt had just had a heart attack. The phone calls about it hadn't stopped.

—But I'm not sick. This is just a pain I'm having.

Harriet said she'd been traveling a lot recently and needed to slow down. Maybe she should pass on going out to that East Side restaurant. She made her mother call her doctor, Annie Baumann, who wasn't in. Everyone was frightened of Dr. Baumann, she said.

After a while, the pain subsided, and Professor Hardwick felt well enough to have a drink and laugh at the news about Watergate. I remember that Devie arrived, looking beautiful, and I put them in a taxi, saying that I'd miss them, thanking her for everything.

—Professor Hardwick. That's cute. I'm no more a professor than I am an M.D.

I'd seen those rhinestone-topped heels before. It must have been a month or so earlier. I could maybe find out from Ian Hamilton's biography of Lowell exactly when he was in New York in the spring of 1974, if I got up from this chair and went in search of it. But Professor Hardwick was wearing them the evening Robert Lowell came for a visit. They went with a purple skirt, heavy, odd, and floor length. It was finished in pennants, a hem of downward facing triangles.

Professor Hardwick was nervous. Harriet was cool. They had an argument about the SLA, the Symbionese Liberation Army. The daughter propped her feet up on the furniture and provoked the mother by using words like 'pig,' 'trash,' and 'waste them.' Harriet's best friend from the Dalton School was late, which made me nervous, because the atmosphere hinted that I was intruding. Where was Devie?

Robert Silvers's office called. Lowell had taken a later plane than expected and Professor Hardwick thought maybe I should come back when he wasn't so tired. Was he coming from Harvard? Then she decided I should stay and gave me another drink, trying to tell me what to expect.

—Well, he's mad. You'll see.

Harriet leapt to his defense.

Professor Hardwick returned with plates.

—Well, not mad, honey. I didn't mean he was . . . Yes I did. Papa's mad.

We listened for footsteps, for the elevator, and talked in short sentences.

I remember how he dropped his suitcases and zeroed in on Harriet, this large balding man with long white fringe, a father in thick glasses aiming his eyes at his daughter. He hugged her. He and Hardwick brushed hands. I don't remember if he ate. His leg is crossed high over his knee and he is fingering a glass of milk and muttering in the gathering dark in the direction he last saw Harriet sitting.

(I wish I'd written down more about that evening and that parts of what I did write down, like what he had said about Bacon, hadn't got destroyed. When the journals from your student days burn up and years later you open a sooty box of remains, the burned pages are the size and shape of Ping-Pong paddles. They are stiff, browned, flaking at the black edges. They still smell of that fire. I can see how many different handwritings I had.

James said, —This is why you're making up your idiom as you go.

Luc used to throw a strand of spaghetti against his wall. If it stuck, then it was ready. Friends used to read to friends. Jim, Phil, Suzanne, coming over with something that truly impressed them. One night, Luc read aloud in its entirety Elizabeth Hardwick's essay 'Memoirs, Conversations, Diaries,' from that early collection, *A View of My Own*:

> Dr. Johnson is treasured, but odium attaches to his giddy memorialist. Grateful as readers have always been for the book, they cannot imagine themselves stooping to this peculiar method of composition.

Luc was into it:

> There is no doubt that the diarist is the most egotistical of beings; he quite before our eyes ceases to take himself with that grain of salt which alone makes clever people bearable.

What Valéry said to Mallarmé; what Mallarmé's pipe smoke said to Valéry. Self-regarding Gide; Pepys, the amateur; De Quincey overawed by Wordsworth; the Goncourts freaking out that soft-boiled egg, Henry James.

'Gorky's reminiscences of Tolstoy—a masterpiece,' she said toward the end of her essay.)

I remember Lowell chiding Hardwick for not liking Ezra Pound. The Pound Question: whether to forgive his wartime fascism and was that in fact fascism or the early onslaught of madness. The answer divided along gender lines, as far as I could tell. On one side of Broadway, at Columbia, Kenneth Koch recommended Pound's *ABC of Reading* and David Shapiro excised *The Pisan Cantos* for us, like a big brother who'd removed a harmful thorn. On the other side of Broadway, however, at Barnard, where I read *The Golden Notebook* as if in secret with Catharine R. Stimpson in order to get away from so much grain-by-grain analysis of Beckett, Professor Hardwick was clear that Pound's poetry was just the randomness of

—a little old idea monger at a machine.

She said when Lowell went to see Pound at St. Elizabeth's in Washington, D.C., where he was confined after the war, she flatly refused to accompany him.

(In Italy, after Pound was arrested and transferred to Pisa, he was held in a cage and guarded by black soldiers. Or was it that he was the only white prisoner?)

One minute her butterflies were up on the coffee table while Lowell was a ways off, huddled over a photo album with the girls. The next minute Professor Hardwick was in her magic shoes, saying that she had to go to Barnard in the morning and he was going to Saratoga. She handed him his keys to the studio downstairs. They said good night and he made one last comment about her essay on Sylvia Plath, reprinted in *Seduction and Betrayal*.

—You've ruined Plath for everyone.

What if she were alive? Professor Hardwick in her essay on Plath made the effort to read the poems as if she'd failed to kill herself or had changed her mind:

> Her poems have, read differently, the overcharged pre-
> occupation with death and release found in religious
> poetry. For indeed she saw eternity the other night,
> also; she cries out *No end?* as Herbert does.

Professor Hardwick went upstairs, right hand on banister, inches of skirt balled in her left fingers.

Later, Mr. Lowell read to us some new poems about Harriet's half brother. Then I was carrying his bags downstairs, one floor below. I was saucy for a reaction to Babu, or Babo, depending on whether I was from Melville's short story 'Benito Cereno' or from Lowell's adaptation of it for the stage. The American captain boards the Spanish ship and doesn't realize that the unctuous black servant is actually the chief slave rebel. But Lowell knew perfectly well who I was.

COME SEPTEMBER, CLASSES were again in session. Life was new, a do-over, which meant that I was across the street from campus, back in a side booth in the West End Café. Luc and I had had a feud and hadn't written to each other all summer. But here we were, and the West End was our office. The drinking age was eighteen, and soon he was lamenting that by the time Rimbaud was his age he'd stopped writing.

I was reading Quentin Bell. The birds were speaking Greek. Bloomsbury was British, gay, and upper class, everything a black American queer could want. I worshipped Virginia Woolf, foolishly sent her into battle against Joyce, failed to get Strachey's humor, and didn't understand Keynes really or G. E. Moore at all. I had a professor who talked about Bloomsbury and androgyny, and that professor had lost me immediately. I liked my Bloomsbury butch-bewildered, with female sacrifices, like a Columbia senior seminar before the undergraduate college went coed. I found symbols, myth, masculine-feminine conflict, and a theory of latent class war inside the pleasure of *Howards End*. Professor Hardwick shocked me by suggesting that E. M. Forster could be read twice, but not a Virginia Woolf novel.

Meanwhile, I was deep into my own private suicide cult, reciting *The Waves* while up all night on clinical speed. My clacking tongue misremembered:

—Against thee I will fling myself O death!

English literature was one thing, the British themselves very much another.

—How revolting, Elizabeth Hardwick said when I confessed my reverence for Elizabeth II. She also had no interest in Bess of Hardwick, the Tudor widow who got richer with each dead husband.

She remembered a visit to the Eliots years ago. Mrs. Eliot asked,
—Now Elizabeth, would you like to see our bed?

For the most part, she found the British unbearable. They did
not like her. They did not get her.

—The feeling is richly reciprocated, she said.

She'd been unhappy at a London lunch, seated next to someone
who had no idea who she was and didn't care to find out.

—John Bayley was filthy. Absolutely filthy.

This was weird: to care about a snub didn't fit my idea of her,
she who faced down the woman Dashiell Hammett had been unable to stand up to.

In the West End Café, I could subject my completely straight
best friend Luc to performances of bits from Elizabeth Hardwick's
essays, the way an old dear back in my home state of Indiana after we'd shared two pitchers of vodka gimlets used to treat me to
extracts from Tennessee Williams or Somerset Maugham. From
Hardwick's essay on Bloomsbury:

> Certain peripheral names scratch the mind. To see the
> word 'Ottoline' on a page, in a letter, gives me the sense
> of continual defeat, as if I had gone to a party and found
> an enemy attending the bar.

The source of her dislike of upper-class Britishness, including
Bloomsbury, was probably obvious to her friends, but was not to
me. England meant Caroline Blackwood, the writer whom Lowell fell for in London in 1970. The woman he switched countries
for. Did Professor Hardwick suspect everyone she met over there?
Everyone in literary London had known about the affair that she,
the American wife, did not.

An abandoned stable of white brick stood across from Hardwick's kitchen and dining room windows on West Sixty-seventh
Street. Did horses go up ramps or in elevators? She said she hated

to think of Thoroughbreds raced to death, lashed with whips and kicked with spurs. She was from Lexington, Kentucky, but the bit in a horse's mouth seemed to her cruel.

Lowell gave her the name Old Campaigner. To call her Old Campaigner never failed to bring forth a smile. Maybe Lowell thought of that nickname for her because she and her father had held hands in front of the radio and cried the night in 1937 when Joe Louis lost to Max Schmeling.

> *Shall I say, I have gone at dusk through narrow streets*
> *And watched the smoke that rises from the pipes*

The whole campus was drunk. I heard my cousin leading the chant on Columbia's Law School Terrace laid over Amsterdam Avenue. I admired my cousin and felt myself a homo scandal to him, to his Talented Tenth fraternity, the whole black firmament of bright, gleaming male disdain.

> *Ali boma ye!*

It was definitely his voice. I'd never heard him so loudly, publicly soul brother. He lived in the law library. The champion, Muhammad Ali, had been triumphant in Kinshasa, regaining his crown.

High and Southern and sounding sinusy, like she needed to blow her nose; she would mind the bodily detail.

> *Is this the proud City? The scorner*
> *Which never would yield the ground?*
> *Which mocked at the coal-black Angel?*
> *The cup of despair goes round.*
> *Vainly she calls upon Michael*
> *(The white man's seraph was he),*
> *For Michael has fled from his tower*
> *To the Angel over the sea.*

I'd no idea Melville wrote poetry. School and refuge was West Sixty-seventh Street.

On a darkening Sunday evening a month or so after Anne Sexton's suicide, we were talking about John Berryman. Poets came alive in the room when she spoke of them. Robert Frost had the most beautiful eyes and the vanity to match, but about Berryman she couldn't find ready words. It was soon to be the third anniversary of Berryman's suicide. I had in my head the last poem of his posthumous collection, *Delusions, Etc.*, ready to dance its blue head off as we sat side by side on that long red velvet sofa, but I'd learned to watch her before I replied, to get the face after she spoke, to see what her eyes intended to do. I did not understand what she meant when she said that he said Shakespeare was a wound. She had a way of saying, —Uhm, and stroking her throat and letting her right hand eventually find her necklace, the choreography of reflection. She said that toward the end of his life he would phone her late, utterly drunk, and she would plead,

—John, why are you doing this to yourself?

WE CALLED Mr. Lowell, alone at Harvard, on his fifty-eighth birthday. At first Professor Hardwick wondered if we should.

—You know, he was pleased, she said. No kindness is too small to offer.

But around the time Cambodia fell, a Saturday night, he went into the hospital. I don't know how I heard. I didn't know what to do. When I phoned Professor Hardwick, I hung up.

Ian Hamilton's biography said that Lowell collapsed in New York in the spring of 1975, from toxic shock, a reaction to the lithium he took.

Some night before then or around then Mr. Lowell was in town again and we were roaring over his version of when he and Elizabeth Bruce Hardwick first met, at a party given by *Partisan Review*. He said she was drunk on martinis and kept repeating,

—There is no such thing as the South.

Later, she was crying and saying that she wanted to go home:

—home to Mama.

He said he told her:

—Madam, by definition you have no home.

Devie got adamant with Mr. Lowell about *The Faerie Queen*.

I dared to interject that the Alexandrine swing of the Spenserian line was easy to hear.

Mr. Lowell pivoted a smile at me. In my heart I thanked Kenneth Koch for his class in which we had to imitate various stanza forms over and over again, week after week. Daphne Merkin was in that class, too, always disagreeing with me.

(Let me interrupt here to remember a classmate, Richard Horn, who died of AIDS. He was famous in that campus way for having written 242 Spenserian stanzas for Koch.)

Professor Hardwick would say later that Cal had been more like himself that night, but even so she went up to bed early. Barbara, Harriet, Devie, and I gathered around as Lowell read a new poem, about Caroline, 'An Ear of Corn.'

Even when sitting next to me, facing the red sofa where Lowell took up all the room, Barbara steered clear of me, unknown, too curious.

THE SADDLE-TAN 1911 edition of the *Encyclopaedia Britannica* shared a tall bottom shelf with thick red volumes, bound copies of the first ten years of *The New York Review of Books*. Professor Hardwick made me start at the beginning, with heroic F. W. Dupee writing on James Baldwin. Jimmy, she called him.

—Typical honky, she said of herself.

Because of her old friend Mary McCarthy's review of *Naked Lunch*, 'a musical comedy inferno,' I could follow what Luc was talking about when he went on about William Burroughs. Even though I'd read him in Catharine R. Stimpson's class, I didn't

understand his attraction. Sunday after Sunday I promised to return back issues.

The *Review* got started in 1963, when *The New York Times* was
on strike. Publishers had nowhere to advertise their books, Jason
Epstein was telling people. If there was a time to do something
crazy, then that time had come, the Epsteins and the Lowells decided. Whitney Ellsworth was to be the publisher. Robert Silvers
was brought in as co-editor, along with Barbara, but from the beginning he was in the office more than she was because her two
children were still very young.

—The first issue was laid out on that table, Professor Hardwick said one evening, gesturing toward the dining room. Arthur
Schlesinger's wife, Alexandra, had been the first editorial assistant,
she added.

'History begins at midnight,' I read Schlesinger said at Truman
Capote's Black and White Ball in 1966. Capote's glittering party
had been news, even in the backwoods of adolescent Indianapolis,
Indiana. In *Esquire*, a double-page drawing by David Levine came
with a key identifying the notables depicted. Camelot's economist,
John Kenneth Galbraith, towered over someone named 'Barbara
Epstein.'

The story I'd heard was that when she was a mere secretary
the woman who was paying me no attention pulled Anne Frank's
The Diary of a Young Girl from a slush pile and got it published.

Otto Frank was touched by her company, in part because his
daughter would have been Barbara's age. To him she looked like
her as well. My father had Jason Epstein's *The Great Conspiracy Trial*,
a complicated examination of a notorious political trial stemming
from the riot at the Democratic National Convention in Chicago in
1968. Because the Black Panther defendant Bobby Seale would not
stop shouting, the judge ordered that he be gagged and chained to
his chair. Jason Epstein had been Allen Ginsberg's roommate at
Columbia and a pair of Ginsberg's sneakers were supposedly still
somewhere in the Butler Library stacks.

The first time I had an issue of *The New York Review of Books* in my hands, I didn't know what it was. In 1971, a high school teacher wanted me to see James Baldwin's 'Open Letter to My Sister, Miss Angela Davis,' reprinted in the *Review*'s pages.

> *For, if they take you in the morning, they will be coming for us that night . . .*

In my reading of the back issues in those red volumes, I'd only got up to 1966 and Stokely Carmichael's statement of SNCC's aims. I'd no idea before that Professor Hardwick had gone to Selma in 1965 and I felt in her report that she was trying to tell us how alienating the hymn singing and praying at the march were for her and how strange it was to experience distance from a movement she supported.

I read, uncritically, pieces by white contributors on the new scholarship about slavery, Malcolm X, the urban riots, including hers.

Robert Silvers had sent Professor Hardwick to Watts in 1966, around the time that the official McCone Report on the unrest was published. She read the report as yet another ineffectual, dishonest document that reflects the wish for and the reality of the distance that bureaucratic language put between white and black. The truth of jobs, housing, head starts, reading levels, dropouts, and woman-headed families had decayed into rhetoric, she said. Watts, she discovered, was 'an exile.'

> You tour the streets as if they were a battlefield, our absolutely contemporary Gettysburg . . .
>
> The Watts riots were a way to enter history, to create a past, to give form by destruction. Being shown the debris by serious, intelligent men of the district was like being on one of those cultural tours in an underdeveloped region . . .
>
> The months have gone by. And did the explosion in

Watts really do what they thought afterward? Did it give
dignity and definition? Did it mean anything in the long
run? We know that only the severest concentration will
keep the claims of the Negro alive in America, because
he represents all the imponderables of life itself. Anxiety
and uncertainty push us on to something else—to words
which seem to soothe, and to more words. As for Watts
itself: the oddity of its simplicity can scarcely be grasped.
Its defiant lack of outline haunts the imagination.

I continued, reading pieces on the philosophy of Black Power,
the biography of Adam Clayton Powell, Jr., going back when
I'd missed something. In one back issue from 1964, Philip Roth
was saying that in Baldwin's play *Blues for Mr. Charlie*, the author
showed a sense of duty to a variety of causes, but not to the cause
of art. That might have told me how unconfident I was about my
own opinions when white writers regretted that radicalized black
writers fell short. In 1963, Ralph Ellison disapproved of LeRoi
Jones's sociology in *Blues People*. He said that Jones, soon to rename
himself Amiri Baraka, treated black music as cultural politics; the
music that for Jones, Baraka, was an expression of the black condition was for him a transcendence of that condition. For Baraka,
black music took place on the margins, while Ellison countered
that black music was mainstream American culture.

Professor Hardwick hinted that Ellison was not someone you
wanted to mess with too much, whether in an alley or a committee
room. He was difficult, prickly. He could be any way he wanted:
he'd written *Invisible Man*. Professor Hardwick, everyone, just assumed I'd read it. Baldwin was my father's contemporary, and my
father never seemed as young as Baldwin, but Ellison struck me
as antique, like the Truman-era race men I met at NAACP mass
meetings who supported our troops in Vietnam. I stopped being
intimidated by Baraka's black macho because Frank O'Hara had

such a crush on LeRoi Jones, I decided after reading Donald Allen's glorious, huggable edition of O'Hara's *Collected Poems*. Meanwhile, Baraka told a large Columbia audience that spring that he'd renounced black nationalism and become a Marxist.

I MAY HAVE abandoned Marcuse for lyric poetry, but it was most important that the *Review* had been against the Vietnam War from the start. Dwight Macdonald surveyed the White House gala for the arts in 1965 at which Ralph Ellison was bombastically, patriotically present, while Lowell had written an open letter to President Johnson declining the invitation because of his escalation of the war:

> When I was telephoned last week and asked to read at the White House Festival of the Arts on June 14, I'm afraid I accepted somewhat rapidly and greedily. I thought of such an occasion as a purely artistic flourish, even though every serious artist knows that he cannot enjoy public celebration without making subtle public commitments.
>
> After a week's wondering, I have decided that I am conscience-bound to refuse your courteous invitation. I do so now in a public letter because my acceptance has been announced in the newspapers and because of the strangeness of the Administration's recent actions.
>
> Although I am very enthusiastic about most of your domestic legislation and intentions, I nevertheless can only follow our present foreign policy with the greatest dismay and distrust. What we will do and what we ought to do as a sovereign nation facing other sovereign nations seems to hang in the balance between the better and the worse possibilities.

We are in danger of imperceptibly becoming an explosive and suddenly chauvinistic nation, and we may even be drifting on our way to the last nuclear ruin.

I know it is hard for the responsible man to act; it is also painful for the private and irresolute man to dare criticism. At this anguished, delicate and perhaps determining moment, I feel that I am serving you and our country best by not taking part in the White House Festival of the Arts.

Yours respectfully,
Robert Lowell

Lowell's voice was made for the enclosed room, and the voice I'd heard reading his poems on the red velvet sofa wasn't easily matched to that of the protester my sister Pat found evoked by Norman Mailer in *The Armies of the Night*, on the eve of the march on the Pentagon in 1967, when young men like her gentle hippie boyfriend who killed himself were preparing to turn in their draft cards:

We will protest this war by every means available to our conscience, and therefore not try to avoid whatever may arise in the way of retribution.

At the last big antiwar demo I went to, in 1972, in front of the Americana Hotel, my high school classmate Mary Evans, *diva assoluta* of Columbia antiwar protest, was barefoot and shouting street theater at couples in evening dress as they stepped from black sedans and walked our gauntlet toward their fundraiser for Nixon.

She turned fast; her sweating blond hair whipped her face.

—Go.

Behind her, mounted policemen, horsemen of the apocalypse, giddy-upped toward our lines.

(James told me that demonstrators in the UK threw marbles under the police horses that made it difficult for them to charge.)

I was in the last draft for the Vietnam War in 1971 and my number was low, 19. I was in my lost freshman year at Indiana University, before I ran away and ended up on a path I'd not intended. My parents knew one of the board medical examiners, and when I came back from New York to report to the draft board in Indianapolis in 1972, I was taken straight in for an eye test that I failed.

I remember the miserable white farm boys in their underwear who had completed the physical. Then the draft was scrapped and student politics went flat. The Jewish Defense League became the loudest group on campus. We bought any number of radical pamphlets and socialist newspapers at the College Gates, but student protest had become insignificant, the accusatory legacy of '68 nipping at the so-called Me Generation and its inability to show up.

One damp Sunday in her kitchen Professor Hardwick was talking about Simone de Beauvoir, and how she regretted the rough treatment she'd given Beauvoir's *The Second Sex* when it came out in 1952. Everything that had become possible for a woman only recently was not the case back then. She demanded that I learn how to make Bustelo. Harriet sat back down.

—Cold water.

I'd read an account somewhere of Beauvoir's antiwar activities and the Russell Foundation war-crimes trial and was sorry I hadn't known about it before, but I was still a kid when Bertrand Russell convened the meeting in 1966. Harriet said she wasn't yet ten years old when she was taken by her parents—By those two, she laughed—to her first demonstration. I said I was still writing pro-war editorials for the junior high school newspaper in 1968 because I, Dr. Tom, was assigned to. But Professor Hardwick wasn't listening. She was saying as I looked for filters that Mary said everyone in Paris knew that Sartre saw de Beauvoir only once a week, ceremoniously, like she was his mother.

—And she writes all of this, If-Sartre-should-die-life-would-have-no-meaning thing, because it's a story.

The Left didn't like the Russell Tribunal on the Vietnam War at first, but the charges turned out to be true, she said, circling back.

—We knew something was wrong but not really, it was just a feeling.

And then we were talking about Lowell's open letter to Lyndon Johnson, and she said something about someone named Edward Goldmund (I can't read my handwriting from then), who called them, presumably about the White House festival.

—I said you can't go, because it will be Carol Channing and Sammy Davis, Jr. And, well, you know how irritated he gets.

She said he asked was he supposed to call them and tell them he couldn't go. She said he was on the telephone and she said, well you can't go because of the war.

—And he said, that's right, and that was it. We hadn't dreamed of the sensation it would cause. Saul Bellow was absolutely furious. Well, that was the beginning of the whole thing. Then we decided he should write a letter. I said, no, it's not good enough and he said, okay, you write it, you know how busy and irritable he is.

She said she wrote the letter and then told him he had to send it to *The New York Times*.

—You know how they are in Washington, they'll just throw the letter out, and that's how it started. Isn't that strange.

(Until today, I'd only seen a few quoted phrases from Lowell's open letter. Now that I have read it in its entirety, the sound of Lizzie is suspiciously clear, her adverbs, and she has him open in a somewhat self-accusatory vein. Some writers we know by voice, like singers, and she was one of them, and one of the several things that made reading at long last *The Dolphin Letters* so sad was not only the evidence in them of the pain of her divorce, but Lizzie does not sound like herself in them for a long time.

The *Dolphin* letters begin in 1970, with Lizzie writing to Lowell in London, having to pretend that she hasn't sensed or hasn't heard that some trouble was up, as the poet Saskia Hamilton tells us in her sensitive introduction to her edition of these letters. It's hard to explain why the end of marriage unfolded between them by post, by letter. But they'd got engaged by mail.

> *O you could not know*
> *That such swift fleeing*
> *No soul foreseeing—*
> *Not even I—would undo me so!*

Lizzie does not sound like herself in those pages of hurt and years of rage until December 1973, when she's writing to Mary Mc-Carthy about Philip Rahv's funeral. I recognize her voice then. She sounds like herself. The writer I knew. Maybe this is a reflection for later, that and how melancholy to look back and see what I did not know she was going through. How could I have? I was a student, and Barbara was a phone call away.)

Back to that dark late winter afternoon and Beauvoir and Lowell's letter. We had to go to a Lincoln Center matinée, and she was unconvinced that I really preferred diner coffee to Bustelo.

—How boring of you. She'd said the same thing when I said I wasn't sure about Hardy's poetry.

The *Review*'s tables of contents were glamorous; they listed writers I'd seen on *The Dick Cavett Show*. Jason Epstein and Robert Silvers had even been at Leonard and Felicia Bernstein's fundraiser for the Black Panthers in 1970 that Tom Wolfe spent a lot of time making fun of in *Radical Chic & Mau-Mauing the Flak Catchers*, one of those things everybody read back then. Wolfe wondered if a Black Panther with an Afro that was Fuzzy-Wuzzy in scale ate Roquefort cheese morsels wrapped in crushed nuts. He condemned *The New York Review of Books* as the theoretical organ of radical chic.

I read the *Review* because my Afro was Fuzzy-Wuzzy in scale. I read it for an interview with Stravinsky, the wickedness of Gore Vidal, or a plea to Auden's friends not to heed his wishes and

destroy his letters. Even after I caught up to 1967 in the back issues and Andrew Kopkind's dismissal of Dr. King for being out of
touch, I kept reading it in order to read her.

—There are two types of criticism, she laughed. The first word
and the last word. But even Edmund Wilson was dumb once.

BY SPRING I'D stopped talking about *The Savage God* and suicide.
I was in love with a leftist jock who didn't know it and in denial
about how far behind I was in the class I needed in order to meet
the science requirement. Final exams and commencement were
just weeks away. None of it mattered yet. Saigon had fallen and I
was in Professor Hardwick's living room with Susan Sontag.

I see her right leg tucked under her, a black boot on the red velvet sofa, her right arm in her yellow turtleneck extended along its
back. A half-empty pack of Marlboros sat on the oval coffee table,
among the ashtrays, silver boxes, and a dish of agates. Sontag, like
Lowell before her, took up all the room. Professor Hardwick was
far to her right, the side of the sofa where I'd never seen her sit.
In my mind, I can see Susan Sontag's lustrous dark hair, and her
incredulous look as she talked. Devie was in whispered exchange
with the surprise of Nicole Stéphane, legendary screen star, French
Rothschild, Susan's girlfriend, and film producer in one, as Professor Hardwick would explain to me some time later.

I was cross-legged on the floor, in front of the television with
Harriet. We were waiting for the Rolling Stones.

I didn't know that Barbara Epstein was even there until she
came back from the kitchen with three stapled pages that Sontag
had wanted to show her, a short story not by her but by her son.

—It's charming, Barbara said as she marched in skirt and low
heels across the carpet and gave the pages into the waiting palms.

When the televised concert was over, we, the kids, got up to
start on our Friday night rounds of, say, a nitrous oxide party up
in Morningside Heights, followed by maybe a drag show at Peter

Rabbit, our favorite dive down in Greenwich Village, across from the piers and the soundless river.

Professor Hardwick didn't want to know too much about our circuit. She accepted our vagueness, because nothing untoward had happened thus far and her daughter shrewdly respected curfew. She went everywhere in the same gang of four girls, and only by taxi. Most of the guys in the girls' orbit were my former roommate's friends, surrogate big brothers and known quantities, scruffy Jewish intellectuals in army-surplus green covered with political buttons, but prep school boys nevertheless. Even so, it amazes me how freely we ran about Manhattan, the Manhattan between Houston Street and West 122nd Street and East Ninety-sixth Street, completely unafraid, never believing anything bad was going to happen to us in our festival of skipped classes, adored classes, weed, burgers, book quotation, booze, films, acid, music, and staring at a quietly pulsing candle on the floor when there was nothing left to say and still everything to wish for.

—No, you stay, Professor Hardwick said. —My cub! she exclaimed over Harriet's wad of taxi and pizza money.

Mrs. Lowell and Har, not smoking in front of her mother, who had not yet begun to smoke again herself. The group, high school seniors, did not need a chaperone anymore, and I, soon to be ejected from paradise, did not need to hang out on weekends with teenage girls. So here was a chance to meet not just anybody.

—There isn't a bad book in these shelves, she had answered when I asked how she decided what would go into her library.

The writer who composed prose like poetry and who would show me that a life of writing was possible for me, too, got up to see to whatever she was going to make in the kitchen and said she didn't need help. The editor with a poet's sensibility who would save that writing life for me was curled up in her chair, listening with her chin on her fist. The writer mocked as the most intelligent woman in America who would one day introduce me to the gentleman I live with was spread out, centered in front of a white bust of a Greek youth crowned with laurel that sat on the cluttered library table behind the red sofa. Professor Hardwick once told me she didn't know where the bust came from.

—Cal just brought it home one day.

(It's not a Greek youth. It's a ceramic bust, probably twentieth century, in the Della Robbia style, of a young man, James, my poet, has just informed me, after all those years of sitting with my back to it. There's no wreath.

—It's mentioned in the Ian Hamilton biography, he said. Look it up.

He reminded me of a poem of Lowell's that begins:

My namesake, Little Boots, Caligula . . .)

In Professor Hardwick's stage set of a living room I was unheard, on a wicker bench, out where the hypotenuse of our configuration began, while the women, adjacent to the right angle, discussed X in earnest.

What X could have been in the spring of 1975:

the fall of Phnom Penh
the fall of Saigon
the mental condition of Patty Hearst, wherever she was

What X would not have been:

writing by Brendan Gill and Tom Wolfe about *The New Yorker*

'In that other place': the murky way members of the Upper House referred to the House of Commons.

—The New York Review of Each Other's Books, a tenured professor who had not been reviewed in its pages said, resigned, without malice.

The *Review* was snobbish about everything, including split infinitives. Academics read it; plenty of its contributors were academics; yet it was not academic. Barnard girls lost evenings blasting away at what they hoped was a flaw in Susan Sontag's argument in her latest essay. Fights almost broke out in narrow back kitchens at off-campus parties because of her 'Fascinating Fascism,' which had appeared in a winter issue of 1975. Sontag argued that a new volume of color photographs of beautiful, striking Nuba warriors, taken by Leni Riefenstahl, the legendary Nazi documentarian, was but a continuation of the same fascist aesthetic.

What X was that evening: Adrienne Rich's letter to the editor concerning Sontag's Riefenstahl piece.

Rich complained that Sontag had failed to interpret fascism for what it really was, 'the purest form of patriarchy.'

Professor Hardwick said that Rich was a very nice girl and greatly gifted. She remembered when she and Adrienne (pronounced by her as Aahdree Anne) would wheel their children to the park in Boston.

—I used to think, If your boys hit my little girl one more time.

(Before he went into teaching, one of the bashers in question, Rich's eldest son, Pablo Conrad, was for many years an assistant editor at *The New York Review*.)

I hardly dared to join in the laughter.

(One evening, years later, Barbara confirmed a story that her daughter had told me. Out in Sag Harbor she, Barbara's daughter, then five years old, played with Lillian Hellman's hairbrush and broke it. Hellman bawled her out, yelled at her, a child, —You little bitch, she said Hellman screamed.

—I wanted to kill Lillian, Barbara said. Not my little girl.

The first rule of friendship between women: you cannot gossip about your friends' children. Do not tell stories about your friends' children.)

Professor Hardwick said that it was Rich who arranged for her to hide radical fugitive Jane Alpert in Cal's studio. She never asked who it was. She just trusted her.

Susan said something about Rich having become a polemicist for unforgiving feminists.

—She is reaching toward enormity, like every moralist, she said.

In her reply to Rich, Sontag defended *Seduction and Betrayal*, which had taken some knocks from feminists for being male-identified in its definitions of great literature.

(I think it was Devie who told me that one feminist critic writing about *The Dolphin* said that from the sound of her in the poems, Lizzie had got what she deserved.)

It would have been in character for Susan to bring up what she had said about *Seduction and Betrayal* and it would have been in character for its author to thank her, gushing and false, in order to shut her up. Professor Hardwick had tried to convince Bob and Barbara to take that part out, to talk to Susan and make her see. But Susan was proud of her capacity for loyalty. It was genuine, a trait the three of them shared, though the two older women never called attention to this in themselves, much as they treasured it in others.

I don't remember who smoked and who didn't, but I could feel that the men in their lives, editors, husbands, lovers, friends, weren't present and therefore these extraordinary women, particularly the three stars of the great table of contents that was Manhattan, were talking without the need to calculate, comfort, or defer, even if Professor Hardwick said she'd been honestly on Cal's side when it came to feeling disappointment in some of the poems in Rich's volume of feminist proclamation, *Diving into the Wreck*.

—After Cal left, Adrienne wanted to say we'd been closer than we were. I do admire her. But I said, Adrienne, it's okay. You came for him. You're a poet.

(If we ever talked about Rich's review of *The Dolphin*, in which she said that Lowell's appropriation of his former wife's letters was an expression of his masculine privilege, I don't remember it.)

I can see myself putting the dishes in the dishwasher. Outside, branches barely scratched the window, or something that I took for that sound. I can remember that. From time to time, I could hear voices, then mostly a trio of low, middle, and high laughter, the whole evening taken from Colette's *The Pure and the Impure*:

> In a certain period of my youth, I associated for some time with various homosexuals, thanks to one of Monsieur Willy's ghost-secretaries. I am recalling now an epoch when I lived in a singular state of neglect and concealed wretchedness . . . I therefore took great pleasure in the companionship of the secretary, like me a 'ghost.' He was young, wellborn, cheerful, impish, and he made no secret of his homosexual inclinations.

The Pure and the Impure, translated by Herma Briffault, was one of those books I'd got on a ladder to bring down from Professor Hardwick's French section. Over the dishes, that part about working for her husband and spending hours in the company of boys who ignored her came to my mind:

> My strange friends discussed all sorts of things in my presence—violent deaths, inevitable blackmails, fleecings, shameful lawsuits, cravats, cuffed trousers, music, literature, dowries, marriages—avoiding no subject of conversation in front of me.

They didn't include her or exclude her, but their cool friendship let her listen, take in their fierce critical sense.

PROFESSOR HARDWICK WOULD sometimes laugh to think what her somewhat conventional friends like Mary McCarthy would make of her bohemian life as a single woman, her ragtag family of Harriet and her Dalton gang, and Devie, and me, with guest appearances by Barbara.

Alison Lurie had been Barbara's big sister at Radcliffe. Barbara knew Jimmy Schuyler, that rare bird of the New York School whom one never saw, and Kenneth Koch, who had been at Harvard when she was at Radcliffe. She met Frank O'Hara her senior year. John Ashbery had been the passion and friend of her undergraduate days.

I wanted to say to her, Okay, most of the muses don't love me, but I really only need one.

And yet, in her best friend's house, on a Saturday evening, when she had stopped by on her way home from the *Review*, she could not resist being herself, not the tough, unyielding bruiser of the office. Off-duty, she was so vulnerable and quick. I remember that I had a vodka martini.

—They explode the whole head, Professor Hardwick said of martinis and not for the first time. She remembered how under the influence of martinis she would

—bawl everybody out.

The carved, painted wood head on her mantelpiece I learned was a present from Elizabeth Bishop, after she had come for a visit and ended up staying three weeks, because, smashed, she'd fallen and broken her hip. Professor Hardwick said during one visit she resorted to hiding the booze, but Bishop hunted out the bottles in the night.

I once brought a vodka gimlet to class in a Styrofoam cup. Somehow Professor Hardwick needed a sip of something restorative. To accept a cup from a student, she must have been desperate. Her eyes blazed. She left the room. She did not forget the incident. Much later she confessed that she'd had the worst hangover that afternoon, having been up the previous night drinking with Barbara.

The night I am thinking of, when Barbara stopped in, Professor Hardwick described a scene in which she got drunk on martinis at the home of Roger and Dorothea Straus, the publisher of Farrar, Straus and Giroux and his wife.

—Jewish Tories, Barbara interjected. She didn't mean to be funny in front of me.

Professor Hardwick said the next thing she knew she was crying and got sick.

She, Barbara, the beautiful jock, and I got plastered anyway. I don't think Harriet drank in front of her mother any more than she smoked.

Then Barbara and Professor Hardwick were in the kitchen.

—I hate big tits.

—So do I.

—Philip likes them. He thinks they're shiksa.

Harriet, the Dalton gang, the leftist Jewish jock who guessed how I felt about him, and I took over the red sofa and slowly passed the reefer around. Devie leaned out of the way rather than touch it. Plumes of Thai stick smoke stretched up to the wooden chandelier in the living room. Maybe we were going to pretend that only I and the Jewish jock who looked like a mounted colonel in an Isaac Babel story were smoking.

Once upon a time the living room had seen the arrival of William Empson, with chewing gum stuck in both ears. He'd tried to block out student noise in the dormitory at Kenyon College, where he was housed as a visiting professor. But then he couldn't get the gum out.

—It is so boring, Barbara was saying, leaning on the doorframe.

I knew already Professor Hardwick would say, when she closed the door, that she couldn't talk about it, so there was no point in my asking her. Colette respected secrets.

THAT SUMMER Professor Hardwick phoned me from Maine for the first time. I had stayed in New York and not gone home to Indiana. My parents had come for commencement and had thanked her by taking us to lunch at a strained French restaurant in her neighborhood. I've always said that I was lucky that my father and mother supported my dream of becoming a writer, but I have found just recently my damaged journals, their faded letters, and they say that they were upset when I announced my decision not to take the law boards, as if I could have.

We asked to be obsessed with writing
and we were

I was attempting a novel, ignoring the incomplete in Science I needed to make up in order to get my diploma. I would have to do it.

—You're the first person in the family since slavery not to have a college degree, my mother said.

(Years later I read a letter from this time in which Lizzie tells Mary McCarthy how terrible things have been, but Professor Hardwick had written to me from Maine at the same time, her first to me, to say that she was fine, not at all unhappy. I was not a peer.)

—I hope you don't have any plans to go out today, Professor Hardwick said. If I were you I wouldn't.

A poem I had sold to a national magazine three years earlier had finally appeared in print, an imitation of Mari Evans, a militant but reserved black poet back in Indianapolis. My father and mother called to congratulate me. They had a subscription to that magazine.

'Making a living is nothing,' begins 'Grub Street: New York,' Hardwick's essay in the first issue of *The New York Review of Books*. 'The great difficulty is making a point, making a difference—with words.'

── Part 2 ──

Sunday evenings at the end of press week, Robert Silvers would send up by messenger to Elizabeth two copies of the new issue of *The New York Review of Books*. She would give one to me and wave me on my way.

She said she did not believe in Maxwell Perkins or Bennett Cerf. She didn't know Mr. Shawn, but she didn't believe in him either. You had to be your own editor. It was a part of writing.

—You believe in Mr. Silvers and Barbara, I said. I called her Barbara because Elizabeth did, but I called him Mr. Silvers even though she of course called him Bob.

—You will never encounter editors quite like them. Or Jason.

I wasn't calling her Professor Hardwick anymore. I'd tried Mrs. Lowell for a while, as in Harriet's mother.

—Elizabeth Lowell never wrote a thing, she said.

Practically everybody in literary New York called her Lizzie, but her remaining family back in Kentucky, her one sister out west, they called her Elizabeth, as did her old friend Harry May.

They'd been in graduate school together. He dropped out before she did. He returned to his native Virginia, but to the other side of the tracks from where he'd come, to a life of loving railroad men. He grew old with the unions and then the railroad lines themselves began to disappear. He liked his rail hands rough. He was shocking. Yet we guffawed at his stories of drunken injuries.

Since her divorce, which became final in 1972, she and Harry had found each other again. He came for a short visit every year. I remember a lanky, silver-haired gentleman with his bony hands in his lap. It was that important spring of 1975.

—I'm like you, he said. I think Elizabeth is the bee's knees.

—Harry, she said, and blew a kiss across the room.

He started to tell stories about what she had been like when she, smoking a cigarette, posed for a photograph in front of Johnson Hall that I'd seen in a redwood chest of drawers full of family pictures.

—I could write your biography, he said.

—Harry Goodrich May, she said in her warning tone.

She laughed at her Communism down at the University of Kentucky, but she didn't want Harry to remember too much. One of her sisters, Margaret, played basketball.

—Everything I am I owe to sitting on that broken bed up in my room and reading, Elizabeth said.

She had a way of dusting off a record on the backside of her skirt. I could not learn the box step, but Harry guided her around her living room, and when they broke apart, they were inclined toward each other, bent at the waist, dropping into easy recall of the dance moves of their era. They cut a rug to Ella and Louis, but when Elizabeth dusted off a Billie Holiday record, she sat and concentrated, even on up-tempo numbers, often with her chin in her palm and her elbow atop her crossed leg.

—Louis Armstrong taught everyone to sing behind the beat, she said.

Elizabeth liked Billie Holiday's early recordings from 1935, but it was the Billie Holiday of the 1940s whom she preferred. Those were the years of her own independent life in New York, of clubs on West Fifty-second Street and fleeting romances with the most surprising but dashing literary men. She couldn't play that record of Billie Holiday late sessions I'd given her; the sound of what to her was a destroyed voice was too painful.

It drove Elizabeth a little crazy that Harry didn't do anything when he visited. He wouldn't leave her apartment. Then five o'clock arrived at last and before long they would be laughing about the boy back in grad school who wrote papers that contained sentences such as

> In the history of wallpaper the use of wallpaper was
> used extensively.

She told me that in her back-when she and a friend used to search through boxes in record stores until their fingers bled and, lo, there that detail was in a story she was writing about Billie Holiday, as well as other things she'd said, like how their hearts pounded when they with their pale faces went up to see the great singer in Harlem.

Another classmate, Greer Johnson, not Harry May, was the model for J. in that story. Johnson had been her roommate at the Hotel Schuyler on West Forty-fifth Street. J. is something of a fairy and longs for the love of what she calls a normal man. I argued, the phrase seemed to me to belittle gay men, but she insisted that that was true to Greer Johnson's psychology, his vintage.

Elizabeth really minded the sentimentality going around then about Billie Holiday as a woman who'd lived her songs, the whole Lady Sings the Blues thing. In her portrait of Billie Holiday, she wanted to evoke a singularly conscious individual, someone who had worked to perfect her art. She also wanted to get across the tremendous force of Billie Holiday's character, her willfulness, and the size her alcohol and heroin addictions had to become in order for them to cut her down. She didn't want Billie Holiday to have been anyone's victim, remembering her youthful anticipation at the bar in Café Society, waiting for Lady Day.

The bizarre deity

Elizabeth relished Baudelaire's phrase about his brown-skin mistress.

(When I learned the name given to the woman in Manet's portrait of Baudelaire's mistress, I felt caught out to realize I'd always accepted that Jeanne Duval would never have one, a name.)

But Elizabeth was also careful to keep in mind when writing how much of Billie Holiday's life had been hidden away from her, what she as this trembling white girl could not know of the great star's black woman's story, the told and the untold.

(When she showed me the story, did she say it was memoir or fiction?)

Once, completely blotto, I read aloud to Elizabeth Frank O'Hara's 'The Day Lady Died.'

Elizabeth said that Cal liked for her to play her jazz records, but he didn't really get them. Harriet did, and Devie. Elizabeth said that you can listen to opera by yourself, but not certain kinds of jazz. You had to have someone with you when you listened to Billie Holiday. Otherwise you might kill yourself. But then you might want to shoot yourself if you were listening with the wrong person, so why not have another.

BARBARA GAVE ME the nickname Fortunoff, the Source, following the two weeks in the autumn when I worked in the *Review*'s mailroom with Howard Brookner, someone her son knew from Exeter, the guy I was sharing an apartment with on a street sloping downhill from the Columbia campus. My handsome roommate was a senior, but I was supposed to be wading into the real world.

The mailroom was out of control. Employees helped themselves to books, telephone calls to Hong Kong, extra sandwiches during press week. They had a softball team. My duties included babysitting for the publisher's assistant's children. I'd once been babysitter to Barbara's daughter, then a preteen in a Spence School uniform and red high-top sneakers.

(I want to remember Helen Epstein as reading Miriam Rothschild. She is sure that she was doing a bunch of math homework.)

Bob and Barbara were *The New York Review of Books* and then there was everybody else, with the publisher doing his best in the engine room of an outfit famous for getting galleys by messenger to its writers no matter the challenge. It was a poor paper that spared no expense when it came to moving print around the globe. These were the days before desktop computers, before faxes, not that long ago, or maybe by now it is, my youth is longer and longer ago, when George the III was king, and not to xerox a letter from Mr. Silvers or galleys so interrogated they looked embroidered before everything was expressed to Oxford or to Washington, D.C., was to put press week in jeopardy.

The telephone was everything in the editors' hourly reasonings with proud and anxious writers. Meanwhile, the young who worked there were either so terrified or so cunning, their business took place as a humming of heads turned toward walls, telephone receivers cradled, or they hid behind hedgerows of books. The softball team's captain, a tall blond painter, and a modern dancer with a thick mustache were the mailroom staff, one needing some more time off, the other not back yet. The painter showed my fellow temp and me the switchboard, calling out over the intercom for either Robert Silvers or Barbara Epstein on line one or line two, assuring us that after a few minutes we wouldn't give a singing rat how urgent any package was. I knew Elizabeth phoned Barbara almost every day.

—How is Felicia Bernstein? I had the temerity to ask of Barbara one five o'clock. There was no reason on earth why I should have inquired after a friend of hers whom I knew to be seriously ill.

Bob and Barbara are dinosaurs and we're these mammals running around afraid of getting squashed, I, trying to buddy up, said to Prudence Crowther, a satirist who worked as a typesetter in the production studio. She smiled but withheld her laughter. An office of the tensed up went nuts at Prudence's huge laugh, slamming doors or screaming that some people were trying to concentrate and *then* slamming doors. Her hair was cut like that of the actor Louise Brooks, who was then undergoing a big revival, but with Prudence that would have been just coincidental.

Prudence tended the studio door, its layers of bizarre headlines, weird cutouts, clippings about the outrageous. The office style was funky, a work in progress, and that of many hands over time. The mailroom walls were dark collages. The office featured a long, wide central space with doors leading from it, or feeding into it. You saw stained, scrawled-upon whitish walls, boxes of whatever, long metal tables of whatever, file cabinets, stray books, already-grimy galleys of books, a water cooler, walls plastered with photographs, posters, against the back wall a cracked white sofa that people with appointments didn't like to sit on, and beside the unhappy sofa a refrigerator second only to my mother's in the high percentage of rot among the contents.

—How is Elizabeth? James Baldwin had asked politely when I was a student and raced over to his table in the Ginger Man, a restaurant near Lincoln Center. I had a volume of Byron's *Journals* with me and opened it for Baldwin to sign as I announced whose student I was and assured him I'd give greetings he had not yet offered to Elizabeth Hardwick. He wrote down his address and telephone number on a slip of paper that he tore from a small notebook.

She most certainly was not going to call him, very disapproving that I had used her name. She laughed that he was never on time, Jimmy and his inevitable entourage.

I once explained to her the concept of CPT.

—You came to New York to be what you are, she said. A mad black queen.

Harriet's best friend from Dalton said that I'd only read the Monarch Notes about everything, because I was too busy memorizing *Seduction and Betrayal*.

(A few years later, I couldn't keep up my end talking about Joseph Heller with my eldest sister, Pat, except to quote one of

Elizabeth's witticisms about *Something Happened* and Pat said she understood that Elizabeth was my teacher and all but maybe I should go back to reading books for myself.)

I used to haunt the *Review* in the evenings when Celia McGee (née Betsky), Elizabeth's former student boarder, worked for Robert Silvers. I was perplexed when she told me she ironed her clothes for work every morning. She was Jewish, had grown up in Holland, and she knew more about black literature than I did and my junior year she got me invited to the Alain Locke Symposium on African American Literature, sponsored by *The Harvard Advocate*, an experience that changed my attitude toward the subject I was born with, as Baldwin once described writing about black literature. At Harvard, Ralph Ellison had drawn himself up to a great height and explained to the assembled that the reason he would not say he was African American was that he was not, he was a Negro.

Celia had moved on, moved up elsewhere, but I still hovered around the mailroom now that hardworking Sigrid Nunez, another former student of Elizabeth's, was waiting on Bob, Mr. Silvers. Elizabeth was much interested in the question of what Sigrid would go on to write. She'd studied dance. She was in earnest concerning all things Virginia Woolf. I tried to be equally intense and would jabber about, say, the sadness of the boots at the end of *Jacob's Room*.

(But a page from my burned journal says I met Sigrid Nunez in Professor Hardwick's office on April 7, 1975, and then Professor Hardwick went to class. The past in my head can't be all prestidigitation.)

I repeated office gossip to Elizabeth, about staff and contributors and strangers.

I had to learn the rules. Don't discuss someone you don't know well with someone who knows that person better. Don't let anyone know that you have been talking about her or him even if what was being said was praise.

—Gossip is just analysis of the absent person, Barbara and I always say. Then we let the absent person have it.

I PILFERED A copy of the notorious issue of the *Review* from August 24, 1967, with the drawing on the cover of how to make a Molotov cocktail. I presented it to Luc. It was also the issue in which Kopkind assured us that even Dr. King acknowledged he'd failed. Luc was not fazed that back in those days the staff used to get high in the office. Bob and Barbara were said not to have noticed.

—What about now.

(Editorial assistants had no billing on the masthead when Joan Jonas and Deborah Eisenberg and Jean Strouse worked for Robert B. Silvers.)

When his glasses slipped down his nose, Luc wouldn't push them up right away, he'd raise his head and his wire rims made his facial expressions even more inquisitorial.

Columbia's blue flags were at half-mast, English department colleagues were rushing into print with remembrances. Luc and I passed behind St. Paul's, the campus chapel, just as the bells began to sound.

—Hark, hark, the bells are Trilling, Luc said without inflection, looking straight ahead.

Hannah Arendt died suddenly, a few weeks before Christmas. Her name came up often in the pages of *The New York Review of Books*. That sweltering first summer in New York on my own, Arendt had published an essay that I got my *Ramparts*-reading older sister interested in, about the political disarray in the United States after the lies of Watergate and defeat in Vietnam. The tribute to her in the *Review* was by Robert Lowell, not Elizabeth Hardwick, who once told me that everything in Arendt's Riverside Drive apartment was beige, including the food.

Arendt had been a way out of the inadvertent Stalinism that my love for Angela Davis had led me into. But I returned *The Origins of Totalitarianism* to Elizabeth's shelves. Yet I, clown, added Arendt's insights to my bar chatter, such as the distinction she makes in *Between Past and Future* between leisure time, when we are free from cares, and vacant time, which is leftover time after work and before sleep that we fill with entertainment. It was usually okay, because in most of the bars I ran through no one was making much sense, either, or weren't interested in that.

In *Crises of the Republic*, Arendt identifies the information that technocrats and advisers deal in as non-facts. What does it matter if we have the capacity to blow up the world thirty-two times when once will do. Everyone at parties was into that one. But the book caused me some discomfort, not because of her stern analysis of Black Power and violence, but because Arendt argues that minority admission programs represent a threat to universities and put black students in the position of having to be constantly aware of their inferiority.

Men in Dark Times was brilliant, just as Elizabeth promised. The Randall Jarrell essay; doomed Rosa Luxemburg. And I was moved by *The Human Condition*. But the work of Arendt's that I was most curious about was *Rahel Varnhagen: The Life of a Jewess*, which Elizabeth said she'd not read in a long time. Arendt's biography spoke to me, her tale of a not-pretty Jewish girl who came of age in late-eighteenth- and early-nineteenth-century Germany, when Jews were eager for emancipation, but only the privileged among them were allowed limited participation in German society. Moreover, this biography of yearning for unavailable, aristocratic men was full of those things that fascinated me: diaries, letters, and salon gossip. Varnhagen resolved to tell the truth of her experience, loser in love that she was.

But Varnhagen did more than dignify my flight into myself, which her life promised would end in self-acceptance. To read about Moses Mendelssohn and the problems of Jewish assimilation had the effect of making me interested in W.E.B. Du Bois at last. Or maybe I hadn't forgotten my resentment of her *Crises of the Republic*. I had everything of Du Bois's that Herbert Aptheker had edited, like trophies. And that paperback of *The Souls of Black Folk* waited and waited, saying what I thought I needed it to, that the spirits could read.

The abstract, theory, did not interest Elizabeth Hardwick for long. In this sense, she was left out of what had brought her old friend Mary McCarthy and Arendt together, the philosophical quest for the truth behind appearances. She told me that after Hannah's husband died, Mary had Hannah up to stay in Castine, the little town on the water in Maine where Mary and Elizabeth both spent their summers. Hannah was lying on the sofa, her hands behind her head, staring at the ceiling.

—What's she doing? Elizabeth asked.

—She's thinking, Mary whispered.

Elizabeth said she felt not a little put down by the answer.

In McCarthy's 'Farewell to Hannah Arendt,' which was published in *The New York Review*, she says that Arendt had pretty feet and loved shoes.

I think she only once had a corn.

Elizabeth was terribly put off by the detail, which she thought said more about the state of Mary's feet than it did of Hannah's. In any case, it was somehow indelicate to her way of thinking, she who retreated from too much frankness about the body on the page. It was a minor example of what Elizabeth said could be the obtuseness of Mary's insistence on truthfulness in all things.

She said that up in Castine, friends fell out with one another from time to time for silly reasons. Mary would march past the someone she was on the outs with and get in the car without speaking, while Elizabeth waved to the banished party behind Mary's back.

—Just as two-faced as I can be.

Elizabeth was glad her visiting professorship for a term at Smith College was over. To employ me, she had me drive her up with her bundles, her typewriter, and her orange plant. We rented a car and she tried to jump from it when someone speeding along next to us gave some mysterious signal that made her panic. She opened the door, at seventy-five miles an hour.

—Are we on fire?

On my command she yanked the door shut and I sped up. I was no driver. We never did that again.

Northampton, Massachusetts, was too far to commute and life at a small liberal arts college was not to be believed. She recommended Randall Jarrell's satirical novel about just such a place, *Pictures from an Institution*. When I came back with it, we went over some favorite scenes.

—Ass kisser, Harriet, the college freshman, said as I prepared to do the dishes.

—No, he's not, Elizabeth said. We're just mutually supportive.

I asked if the battle-ax character of Gertrude Johnson in the novel was based on Mary McCarthy, and she said, no, she didn't think so, and Jarrell never 'got' Mary McCarthy anyway. She said she had been surprised to hear that Mary told people she suspected Gertrude Johnson was modeled after Elizabeth Hardwick.

Nabokov's academic parodies were of an entirely different order, she warned in answer to my question.

(A few years later a biographer of Jarrell came to see her and the only thing he got right, she said, was that Mary Jarrell didn't like her.)

MR. LOWELL WAS recovering. He'd fallen ill when winter came on. I imagined him sounding like a book from their shelves, like Gorky's drunken manic friend, Andreyev:

I want to expand . . . Nothing should be restrained; let
everything be destroyed.

His breakdown, in England, in November and December of
1975, was severe. I don't think she went over to help this time.
Not anymore. After all, he had a wife. This episode went on into
the New Year. But she said she didn't mind him during his breakdowns. She was never afraid of him, more worried for him, that
people would take advantage of him in his confusion and enthu-
siasm. His hospitalizations were something of a relief. At least he
was safe, and even in his mania he could be endearing.

—Bring me my Dante, she said he'd demand.

His breakdowns followed a pattern. He'd get excited, she'd
worry about where he was, who he was talking to, maybe offending
someone, but not meaning to, innocent somehow as he was. Then
there'd be some girl from a poetry reading and that meant he'd
gone over the edge. Once in the hospital, they'd bring him back
down. Afterward, he was exhausted, meek.

One of the worst times with him happened in Europe in the
early 1950s. He went off in Salzburg and was taken to a military
hospital in Munich. When the officer in charge at the admitting
desk found out that Lowell had been a conscientious objector, he
yelled over his shoulder, she said, quoting him,

—Get that son of a bitch out of here. Can you believe it? He said,
Get that son of a bitch out of here.

('A Mad Negro Soldier Confined at Munich' is a poem impossible to understand, I just said to James on our stairs.

—That's because he's talking nonsense, James replied. And, no,
no English translation as poetry can give a sense of what Dante is,
the *terza rima*. The plain prose translation is the most helpful.)

She once hid in a doorway on Second Avenue rather than run
into him, so great was her attraction to him.

—He was more experienced at having wives than I was at being
one in 1948, she said.

They got married in 1949, at Beverly Farms, an old Yankee sum-mer place on the ocean not far from Boston and where his parents had a house. He was high.

—On simmer.

She said that she did not regret the first twenty years of her marriage.

—But the last one . . . , she said, not finishing the sentence.

She said something obscure, about how women weren't one of his privileges, but they were accepted as part of his birthright.

A high-yellow black doctor was on trial in Boston for manslaugh-ter, because he had performed an abortion on a woman six months pregnant by separating the fetus from the uterus, rather than by in-jection of saline solution. Elizabeth said it was like the Scopes trial.

I said that I had a high-yellow great-uncle, a physician in segre-gated Alabama, who made a living performing abortions on white patients throughout the secretive South.

She revealed that she'd had an abortion as a young woman, up in Harlem, operated on by a black doctor who smoked a cigar the whole time, a detail that surfaced in her Billie Holiday story.

She was having trouble with a story based on the work of Valery Larbaud. She wasn't quite sure what it was, maybe an homage to ridiculous narrators. She liked his novel *Diary of A. O. Barnabooth*, but I didn't get his rich boy's jokes:

> Would not the poster telling of an insect powder stand
> for the indifference of nature.

He regretted that he could not finish his essay 'How Cats Spend Their Time.' Some of his journal entries consisted of single words: 'Headache,' 'Toothache,' and the next day simply, 'Toothache' again.

Elizabeth said that at first people thought H. G. Wells was the author of W.N.P. Barbellion's *The Journal of a Disappointed Man*. Barbellion was a pseudonym, but not for Wells. It is a diary, not a novel. When I brought the book back, she was surprised, even

concerned, that I hadn't fallen for it. H. G. Wells is, indeed, hard
in his introduction on those of us who could not appreciate Barbellion, a young Edwardian who, when he found out that he was
dying, felt as much as he could as a naturalist, husband, and father
in the little time he had:

> March 22
> I waste much time gaping and wondering. During a
> walk or in a book or in the middle of an embrace, sud-
> denly I wake to a stark amazement about everything.
> The bare fact of existence paralyses me—holds my mind
> in mort-main. To be alive is so incredible that all I do is
> to lie still and merely breathe—like an infant on its back
> in a cot. It is impossible to be interested in anything in
> particular while overhead the sun shines or underneath
> my feet grows a single blade of grass. The things imme-
> diate to be done, says Thoreau. I could give them all up
> to hear this locust sing.

In my memory, the Barbellion I see is a black volume with no
dust jacket. Elizabeth and I were reading together a part of it. She
was the fastest reader I have known and she didn't skip a word. She
had to wait for me to catch up so we could turn the brittle page.

—Why, you're like a deprived child.

I said that sometimes life was so weird I was afraid to get up.
She said that life was often so strange to her she was too nervous
to remain in bed. When she'd given up her idea on eccentric narrators, saying that I had to be careful of fragments, of unfinished
things in a drawer, because they could prove undermining of one's
confidence, she was disturbed to find she was having equal trouble
with what she'd thought less ambitious and more straightforward,
a story about Holland and a love triangle. The real-life models in-
hibited her.

———————

ONE SUNDAY ELIZABETH opened the door and went back to the red sofa. She'd had an unrestful night. She sometimes said things on the order of insomnia being so boring there was no point talking about it. She had saved *The New Yorker* for me, in case I hadn't seen Elizabeth Bishop's poem 'One Art.'

She said the experience of literature comes fullest when you can admire what's in your hands. She called attention to Bishop's control, noting that the villanelle was a difficult form, but her rhymes were interesting. Then, too, though Bishop was far from the confessional in temperament, 'One Art' struck Elizabeth as much more direct about her experience than most of her other poems.

—Let me see to this meager bird.

She pushed off wearily, with a characteristic, slightly comic noise, —Umph. She wore heels, not fancy, even when at home. I never saw her in a pair of slacks. I don't think she even liked the word. She never looked tired, soft cheeks and nervous hands, tall enough and self-conscious about what she dismissed as hips too wide for her shoulders and shoulders too narrow for her hips. She let her hair grow again in the late Sixties, photographs said. She escaped the helmet-hair look of her 1950s photos. She called me into the kitchen, because she was thinking about Bishop's descriptive powers and the Brazilian landscape, especially in that poem where the Christians come and find it all.

I said I liked her essay 'Sad Brazil.'

—Mine?

> In Brazil the presence of a great, green density makes
> the soul yearn to create a gray, smooth highway.

She didn't see why I found that such a scream. She said Harriet was probably too young to remember their first trip to Brazil.

She hoped. In those days, everything was the Congress for Cultural Freedom. No one knew anything about the CIA. They left Lowell in Rio and came home.

—Cal got into difficulties. South America was not prepared.

The meager bird and dark vegetables were on the table, but we were looking for Bishop's slender edition of Portuguese poetry in translation in the living room shelves.

Elizabeth said there was no question that Bishop was Cal's friend, not hers, deep as her respect was for her. I got the impression that she considered Bishop's friendship with Lowell an honor Bishop had bestowed on him or let him keep. I didn't know, and wouldn't for years, until books about them began to come out, as well as their letters (also edited by Saskia Hamilton), that Lowell had a history of declaring himself in love with Bishop, a love mixed up with his poetic gifts, the floating fingers of his madness, and having as a poetry competitor a woman. Elizabeth did say back then as she asked for my plate that there was no chance of romantic feelings on Bishop's part. Bishop wasn't crazy, Elizabeth almost said with a look.

She said she had really adored Bishop's Brazilian love, the refined Lota de Macedo Soares. They had an airy time with her touring a yellow house of old walls up in Maine, on one of the un-famous islands. They moved around by candlelight. The wind got in. She wrote something about it quite a bit later, she said, in 1971, in an essay, 'In Maine,' one of the first things she wrote after Cal had gone. She said that about more than one piece from that time, as if each had been a starting over.

> Some years ago we took a friend from South America to an island quite a distance off Machias, Maine. The launch pulled up to a long, wooden pier to which the owner's sloop was moored. The house was a large yellow frame with two graceful wings and inside there were

beautiful dishes, old maps on the wall, fine painted chests, and handsome beds. We lived there in silence and candlelight for a few days, stumbling about with our guttering tapers, coming upon steep back stairways where we had been expecting a closet with our nightgowns in it. 'This is madness! No, it is not one bit amusing!' the Brazilian lisped in fury.

She said she was crushed to get a letter from Bishop about the essay two years after it was published. Bishop was sore at her. She'd brooded, obviously. Lota wasn't like that; Lota didn't talk like that, Bishop complained. Elizabeth hadn't imagined that there was anything unflattering in what she'd intended as a humorous anecdote illustrating a point she was making about Yankee houses being uncomfortable on purpose. She promised Bishop she'd take out what was only a paragraph should she ever reprint 'In Maine.' She said she felt she had to, considering the unequivocal stand Bishop had taken with Cal about using a wife's letters in *The Dolphin*.
—The one about the woodchuck. I did write that. I remember looking out the window.
She herself had the slightest lisp when a little tight.
But what annoyed her almost as much as Lowell's treating her words as his was not being able to see what she'd written, to check her memory against the factual evidence. She'd asked him for them, just to let her see her letters.
—He came once and held out a few damp pages. I said, Cal. I refused to take them. He knew better.
Everything was in her eyes.

MY ROMANCE WITH madness was over. My sister Donna, the middle child, had a spectacular nervous breakdown that spring. She battled schizophrenia for the rest of her short life.

I went back to Indiana to see her in the hospital. I came upon her by surprise, seeing her reflection in the hospital bathroom mirror. She was about to brush her teeth. Soon, it was she who was reassuring me, confiding that she and a friend had a plan to get her out of there. They were able to communicate, telepathically. She held up her hands and showed me how her fingers could channel her thoughts to her friend on the outside. I let her down. I flew from her room. I should have at least gotten it together before I came back to where my grieving mother waited.

My father said that of their children he and my mother had expected Pat to be the one to fall apart. Fresh from law school, she had the chance to work on Capitol Hill during the Watergate hearings but was so terrified of living on her own, my father had to go to D.C. and bring her home. They hadn't told me the truth. I just thought she'd been on a program that then ended.

I'd changed my tune.

'It is only for the sake of those without hope that hope is given to us,' said the wayside robber who shot himself on the border between Spain and France when he had no escape from the Nazis.

My mother's only sister fell dead in Los Angeles not long after Donna's release. My mother wanted my sister alone to accompany her to the funeral. My mother's father died next. Elizabeth was appalled; she sent flowers. My mother did not talk of herself with outsiders, as she called the rest of the world, and Elizabeth was embarrassed to repeat her condolences when they were on the phone weeks later.

We talked about Gayl Jones, a young black writer who to me seemed to have turned up out of nowhere, or from Toni Morrison's list. A year or two before, Elizabeth had urged on me Jones's first novel, *Corregidora*, an angry, hypnotic story of enslaved Brazilian women told as three generations of incestuous rape.

Here already was Jones's new novel, *Eva's Man*, even stranger than the first, full of beatings that go beyond what a black woman puts up with from her man's fist in Langston Hughes's blues. Jones has no scenery, no description, not even a black side of town in the Southern no-place where the short novel is set. Obscene and, at the same time, riveting, spare dialogue. A woman kills the tormentor she loves, castrates him, takes the time to eat afterward, and is then locked away in a mental ward.

Elizabeth wanted me to have it and handed the novel back to me, telling me to put it by the door so I wouldn't forget it. No, she hadn't told me how she knew about Gayl Jones.

In the kitchen, she said one time she went back to Lexington, for some reason, maybe to see her old friend Susan Turner, and she visited Henry Clay High School, where she still knew a teacher, who in the course of their chat about how integrated the student body had become mentioned that they did have one real smart colored girl. She was so smart that at first they thought she copied her papers. Elizabeth asked if the senior had any plans, was she going to college.

—She said, I guess the University of Kentucky. I thought, Come *again*. This was 1969. June already. When I got back to New York, I called Bill Alfred and told him about the papers she'd written. He got her into Connecticut College immediately. I don't think anyone ever told Gayl Jones. I don't care about that. I never knew what happened to her. But it was Lexington, my old high school, and this extraordinary girl. I figured out she lived a block away from our old house. I thought, We have to get her out of here.

LUC HELPED ME to sneak out of my Columbia-owned apartment that my handsome roommate had sublet but not legally from his cousin. Howard and I used to have martinis for breakfast. His mother would call his waterbed and I would have to be quiet. We danced to Aretha. We sang 'Una furtiva lagrima' on the snowy banks of the Hudson. He was an usher at the Met and would slide me in. One night, Elizabeth and the poet Howard Moss came to dinner and got staggering drunk on Hungarian plum brandy when the meal on the stove congealed into a yellow and pink mass. Whenever it was Howard's turn to do the dishes, he simply threw them out.

I once woke up on the sofa to see Howard conducting firemen through smoke to the front door. He'd found them there when he came home. I'd put an egg on to boil and then passed out.

One morning I broke into the small safe in his closet with a fingernail file and found he'd made a copy of my unpublishable novel. I read what he said about me in his journal; I read that he'd read what I'd said about him in my journal. He was categorical. He'd finished his thesis early and was going to Paris. He left.

After he had gone, I discovered that he hadn't paid the rent in our six months of merriment. That was why Luc was helping me to carry boxes and a coffee table down flights of stairs. I see Luc in high-tops on the empty Broadway local subway train at three in the morning, sitting in a rocking chair that had belonged to my former roommate's Eastern European grandmother.

—Only young people and boys want to get married these days, Elizabeth said as she reached for ice in the battered aluminum tin she kept in the freezer.

She said she suspected that I was condemned to live through a number of these one-sided episodes.

Leave me, O Love, which reachest but to dust

Luc was high on Brecht. Cool New York was into Weimar Germany. You checked off films like *The Cabinet of Dr. Caligari*, *Metropolis*, *M*, *The Blue Angel*. You went to see Raul Julia in the new translation of *The Threepenny Opera* at Lincoln Center, passing a joint through the Calder sculpture outside at intermission, and then you repaired to a Chinese Cuban restaurant back up Broadway to talk about why Lotte Lenya was hostile to Richard Foreman's production. Brecht was lumpenproletariat, free of illusion, and a womanizer, though he wrote his own *Edward II*, after Marlowe.

I was beguiled by Weimar, because of *The Berlin Stories*, *The*

Damned, and *Cabaret,* which I'd seen thirteen times back in Bloomington, Indiana, the summer it was released. The narrator of the
novel *Prater Violet,* 'Mr. Christopher Isherwood,' stretches like a
cat, knowing that: 'After J., there would be K. and L. and M., right
down the alphabet. It's no use being sentimentally cynical about
this, or cynically sentimental.'

He was not on any reading list. He'd been my own student hunt.
It was winter outside the grub room. I should have been writing
something like a paper on Stendhal for Michael Wood. The graduate student sitting on the floor near the dark window said that by
coincidence she was discussing *Prater Violet* in her dissertation on
Isherwood as his coming out, significantly early, in 1945.

I heard only Isherwood's romantic promises, although the sexy
side of Weimar was dark, we said, decadent, we said, but what did
we know. Josephine Baker is dancing at Max Reinhardt's house in
Berlin.

Count Kessler didn't say anything explicitly homo in the English edition of his *Diaries* from the 1920s, as far as I remember,
intrigued by the volume at the Gotham Book Mart near Times
Square. Yet somehow I knew about him.

(How would I have known?

—The Homintern, James said just now, down in the kitchen,
wearing shorts, reading the *TLS,* and having a white wine spritzer.

—That's Auden, right? The Homintern.

—I don't know. He certainly loved the term.

It was an echo of Comintern and referred to a gay mafia in the
arts or supposed gay control thereof.)

Your literary pedigree because of being a homo was important.
Histories of sodomy, popular works about prominent homosexuals in European history, were beginning to appear. Or someone
older let you in on the secrets of the tribe; it was something you
pieced together. Verlaine shot Rimbaud.

I knew about Shakespeare, Marlowe, Bacon, Michelangelo, but
not the rogue Caravaggio. Not one of the English Romantic poets

was gay, or bi, though Byron's heart filled when he happened upon the chorister he used to love as a boy.

Oscar Wilde had always been around, if you were my age, because of films like *The Importance of Being Earnest* and *The Trials of Oscar Wilde*. And PBS and H. Montgomery Hyde had a Wilde industry going.

(—Every actress wants to play Hamlet, just as every actor wants to play Lady Bracknell, James remembered Auden saying.)

The Letters of Oscar Wilde, with the complete text of 'De Profundis,' Wilde's excoriation of Alfred Douglas, was a rare prize, in those secondhand-bookstore-hunting days, though Auden observed that Wilde was a talker, not a letter writer. Not enough of an audience for the performer that he was. As for Douglas, Auden judged him 'an untalented little horror.'

(The art historians John Fleming and Hugh Honour said they could not forgive Wilde his reckless lawsuit against Alfred Douglas's father. English literature paid a price, they said. After Wilde's conviction on morality charges, a whole generation of Victorian queer men destroyed incriminating papers, their love letters and diaries.

I didn't know then about the writers Edward Carpenter and his boyfriend, George Merrill, or the two painters, Charles Shannon and his boyfriend, Charles Ricketts, Victorian men who managed to live together a long, long time, right under society's noses. James said just now that the Shannon-Ricketts story was not so simple. They survived through their social invisibility. Though plenty of men lived together in those days, Shannon felt vulnerable, as the illustrator of Wilde's books, and Ricketts's sexuality was probably complicated.)

'The Love That Dare Not Speak Its Name' is from Lord Alfred Douglas, not Wilde.

Barbara Epstein coined the phrase 'The Love That Won't Shut Up.'

The dandyism of Wilde and the *Yellow Book* aesthetes became antique to me. So, too, Bloomsbury and wanting Rupert Brooke to be one of us. There were more thrilling, anti-bourgeois antecedents for what was being called the gay subculture.

I was going to be quiet in my old West End Café side booth with Isherwood's memoir, *Christopher and His Kind: 1929–1939*, in which he went back to the time of *Lions and Shadows*, the autobiography of his youth, and *The Berlin Stories*, and angrily asserted what he had had to say in code back then. He could scarcely forgive himself. The boy's real name was Heinz. He tried to get him out of Germany, but couldn't. They met again some years later, but there was something disappointing about the reunion for Isherwood, and not just because Heinz had married and become this ordinary guy.

I would try to write about *Christopher and His Kind*. Elizabeth was not encouraging. When I read in the *Review* Gore Vidal's complex and thoughtful examination of Isherwood's narrative style, his invention of himself, his conception of the novel, and his rebellion against the culture that shaped him, I understood.

Isherwood was still alive out there in California, but I hadn't Vidal's interest in his later work or his Vedanta ruminations.

Elizabeth imitated his high-pitched voice: —*Goodbye to Berlin* by Christopher Isherwood.

Her review of Isherwood's *A Single Man* in a back issue got me to read Gide, but it was one piece of hers that I didn't know what to do with. Isherwood follows an English professor through a day of grieving for his lover, killed some months before in a car accident. He plans to commit suicide that night. He has what she called a mystifying, exhilarating encounter with a normal man.

She meant a student who plans to save him from himself. But there was that phrase again, 'a normal man.' However, the book was published in 1964, set in what was then the California present day. What was vintage about George's psychology, he who would die of a heart attack at the end of the book instead of a gunshot wound? It bothered me, that and her description of Isherwood's novels as campy. What she really minded about *A Single Man* was what she called its 'brute biology.' The novel opens with the protagonist on the loo. That was already ten strikes against the book for her.

(In that essay, 'Memoirs, Conversations, Diaries,' Elizabeth Hardwick is merciless toward Frank Harris, observer of Wilde, pursuer of the famous, scavenger of anecdote. He is so vain a wine bearer at the banquet of life that not only does he give us what Shaw said about preferring his Caesar to Shakespeare's, Harris reports his own long-winded defense of Shakespeare, she said.)

Normal: the sort of masculine guy Baldwin made the narrator of *Giovanni's Room*, I said. I used Catharine R. Stimpson's example of the middle-aged gay character in *Sunday, Bloody Sunday*. His equality is implicit. He doesn't have a problem being queer; his young boyfriend who has an older girlfriend is his problem. Elizabeth said merely that the screenwriter, Penelope Gilliatt, had been one of Hellman's friends who attacked her.

The new day had come, but it didn't really interest her. Lowell had been to New York that spring and she had been to London.

She could have said, but didn't, that she was probably the only reader of Hart Crane's letters to suggest that he had a happy life, that he loved to be drunk, that the only problem he had as a lover of men was lack of opportunity, and that maybe he hadn't jumped. Or she could have pointed out that Auden himself used the expression: normal men.

Marlowe, the known homosexual, some book called him. But Marlowe went with suffering Thomas Nashe and both with Shakespeare, high lone in thought, the subjects of Berryman's posthumously published essays, *The Freedom of the Poet*. She said I should have heard Berryman on Shakespeare.

—Have you ever been to a lecture that was so unforgettable . . .

(In regard to

the onlie begetter of these sonnets . . .

James said: —To believe you have identified W.H. is a sign of madness.

I found James's dried-out Signet Library paperback of *Shakespeare's Sonnets* from his schoolboy days, with Auden's rather angry and willful introduction. It's reprinted in *Forewords and Afterwords*. There are those who love poetry for its own sake and those who look at a poem as a historical document, Auden writes. For Auden, the relationship between the life and the work is too self-evident for comment. Art is self-disclosure too complicated to unravel. The personal life of the artist was of no concern to the public. He even says 'begetter' refers to the printer, W.H., not to a boy inspiration.

—It means, Pay no attention to what I'm saying while I strangle Chester, James said.)

Luc told me about a lecture Foucault gave, 'Masturbation in the Seventeenth Century.' Foucault projected incredible diagrams. Graduate students lunged as he dropped sheets of paper to the floor.

PEOPLE WE KNEW were signing up to be extras on the remake of the film *King Kong*, which was being shot in part at the World Trade Center. I'd been to Windows on the World with my parents and stood on the observation deck and felt the tower sway.

One Friday Elizabeth phoned after eleven o'clock in the evening, surprised to find me in. She'd returned from dinner at Windows on the World, the guest of someone whose contradictions as a rich man and Stalinist tempted her into accepting more invitations from him than she really wanted to. She was studying him. In the novel she was working on, *The Cost of Living*, what he represented is given to a woman character. Dinner had been awful; her date refused to tip.

They'd been driven uptown and had passed the edge of Greenwich Village, along the Hudson River. She hadn't believed the outrageousness of the scene I'd described. Now she'd seen it for herself: hundreds and hundreds of boys, mostly white, strolling arm in arm under the streetlamps, sitting on cars, dancing to radios, milling around the piers and fading down side streets.

'I must set out,' Gide said in his *Journal*.

Elizabeth said that there were no bachelors anymore and divorced men and widowers expected the next girlfriend to look after them like a wife. Therefore, gay friends made possible the life of the single woman in the city and up in Maine by doing those social things the husband used to do: tend bar, for instance. Mow the lawn. That was a Castine problem.

She said that sometimes in restaurants waiters asked who she was. In her sheer vivacity she had to be a former movie star. It was a West Side problem.

—They think I'm Betty Grable.

Help from a man, she would call it. The problem of her life: looking for help from a man. To open bottles, jars, doors, change lightbulbs.

—My hands are like flippers.

She had her favorites among the elevator men: light-skinned Cuban Louis; dark-skinned North Carolinian James. They were the kind of New Yorkers whose stories Elizabeth was interested in hearing ever more of on her way down and back up.

We reorganized her books. Every year she went up to Maine early, as she called her flight in May, to open up the house. Then she came back to New York and did anxious packing and unnecessary putting-away for the summer. I was to sift through the mail and send on the important items. (Castine was *hers*, she underlined. Lowell's cousin Harriet Winslow had left it to her, not to them both. She sold Cousin Harriet's big house on the village green to a difficult contemporary composer's brother and had the barn down on the water redone. Modernized. The word amused her.)

There were ships with great sails jamming the Hudson and the harbor for the Bicentennial fireworks. The queen of England had gone to Trinity Church.

When I called her in Maine on her sixtieth birthday, she said,

—My true friends would not have remembered.

THAT SEPTEMBER LOWELL was again in the hospital in England, but I remember him signaling for me, grubby, nervous, alone, to come into the greenroom after his reading at the 92nd Street Y maybe three months later.

In those days, someone returned in a page, or was back in just a paragraph. We called it a long time. Howard Brookner, the vanished roommate, was back from Paris, more handsome than ever. He was enrolled in film school downtown, like others of our classmates. He put me in his class projects, shoots in unoccupied rooms in the murky Empire Hotel across from Lincoln Center, even though he knew I couldn't act. I was so bad at portraying a cabbie, Howard rolled around with camera and sound equipment in the back seat of a Checker, trying to breathe.

Howard had changed. He could be crazy fun still, but he was without a trace of the opera queen or preppy in corduroy of his senior year identity experiments. He'd moved to SoHo, nobody's bottom anymore. The gallant in him stood sentry at the curtain that led down the steps to the new Howard. Somehow, maybe because of the Homintern, he knew that Ginsberg had not been above begging Neal Cassady to love him just one more time.

It was as though while I was off at an NAACP convention with my family, the excited, overheated people from school, every single one of them, had become cool. The black people I knew were debating the merits of Jimmy Carter, but Luc was talking about the Baader-Meinhof Gang.

I had heard A. Philip Randolph, the eloquent, fiery labor thorn of presidents, hold forth at NAACP headquarters the spring before, and my parents were ashamed I didn't know that the other elderly man whose hand I shook afterward was Clarence Norris, the last of the Scottsboro Boys. In the hallways of my parents' rank-and-file life, people were still arguing about Paul Robeson. I didn't understand at the time, or I was too impatient to let myself be detained by the old secularizers and sanctifiers. The conversations I stood next to I treated as fields to be harvested later, if at all, which helped me to keep my distance from error, or to think that I was doing so.

Elizabeth had had a dinner back in March for Lowell's sixtieth birthday. In early April, we were watching Irene Worth in a television production of Flannery O'Connor's 'The Displaced Person,' but still talking about Lowell's call the Sunday before.

She'd gone to the kitchen and when she picked up the wall phone, I hung up the phone on the little table by the front door and let myself out. Lowell was at Harvard, safely back from Ireland and a most unhappy visit with Caroline. She blamed him for her madness, threatened to kill the children, to take her own life. Drunk, depressed, writing in chaotic surroundings. Caroline had seen Plath's daughter and said she was a mess and she didn't want that to happen to her children.

He once confessed to her that Caroline represented

—Aphrodite and ruin.

Elizabeth said she was in a quandary as to what to do. Ironically, she was his confidante and wanted him to know he always had a place to go. But she felt uncomfortable, she said, if she seemed to press the point. She said she didn't trust him, but in his defeat, she, of course, would take him back, if that were a viable solution for this sad figure's homelessness.

She said she told him it was his house, those were his things.

Elizabeth said most everything she had had come from him, from being married to him. The settlement was generous, though she had to work. After the divorce, she was determined to get along with everyone, for Harriet's sake. There had been summers of Harriet and her best Dalton School pal going over to Millgate Park, Caroline's country house in Kent. Elizabeth said she'd been afraid Harriet's father would drift off and lose any meaningful connection to his daughter.

(Somewhere in a letter Lowell notes that Lizzie speaks as though he has left them both, instead of his having left just her, not Harriet.)

Elizabeth remembered that she decided it was time to get pregnant when she overheard a girl at a party tell Lowell that she wanted to have his baby. A Catholic convert, because of Jean Stafford, his first wife, he had never been with a woman who patted his rear as he walked by, Elizabeth said. But there was something ridiculous about the sex act, she said, even for the most beautiful of couples.

She admitted that it had brought her low when during one of Cal's breakdowns a doctor would blame her or agree with Lowell that his problems would be solved if he got away from her. She viewed the girlfriends as symptomatic. But when she heard he'd taken up with Caroline Blackwood she said she gave up. She said Bob, who thought at the time that *he* was seeing Caroline, had to come up from the *Review* and tell her what was going on. She stopped struggling to get Cal to come home. She knew this wasn't some poetry fool hanging around at a reading. Caroline Blackwood had been married to the artist Lucian Freud and the composer Israel Citkowitz, by whom she had three daughters. She herself was a skilled novelist with a streak of aristocratic heartlessness. Then, too, she was a Guinness, as they say, meaning she had money to burn.

—It wasn't like he had to find an apartment. Caroline was already more than set up, she said.

(Those letters of hers to Lowell that went into *The Dolphin* that to her death she thought lost sadly contradict her version of herself as immediately resigned once she found out that the woman he'd taken up with in London was Blackwood.)

—Robert Lowell never married a bad writer, she said.

We hadn't noticed how much wine we'd had with dinner and were reeling.

My sister Donna blithely reported that she'd quit her job, quit graduate school, and was back in the hospital for three weeks, just to get her medicine straight, as she put it. No one wanted to tell me, I who still had to phone home every Sunday.

CUT TO A ceremony in May at which Elizabeth was to be inducted into the Institute of the American Academy of Arts and Letters. Lowell was to get the Gold Medal in poetry from the Academy that afternoon. According to Ian Hamilton's biography, there had been some trouble. I can see a flickering image, a teasing on the retina, of trouble's wild blond hair in a throng of people. Caroline Blackwood, arresting and tense. She'd insisted on coming over from London for the ceremony. Elizabeth, Harriet, and I scooted down a side staircase. Caroline had thrown Lowell out, but then changed her mind once he'd agreed with her that their marriage was over.

Two weeks later, a beautiful weekend, Elizabeth called to sum up the phone calls with Cal. They determined that when the term ended, he would come to New York and stay in the studio, most likely. She said they talked of many things, indirectly, and this was best, to be gentle and cautious at first. Anything could still happen and his divorce from Lady Caroline, for purposes of his will, was a long way off.

This was his home, but Harriet was in college, on her own, and she, Elizabeth, had made a life. Her life as a single woman was not nothing. She said she treasured his genius, but some things she wasn't looking forward to: six o'clock cocktails, having to make dinner, and then listening to him hold forth brilliantly for the rest of the evening.

—He takes up all the air.

She felt guilty, conflicted, because she loved her single life of reading through the evening, drinking in front of the television, talking on the phone with Barbara and the rest of us.

(Did either of us mention that she had redefined, reasserted, herself as a writer in his absence as well? Some feminist conclusions applied to her, after all.)

It was not that she wanted revenge on Caroline.

—There is no credit in suffering these days, she said.

Mostly, she was sorry for him in his exhaustion, his humility. Her wish had always been to help him. She said he said,

—I'd like to go up to Maine if you'll have me.

LUC HAD A new job at the Strand Bookstore, on Broadway down from Union Square, where friends of mine on a visit from Indiana were mugged.

New York was cheap enough to shelter the young and sufficiently unpredictable to discourage most tourists. Back then, not every downtown Manhattan street was crammed with bars and restaurants. Downtown especially, you moved through darkness until you came to little pools of light, corners of activity. A friend's place was a safe house.

—You're not really part of youth culture, Luc said.

I didn't know much about photography, wasn't into CBGB's or Godard, and had not studied French, gone to Reid Hall, Columbia's summer school on the Left Bank.

(—Reid Hall is disastrous to one's patriotism, Professor Hardwick had said.)

The actor Suzanne Fletcher told me that when she studied literature at Reid Hall her tutorial with Hélène Cixous consisted of the two of them silently weeping in her office for an hour every week. Meanwhile, Belgian-born Luc, prey of Jesuit teaching, only child of immigrants in Cherry Hill, New Jersey, got into a screaming match in French on the phone every Tuesday evening with his very Catholic mother.

It used to hit me: here I am at the Elgin Theater for the midnight showing of Max Fleischer cartoons; here I am sitting in a balcony of Acapulco Gold.

I was seduced by New York City at an early age, when the historical temperature of the country was going up month after month, as Norman Mailer said.

New York touched me first as a tourist, and every time I am on the expressway in from JFK, going through Flushing Meadows, I see the old Unisphere and remember the crush of the 1964 World's Fair and the compartments of pie in the last automat in Times Square. But it was really television that did it for me: *East Side/West Side*, *Naked City*, gritty black-and-white TV dramas I was up late quietly watching because my parents thought I was in bed. When I was at last alone in Manhattan, where the drinking age was eighteen years old and you didn't have to drive to get anywhere, I raced to place myself in the window of Julius', the gay bar in the West Village featured in the opening title sequence of *The Boys in the Band*.

My father always stressed that my white friends could hitchhike, but I could not. I would end up dead. They could get arrested at demonstrations, but I would end up beaten. (What about Chicago, I once dared.) I was maybe not a part of youth culture, but I was gathering up loose change from Baldwin's jackpot, as he called it, of being both black and queer. Plus, I was into Weimar.

I stayed on the Upper West Side and in the late spring of 1977, I finally managed to burn down an apartment. This one was on West Eighty-seventh Street, near West End Avenue.

The rolling clouds of black smoke.

—You're more trouble than the law allows, my father said.

The heat; the looks of your fellow tenants who have had to flee their homes.

My journals burned.

—A happy event. Probably everything I ever said, Elizabeth said when I got back from Indianapolis.

—It's funny what will make you snap out of it just before you snap period, Felice Rosser said.

Felice, the beautiful black girl from Detroit who followed the rock music at CBGB's, another student of Elizabeth Hardwick's. My mother and her friends would have called Felice a nice girl, even though she came to the Suicide Party that Howard and I gave on 115th Street just before he left for Paris.

I was crashing at Luc's place in a mostly Hispanic street in Morningside Heights that he shared with Jim Jarmusch, Phil Kline, and George Winslow, the filmmaker, the composer, and the political journalist. They worked on things at lonely hours; they only went out to interesting places. The women in the lives of these cool guys tended to be anarchic. I slept on the floor in a room empty of anything except a collection of both working and defunct televisions and an early heavy computer monitor piled along a bare wall.

When the list of Janeway Contest winners was announced, Felice tossed her writing out of her Barnard window into 116th Street. Elizabeth, as Professor Hardwick, talked her down. The Janeway judges were notoriously middlebrow, even Sigrid Nunez would say so, she said, and she'd won top prize her senior year.

Felice had given Luc a black nickname: Earle.

—Just wait.

Sure enough, Earle, in the middle of an apocalyptic monologue, threw books out of his window, toppled bookcases, and smashed his fist through a glass door, tearing an artery. He said when he took the bandage off, he nearly gagged at the stitches.

I'd snapped out of being untogether, too. I found an apartment on the Upper West Side and a job in a secondhand bookstore only six blocks away. I'd happened to be there on the night the clerk absconded with a great deal of the store's money. The two owners, white guys with ponytails, offered me work. Luck used to be like that in Manhattan.

My bookstore was just off Broadway, a front room, back room, and grotty bathroom, everywhere tight with wall shelves and large wooden bookcases, a wooden hole impossible to clean. There wasn't enough room for the stock, which ranged from discounted *Valley of the Dolls*-era paperbacks to collectors' items, such as Mary Wollstonecraft's *A Vindication of the Rights of Women*, printed in Dublin in 1793, or an edition of *Moby-Dick* illustrated by Rockwell Kent. They did a brisk business in dictionaries and classical and Broadway recordings. Bibliophiles and obsessives could get as comfortable as mice in the debris. Wax paper and empty rum bottles and drawers of rubber bands and Scotch tape. There was an old-fashioned kosher deli around the corner. Its owner and one of the bookstore bosses would sit in front of their businesses with candles at their feet and shotguns across their laps during the science-fiction-level citywide blackout later that summer.

One evening Susan Sontag; her son, David Rieff; and Sigrid Nunez, his girlfriend, came into the bookstore. I'm sure my teeth were huge. They'd come into my long hot day of wrapping packages, addressing labels, sweeping the floor, alphabetizing volumes, shoving books, rearranging prints. Pipe and cigarette smoke, tubes of glue and leather preserver. The bookstore owners took a while finishing whatever they were doing before they came over.

I felt I had to make up for my bosses in the absolute deference department and said I heard that she and Donald Barthelme had read at the recent PEN conference in California.

She smiled, pressed my shoulder, and fell to ordering books, giving the owner her details, which was usually my job. Other lovers of books warmed to her presence. I offered everyone a Scotch. Everyone declined.

Elizabeth had been at that PEN conference and said she found it taxing: continuous appointments, interviews, dinners, cocktails, lectures. She said she worked very hard on her lectures.

—I can't just arrive like some star and go on impromptu. Appearing isn't enough.

Sigrid had seen twenty-seven films in ten days at the remarkable Pacific Film Archive.

The night I burned down my apartment I had gone to see Sigrid. She and her boyfriend were living with his mother on Riverside Drive. I told Sontag how depressed I was. She laughed and went back to her typewriter, she who had gone off treatment for breast cancer in order to finish her long essay for *The New York Review*, 'On Photography.'

ELIZABETH AND LOWELL returned from Russia a week earlier than planned. They were both exhausted after an eighteen-hour flight. St. Petersburg was wonderful, she said, the blue and white Winter Palace, the art collections. But the rest was dreadful: visas, escorts, simultaneous translators, hunks of bread but no butter or fruit.

—The hotels in Moscow are like Macy's closed down. Science and arms are all the Soviets have.

The conference itself was horrible: meeting after meeting, she said. They wanted more Soviet literature in translation and talked endlessly of six million copies of this sold, six million copies of that. She said there was a gasp in the audience after her opening remark was translated:

—There are books, and then there is literature. They are not the same.

He, Lowell, came up from the studio. Her door was unlocked. Yes, they were back together.

They gave me a small hard box of matches with Pushkin's self-portrait on it and we drank Russian vodka. I'd read at my desk in the bookstore Pushkin's first attempt at prose, an unfinished novel about his great-grandfather, *The Negro of Peter the Great*. Hannibal had come from the slave markets of Constantinople as a present for the tsar, who sent him as his favorite to military school in Paris.

Pushkin was proud of his African ancestry, or defiant enough about it, and talked of his 'Brother Negroes.'

Lowell hadn't read that work, but spoke almost in a whisper of *Eugene Onegin*, the Pushkin stanza, and Vladimir Nabokov's edition. Nabokov's quarrel as a native speaker with a presumptuous

Edmund Wilson about problems of Russian translation was one of those intense, dragged-out exchanges that *The New York Review*'s end pages reveled in. But I'd not caught up to that in my survey of its back issues.

Elusive Pushkin!

It was Avrahm Yarmolinsky's 1936 Modern Library edition that I'd got on an employee discount from my bookstore.

—The five-finger discount, Luc called it.

To this were fribbling hours devoted, Babette Deutsch's Pushkin stanza translation says.

Nabokov's three types of translation, the literal ones, those that try to reproduce the form, and those that chase the spirit of the verse, were also a hierarchy. Lowell's translations had never come up in any class of mine and I think I read them with the sense of just doing enough to follow Elizabeth's remarks about them should she ever refer to one of them. They were not my thing.

I want this to be the afternoon Lowell said he didn't think Hart Crane knew what half the words he used really meant.

Lowell was reading *Native Son*. Elizabeth had once said she found it interesting that we forget the second murder victim in *Crime and Punishment*. We forget the second murder in *Native Son* as well, I said. She didn't think the Communist lawyer's speech at the end of *Native Son* anywhere near the Christian philosophy at the end of *Crime and Punishment*.

(I am no better than Frank Harris thinking that he had kept up his side of the conversation with the greats.

My *Crime and Punishment* was translated by Constance Garnett. Someone asked Elizabeth who was the greatest novelist of the twentieth century and she came back swiftly:—Constance Garnett.)

We went from Ralph Ellison's paranoia to the awfulness of Georges Bataille's *Literature and Evil*.

My memory of the long afternoon was that it was not a runaway success. Several subjects got launched but nothing stayed afloat. I had no background in Greek or Latin. It was as though I'd never read anything and was letting down Elizabeth and proving Arendt right about us minority admissions types. The vodka wasn't doing its job.

—Guess which American writer is most admired in the Soviet Union?

—Richard Wright?

—Faulkner, Lowell announced.

With that, we got up to go see Fassbinder's wonderful *Effi Briest*. The Alfred Kazins were in the movie lobby afterward. We walked slowly. ABC, one of the three major network television companies, was building new studios on the corner of West Sixty-seventh Street and Columbus and also putting up an office block directly across from Elizabeth's, and now again Lowell's, windows, on the site where the abandoned stables had been.

> *Tonight, though, I see it shine*
> *in the Azores of my open window*

They were going to Maine in a few days. A sad Saint-Saëns was waiting for me on the radio in my new place.

I READ THE galleys of *Day by Day*, Lowell's new collection, due to be published at the end of the summer. Several of the poems had been in *The New York Review*. There was a surprising one about the convicted abortion surgeon in Boston. Lowell had stopped writing those sonnets.

> *But sometimes everything I write*
> *with the threadbare art of my eye*
> *seems a snapshot,*

> *lurid, rapid, garish, grouped,*
> *heightened from life,*
> *yet paralyzed by fact.*
> *All's misalliance.*
> *Yet why not say what happened?*

She said that they had been abroad for some time, he hadn't written anything, and she suggested that he write about his family in prose. She typed some of it and the next thing she knew he was upstairs breaking paragraphs into stanzas. Yes, the pope had a canary, and His Holiness did get a shave; it had been in the newspaper when they were in Rome.

But what did '*the black classic*' in the penultimate line of the poem 'Beyond the Alps' refer to? Rimbaud, and also Baudelaire, she always said, but couldn't explain how he meant it, only that he did.

(Lizzie and James once had a very acrid exchange over that line. Some speculated that the black classic referred to a Paris covered in soot, but I never heard Lizzie offer this gloss. She said it was either Baudelaire or Rimbaud or both and you either got it or you didn't. James didn't think that satisfactory. That angered Lizzie.)

'*Etruscan cup*' she thought just sounded good to Cal.

You cannot write by committee, she would say. Writers must be free to make their own mistakes. But it was this weird thing, she often noted. It was much easier to tell someone else what was wrong with what he or she was doing and much harder to see these things for yourself.

She said that *Life Studies* had not been well received at first. The wave started with what she called the New York Jewish intellectual set.

In the West End Café, David Shapiro had insisted that if I was going to admire Lowell's poem 'Skunk Hour,' reprinted in several anthologies and taught in classrooms, then I had to accept from him a little paperback volume of the poems of Francis Ponge in

facing-page translation, because this poetry didn't want to do anything other than sit in my pocket on my walk home.

For the Union Dead is the Civil War. The poems themselves have
the tightness of troop formation. The culture in which Lowell wrote
the poems, that of the United States of the early to mid-1960s,
could still communicate with that of the U.S. in the 1860s, or so it
seemed in the days when Carl Sandburg's reverential biography of
Lincoln was popular literature. At the same time, Lincoln's simple
letter to the mother of five sons killed in battle was given in schools
as an example of the beauty of the language.

(Decades later Lizzie said that when she and Harriet went to see
Glory, the film about the young Colonel Robert Shaw and the val-
iant death he shared with his black troops that Lowell celebrated,
tears poured down their faces just with the opening credits.)

The volume of Lowell's I liked most, and still like most, is *Near
the Ocean.*

> *Is it this shore? Their eyes worn white*
> *As moons from hitting bottom?*

Back then I liked what I took to be the political overtones or un-
dertones of *Near the Ocean*. Elizabeth herself was proud of the man
who had ended his poem 'Waking Early Sunday Morning':

> *. . . peace to our children when they fall*
> *in small war on the heels of small*
> *war—until the end of time*
> *to police the earth, a ghost*
> *orbiting forever lost*
> *in our monotonous sublime.*

She said it was about more in the end than LBJ, it had to do with
our politics, our culture, the monotonous sublime.

Near the Ocean also has Lowell's translation of Canto XV of the *Inferno* and Juvenal's *Tenth Satire* and free versions of Horace's *Odes*.

(I was about to say that I could never get into them, but then James said just now that the point of translation was to give the pleasure of a work to those who cannot know it in its original. That felt like a reproach.)

—His learning, I said.

—You could call it that, Elizabeth said.

The years between 1955 and 1967 had not been calm ones. She said they ended up in New York because of one his manic episodes. It was 1961. Their beautiful house on Marlborough Street he traded in an instant for Eric Bentley's tiny apartment on Riverside Drive. Fortunately, they found West Sixty-seventh Street quickly, once it was clear they weren't going back to Boston. They put a deposit down for an apartment in the same building for Devie's mother.

When in 1970 Lowell said he wanted to move to Oxford, Elizabeth resigned her position at Barnard and withdrew Harriet from school. She made plans, but got no direction from him. For months, he didn't tell her about Caroline. New York turned out to have been the best thing for her as a single mother, she once joked.

—He stands committed in his own mind, and there it all is, she said.

THEY WERE IN Maine for the rest of the summer. We were on the telephone. She was having a quiet summer: few guests, many household chores into which she put most of her nervous energy. Lowell had found a shed near the water to use as a studio, so perhaps she would be able to work on her novel, though this was already the end of July.

She said she was having trouble imagining how all the pieces would fit together. Some chapters she had to revise in order to meet the intensity of the opening part of the novel, which she had published in *The New York Review* four years earlier. I was thinking of her book as autobiography, which perhaps annoyed her. It was certainly cultural history for me. One section she'd shown me began,

> The tyranny of the weak is a burdensome thing, and yet it is better to be exploited by the weak than by the strong. With the weak something is always happening: hypochondria, secret drinking, jealousy, lying, crying, hiding in the garden, driving off in the middle of the night.

She said it was about her freaking out one weekend in Connecticut and driving off in the middle of the night. Yes, she wanted me to find it a scream, because it all happened, including her running behind some bushes. She'd not much confidence in her novel, and only half kidded that she was worried it would be received like an odd Polish memoir in translation. Still, the work drew her on, because for her it was turning into a work of fiction that asked questions about the novel as a form.

Elizabeth had no desire to write a memoir about the literary side of her life or the high life in New York, whatever that was.

—The rich, their rich dishes, and frequently poor characters, she said.

She said he, Lowell, had made so much of his marriages and breakdowns she refused to write about him, or those years of her life. Many of his poems had caused her embarrassment or pain but the record, so to speak, could never be put straight by her setting her own version down on the page. Injuries from those we loved were to be endured. Not stoicism exactly, but no relief would come from rebuttal.

In another phone call, she reported that she'd been working every day on her novel. She was not doing dinners anymore and reading *Anna Karenina*, a chapter a night, before bed. She and Cal were getting on well. Maine was peaceful. It was nice for her work to have him out and down at his boathouse by the sea. She confessed that she'd been miserable the last few summers alone, had wanted to sell it. But she had come to love Castine again.

The following week a bold review of *Day by Day* appeared in the Sunday book section of *The New York Times*. Many of the poems about England are quite opaque, Elizabeth noted, yet the review referred to the attrition of Lowell's marriage to Blackwood and his return to America,

—Which is not in the book.

She thought maybe Caroline didn't have to see the review, though she, Caroline, had sent a clipping of an interview she'd given, peculiar in its meaning. She is photographed on the lawn at Castletown, in Ireland, with some of her children, and throughout is called Lady Lowell. He is said to be touring in Russia at the moment. Apparently, she was ignoring the fact of their separation. But he didn't seem inclined to visit Ireland, except briefly, and he probably had no intention of letting her take a house in Cambridge for the term coming up. In the interview, she said she spent three months of every year there. She'd always been obstreperous about going to Harvard.

The *Times* review was a great send-off. Elizabeth said he was quite removed from his work once it was finished: rewriting things, new phases; renewal one volume, depression the next.

> *The Queen of Heaven, I miss her,*
> *we were divorced.*

—His search for material, she once began, and did not continue.

She said Lowell was reading my piece on a very shallow book about class in black America in the new issue of *The New York Review*. I pretended to play down my debut.

(At some point back there, Elizabeth must have shown Bob and Barbara something I'd written elsewhere. One day a book arrived at my apartment in the mail with a brief letter from Robert Silvers asking if I'd maybe see what could be done. After I'd handed in the piece, Elizabeth broke the *Review*'s code of Vatican Silence about its deliberations and told me that Barbara had tossed off that they might use the piece.)

—The only joy in these things is thinking how miserable you'd be if you weren't doing them, she said.

A while back we'd had a session concerning my short stories, not unlike the evening when my poetry was on trial. She said my stories seemed to be about one thing: yearning for some abstract boy. My black family would be a more interesting subject. She didn't think I needed to burden myself with trying to be a gay novelist. She preferred to say 'queer.' To her it was old-fashioned, but back then there were guys already using the word in a militant way.

—Sex is comic and love is tragic. Queers know this, she told me.

She said I didn't yet have the experience for what I was writing about, and the writing itself was immature, because I was imitating her, which, she could assure me, was a dead end.

—Better stay away from gay lit, honey.

In her view, I had a more immediate future as a critic. I was horrified. She was offended. She wasn't talking about anything French.

(By French, she didn't mean Montaigne; she meant postwar theory.)

—Listen to me.

Mary McCarthy believed that a young writer should work at reviewing. For one thing, it offered the validation of seeing your name in print.

She prescribed heavy doses of Edmund Wilson and got a canvas bag for the small Farrar, Straus and Giroux volumes that she was only lending because she wanted them back. Wilson was someone she used.

(She'd forgotten that I still had *Patriotic Gore*. I sneaked it back with the others and put off reading it for a while.)

And had I not read Emerson in high school? The essay was as noble as it was American. It was imaginative prose. It was a chance for American language. What did I know, she asked, really vexed.

Elizabeth always said that what she liked best about finishing a piece for Bob was cleaning up her desk and putting away the books she'd pulled out. She never expected to hear from him quickly, she said, but in all the years I knew her he never kept her waiting. When she handed something in, he read it straight off.

—Of course, it's very assumptive, I once heard him say into the telephone in his office when I was in the mailroom. I was sure he was talking to Elizabeth.

She really didn't like to be rewritten by editors. She trusted Barbara's ear, but few others. Bob Silvers could describe what sort of correction or addition he thought was needed, but she had to hang up and write it herself. Her style mattered.

Barbara was Elizabeth's best friend, but Bob was her editor. Elizabeth noticed once when he was abroad and she sent something to Barbara that she didn't hear from her right away, not like when she phoned Bob's office to have them send a messenger to pick up a piece. He knew how anxious she'd be. So did Barbara, but she still took her time, and when she did call, she was never as praiseful as Bob. He got around Elizabeth's natural diffidence, talked her into writing. Whereas if she said to Barbara that she didn't feel like doing a certain subject Barbara always said,

—I don't blame you.

Elizabeth said she was afraid it was because they were girls, and not supposed to put themselves out there.

My father congratulated me, though he was not yet ready to believe. He said my mother excused me for quoting her in my piece.

He said she said her friends wouldn't see *The New York Review of Books*. It had been a while since we were all okay at the same time: my sister Donna was out of the hospital, back in her apartment, going back to school; my sister Pat was out of town on business, getting married in the autumn; and my mother was losing my father's money at a blackjack table, because he was calling from an off-season hotel room in Las Vegas, in case I'd tried them at home earlier.

My father still hoped I'd get my education together. He wanted me to go to graduate school, to have a backup plan, but he took out a subscription to *The New York Review of Books*.

THE TYPEWRITER IN the bookstore kept sprouting roaches. Elizabeth had broken her last pair of reading glasses up in Maine. That chapter of the novel on Communists wasn't working at all, she said, but Lowell returned and she couldn't talk anymore.

It was cool enough to wear a sweater to Felice's. She and Luc were fairly stoned, listening to popular music from West Africa. I was very blank by the time we were in a taxi heading for the Loft, a fierce after-hours club Howard had first taken me to. There were many checkpoints and much referring to guest lists but using Howard's name got us in. I wasn't hip, but my friends were.

The Loft was large, and very mixed: white, black, Hispanic, men and men, women and men, women and women, groups, solitary figures. Downstairs the music was cool, there were places to sit, to nod, and plenty of water, grapefruit juice, cookies, popcorn, bananas, peaches, potato salad, grapes. No alcohol was served at the Loft and that was why its atmosphere was so civilized and calm on the one hand, and on the other so concentrated on the wordless language of the body, even though people snuck in booze.

Upstairs was filled with people intent on nothing else for the moment but dancing, no matter for how many hours the moment

was going to go on. They shook and dipped. The music was bump-
ing and by three in the morning the whole place had gone wild,
had, as Felice said,

—Gone off.

Lights blinked everywhere; balloons dropped from the ceiling; a
tall, elegant black queen in layers of red chiffon was on a dais dancing with gods, while around the high priestess, the hand-clapping
of joyful hearts ebbed and built again.

Daybreak. Mercer Street was refreshing. I could feel nothing in
my legs and I was incapable of hearing. I woke around dusk and
met Catharine R. Stimpson and her partner the musicologist Liz
Wood in Central Park for a performance of *Agamemnon*. They introduced me to an Australian doctor who was worried about his
American qualification exams. He belonged to a motorcycle club.

I must borrow from Walt Whitman to praise this night.

He and I were happily surrounded on Christopher Street, and
coming toward us in the opposite direction of traffic, threading
through the stalled cars, was Rollereena, the radical fairy, a mad
old white queen in white roller skates, dressed in a white tulle
skirt. He was wearing a pinkish-white wig and white, begemmed
butterfly glasses. Rollereena carried a wand that ended in a puff
and smacked the hoods of cars packed with bellowing bridge-and-
tunnel types, and performed circles in headlights, and told them
off, driver by driver.

(The anxious Australian doctor, a nice Catholic boy from Sydney, was named John Brennan. Ten years later he died of AIDS, but
would never say to me that that was what he had.

His partner, Phillip Drummond, a musicologist, died of AIDS
two years before him. He was so sick when John finally got him on
the plane home to Australia that the airline kicked them off in Los
Angeles. Phillip died soon after and another airline refused to take
his body from California to Sydney.)

—I loathe the Upper West Side, Elizabeth once said. Midtown is my idea.

In the ten years I would live on West Ninety-fifth Street, it never crossed my mind to invite her up.

I always dreamed of the Village.

John hated the Village, camp though he was.

—Mary.

Not even Howard called me Mary. The doctor's favorite place was the Nickel, a riotous black gay bar with a little square dance floor on West Seventy-second Street between Columbus and Needle Park, the intersection with Broadway where Amsterdam began. Professional black dancers liked hanging out at the Nickel; the clientele was the floor show; bedecked women like the singer Taka Boom would stop by to holler at the boys. It surprised me that John was so well known in there, so comfortable as a Dinge Queen, as he called himself. (Rice Queen bars were on the Upper East Side; Snow Queens were sometimes humiliated at Clone bars because the doormen thought black men would prey on the white boys inside.) The Nickel's manager was a magnificently built black guy rumored to have a mob boyfriend. Real fights could break out in that bar and spill into the street along the façade of plaster carved to look like pinto hide.

My doctor's boyfriend, the Australian musicologist, was conveniently away in San Francisco for weeks, and I had something not from my usual playbook of the one-sided to go on and on about when Elizabeth was at last back from Maine that September and making Sunday dinner.

But when she let me in, she said Cal had just called to say he was coming back early from Ireland, not to Harvard but to New York.

—It's been sheer torture, she said he said.

Caroline had run off to London.

All year Elizabeth had been cautious with her feelings, she

said, aware that something could still happen with Caroline. He'd been writing to Caroline over the summer. Giving up love is hard, she said, and being alone is much worse.

She'd said to him that he didn't have to write or call from Ireland the two weeks he would be there, but because of this dramatic decision to come immediately to New York, she felt now the time had come when they could talk about how they wanted to live.

Part 3

Elizabeth was on the phone early, asking, —Where were you last night? I tried to call you.

I wondered what she was still doing in town. She hung up, horrified I hadn't known.

The line was busy when I phoned back from bed, busy when I phoned from the bookstore. I had Tuesday's paper. It was front-page news. It was on the radio all day. Sunday he was on the phone saying that he was on his way; Monday he arrived dead at her front door.

'Grim, gallant, and tender,' Norman Mailer said of Robert Lowell.

I called Barbara Epstein, who was chewing gum, not smoking, not saying much, and suddenly she asked if I was afraid to call Elizabeth.

I'd tried to call Elizabeth on Monday, because the day before I'd forgotten the pages of *The Cost of Living* she'd set aside for me to read. I was going to ask her to leave them with her doorman before she went up to teach her class in Connecticut. At first there was no answer. I assumed that she and Mr. Lowell had gone to dinner. I remember being surprised that her number was busy all night. Then I met Luc, late, to borrow what we all referred to as his exquisite typewriter. He was getting over a cold and a funk, describing periods of sweating lethargy and sweating energy. Elizabeth had called when I was out.

The taxi driver couldn't rouse Lowell when they reached her door on West Sixty-seventh Street. The doorman fetched her and he was pronounced dead on arrival at Roosevelt Hospital. She told me much later that she called to him all the way to the hospital, though she knew he was gone. His fingers had fastened over a parcel, Lucian

Freud's portrait of Caroline, and emergency staff had had to separate the no-longer-living him from it. (Was it the portrait entitled *The Idle Woman?* The eyes wide like a sea creature's?) Back then, after Caroline had gone back to England, Elizabeth told me that she carried that portrait around the hospital's chaotic corridors, along with his satchel rattling with the odds and ends of a life in poetry.

She showed me a notebook and a gold medal and put them back in the faded leather satchel, saying that perhaps she ought to have given these to Caroline as well. I said no and she shoved the moral dilemma back into the closet where she kept, among other treasures, a scrawled-on copy of his very first collection, privately printed, *Land of Unlikeness.*

In the hospital, Elizabeth had her purse, his things, and no change. Even when she explained, the emergency desk could not make change and would not let her use a hospital phone to call her daughter. She said she bought a dime for five dollars from someone sitting in the waiting room. I couldn't believe that guy hadn't just given her the dime.

—Neither can I.

Harriet's Dalton School friends, Cathy Grad, Melissa Brown (where was Lisa Wager?), came over that Tuesday evening and gave Elizabeth a tranquilizer. We got her up to bed.

—I am utterly prepared to live alone now.

Her head hit the pillow.

—This is the worst thing that has ever happened to me.

I DIDN'T GO to the funeral in Boston. I didn't have any money. I couldn't ask my parents. The conviction had taken root in my family that I was unable to cope with funerals, with death. I couldn't then turn up at some white family's farewell, not even Elizabeth's. That was something my father's father would have done.

I'd not gone to my mother's funerals the year before. My mother's father broke apart shortly after my grandmother died. My mother had to go to Atlanta and bring him like pieces in a bag back with her to Indianapolis. He seemed to think he was playing for the Atlanta Black Crackers and had transferred with them to Victory Field in Indianapolis. The nursing home where he sat for years, forgetting who Hank Aaron was and how much he hated the crackers who tried to own him, really smelled, and was not far from us, on the old Michigan turnpike that was becoming a strip of black businesses. I did not want to go to funerals.

and everyone and I stopped breathing

Maria Callas died the day of Lowell's funeral.

—I promise you Cal was buried in papal style, Elizabeth said.

But the ride to the family graveyard in Dunbarton, New Hampshire, she said was a nightmare. Caroline insisted they ride together. The hysteria. Elizabeth said she was not going to fight with her over the body. She had no intention of being the widow.

The memorial held for Lowell at the American Place Theatre in New York ten days after his funeral was her next big thing to get through. It was going to be more like a party than a wake, my excited guess.

When everyone was gathering at the bar of the theater, I looked across the room for Elizabeth. She was standing, alone for a minute, a lock of hair almost covering an eye, cigarette between forefinger and thumb, with the palm turned upward. Her left hand rested on her hip. Dressed in gray, she saw me, smiled, and shrugged.

—I'm not going to wear widow's weeds, she'd said.

Sigrid had broken up with Sontag's son some days before and was trying not to speak of it.

The mother of one of Harriet's Dalton School pals appeared before me:

—I didn't recognize you. You look respectable.

In the theater, I saw Barbara sitting by herself. She didn't have a chance. I pounced, abandoning Prudence Crowther, satirist in the production studio, and Michael Johnson, painter in the mailroom.

Fifteen or sixteen eminent readers of Robert Lowell's poetry, including Robert Giroux, Jonathan Raban, Susan Sontag, Norman Mailer, and, in person, Meyer Schapiro. It had been a ritual of Columbia life, to try to infiltrate one of his lectures closed to undergraduates. Joseph Brodsky was up before his turn and blinking back tears. Irene Worth stood aside from the microphone, became for a few seconds Lowell observing rehearsals for his version of *Prometheus Bound* at the Yale Drama School, and then she became Io, pursued by Zeus.

> I shall never stop running. Prometheus, tell me where I
> must go, and how far I must run before I die.

Twice a trio, with Lukas Foss at piano, played a movement from Schubert. As Lowell's friends read, I would glance at Elizabeth, sitting toward the front, her cheek meeting Harriet's now and then. Harriet looked a lot like her mother. There were Devie and her sister and their mother. Susan's great head of newly salt-and-pepper hair would turn and she'd squeeze Elizabeth's hand. Eugene McCarthy read from 'Waking Early Sunday Morning' and gave gentle anecdotes of the '68 campaign. Elizabeth Bishop, the hem of her blue suit well below the knee, also read from 'Waking Early Sunday Morning'

—With the political allusions removed, she mumbled. After that, nobody could make out a single word.

Caroline Blackwood herself rose in a black velvet suit and black cap and read a poem from *Day by Day*, 'For Sheridan.'

We listened to a recording: the dramatically civil voice, the unlikely pronunciation of vowels. It was as though Lowell were on the little stage, reading his poem 'Dunbarton.'

> *Grandfather and I*
> *raked leaves from our dead forebears . . .*

Next to me, Barbara struggled; next to her, I gave in.

I borrowed Grandfather's cane . . .

Afterward, I walked Elizabeth in the rain, around puddles, to the Coffee House, a club in the West Forties that Bob Silvers belonged to. Mailer tried to have a conversation with Susan about karma. Brodsky and Derek Walcott were playful, pretending to stash objects inside their jackets. Soon the bar was very busy and the crowd's laughter real.

Elizabeth and Barbara were hungry. They ended up in a neighborhood restaurant, their neighborhood, the corner of Columbus Avenue and West Sixty-seventh Street, with Susan, John Thompson, and me. Jack Thompson sang a lot and Susan Sontag was not a drinker, but his book *The Founding of English Metre* was held in such esteem he could tease the ladies if he must, friend of Cal's since Kenyon College that he was. In all that time, he'd published only one book of poems. He couldn't keep in his head why I was there. Something about him was entirely sympathetic.

It was a Monday, two weeks since Lowell's death. September was almost over. Elizabeth was touched and surprised by the letters that had come.

She was most sorry that she'd not had a chance to speak with him before he died. That phone call from Ireland had been so short, two weeks and a lifetime ago.

Elizabeth said Cal had said to her in Maine:

—Don't think I don't know when I have it good.

CAROLINE APPEARED AT Elizabeth's door and stayed. Her children must have gone already. Elizabeth telephoned, breathless and worn out.

—I can barely talk.

Caroline had been sleeping in her clothes all week.

—Has she been drinking?

—Drinking?!!

In her grief, Caroline was up until four o'clock in the morning, talking maniacally. Elizabeth said she said repeatedly that Cal wanted to die; he was torn. Everyone was in deep shock, she'd say again and again. Late in the night, you got the truth, but otherwise she was carrying on, deeply angry, Elizabeth felt. Caroline said she couldn't bear to go back to Ireland, to the rooms where they were last together. Elizabeth said she wanted to ask, Then why are you so comfortable on West Sixty-seventh Street?

I'd been in Indianapolis, dancing with my sister at our sister's wedding, standing with our cousins in a circle of remembrance for my mother's sister.

> *Between farewell and the absence of farewell,*
> *The final mercy and the final loss,*
> *The wind and the sudden falling of the wind.*

ELIZABETH FORGOT HER rules about gossip and not talking. Susan had been through a terrible scare. Blood in the urine, refusing a biopsy, on the phone to her doctor in Paris, exams with her doctor here, thinking it was one thing on Wednesday, being told on Thursday the kidney had been invaded, discovering on Friday it was a cyst. She said Susan's voice was shaking Thursday. Elizabeth was always anxious when in Connecticut for her class, unable to go to sleep, waking early, and whenever she had finally slipped under, the phone would ring, and it would be Barbara calling with another report. Nicole Stéphane was coming from Paris. It was Susan's worst crisis since her surgery two years before.

Elizabeth said she once asked Susan if she ever woke in the middle of the night in a panic.

—No, she said Susan had answered in a flash.

(—I bet she did, James said at lunch this afternoon. —I bet Susan just did. He made a Vietnamese soup, pho.)

—Susan is a winner, Elizabeth said. She's happily demanding, quite so, and a big child at times, but worth it.

From time to time, Luc slipped me old issues of *Partisan Review* that he'd come across. In 1947, Elizabeth Hardwick said of Jean-Paul Sartre:

> No matter what their final value may be, these people, by arousing gossip and controversy, disturbing Philistines and exhilarating college students, help to keep alive the interest in art and remind the world of the excitement of the intellectual life.

Susan was having her moment: a collection of stories was soon to be published and *On Photography* had come out as a book. She gave an astonishing lecture, 'Illness as Metaphor,' at New York University, in a distinguished series. It was impossible to think of her as ill, she looked so healthy, so vibrant and undaunted, pulling at her hair, sweeping it out of her face as she spoke. A thinker, not an artist, we young folk said, maybe a little glad to have some reservations about this impressive woman.

The whole of the *Review* turned up for Susan's lecture, and Sigrid, with Brodsky and Barthelme, and Susan's house cleaner, a young actor. A lecture you wanted to pay attention to, followed by an adult party, hot, smoky, the kind of New York evening when it was gratifying to be another young observer in time, noshing away and ready to hear everything inspirational.

Elizabeth: —I would never be able to bring myself to face a New York audience.

Mr. Silvers: —Lectures are for the provinces, sort of.

Elizabeth, nodding at me: —Tickets are always sent to couples.

Grace, Lady Dudley, the ramrod woman by Bob's side: —Marvelous.

Maxine Groffsky introduced me to Margo Jefferson. A memory pinched me: Professor Koch sent me as a student to meet Groffsky, newly established as a literary agent. She gave me a drink. I'd had a fortifying few beforehand and at the end of the John Cage concert she took me to, I woke in the front row to the sound of applause and my final snore.

One evening before Thanksgiving, Elizabeth got on the phone with Barbara while I was sitting there. They'd been to Robert Fizdale and Arthur Gold's party, then to Gore Vidal's birthday party, and were discussing the next intense party on their calendar.

Elizabeth said, —I'm ashamed to be at three of these in one week, aren't you? I mean I feel like a fool.

SOME WINTER MORNINGS found me hungover in the same Upper West Side diner around the corner from my apartment. The counter's dust was oily. I was already late to my new job. The sole waitress added slowly, incorrectly, her Bavarian accent thickening as she rushed between toast and more syrup to scribble for a hardened white couple the address where her congregation met. It was an effort for her to balance four glasses, one pencil, and keep her expression of serene understanding. Her Greek boss fumed. She wanted to testify, but the couple stood up.

—Have you got a boyfriend? I'm trying to find out if you love anyone besides Jesus.

I stood up to get on my way as well. I was working for Elizabeth Hardwick.

Cal's letters and remaining papers. She did not want a stranger for this work, but she was uneasy about having a secretary, taking letters and answering the telephone, things she did herself.

—It's a travesty to face instant coffee in the morning.

The shrill voice that could scorch the traditional South in which she did not believe belonged to her domestic persona. Not only did she, a hysteric about debt, pay taxes well in advance, she got on the telephone with utility companies and made sure they knew what kind of customer she had been for years. Then the phone might ring and she'd pick up herself, her social dial already spun to the lost-dove channel. Old-fashioned charities such as the Patrolmen's Benevolent Association were charmed to be in touch with Mrs. Lowell around the bourbon and lemon hour.

But first the articles on Lowell's death had to be collected and filed. Then I had to sort through the letters and telegrams of condolence. (Nicolas Nabokov wrote one of the most beautiful.) From the closets in a little office next to the kitchen came old Mrs. Lowell's scrapbooks, including one she kept of her brother, Devereux Winslow, the uncle in *Life Studies* dying of the incurable Hodgkin's disease, as well as a notebook of Lowell's from his Kenyon College days, and numerous worksheets. He went over and over his lines.

She said that after a breakdown, ashamed, though he'd no reason to be, Lowell would retreat to his study. It was his male preserve, his garage. Only he didn't have a car to tinker with, only his poems. The year Lowell published *The Dolphin*, two other volumes also appeared, *History* and *For Lizzie and Harriet*. And those sonnets are what he would describe as a rearrangement and rewriting of *Notebook*, itself a work published in two versions.

(I just misremembered on the street:

—The birds sing revise, revise, revise.

Elizabeth Bishop's poem for Lowell. It's 'North Haven,' but I had it wrong. It goes:

> *Nature repeats herself, or almost does:*
> *repeat, repeat, repeat; revise, revise, revise.*)

My separating a box of letters from Lowell, chronologically, proved difficult for Elizabeth to take. There were lots of them to get through, so I looked at the dates, and didn't read them. I didn't take in at the time what those letters were: when he left and wouldn't come back; his new family; their divorce; maybe even *The Dolphin*. Several times I had to ask her to read undated ones so that they could be filed.

—And what does it all mean? she exclaimed one day, looking at the rows of envelopes lengthening down the dining room table.

There was Lowell's long letter to Roosevelt explaining his decision to be a conscientious objector after the bombing of Dresden; Madame Mandelstam's letter defending Lowell's adaptation of a Mandelstam poem, an adaptation Vladimir Nabokov had attacked; and several letters from Elizabeth Bishop. There were his unfinished essays, on New England writers, on Eliot, that were really good. She said he wrote them in his shed, with no books around him to consult. The late things belonged to the estate and she had already shipped off to Boston the manuscript of *Day by Day*.

She said the Lowell Papers were largely a product of housecleaning. She'd empty the trash, smooth out the crumpled sheets, and put them away.

(I told James this story and since then James Fenton has never let me near the wastepaper basket in his study.)

It was a casual arrangement. Often Elizabeth would cancel our workday so that she could write, or run errands, or go to the hair salon, or meet with Harriet.

—You're the only child of an aging parent who suffers from an exaggerated case of mother love.

They'd laugh and embrace.

Or sometimes we'd quit early, have drinks, dinner, play an Ivy Anderson recording, look down our noses at the doggedness of the black critic Nathan Scott's Christian interpretations of modern poets.

ELIZABETH WAS AMUSED that everyone went on about Allen Tate's influence on Lowell, but Tate wrote to her before *Life Studies* appeared and accused her of trying to ruin Cal. The odd thing to her was that Tate was certain she had put Cal up to doing the book. I didn't realize that Allen Tate was still alive. 'Ode to the Confederate Dead' was something I was excused from having to read.

—Feeble-minded, she pronounced. —Of a fatuity, her voice going up steps before it glided into her light laughter.

I hadn't heard that from her in a while. Something gentle settled on us, on the sofa, the oval coffee table that hinged up into a rectangle, on the carpet. She got up and turned on more lamps and remembered the time when the first Mrs. Tate (I wrote Christine in my journal, but I meant Caroline Gordon), a Southern writer who believed all the myths about the South and its Whig characteristics, was breaking up with Tate. Jean Stafford, a big Catholic and an even bigger drunk, summoned Elizabeth to the Hotel Earl.

—They've been together forever, Stafford charged.

—I hope they stay together forever, Elizabeth said she whimpered in reply.

Jean got drunk; Cal took Elizabeth to a taxi. She made a plea about her innocence.

He said, —That's all right, very tenderly. She said she was already falling for him. Once she saw him on Sixth Avenue and just swooned.

(Was Lowell married to Stafford at the time? Didn't she also say she saw him coming up Second Avenue and hid in a doorway, she was so attracted to him?

And when had she thrown up on Cal, or nearly, on his shoe, as he handed her into a taxi?

I thought her summons to a midtown hotel was to appear before a tribunal of literary wives and any number of martinis. A cascade of tears when Cal rescued her and led her away. She suffered curbside sickness, just when she should have been thanking him. A story I've told often enough turns out to be different when I find it written down in an old journal, like how much smaller that historic house is in real life compared to the film version. Or a story she told often enough turned out to be changeable in the dominion of memory.)

I have her saying that that trial was probably why she and Tate never really got on. She laughed some more, saying it had been unnecessary of him to have made her sick.

Tate's clueless biographer had been by to interview her. He informed her that he heard that she and Tate had had an affair.

—Allen said that, didn't he.

—Yes, he did.

She said Tate could have an affair with her for his biography if it meant that much to him.

Because of Lowell's opposition to the Vietnam War, and his having been a conscientious objector, I didn't really think about his involvement with the Fugitive Poets and what they stood for. For all his Union heritage, he flirted with the South quite a bit. In the late 1930s, as a student giving up on Harvard, Lowell had gone down to Tennessee and pitched a tent on Tate's lawn, offering himself up as a disciple. Then he followed Tate and John Crowe Ransom, the leader of the group, to Kenyon College in Ohio. After graduating with a degree in classics, he taught in Louisiana for a spell.

It meant nothing to Elizabeth that Tate was also from Kentucky, or Ransom from Tennessee. The claim in the Agrarians' manifesto that Southerners were the natural defenders of English culture irked her. She disliked 'the false cavalierism,' as she called it, in this picture of the South. For her, the South was small-town America, a state of mind you wanted to get away from.

—It's better than it used to be. Looking through people on the street, pretending they did not exist, she once said about the progress U.S. society had or had not made concerning race.

She understood what Ransom meant to Lowell, what American academics liked to call a formalist approach. Bishop admired things about Ransom's poetry, and although Elizabeth seemed to have the respect for Ransom that she did not for Tate, she never recommended I read anything by him, either.

Much as she might respect I. A. Richards and C. K. Ogden they didn't speak to her. She was distant from the deconstruction and poststructuralism that were burning through American universities at the time. She also had little interest in the New Criticism. We were all descended from the New Criticism, if you wanted to say it came from T. S. Eliot, she conceded, adding that that was such a dreary observation.

And it wasn't that she was against close readings. Discussion of a novelist's or a poet's language could be very thrilling. The wildness of Dickens. It's just that most theory was, for her, badly written, a bore to read.

—The difference between Roland Barthes and his imitators is that he has genius, she said.

Moreover, *Partisan Review* had been the anti-Stalinist Left. It was a matter of relief, even pride to her that as an undergraduate she had been against the Moscow Trials. Marxism made her distrust ideologies of criticism.

Elizabeth remembered that Tate became jealous of Cal after the publication of *Life Studies*.

—Surely he has met his ruin. Tate's favorite line, as if he hoped he would, indeed.

Sterling Brown despised Tate for his cultural racism, including his saying that too much education was bad for a black person. I got the impression that Elizabeth regarded the Agrarians as Lowell's disheveled youth and he had of course grown out of all that.

ALFRED KAZIN'S NEW memoir, *New York Jew*, irritated her, for Lowell's sake. Kazin had written of something that happened at Yaddo thirty years before in the time of McCarthyism, witch-hunting, and score-settling that she preferred not to remember.

In 1948, Lowell asked if she was coming back to Saratoga. She did, and Flannery O'Connor was there. (O'Connor had been high on Professor Hardwick's list of writers our Barnard class had to read.) Another writer, Agnes Smedley, was also there at Yaddo. In 1949, an article appeared in *The New York Times* saying that Smedley was a Communist.

(She had been a spy, it was discovered decades later, but neither for nor against the U.S., rather in China, on behalf of the Soviet Union.)

Elizabeth Ames, Yaddo's longtime director, was investigated for harboring her friend Smedley for such a considerable amount of time. Ames was exonerated, but Smedley left the U.S. for English obscurity and soon died.

Kazin remembered that he was having trouble writing at Yaddo for the first time in his experience of the hallowed retreat for writers, which made Lowell's excited presence hard to take.

> Lowell and Elizabeth Hardwick were a brilliant couple,
> but Lowell was just a little too dazzling at the moment.

Kazin was clear that it was Lowell who went to the FBI with the allegations or reservations about Ames's political allegiances. Lowell, who had already emerged as an important figure in American poetry, used what Kazin called the authority that his reputation gave him to convene Yaddo's board and demand Ames's dismissal. Kazin said he and other writers moved to support the director, but plenty of people were afraid to risk their positions defending someone who had been denounced, or to go against Lowell.

—Cal comes off as reactionary. I could no more have married a Republican than I could have a Nazi, she said in an unfamiliar voice.

Elizabeth had given me her old copy of Kazin's first book, *On Native Ground: An Interpretation of Modern American Prose*, published in 1945, when he was twenty-six years old. Kazin read the history of American literature from Howells to Faulkner as the coming of realism. His interpretation influenced my view of black American literature as a historical progression, a constant push for the realism that could open up in literature a truer picture of the black condition.

Elizabeth and I argued over Kazin's criticism that the lawyer's speech in *Native Son* in which he explains Bigger Thomas's murders in the context of his oppression almost undoes the novel. It was our ongoing debate over the dangers of trying to oblige ideology in fiction. It was not, for her, the abrupt change of tone, of point of view, that was the problem. After all, she appreciated weird things on the page, provided they worked. Max's plea to the jury was too easy. And she agreed with Kazin: it was too party line.

(Kazin would eventually reassess the novel's closing argument, but Elizabeth didn't. I had from my secondhand book job, on Luc's five-finger discount, Wright's nonfiction books about Nkrumah, Protestants in Franco's Spain, and the Bandung Conference, written in his last years in France. They were of much more interest than his novels of the same period. *Black Boy* was Wright's great work, Elizabeth always said, and his early stories.)

That was not the moment to remind her of her often-repeated line: that her ambition when she was young had been to become a New York Jewish intellectual.

Kazin opened *New York Jew* with the publication of his first book, getting his first job, being in his first marriage, finding his first apartment in Manhattan. He had a lot to say about *Partisan Review* and its parties. He identifies Elizabeth Hardwick as the author of sensitive short stories and essays, but his attention is on Lowell, on Hannah Arendt's doting on Lowell and how it went to his head. Kazin blamed Lowell for the witch hunt at Yaddo, blamed his inflated, unbalanced ego. He said when years later Lowell told him he didn't remember the episode, he believed him.

Elizabeth blamed herself. She said someone had turned up recently with the minutes of that meeting. She said she had something to do with starting it, then forgot it, but the thing had already mushroomed. She attributed the incident to what she called her volatile nature. She had these explosions and retreats.

—I was always organizing kids to run away from home. They got ready and then I wouldn't go.

She scarcely figured in Kazin's account, but I had to leave it alone and was happy to. It was not nothing.

(In Ian Hamilton's version in his biography, Yaddo was already being investigated by the FBI when Lowell somehow latched on to the Ames-Smedley story. Apparently, Lowell's remarks to the Yaddo trustees' meeting run for several pages. What Hamilton quotes has Lowell nattering on the edge of his mental rocker. Lizzie is quoted as smearing Ames in a line, saying she seemed dishonest on the surface, but she couldn't read what was in her heart. Defenders of Ames at the time pointed out that Elizabeth Hardwick was a former Communist and her type was predictably energetic when rooting around for possible traitors.

Looking back, I think her harshness had been toward herself, for the smear, much as she maybe tried to make it sound like she was saying nothing, and for not having done more to protect Lowell from himself. But she wouldn't have known what his rhetorical grandeur portended.)

It was a manic episode on their way to the altar, perhaps. Bishop warned Lowell against Elizabeth; Lowell's doctor advised her not to marry a man so tormented in mind; Mary McCarthy considered Elizabeth to be getting above herself.

One night she called to read me something she'd written on Solzhenitsyn. The next morning she called to say Random House had sent her Stokely Carmichael's mail by accident.

ROBERT GIROUX QUOTED Lowell on the death of Eliot in his citation for *Day by Day* at the National Book Critics Circle Awards at the Time-Life Building.

—It's like old home week, Celia McGee said.

Toni Morrison wore a striking black dress that caught the light. John Leonard was rapturous in his speech about her, so excited he briefly stood on one leg. Was it then or later that Erroll McDonald, the young black star of Random House, pointed out to me that in *Song of Solomon* a black person flies for the first time in African American literature? Erroll said that Morrison had written her dissertation on suicide in the works of Virginia Woolf and William Faulkner. He said that Faulkner's influence on African American literature could be traced back through the magic realists of South America who read Faulkner in translation.

Elizabeth read the citation for Sontag's prize that she'd written. She took out her glasses, said, —Umph, which made everyone laugh, and then began:

—In reading *On Photography* today we are also reading a classic of the future.

Her public voice once again a surprise to me in being high, loud, and so very Southern. She did a seesaw dance with her shoulders, as if ambivalent word by word about how she'd expressed herself. She'd say 'perm,' in the most countrified accent—'purrm'—on purpose. Right after a visit to her hair salon, her layers were more like curls, and they were set in motion as she spoke. She was warmly applauded.

Susan was so pleased it made her bashful. The room was buzzing; people were knocking them back and smoking everywhere. Elizabeth left to have dinner with Susan, Susan's son, David, back with Sigrid, and Roger and Dorothea Strauss. Then, when I was talking to Eliot Fremont-Smith, book editor of *The Village Voice*, a memory tapped me on the shoulder, about how I'd shared my wonderfully vehement opinions with him at the last cocktail party where he encountered me.

John Ashbery, on the wagon, said as he was leaving,

—Call me.

—Sober this time, I said, remembering that one, too.

—Drunk or sober, I do it all the time, he said, a gracious guy.

(Almost every encounter with that old self can be rough. Just now, I had to get up and go hold my head in the hallway. I leaned over the banister and told James, known east of Suez as 'Jimbo,' how embarrassed I was to look back. He said: —Well, Frank Harris did a useful thing. He was nice to Oscar Wilde.)

Days later, Elizabeth said that reading was such a wonderful thing that to have made a life around the experience was almost criminal it was so fortunate.

I said I couldn't imagine being George Sand and writing thirty pages a day from necessity. She said she was glad I couldn't see myself as George Sand. Who would be Chopin?

—I swear it's almost a bodily process. And you wonder how you wrote that today and why you couldn't last Monday.

She reminded me how much Byron and Pasternak she had been taking in. That kind of reading was a pleasure. She expected me to know more than I did.

(Recently, I was surprised to hear James say to someone who asked him what's the best poem in English that he thought maybe *Don Juan* was the most complete poem.)

I found a blizzard hopelessly distracting from writing and then when the curbs were full of sooty-snow remains I caught a cold and laundering handkerchieves kept me from sitting down to that review or making the trip down Broadway to West Sixty-seventh Street.

—Not to mind.

Elizabeth was working, telling me again that writing turns into a matter of plodding along.

—My first drafts always read as if they had been written by a chicken.

I remember her talking about the joy of revision, but she also said that anyone who can't bring himself to the pain of revision can't be a real writer. She said nights of restless envy were a part of it and showed me what she thought was a brilliant essay in the *Review* on the kabbalah by a classmate whom I didn't much care for.

It was a relief not to be teaching, she noted. And to write about Olga Ivinskaya's memoir of having been Pasternak's mistress clearly gave Elizabeth a way to address the experience of survival and the unreality of literary legacies that had been on her mind since Lowell's death, emotions that she found herself either living out or trying to avoid.

She'd been to Eleanor Perenyi's for a night in Connecticut and, needing to work, canceled the workday. I stayed home. Bob sent her *Tolstoy Remembered* by Tatyana Tolstoy, Tolstoy's eldest daughter. Elizabeth encouraged me to stick to the assignments and pledges on my own table. I stayed in; she phoned again to push me to finish what I was working on. I did and, pleased to be reading something not related to an assignment, moved on to Pasternak's stories, which enabled me to get Ashbery's quip about wanting to holiday on Tula.

Elizabeth had a way of talking to young writers that assumed we understood what was involved in the production of: anything. Part of what made her such a powerful example that a writing life was possible for you, too, was that she took your anxieties seriously. But all problems about writing had one solution: you had to, you said you would, it was the contract you made with yourself, it was your life.

She said she felt renewed energy from having something to write. She said the past few months had felt like a moral collapse. She said it again. Her mood of the past few months had been one of moral collapse.

ON THE LAST day of February, Elizabeth came back from a weekend in Princeton. She had the Sunday newspaper, but was tired, so she went downstairs to make coffee. She reasoned afterward that some of the newspaper must have covered the ashtray on her bed-side table. It caught fire. By the time the firemen left, the master bedroom was in ruins, most of the upstairs blackened, and the walls of her living room, two stories high, streaked with black wa-ter so that in the daylight it had the timbered look of a Stratford-upon-Avon type of inn.

—What have I done to my beautiful home, she said, in borrowed clothes, rubbing a small silver dish with an ineffectual sponge.

She said the clothes she hated survived. She lost her best clothes, a signed Eames table, a drawing by Elizabeth Bishop, two by Sidney Nolan, nineteenth-century Goya prints, and books, including the privately printed memoirs of Cassie Julian-James, née Myers, from which Lowell drew a great deal for '91 Revere Street.' We did find the volume of poems by the original Robert Traill Spence Lowell, badly damaged, along with one of the two drawings of Ezra Pound done by his girlfriend at Rapallo. Elizabeth gingerly inspected the inscription in Lafcadio Hearn's *Glimpses of Unfamiliar Japan*, a book mentioned in the poem 'Father's Bedroom':

This book has had hard usage on the Yangtze River, China.

Those sets of James Russell Lowell that had been in the upstairs hallway, black, warped, common enough, yet still there, with sweet, handsomely bound volumes by his wife, Maria Lowell, who died young and whom many considered the better poet. A. Lawrence Lowell, Percival Lowell, Amy Lowell, John Lowell, General Stark (one of Lowell's Revolutionary War ancestors), privately printed histories of the Winslows, and our hands got covered with ash just from touching them. Her work and manuscripts in what had been Harriet's bedroom were fine, stored in drawers. Safe were those chapters of *The Cost of Living*, as Elizabeth was still calling her novel, and a diary.

(Until working on Lowell's papers, I hadn't known she kept a diary. Maybe to keep a diary wasn't the correct phrase. She began it when Cal took up with Caroline, and, in not wanting to write anything awful about him, she didn't feel she had written anything. Those pages had long been torn out and destroyed. In that heavy, brown leather book, in her large handwriting, there was only a brief beginning of a portrait of I. A. Richards and his wife. Blank pages followed.)

Sturdy boxes and drawers had saved her jewelry, but the guilt was terrible for her. Fortunately, no one was injured; no other apartment had been touched. It would take months for her and Harriet to put their home back together. I thought Elizabeth might write a story about a claims adjuster; crooked competitors called her in the middle of the night, bullying.

It was never meant to be a permanent position. When she first took me on, she smiled that she got a cut of the first sale of his papers and rightly so, because she had done all the work.

(I see now that she did not say then that when she was first working to get his papers in order, Lowell met Caroline Blackwood.)

My job on the Lowell Papers, as she stressed I must call the effort, turned into a cleaning job. We never resumed work on what was in those file cabinets and closets, my lists of works, articles by and about him, tedious to compile. (Saskia Hamilton would finish the work on the Papers for Lizzie.) While Harriet answered the telephone, Elizabeth typed her own work. She finished an article on Susan for *Vogue*. We'd assembled a little bed in the office next to the kitchen. Harriet made her mother lie down. I typed the quotes from Susan's work that Elizabeth had chosen to go with the article. She praised the fantastic energy of Susan's thinking and her accomplishments. I thought, Old Campaigner.

The unattractive ABC building was going up and up across the street, a terrible racket, a grinding and knocking that went on until the whistle blew shortly after four o'clock. The skeletal steel frame already blocked out the light she used to get in her kitchen and dining room. She commented often on the new gloom of her afternoons. She had her moments of worry, helpless, sinusy melt-down. You couldn't blame her, bathing next door, her cosmetics on a kitchen counter by the mirror.

The inscription for Lowell's tombstone had been decided on. I thought it was going to be from 'Endings':

> *The immortal is scraped unconsenting from the mortal.*

Elizabeth said he was writing about Cousin Harriet and she particularly liked the use of the word *'scraped'*:

—Its modernity.

Both she and Lady Caroline agreed that the more rhetorical and public lines would not do. But Caroline decided that *'scraped'* sounded too much like an abortion and Lowell's literary executor didn't like it, either.

The ending of 'Fishnet,' a poem about writing, was finally chosen.

—It's from *The Dolphin* but has nothing to do with anyone, Elizabeth said.

I typed it for the workmen. The punctuation was difficult for a stone.

Cal wrote the lines or chose them for his family buried at Dunbarton. —He did not choose his own, no one can, she said, which struck me as odd, but she hoped he'd be pleased. —One error would mean disaster, Elizabeth kept saying.

In the office next to the kitchen, in the white file cabinet, were sheets he'd worked and reworked, among them:

> *Christ,*
> *May I die at night*
> *with some semblance of my senses*
> *like the full moon that fails.*

Elizabeth started to clear things out, giving stuff away. I got books; I got a recording of *Das Lied von der Erde* that forever in my head puts Kathleen Ferrier's contralto together with the winter theater of distressed living room walls.

THERE WAS MORE to having a past as a writer than I knew, for all my collecting of back issues of her *Partisan Review*. After she'd moved back upstairs and the narrow room next to the kitchen was declared an office once again, she had me get down magazines and books that had been stored in its closets for years.

I came across an early story, 'The Temptations of Dr. Hoffmann.'

—Oh, God. That story's terrible. She looked at the little stack I'd put together. —Oh, those were the first things I ever did. I was too scared.

(A professor, Charles Riggs, just wrote to me to say that the character of Dr. Hoffmann may have been based on Paul Tillich.)

I'd found in Barqu Bookshop, the secondhand bookstore I left in order to work for her, *The Ghostly Lover*, her first novel, published in 1945. Here she was presenting me a copy that still had the dust jacket. A smooth hand is on a soft cheek in the blue-washed author's photograph. The copy says she is one of eleven children and has an interest in Billie Holiday and Paul Klee. Who was John Woodburn, the name she dedicated her first book to? Her editor. Somehow, she had felt it was expected of her. She said people thought the bad girl in the novel was her; but the bad girl was modeled on the girl who lived next door to her when she was growing up.

I had to read on-site those fragile postwar anthologies of modern writing in which she had short fiction. Her voice was already there, immediately recognizable as hers, even then. Her youthful narrators dream of getting away, yearn for the city, and not just any city. They are conscious of being female. If you can say what is happening to you, then you have something. She did give me, almost as a joke, one of her last copies of *The New Mexico Quarterly* of 1944 in which her very first published story had appeared.

Another day she had waiting a folder of attempts at fiction she'd dug up that she wanted to show me.

—Just for fun.

> This is going to be a long evening. What I am thinking about, I will not be talking about. Aren't my eyes looking odd, feverish as they would say about Raskolnikov, when he is walking along the street, before or after the crime.

> Second plot: I came here in 1960, yes, to my small little retreat, where I meant to live quietly, as they say in old novels. It is a strange place, stranger than you think . . .

> How to use cinematic technique? Interviewing. But how would the narrator know?

> What does the narrator do, just look? That won't work. I hate making up things. Could one imagine a lot of characters, and just have it told in a general way, not confined to the street, to the apartment house, some central situation. Try this, for a change . . .

The folders of fiction ideas were about marriage, infidelity, divorce, property. They were attempts that came from the collapse of her marriage and said that she was writing about things from the perspective of a certain class and age, hiding out in another gender, even, but she could not bring her thoughts together, or sustain the story of her characters.

The fragments show her trying to find an attitude. Lowell did not come back, the city was an abandoned woman's ally, she sought to conquer experience through the writing of fiction, and she decided not yet, she who was such an enemy of the unfinished. She explained, maybe not at this point, but later, that she couldn't sit down and start a story with 'The sun was shining.' She had to have an idea, a way in. The essay form, however, was another matter, because the essay was already put in motion by an occasion, a question.

The first essay of *Seduction and Betrayal* that she published, in the *Review*'s September 24, 1970, issue, said no, Zelda Fitzgerald hadn't enough talent, but she had some, and it was sad how discouraging of her wish to be creative as a dancer or a writer those around her were, meaning F. Scott Fitzgerald. The husband's concern that his wife not risk disappointment hastened her disintegration.

(Baldwin's dismissal of *The Great Gatsby* surprised me. Murray Kempton once said he found it the perfect novel. I minded the yellow Cadillac of 'negroes' rolling their eyes at Gatsby on the highway into the city. Elizabeth said she thought Gatsby's secret was that he was Jewish. Celia McGee told me a while back that articles have appeared saying his black ancestry was his secret. Hence, the Cadillac of souls.)

The spoiled, corrupt Fitzgeralds did not appeal to Elizabeth as a couple. Their excesses made the existence of his work a miracle, she said. The note in her essay of wanting some respect for the lost woman carries an undertone of speculation that genius also pays a cost for having had its way. She wrote and published the essays that make up the book one right after the other, confident of the shore.

SHE GAVE ME the latest issue of *Daedalus*. It had in it her essay on the Sixties and their aftermath, 'Domestic Manners.' She'd written it for a symposium the magazine sponsored. She did get up in front of New York audiences, contrary to what she claimed. She felt the essay was just nonsense, her typical chat:

> The arrival of women's ambition, transforming as it
> does private life, inner feeling, and public life is not at
> all simple but instead resembles the subtle shiftings of
> human thought and life brought about by enormously

challenging ideas such as evolution and Freudianism. Many hang back; just as many would stand on the literal truth of Genesis; but no matter what the ideological reluctance may be, every life is an inchoate but genuine reflection of the change.

She wouldn't hear a good word about the essay.

The 1970s have passed their zenith. Did they take place—this handful of years, somewhere else, in another land, inside the house, the head? Fatigue and recession, cold winters and expensive heat, resignations and disgrace.

An important person in cultural television whom she didn't know phoned to suggest she make a book of the subject. She begged off cheerfully.

—That dunderhead.

The debris in the burned room had been carted away. She was pleased with her contractors, with the energetic European workmen talking on the kitchen telephone as charred drawers were lowered on pulleys outside the window. She called after I left to say the removal had set up a cloud of dust throughout. She said she raced around snatching paintings from walls, covering chairs.

In the midst of it all, she pressed on with her essay 'Wives and Mistresses.' She was concerned Byron scholars would feel her telling of what was known as the Separation scandal a pointless effort. She was hilarious about Lady Byron, married to the poet for only one year, but from whom she got 'her name and a lifetime of poisonous preoccupation.'

When it came to the Ivinskaya part of the essay, she was afraid people would think she was addressing herself to Caroline. Pasternak did not leave his second wife and those fourteen years with Ivinskaya were that of a triangle. Ivinskaya's love-haunted spirit wanders in the shade without rest, needing always proof of love from him and proof offered to the world.

The Tolstoys' marriage illustrated what she meant when she said that you cannot know anything about someone else from the outside. They, the Tolstoys, husband and wife, left a voluminous record of their strife, each obsessed with the faults of the other. Elizabeth wondered where they found the time for the diary entries and letters, 'the violently expressive record,' as she called it.

(Where had she and Lowell found the time?)

She said that maybe no one could have been married to Tolstoy; the countess was a character in a Russian novel by Dostoevsky rather than by Tolstoy. Elizabeth was moved by the sufferings of Tolstoy's wife, by her humiliation, barred from the room where he lay dying in a stationmaster's house. But she had to pity her, which was not the same as having respect.

—To write is a profoundly solitary activity, Elizabeth said.

Tolstoy, the daughter, started off by saying that to be a writer's wife was a profession, more, a calling. She remembered her mother as a collaborator in the writing of her father's novels. Implicit in the essay that Elizabeth was writing was her judgment that the countess's daughter was wrong: the literary wife is not a collaborator.

Sometimes someone else makes it possible for someone to write, sometimes someone else made sacrifices so someone could write. In the world of husbands and wives, we knew who tended to do more of one than of the other. But if the countess thought that years of taking down Tolstoy's dictation made her a coauthor of some kind, then she had misplaced herself along the way.

Elizabeth ended her essay with a funny postscript about husbands, Colette's last, a much younger dude, and Katherine Mansfield's, the publisher John Middleton Murry, who gave himself a big part in her story. It was a valve, a way to let off the too-much emotion she got from leaving Ivinskaya's weak memoir and going to the sad majesty of *Hope Abandoned*, to the moment when Madame Mandelstam prints a letter she wrote to Mandelstam before she learned of his death.

> You came to me every night in my sleep, and I kept asking what had happened, but you did not reply. In my last dream I was buying food for you . . .

Elizabeth canceled a trip to Israel in order to work. I could not have said to her that the essay was most certainly about what was going on with her. Because of her own story, she could look at another woman's story with a profound and illuminating sympathy. To write the essay somehow clarified for her that she was not a casualty.

She said she liked Gorky's description of Tolstoy as the old magician, or a stone found on a beach. She warned that there were no ideal circumstances for writing. She liked best to think of Chekhov writing at a little table in the middle of his zoo of a family.

—Writing is a profoundly unmarried activity, she said again.

I hadn't known her when she was first writing the essays on women and literature that became *Seduction and Betrayal*. (I'd only read them in book form. I skipped through them in the red volumes.) But I understood that what she offered novels and poetry and drama and biographies was her own experience, not as a comparison, but as a way to imagine what the sum of experiences means to literature, a human drama.

(—What do you mean? she would ask, light blue eyes emphatic, like those of someone in a book. She didn't let you say just anything, even if you were tipsy.

—So what did Chekhov say about small-*n* negroes?)

It moves me to think of her sitting in the dust of her red sofa, surrounded by books on Byron opened to different pages. The grind of construction noise was not enough to make her not hear her own music when she sat down at the typewriter on the dining room table. When the A galleys arrived one evening, she sang the fourth paragraph of the piece, including the punctuation marks, in the style of a bel canto aria.

—The determination of footnotes cries to Heaven period

—Lady Byron *riventicata* exclamation point

It was the anniversary of the Triangle Shirtwaist Company fire near Washington Square in 1911. The workers were locked inside the sweatshop. Many jumped in flames from windows.

Dusting books that same evening, she said, —I just can't accept it.

She meant Lowell's death. She remembered how Cal used to tease her. He convinced her that there really was a book called *The Wonders and Horrors of the Vatican.*

In the early spring of 1978, *Some Trees* by John Ashbery was reprinted and Nicolas Nabokov died.

Elizabeth called, embarrassed. It had all caught up with her and even if anyone would understand she still felt funny about it. She said she couldn't believe it, but it had happened. She fell apart at Nicolas Nabokov's funeral. She had to be held up by someone. She said she sobbed and sobbed.

ELIZABETH FEARED BARBARA'S disapproval, but that did not stop her from accepting the invitation from a former suitor to take a break on St. Croix. She came back recovered enough to regret she'd gone.

The blueprint for Lowell's tombstone had come and been returned as unacceptable and then another. That, too, wouldn't do, and 'Fishnet' was discarded. 'Endings' was chosen, after all, and a type, like Commander Lowell's, Cal's father. A final set of blueprints came. That was settled.

Elizabeth ordered two more file cabinets and finished a talk for a symposium on Ibsen at the Pratt Institute while I assembled a new table. She was very discouraged, reading through the plays, not wanting to speak on those she'd dealt with in *Seduction and Betrayal*. Her idea was to talk about how Ibsen's plays hinge on secrets, the nature of them. But, as usual, she felt it was a very small idea and putting it together would be a chore. She said Ibsen was maybe only engaging to a certain age group: the plays are about marriage, the domestic, conventions. It was maybe too suggestive, not really developed, but it was what intrigued her.

—Nora and Hedda were different from other Ibsen women. One left and the other shot herself so that, one might say, she wouldn't end up in another Ibsen play. Is that okay? Should I say that?

The week before Elizabeth had lectured on 'The Artist in an Alien Culture' at City College and said that it went all right. Much trepidation before appearing in front of a New York audience; just as much casual writing off of the event afterward. I wanted to see her perform but she refused to let me attend anything, waving her hands and insisting that I wouldn't hear anything I hadn't already heard from her. She'd spoken around the same time at a Rutgers Founding Day celebration, on women and education, which meant Simone Weil, Arendt, and Margaret Fuller. She knocked her recycled lectures, saying that she had one on fiction that she'd given a thousand times across the country.

—In St. Louis, they call me Betty. Great talk, Betty. How about a highball, Betty.

She went to St. Louis, she said, mostly to see her old friend Sally Higginbotham.

And then without need of transition she was talking about *Safe Conduct* once more, 'the chilling purity' of Pasternak's prose.

Rilke's *Notebooks of Malte Laurids Brigge* interested her for formal reasons, and she would read from it as she did from Pasternak.

> It will be difficult to persuade me that the story of the Prodigal Son is not the legend of him who did not want to be loved.

She liked to talk about the Bible. For her, Scripture matched Freud when it came to abundance of case studies. She would joke that we were the only Protestants the other knew; everyone else in our lives was Jewish. I mentioned Luc, because once in school I'd gone to Mass with him at his mother's renovated church. She laughed that Catholics were not really Christians. Renan she didn't like, he was too sentimental. She urged me to try Karl Barth. She liked the Albert Schweitzer of *The Quest of the Historical Jesus* but the honky doctor in the jungle with his barefoot charges not at all.

She said that when she was a teenager, she was addicted to getting saved. She accepted Jesus as her personal savior in revival tents all over town. She kept different notebooks on the coffee table and reached for one of them, to jot down something that had just come to her.

And once again, watching her at work, deep into her world of great books, the lesson of perseverance, even though writing as an act was the last thing you wanted to do.

Heine was someone she often read before she tried to write, just to open herself up.

She didn't write poetic prose, but rather she composed somewhat like a poet in that she could not move on to the next line until the one that would stand before it was okay. She went line by line. She said it had to do with her not knowing what she thought until she wrote it down.

ELIZABETH TOLD THE Soviet writers who'd come for a conference that she was from Siberia.

—In America it is known as Lexington, Kentucky. My dream, in my youth, was not to be a famous writer, but to escape to New York. My dream, in my old age, is to remain here.

She said the humor and cordiality did not last long. Kurt Vonnegut walked out of the meeting. The Soviet representatives were offended at the patronizing tone of the American publishers: now we want to publish more Soviet literature and if it's any good, if it has anything to say, we'll back you up.

The Soviets rose and made angry speeches. They talked of their historical suffering and their great literary past. To this Edward Albee, intelligent and nervous, she said, raised the question of censorship. He was roundly put down. More nonsense from American publishers. More Soviet retort. Elizabeth said she decided she had to get out of there, but she couldn't leave Albee out there all by himself, shaking. She told the gathering that the publishers behaved exactly as she thought they would, but she wanted to return to the question of literary heritage.

—Censorship does not honor the dead.

It was splendid when she got going.

—Henry James's inanities, she announced as I unloaded the dishwasher she'd ignored for two days. She was going to keep a ledger of James's silliness. She said for some reason she disliked unloading the dishwasher. Loading it was fine.

I was reading Lattimore's translation of *The Iliad*.

—How lucky you are. I do think anyone reading it very fortunate.

She worried that maybe she had an ulcer. The pain would come and go without sense or pattern. She'd clutch her waist in the middle of a sentence. She didn't want to call Doctor B., who would scold her for not having made an appointment sooner or for taking aspirin before an examination. Finally, Doctor B. gave her medication for spasm of the colon, blaming the pressures and crises of the year, the sleeplessness because of work crews hammering away across the street. The medication seemed to have an effect. The sharp, burning sensations stopped.

She went up to Maine, landing in Bangor, picking up the car. I'd let myself into Elizabeth's place toward the end of the week, sort the mail, settle in on the red sofa, and discover that I couldn't sit there comfortably without her. I couldn't steal a vodka and flip through her magazines.

———

I'D STARTED A temp job that summer as a waiter at the Columbia University College of Physicians and Surgeons Faculty Club. As a black person, I didn't want to serve white people. Elizabeth said,

—I don't see that. You're a youth. You do anything to make your life.

I was lucky to get the job, way up in Washington Heights. I didn't tell my parents. I got it through a bookstore friend, Linda Melisano, the Italian American half of a beautiful interracial couple. In the Faculty Club, she played tapes of Umm Kulthum continuously while chef David Higginbotham talked philosophy to the skillet.

Elizabeth said she had changed the title of her novel.

CBS was sending Felice to Paris. There was a party for her back near campus. Everyone was there. Suzanne and her boyfriend weren't speaking to me; Harriet and her boyfriend weren't speaking to me.

Every white guy who had long hair cut it. No matter where he was on the Kinsey scale, off it went. Luc, Phil, Jim, the other Phil, Lewis, and Clyde Moneyhun with the da Vinci locks, the future translator of Catalan poetry.

(Joe Donovan cut his long hair because the Age of Glitter was over, he said. He got a punk fade and I lost touch with him. Luc told me he was singing in an Anglican chorus, a repertoire Joe had always enjoyed, even in his Bette Midler days of platform shoes. Then Luc heard some time after it happened that Joe had died of AIDS.)

Jim had finished a film based on a short story by Apollinaire. He said he wanted to do a treatment of the last fifteen minutes of Webern's life.

George Winslow told us that he'd had an eight-hour dream that consisted entirely of him building roofs.

Aldo Moro was still good for a few macabre cracks, the former

Italian prime minister, kidnapped by the Red Brigades, his body found wrapped in blankets in the back seat of a Renault parked at CP headquarters in Rome.

Boswell believed that if he practiced at being cool, easy, and serene he would become those things.

Eva Pierrakos arrived, a small, dark-eyed young woman whose Greek American parents were Reichian therapists in New Jersey and themselves certifiable. Back when we were in school, she charmed my father, explaining the absurdity of Wilhelm Reich's lenticular clouds. She was wearing two-tone heels with laces, a pleated Lindy hop skirt, and a black jacket. She rolled her own cigarettes. Her skill made my father think of Naples after the war. Other people's parents were terrific.

Luc had a book on Jacques Rivette and wanted to argue about revolutionary art forms. Mainly he wanted to attack individualism. You could tell when Eva was around.

When I told Luc about some revisions Silvers had asked of me on my next piece, he said he would have walked out of Bob's office and never come back. I told him I was tired of being thought of as a collaborator.

—Good.

We didn't speak for two weeks and then when we did, we argued over whether the bombing of Versailles was a good thing. In a picture book from his early youth one of the paintings that affected him most strongly was a Courbet. He'd learned that it had been destroyed in the bombing of Dresden, from which he concluded that his knowledge of a thing was as important as the thing itself.

LUC AND HIS bookstore colleagues were putting out a magazine, *Stranded*.

Howard returned from Florida.

—With syphilis, of course.

Howard wanted to make a documentary about William Burroughs. Howard's loft on Prince Street looked like a tornado hit it, like Howard lived there. He stayed in Burroughs's loft whenever Burroughs was out of town. Burroughs's building, the Prince Hotel, was once a YMCA. Howard claimed that it was haunted.

I sat in Burroughs's orgone box. It didn't energize me. Howard said I had to come back and sit in complete darkness and take drugs, for hours, as Burroughs did. What windows there were in the Bunker, as everybody called it, were boarded up. The walls were white, a lithograph here, a photo of Burroughs and a friend over there. A few pieces of furniture. File cabinets, a desk for an old typewriter, several office chairs in a tight row, and one massive table.

The bedroom had a bed low to the floor and a bureau; the office a high clerk's desk with a nook for a typewriter and steel shelves with boxes, some marked 'Huncke,' and magazines and papers. Large studio bulbs lit the rooms. The bathroom had two urinals and two stalls, the last one a shower.

Howard liked to stay up late working. He'd stand at the foot of Burroughs's bed and fall on his face. The impact woke me. He could sleep and sleep.

One time he came uptown with a red rose and said,

—Let's talk lying down.

Howard would phone up from someplace like the cloakroom at the Hungarian consulate, come by, and pass out in the middle of a story about another one-night stand he'd had or a crush he was contemplating. We took mild doses of LSD and went to movies. We listened to Taylor Mead rant in Phebe's about second-rate artists and I got numb again at CBGB's. We broke bottles in the moonlit rubble of a partially collapsed building. I'd get up early and read Burroughs's books, in order not to be lying fully clothed next to him.

He took me to the Mineshaft. I wasn't going to be let in, not in my green clown shirt with white polka dots. Howard had to lend me his T-shirt, because I wouldn't go in shirtless either. Two hushed floors of sticky dark and the sound of feet; a man in a bathtub getting pissed on and dicks being sucked in stalls. Foucault loved the joint, I heard much later, and Susan had been the only woman ever to cross its threshold. She tried to tell a *Review* dinner that she saw a guy with his fist up some other guy's ass and both guys were facing away from each other, in conversation with other guys, as though nothing special was going on back there. The girls stopped her before she got to the end of the picture. She finished it for me some time afterward.

(James remembered Susan telling him of course she went to Plato's Retreat back then, a straight sex club in the basement of the sketchy Ansonia on Broadway just above Seventy-second Street. She said you reclined on Roman-like couches and either accepted or rejected the someone or someones who approached you.)

Outside the Mineshaft and then the Anvil, taxi lights stretched along the loading zones of meatpacking plants ghostly at that hour.

(I forgot that Foucault died of AIDS.)

The summer was for Claude McKay, Cavafy, and Lord Hervey's memoirs. Howard had a picnic framed by a reddish sunset back on his own roof on Prince Street. He handed wine and cigarettes up to the men in the derelict building on the Bowery behind his. They knew him. It would take him a long time to admit it, he hadn't told me they'd met, but Howard had fallen in love, had found the love of his life, in the young poet wandering around the barbecue, Brad Gooch, already famous back on campus for his beauty.

Felice was back. Eva was having a party for her at her sister's loft. Luc was keyed up because it was the first party he'd ever had anything vaguely to do with as a host. He went all over town getting the music together. Then the night of the party the sound system went on the blink. Nobody left. Some guys doo-wopped at microphone beer bottles, waiting for Luc, who managed to locate fifteen-inch woofers somewhere. There was a large pan of scrambled eggs in which we stubbed out cigarettes. Howard introduced Brad to everyone. Everyone already knew who he was.

Magdalene, Eva's younger sister, had a paranoid roommate who began to hear barking dogs.

—I am friend to Luc and Eva, a Klaus Nomi voice piped over the intercom.

(Klaus Nomi would be the first person to die of AIDS whose name I recognized. I'd just got off a plane, was on the subway, and looked down at his picture in *The Village Voice* that a passenger was reading. I thought it was a review, then realized it was an obituary.)

—Why are there dogs? Who brought so many dogs?

THE SADNESS OF Maine had gone. It had been hard to come across his shirts and socks when Elizabeth opened the house over the Memorial Day weekend. She got down *Notebook* as she talked about how much of Maine was in his work, which she hadn't realized before.

She spoke about the obscurity of some of his references. The poem 'Mink,' for instance, is really about a Castine character and not an animal. 'For a Friend Across the Park' is Jackie Kennedy. In one poem, they are at the Parker House in Boston for Spock's sentencing, which the reader isn't told. She wondered if she should make a little tape explaining these things. He often referred to her as a gazelle.

There had been a memorial for Lowell in Italy. Two of the speakers told his Italian translator who'd organized the memorial that if he invited Caroline she would come and therefore they would not. He didn't and she was furious. Elizabeth heard that a friend of theirs from way back had spoken about two Cals. After he went on lithium, around 1965, he was, Elizabeth explained again,

—on simmer. He wasn't mad quite, but he wasn't really calm. Mary used to say, I don't like Lithium Cal.

He was teasing, careless, irresponsible, somewhat manic, making crazy decisions. Their friend in Italy said he was in this state

for some time and it led to some errors in judgment in both his life
and his work. The old Cal returned in his last year, tender, recep-
tive, letting others talk.

Elizabeth said, —When I gave up Cal for good I used to think
too bad for Caroline. She doesn't really know what he's like, since
in the early Seventies he was well into simmer.

One of the things that made her decide to take him back was
that she felt the old Cal had returned, that he had suffered so much
over Caroline he could feel again. It made him more real. He worried a great deal about Caroline's threats. Once in Boston, shortly
after Caroline had thrown him out, Elizabeth said,

—You really care for Caroline.

—I do, he said, and then he started weeping.

Hannah Arendt: 'To talk about poets is an uncomfortable task.
Poets are there to be quoted, not talked about.'

Elizabeth was reading Büchner, *Danton's Death* and *Woyzeck*,
stirred by how quick and resolute he is. She rang again to say she
felt better about her novel than she had that morning, and was in
her housecoat, making a drink before she went to Mary McCarthy's
for a cocktail. They gave her a birthday dinner. She'd gone with
Mary and her husband to a volcanic island, Brimstone Isle, and
their boat passed a herd of seals on rocks.

She was working every day. At first, she started new things,
new portraits, but she really couldn't get a sense of it as a whole
thing. Then she began to worry that characters and places were
mentioned, introduced, and never spoken of again; that she had
to explain, in some way, how she got from Kentucky to Boston or
Maine and all that furniture.

She was still at work on the section about Holland.

—A dumb narrative, she said. She read one part to me, loudly, a
sort of break:

In Amsterdam there were many people my husband
could talk with about poetry.

It touched on their nights of conversing about his childhood, and
Commander and Mrs. Lowell. It was quite fine, not at all interrupt-
ing, impersonal and yet not idle description.

The next day this addition was under heavy suspicion. Soon it
was on the cutting-room floor. She didn't say because it was too directly about Lowell. She was nervous about how little time she had
left in Maine. She had fallen in love with it once again. She'd been
very social. James West, Mary McCarthy's husband, had a party on
his boat. She came home and restored to the Holland section the
pillow talk about her husband's parents, but left out the line about
him being a poet.

That was when she said Elizabeth Bishop had written a poem
for Lowell, 'North Haven.' She said it was marvelous.

—Wonderful images and descriptions.

One day she decided she had to attack the beginning, the original opening chapter that had appeared in *The New York Review* under the title 'Writing a Novel.' She had to alter it. It was too much
about the problems of fiction.

—You can't question description and then have nothing but
description.

V. S. Pritchett advised her that as an opening it was very much a
stopping, that it would be hard to go on in that vein. She broke up
her Kentucky sections, and even the one that began

The tyranny of the weak is a burdensome thing

may have been as wonderful as I said but it didn't connect with
anything, she felt. She wanted to blend reflections on Kentucky
into the beginning so that the novel was about the problems of
memory, not the challenges of composition.

Elizabeth felt that it wouldn't do to come on so hard about the novel form in the portrait of Gass.

I thought, That was William Gass?

. . . A short pear-shaped man came onto the stage for his lecture . . .

The author begins to speak of his obsession: the theoretical problems of contemporary fiction. In his life he is a man of reason . . .

Fiction is another matter. He cannot, for us, for himself, accept a simple, linear motivation as a proper way to write novels, involve characters. He does not at all agree that if the gun is hanging on the wall in the first act it must go off before the curtain goes down. No, the ground has slipped away from causality . . .

But how is the man's genius to be made manifest . . . How is his art to become real in my novel? What is a writer's motif, his theme song, except stooped shoulders, the appalling desolation of trouser and jacket and old feet stuffed into stretched socks . . .

An unhappy summer, and yet not a happy subject for literature . . .

Memoirs: felonious pages in which one accuses others of real faults and oneself only of charming infidelities, unusual follies, improvidence but no meanness, a restlessness as beguiling as the winds of Aeolus, excesses, vanities, and sensualities that are the envy of all. I have thought of calling my memoir *Living and Partly Living*. But I am not happy with 'partly living.' It comes down too hard on the aridity of modern life, on the dispirited common folk without tradition, on the dead gods and the banished God . . .

Is it possible for a woman to write a memoir? Their productions often fail to be interesting because there isn't enough sex in them, not even enough longing for consummation . . . Courage under ill-treatment is a woman's theme, life-theme, and is of some interest, but not if there is too much of either.

Maybe the shadows will suffice—the light and the shade. Think of yourself as if you were in Apollinaire's poem . . .

. . . Now my novel begins, no, now I begin my novel—and yet I cannot decide whether to call myself I or she.

(I looked up, not long ago, Elizabeth Bishop's indignation about the description of Lota de Macedo Soares, unnamed, in that essay 'In Maine.' Bishop's letter changes key and ends with her expressing admiration for the last line in particular in that just published opening of a novel:

and yet I cannot decide whether to call myself I or she.

The ambiguity attracted her, perhaps.

I recently read again 'Writing a Novel' in the appendix of Saskia Hamilton's edition of *The Dolphin Letters*, and then in my tattered copy of the tenth-anniversary issue of *The New York Review*. It's been a while; her old opening is different from what I remembered. It is much more compressed.

She once said she used to take essay exams in school and when she finished the rest of the class would still be scribbling away in blue books. She just sat there, amazed. She got bad grades, but she couldn't bear to repeat to teachers what she knew they already knew. She wished she could be more expansive.

Mr. Silvers said at one of his examinations of a piece I was writing, —Lizzie is a champ at this kind of thing. She writes like a poet. The leaps are so precise and dramatic that they open up the mind.)

My memory has been telling me for years that she took that

tight opening chapter, split it in half, and inserted her other chapters in between. No, she scattered the original opening throughout the novel, but the William Gass portrait and her musings about description as the under-layer of a novel are gone entirely. And when had the stables disappeared for real? I don't remember the parking lot across the street from her, before the ABC building went up.

She thought about structure, and, apart from two chapters that had appeared in *The New Yorker*, she went through her existing material and reshuffled paragraphs, which left room for new scenes. Passages fold and fit, as I listened to her explain her new approach that had to do with the deceptiveness of the fragmentary, and because the construction was held together from the inside, she hoped, she could, she said, dispense with a conventional frame.

She identified with the seemingly random, perfect, lyrical work: Baudelaire, Laforgue, Rilke, Bruno Schultz.

Some nights she'd call back and we'd talk for hours. Phone receiver under my chin, I'd pour water in my trash can just to make sure after I dumped an ashtray. On a Thursday, she was worried about the length, that she did not have enough material. The next day she woke certain no one would like it, that it was not making sense. One more night and she was cheerful that she had finished the section on Holland. Then she felt she'd done nothing but rewrite material she already had, and then she found some old things she liked.

I was Brillo-ing pots in my kitchen nook and listening over the radio to the homily for Pope Paul read in St. Peter's Square. Chair bearers were bringing his coffin into the basilica.

—People in Rome seem to be taking his death very much in stride, Elizabeth said.

Come Saturday and there was black smoke twice from the Vatican windows. Courtesy of her taste, I had Jamaican Blue Mountain on my end as she did on hers for phone calls.

A few years before, a mother superior whose extremism had driven everyone from the convent on Sutton Place, except the cook, announced her candidacy for pope. Dressed in khaki trousers and combat boots, a tattoo of a cross on her forearm, the mother superior was solemn about the need for church reform, adding,

—And besides I think being pope would help me to get my head together, Elizabeth and I remembered at the same time.

She had her doors open and was listening to intermittent motors on the water. I had the sounds of delivery vans on Broadway. Across from my windows on West Ninety-fifth Street, a black drag queen in a shiny black wig pelted the superintendent of a building with insult. *Children of Paradise* was to play at the Thalia, the little cinema two doors down from me, so art house the owner kept his film reels in the refrigerator.

She heard that Susan was back, working on an essay on Walter Benjamin for the fifteenth-anniversary issue of *The New York Review*. She asked Barbara, who'd seen Susan in London, if Susan knew anything about Benjamin.

—Susan knows everything.

Elizabeth said she noted but hadn't wanted to how long it took Susan to say anything to her about her last piece, 'Wives and Mistresses.' She decided she didn't want to publish the section of her novel about cleaning ladies in the anniversary issue. It wouldn't do.

(Luc Sante would share the cover of the fortieth-anniversary issue of *The New York Review* with Elizabeth Hardwick and Robert Lowell.)

Elizabeth said she was not anxious to come back to New York. In past summers, as glad as she was to be in Maine, she was always ready at the end of the season to get back to the city. But she couldn't face having to have the living room painted because of the water damage from the fire; she'd broken a filling and had had a temp put in, so the dentist was on her list. She worried that she was just returning to trouble and the past year had been so hard.

Trouble, evidently, had taken an unsuitable house on Long Island, from which self-serving raps were being dispatched on missions. Trouble's canny lying would begin as an outburst but, after a passage of time, become a sudden yet casual revision of events that Trouble no doubt knew would soon be skipping from secondhand to thirdhand conversation.

She wished she had more time. She felt guilty that she wanted the rain to stop, when Maine desperately needed it, and forests were on fire. All summer, in between other things, she'd been reading Herzen in a mesmerized state and one day so would I, she predicted. She thought at least her book had a shape and would maybe work as a whole once it was all pressed together, smoothly typed up.

A novel is always written on the day of its writing.

She read some more of it to me and though it was much changed, the atmosphere was not, the melancholy, the meditative tone.

—Give me a noun and I can image for four more lines.

She was in another mood from when she'd begun the novel five years earlier, and that difference in inner core temperature was a source of doubts. She labored to make nothing sound too worked on; she worked to honor her contract with ambition. She decided she had to write the book so that more than ten friends would understand it. In some ways it was more open, full, less condensed and elliptical. But she never did or said the expected.

—There is not an ordinary sentence in the book.

—That's what worries me.

She came back in September with a cardboard box that contained the manuscript of *Sleepless Nights*.

Part 4

The anniversary of Lowell's death passed quietly. Elizabeth had dinner with Harriet. She was upset in the afternoon because it brought back her waiting for the plane to land, waiting at the window for the taxi.

She said Harriet noted that her father and Steve Biko died on the same day. The photograph of his stone had arrived, beautiful, they thought.

The next day she complained of an aching stomach and I didn't want to keep her.

She had arranged to be buried at Dunbarton. I said I couldn't stand to hear her talk like that. She still hadn't had her hair done and she pressed up on satiny, whitish-brown strands that had fallen during her summer of writing.

She was free. She had her work and Harriet and friends.

—The days aren't long enough. And I've had marriage. I've had a profound experience. I don't want to marry again. That is not my destiny.

She was never much interested in marriage in her life anyway.

—That's not what I'm about.

Still, she was sad enough.

IT WAS THE SEASON. Samurai Mover, we called him, an Irish-looking tai chi instructor, strapped furniture on top of his little red pickup and drove Luc from West 101st Street to his new building on St. Marks Place that had no elevator. Samurai Mover strapped boxes of books on his back and hiked up six flights of stairs.

George, Jim, Charlie, who'd dyed his hair again, from blond to red, Luc, and I, soaked by sweat, lungs pounding, legs aching, struggled upward with monstrously heavy possessions. Luc's proudly stolen library copy of *Charles Baudelaire: A Lyric Poet in the Era of High Capitalism* was safe and dry.

—Comrade, see you in the next absurd situation, Jim said in the evening rain.

Luc said nobody our age missed the newspapers during the strike.

ELIZABETH DIDN'T WANT to talk about why there was still no box waiting on the wicker chair by the door. Its contents would represent the restoration of her narrative freedom and a reconciliation with the past. She needed to work on the ending some more, she said.

I went after Susan Sontag instead, carrying our glasses to the dining room more in sorrow. Because of me, the plants in Elizabeth's windows over Sixty-seventh Street had either practically dried out or been nearly drowned. She sat down to small burgers she would not cook to well-done, and opinions I could be unfair or wrong about in the privacy of her tutelage. Alas, Sontag's piece on Walter Benjamin for the fifteenth-anniversary issue of the *Review*, October 12, 1978, was a disappointment.

—I thought so, too, she said, as if astonished to find anyone who would agree with that.

—Thing, open that window on the left more. Thank you. I'm exhausted. I hate cooking, don't you.

Her approval breezed through me. I had saved up observations I was proud of, yet I knew right away they were not as interesting as her take that started with Susan telling her she was trying to do a kind of character thing, the way she does. Elizabeth said she'd been thinking of those Charles Rosen and Hannah Arendt essays on Walter Benjamin and had noted Susan didn't refer to them.

—I love the little hunchback.

Arendt may have been his mistress.

I didn't know either George Steiner or Charles Rosen and thought repeating a story I'd heard about them would not have me breaking any rules: Steiner sat annoyed throughout a dinner because Rosen was not acknowledging his recent essay on Benjamin. At the end of the dinner, he called him on it. Rosen said he hadn't mentioned it because it was terrible.

—I am joyfully in awe of Charles Rosen.

I said I didn't like Marshall Frady's latest.

She said he was trying to do something Faulknerian with these American figures.

—If you say it's overwritten then you're saying he should write like everyone else.

She pointed out that many of the works cited in Susan's essay are not available in English, implying, through her footnotes, that she had read the German editions. She said Susan told her she looked at them in Italian.

—She should have referred to some famous melancholics, she said.

I cleared the plates. She said she was surviving on what I'd put in the refrigerator on her instructions before she got back, and the takeout leftovers from dinner with Harriet. She hadn't ordered anything, she'd been so agitated.

SHE CHANGED HER mind, for the last time, about whether to use the Hardy poem at the end of the novel. If people thought she was referring to him, then there was nothing she could do about it.

She told me I had hypoglycemia. During the night my blood sugar dropped and I had to eat when I woke. If I didn't, I was faint by ten o'clock.

—I made a sandwich to take to Barnard for lunch. Do you know it was gone by ten. I thought I'd die if I didn't eat that thing as soon as I got there.

She said she just shook sometimes.

She said she and Barbara had tried to call me Tuesday to tell me to come crash the *Review* anniversary party. She said everyone was there. She said everyone was also at the Avedon retrospective and although Sigrid looked beautiful and David was an essay in black-and-white pointed boots, a black suit, a black string tie against a shirt as white as a tablecloth at the Ritz, and a great hat, she had never seen such a tacky-looking crowd.

As I left my new job as editorial assistant to senior editor Frances McCullough at Harper & Row, Publishers, at Fifty-third and Fifth Avenue, I encountered Iranian students chanting in front of Rockefeller Plaza. The voices, the fists, the masks. SAVAK men leaning against trees, dressed in gray polyester suits, wanting to be seen.

Elizabeth said there were Iranian students marching at Columbia. Her fist shot up in the air.

—Right on. No more martial law. There's something really riveting about a demonstration.

She remembered Benjamin, quoting Flaubert: 'Of all of politics I understand only one thing: the revolt.'

She remembered the Biafran war and Chinua Achebe coming to the house. Once she and Lowell on a windy night demonstrated with placards in front of the English-Speaking Union.

—These doddering Anglophiles.

They were joined by a red-faced crew of Irish republicans. One lone, silent figure passing out a leaflet calling for Harold Wilson's assassination. Stanley Kunitz and Alfred Kazin were awful to imply Robert Lowell's politics were right-wing, she said. No one else responded to the bombing of Dresden by going to jail as a CO.

She said the transcripts from the inquest quoted in Hilda Bernstein's *No. 46: Steve Biko* read like dialogue from Brecht. We'd missed the Steve Biko memorial, but I brought the petition for Ngugi wa Thiong'o. I forgot to give her his *Petals of Blood*.

ON A SHIMMERING Saturday, the members of the Homintern who'd assembled for Benjamin Britten's opera *Billy Budd* were knowledgeable older men wearing cigarette burns on their laps, or young men in black leather, one Warhol portrait after another, or nicely toasted middle-aged men in black tie, expectant in the boxes. I listened to Howard complain, he, an animated young man in old, soft black jeans and a carefully ironed black T-shirt. Benjamin Britten's lifelong partner, his survivor, Peter Pears, sang the role of Starry Vere, the captain, and the audience showed how moving it was to hear him. He'd sung it at the premiere of the opera in 1951.

When the crew, spying a French vessel, sang a prayer for victory, the audience pulsated, but it was Richard Stilwell as doomed Billy Budd who drove the men wild.

Howard suggested we concentrate on *his* homo struggle. We had to go to three dank West Side bars to hash out that he felt trapped, angry, and thrilled before he was ready to kick some ass. Then he left.

It was too late to call her. She said that when the chandeliers went up and the lights went down at the opera house she always thought of Baudelaire and his anticipations of pleasure when the chandeliers were hauled up in the theaters. I wanted to tell someone *Billy Budd* was the saddest thing I'd ever read.

Sunday morning, I was up early and dialed the number of the insomniac who found pardon in sunrise. She took me by surprise. She said she would leave it in a shopping bag with the doorman. I was to come back that evening to talk.

She made her friend Lee Gardner's recipe for bay scallops with dill and lemon, and even with us standing over the pan the butter scorched. I tried to reassure her. It meant everything to me then, and it still does, that she asked me to read it.

She said as we ate the bay scallops anyway that in her novel, she left out her brother who gambled at the tracks and paid for her graduate studies with his winnings. She didn't know why. The suicide note that she gives to a local womanizer early on in the novel is her reconstruction of the kind of euphoric letter a crazy, sanitarium-locked brother of hers wrote home to their mother.

(Or was it her mother's brother?)

The Annals of Tennessee to the End of the Eighteenth Century by J.G.M. Ramsey, her maternal great-grandfather, published in 1853, makes an appearance in her novel. She had one copy on the shelf in the office closet, hidden away from that library about the Lowells and the Winslows in the repainted bookcase in the upstairs hallway. But she couldn't answer why she reduced her family from eleven children to nine. It was fiction. She said it had freed her to make the narrator as much like herself as the story needed for her to be, but it also was not herself.

The next day she was already thinking about an idea for another novel, indeed, to be called *Ideas*. About two couples and how their ideas affect them. In her mind, her characters had antecedents. It had to do with the soul of New York.

—Everyone has political ideas now.

She thanked me again for the encouragement the previous evening, I thanked her again for the honor, the exhilarating experience, I promised her, and she hung up.

I had an appointment with Mr. Silvers. I told Barbara Epstein, back from London and Italy, that she looked well.

—I just have Jewish hair, she said with a get-out smile behind a piled-up desk.

I said no way anyone would ever convince Elizabeth Hardwick that she'd written a masterpiece.

—Typically modest about her brilliance, Barbara said, the pencil raised to her ear letting me know that a grown-up was preparing to read what was on her desk. She made herself heard to the assistant at the desk outside her door. She wanted back the galleys that had been taken from her desk before she'd finished with them, please.

Obviously, Barbara had read *Sleepless Nights*, and there I was, full of its locations, Lexington, Boston, more New York, and Maine. The narrator's unperturbable mother and tuneful father, the brothers and sisters, then women on their own in the city. Billie Holiday and jazz, people in rooming houses, a ménage in Holland, bachelors, women of certain temperaments, moments of the phantom Cal, cleaning women toward the end. Memory, a novel that reads like an autobiography, but is also made up.

In my journal, I briefly tried to call her E., but it was a creepy affected something in regard to the last line of *Sleepless Nights*:

> Thus, I am always on the phone, always writing letters, always waking up to address myself to B. and D. and C.—those whom I dare not ring up until the morning and yet must talk to throughout the night.

The end of 'Writing a Novel' has the narrator, Elizabeth, waking to address herself to

B. and D. and E.

Barbara and Devie were easy. I'd asked her back then who 'E.' was. She said 'E.' had just been to throw people off. Maybe it was she who had been thrown off, asking hard things of herself.

The change from 'E.' to 'C.' at the end of the finished novel isn't meant to throw us off. Why should it be any other? It seemed to me at the time a gesture of forgiveness. And farewell. Like she had Lowell in mind with that Hardy poem, after all, but he was not her only loss.

She would dismiss this kind of reading too much into things, but at the same time she deliberated every move, especially after she'd made it, and kept it or not.

—It's immoral to be indifferent to what you put on the page.

The novel is really about poor people. She liked that. Those chapters, fragments, that I had read or heard about, magically unified by her voice.

WHEN I WAS her student, Professor Hardwick told me about a dinner given in 1964 for Simone de Beauvoir. She said the intellectual also famous for being a girlfriend was stubbornly silent, looking down her nose at all the Manhattan wit going on around her. Suddenly she announced,

—I want to see Harlem.

Professor Hardwick said that if Beauvoir and Cartier-Bresson went to Harlem, then I should, too.

I took Luc of the black nickname Earle with me. The colors of Pan-Africanism stood out in the layers of shop signs and crowded sidewalk stalls along West 125th Street. A late autumn evening was coming on. We were where most white kids, and even some black students, wouldn't go, which would make us seem street to others when we got back, should anything interesting happen. The era of student alliances with the ghetto was over. Black Vietnam veterans, the sort who used Swahili words for self-determination and unity, *kujichagulia* and *ujima*, displayed their solidarity at campus rap sessions that attracted few, with the war winding down. But James Brown still came to the Apollo every year. Earle had been to one of his shows, but I hadn't.

The cry of the mighty Aretha slowed us as it soared from a record store's speaker. People were friendly, so much so that we accompanied a cheerful hustler of mediocre-grade marijuana to his run-down Beaux Arts building on West 110th Street. The walls of his one room were painted dark blue and so was his refrigerator, the shelves of which were stocked entirely with packages of hot dogs. The smiles of his roommates, a man and a woman, were radiant in the refrigerator door's light. Our polite host rummaged in a desk drawer. We saw the sleeping gun. We shook hands with our host, as after a good performance. The post office and Western Union were on 125th Street, but when on my own I didn't go beyond the Freedom National Bank. It was enough to know that Harlem was there.

The Harlem that Luc and I expected was the urban landscape of film, sociology, and Baldwin. It never occurred to me that Harlem had been anything else. I listened to jazz haphazardly and didn't know anything about jazz history. I once registered for and quickly dropped Nathan Huggins's Afro-American History because the class met too early. The first time I understood what the Harlem Renaissance was came from reading Ishmael Reed's novel *Mumbo Jumbo*, published in 1972, which had its devotees as an allegory about the New Negro Movement of the 1920s.

(John Oliver Killens told me to read Ishmael Reed. I'd not read Killens's novel *The Cotillion*, and it was a bestseller. There it was again: I didn't know who this black man was, visiting an office in Dodge Hall where the translation center was.

Luc had loved Ishmael Reed's surreal first novel of cowboys and helicopters, *Yellow Back Radio Break Down,* since he was in high school.

Lucy reiterated just the other day that Reed's novel had done something to her brain.)

Langston Hughes and Countee Cullen were Negro History Week poets I'd grown up with. My father knew as much Hughes as he did Kipling. He would quote on nearly every occasion:

Life for me ain't been no crystal stair.

He regretted that when he was a student at Morehouse College in the 1940s, Hughes's appearances around Atlanta were so frequent he took them for granted and missed most of them after a while.

Professor Hardwick did not think much of Langston Hughes really.

—Too simple.

A blues poem from the 1940s by Elizabeth Bishop, 'Songs for a Colored Singer,' was published in a small journal, and I thought Sterling Brown was better at that, though Bishop said she had complicated words in mind, because Billie Holiday sang complicated lyrics.

Go drink your wine and go get tight

Professor Hardwick said she would not answer for Bishop's folly.

She was not impressed by Sterling Brown, either, not even when I said he and my mother's mother were cousins. He'd seen me as a baby, he thought. I shook his hand after a reading at the Guggenheim in 1973 that Celia McGee took me to. I almost didn't know of him. My mother had never mentioned the connection. They had a few other books with dedications. Another elderly cousin let the cat out of the bag one Thanksgiving in Jersey City. She was pleased to see me at that reading. But to me Sterling Brown was historical, filed, in the shelves with the pharmacy-framed photographs and baffling keepsakes in my mother's hopeless family room.

(My father insisted on giving a particularly dream-prone black Vietnam War veteran all such carpentry work, and no matter his real abilities my mother got her notions of 'contemporary design' from *The Jetsons*, the space cartoon show. Mr. King, the carpenter responsible for turning the garage into one of the ugliest rooms in our Indianapolis township, was the handsomest man I had ever seen. But I'd not thought about Mr. King in more than a decade when my sister told me he died of AIDS. I was so startled.)

I'D READ HUGHES'S autobiography, *The Big Sea*. My father hadn't, to my surprise. Hughes's description of the Harlem Renaissance, I discovered, was almost a blueprint for most histories or memoirs I read of the period. In his elliptical, offhand style, Hughes introduced the Harlem Renaissance cast he cared about and what they got up to. For him, Manhattan's black Renaissance began in 1921, with the black Broadway musical *Shuffle Along* that featured Josephine Baker in the chorus, stealing the show. Hughes said the Harlem Renaissance ended in 1929, with the stock market crash, followed in 1931 by the funeral of Harlem's party queen, A'Lelia Walker, the hair cream heiress. In that same year, he noted, black people lost control of the numbers racket in Harlem to the mob.

In Hughes's account, the Negro Awakening was already in full swing when he was newly back from his adventures at sea and in Paris after he jumped ship. He would come up from Lincoln University in Pennsylvania on weekends for the parties, the prizes, the shows, speakeasies, and spectacles. He had a swell time while it lasted, he said. He hadn't expected it to last forever, because the white people who had been going up to Harlem in droves could not have been expected to be interested in black people forever. Moreover, the people Hughes called ordinary black people had never heard of the Harlem Renaissance, he said.

Hughes may have liked uptown best, but he hit downtown as well and some places in between. Hughes's scene wasn't exactly an integrated one, but the Harlem Renaissance had its crucial allies among white people. Then, too, cross-pollinations occurred. Lorca and Nella Larsen, the shrewdest observer among Harlem Renaissance novelists, befriended each other in French in Harlem, that Jazz Age junction. He was getting over a man back in Spain by writing nasty things about queers in New York; she was on an unhappily married woman's binge that would become the refuge from writer's block, but not the cause of it.

The Harlem Renaissance was a Romantic movement, not least because many of the black writers associated with it died young, or gave up, were given up on, and disappeared. When Nella Larsen died alone and lay a day or two unfound, decades after those piano

duets with Lorca, her neighbors in the East Village had no idea who
that retired registered nurse had been. Hughes was right: enough
Harlem Renaissance writers went on trying to publish, but it was
as though their moment had gone by.

Zora Neale Hurston, a great contrarian, published her first
books steeped in black folk culture in the Thirties, in a more political time, when poetry's designs upon us were supposed to be
detectable. When it came to the Harlem Renaissance, she'd just
been passing through. Alice Walker remembered that Hurston was
mentioned but not taught in Margaret Walker's class at Mississippi State in the Sixties, but for the general public Hurston had
not disappeared, she never was. Wherever she'd been, she was back,
thanks largely to Alice Walker. Hurston's novels, collections of
folklore, essays, stories, were coming back into print, along with
the first biography.

Mr. Silvers agreed that Hurston was important. He would over-
look that I had already written about Robert Hemenway's biography
of Hurston for *Kirkus Reviews*, because that was a bulletin of short
notices. But I was not to do something so unprofessional again.

The Harlem Renaissance coincided with the arrival of talkies in
film and recording studios for music; the documentation reached
beyond the page. It was part of the mass escape from the ruralism
that Hurston claimed the black We carried with us everywhere. It
was urban, Modernist, anti-pietistic, and up all night long. And for
me the Harlem Renaissance, my entrance into the history of black
literature, was as queer as Bloomsbury, though the guardians of
black America had too much invested in Langston Hughes to let
his sexuality spoil the usefulness of his legend.

—Have you read Thulani Davis's poetry? Elizabeth asked. She
had suddenly remembered talking to her when she was a student at
Barnard. —She said, Miss Hardwick, Arna Bontemps is my *godfather*.

I had to decide I'd read enough and it was time to write, Elizabeth reminded me. I had more than enough to say about the wild
and original Hurston, she said. She'd been saying it to me since

I first realized how much had been produced during the Harlem Renaissance, how much of it was being reprinted, or sat in little white boxes of microfilm up in Harlem at the Schomburg Center for Research in Black Culture.

She said that she should talk. She'd bolted up one night and had to rush downstairs to see if it was Keats who said 'Sorrow is Knowledge' and Byron who said 'Knowledge is Sorrow' or vice versa.

ELIZABETH ALWAYS ASKED about my family, exchanged enthusiastic, if awkward greetings with my mother on holiday calls. She was so full of praise for my parents that I sometimes worried she was on the verge of calling them credits to the Race. They were correct, attractive, and outspoken, and she admired their NAACP civil rights activism, which in the late Seventies many black people were writing off as exhausted. She respected certain straight people, she just didn't want to be one of them. But middle-class black people and middle-class white people were not to her mind the same. Black people were not conventional, almost by definition.

My parents would have agreed with her. But they did not appreciate being approved of by a white woman from the South, not even a liberal white woman important to me.

I could tell her that Alyosha's speech to the young man at the end of *The Brothers Karamazov* made me want to run through the streets, as though the world had changed. But I held back on that kind of language around my parents. I don't know why. Maybe it was an extension of not being out to them. I hadn't yet read *Crime and Punishment* when Professor Hardwick and my parents first met.

—You're badly educated, my father said. He pretended to be shocked, and after so much tuition cost.

—That's true, said my mother the mathematics major, still blaming herself for the low SAT math scores of two of her three children.

I realized that my father was trying to impress Professor Hardwick. He folded his napkin again in his lap and told her it was a gamble going to graduate school in chemistry at the University of Chicago on the GI Bill. Sure enough, pharmaceutical companies weren't hiring black chemists in 1948. They would begin to in the 1950s. He didn't want to be a professor. But he was married, a Morehouse College and Spelman College match. He had to do something. He went to dental school.

—Like some of the Jews, my father said.

Fortunately, he fell for dentistry at Howard and looked forward to annual classes in new techniques. He said he never missed a day of class anywhere, except for his mother's funeral when he was in high school. He said his father hadn't told him that he knew Howard University's president, Mordecai Johnson, but when my father's brother was graduating from MIT on the same day that Howard was having its ceremonies, his father told Reverend Doctor Johnson when nobody had asked him that he preferred what he considered the better occasion. My father said he was on his way to Denver with his young family when he ran out of money in Indianapolis, a good tale.

He said his father complained that I never visited him anymore, now that I no longer needed his help. My grandfather lived in East Harlem, in one of the projects the residents had been promised would not become the projects, surrounded by his second wife's sisters in nearby watchful towers. He found reasons to make long visits to his children near Boston who were not fond of him. His idea of being a help to me consisted of appearing unexpectedly in Hamilton Hall and requesting a conference with one of the deans in order to discuss my progress. After all, he was an alumnus of an Ivy League school I did not get into.

Professor Hardwick understood that my grandfather was the Mrs. Rochester in my attic. She threw herself into a somewhat circuitous explanation of her family down in Kentucky being poor white, which was not the same as white trash. Her old neighborhood in Lexington had become all black, she went on, oblivious somehow.

My mother was looking at her as if to say, 'I need a cigarette,' she who said I cared too much about appearances. She chose their hotel, in the days when they could stay in such places, for its proximity to the midtown department store she liked best. On her earliest visit to New York City as a girl, even Blumstein's on West 125th Street had white clerks only. My mother and her friends read *Gone with the Wind* that year, the same year the film of *Heidi* came out.

THREE YEARS SINCE that anxious lunch and I was still removing homo titles from my bookcases in preparation for my parents' inspection tours. They didn't take off their coats on this particular fall tour of my two rooms of five windows at the end of Pomander Walk, a loony lane of small mews houses sandwiched between apartment buildings. My mother remembered a restaurant called the Library three blocks away down Broadway, its tables and banquettes sectioned off by shelves of junked books. It had a string quartet on weekends.

My father explained that every sane black person in America understood that the ambiguity of the Supreme Court's recent decision in *Bakke v. University Regents of California* was its danger. He'd also read Ronald Dworkin's urgent pieces in the *Review* on the case, but he was never going to agree that anyone other than himself had the real picture.

I had cribbed enough to talk about either *Bakke* or the upcoming midterm election. They, too, had done homework in preparation for the visit, and had looked into the Zora Neale Hurston books my mother had no interest in that I sent for her birthday. They had some old anthologies of Negro literature that reprinted a chapter of either *Their Eyes Were Watching God* or *Mules and Men*. But they'd not opened a one of them since their school days.

My mother wrinkled her nose at the possibility of being 'common' in public. She understood someone liking to be entertained in private, among your own, by stories of black ignorance that were actually the opposite, although animal tales had never registered with her, even as a child. Other people should do as they pleased, she just didn't want to have to sit through what others enjoyed that she perhaps couldn't. She considered folklore an off-color idiom.

Hurston was interested in the same kind of people that Langston Hughes and Sterling Brown were, storytellers, country folk. On a visit to Opelika, Alabama, the boll weevils Sterling caught in a cotton field got loose in the house and my mother's aunt nearly had a fit. Folkways, like boll weevils, were best kept outside. My father considered himself a Georgia country boy and my mother had summer camp down in Fort Valley, Georgia, run by a poet, Frank Horne, but for them both the Old Country was put here on earth to be left behind.

Moreover, down home was no laughing matter; do not be fooled. Sterling Brown in his review of *Mules and Men* said that in order for Hurston's picture of the South to be true, it would have had to be more bitter. I'd looked things up. If I really wanted to know what the South had been like and was still like in some places, I had to read *Black Boy* by Richard Wright, my father said. I had. Threat of one kind or another was always in someone's air. He said he managed to avoid ever getting himself into a position where he had to yass, boss a white man in Georgia.

The tobacco fields he and his brother worked on between semesters were in Connecticut, he said, and it seemed like everybody was studying something, like the Jews in Richard Wright's Chicago post office, he said. My father remembered that he and his brother had the thinnest cardboard suitcases at the station. I told him Richard Wright had escorted Simone de Beauvoir on her first tour of Harlem in 1946. My mother thought I was referring to that French actor with the cat-like eyes, what was her name.

I said Hughes worked as a busboy in Washington, D.C.; he and his mother were the poor relations of a prominent black family of

Reconstruction lawmakers and educators. My father said Wright was as great as Victor Hugo.

My mother remembered that Sterling's sister Helen had been kind to them when my father was in school. Otherwise, they ate whiting every day. She had not gone near whiting since they left Washington in 1952. Helen Brown lived on one side of nutty Sterling and his saintly wife, Daisy, and the Ralph Bunches lived on the other side. She said Jane Bunche had such pretty hair she stopped thinking too much of her own.

The Hughes my father really loved had been the companion of his segregated army life, the author of the 'Simple' columns syndicated in black newspapers. During World War II, the Red Cross jim-crowed the blood supply, a fact that never ceased to outrage my parents, Charles Drew fans. Look Drew up, they told me. Hughes created a Harlem folk character, Jesse B. Semple, who had comic but biting exchanges, usually about race or women, often in a bar, with Hughes, a book-reading guy.

Maybe he never yass-suhed a white boss, but my mother remembered how disgusted my father had been after he'd had to shuck in R. B. Russell's office in order to secure a signature from the Georgia senator who would soon author 'The Southern Manifesto,' the declaration by Southern Democrats in Congress of their intention to oppose implementation of *Brown v. Board of Education*. My father needed a letter for both his post office job and school that only Senator Russell could sign in the District of Columbia. He said he learned from reading Langston Hughes how to fool self-important crackers.

My father could recall from his reading of Hughes:

> I was so mad I decided to set down and stay awhile. So I did. With my gun on my lap, I just sat—and every time a Southerner came in, I cocked the trigger. Ain't nobody said a word. They just looked at me and walked out. I

stayed there as long as I wanted to—black as I am—in that WHITE latrine. Down in Mississippi a colored soldier has to have a gun even to go to the toilet!

We'd been serenaded by the same Mendelssohn mush as the year before. And we'd not been having another Marshall Plan conference on my development. My mother hadn't needed to resort to her pillbox of punctuating looks. My father hadn't flared up over the bill. He had his very late birthday present under his arm as he opened the taxi door for my mother, a first edition of *The Story of the NAACP* by Langston Hughes that I'd actually paid for. New York was much warmer than they thought it would be.

I was sorry they were going. I wanted to hear more of their memories. I hardly knew them. They had funny set pieces that they repeated on holidays, or in times of sadness, but I'd no real idea what they'd been like when they were our age. They were not our friends. They were our parents, the givers of life, loans, and the law.

A week or so later my mother sent a copy of the summary of the NAACP's symposium on *Bakke* held that past summer and a clipping from the Indianapolis Sunday newspaper medical column on marijuana's harm to chromosomes.

ELIZABETH SHOWED ME the photographs Tom Victor had taken of her for her book.

(A sweet, disorganized guy, Tom, when he got AIDS, vanished, went home to his family in Michigan, or Wisconsin, and wouldn't take phone calls, or his relations would not put through calls to him.)

She favored the shots taken outside, in front of the house, since a lot of the novel was about Sixty-seventh Street. Her rooms she thought looked too grand for a book about poor people.

I'd heard that Jason Epstein loved the book, was planning to print twenty thousand copies, and that the word around town was that it was a marvel. I was excited, but she was fearful, beside herself. I'd seen her tempests before, and I would never get used to them, to her being in a state of real weather.

She was worried that some people might be recognized, that she would give offense with some of her portraits. Mary McCarthy told her she wished ten people would die before her new novel came out. Elizabeth was dedicating her book to her and to Harriet.

—I told Mary, At least you won't have to write a blurb.

Elizabeth had been to Charles Rosen's lecture on the Romantics; to dinner with a persistent suitor (—I should have said I'm not that hungry); to the opera with Devie's mother; to her class at Barnard; and to committees. She did an imitation of Gwendolyn Brooks.

—I shall flail in the HOT time!

(When Luc Sante first came to dinner at Professor Hardwick's, they bonded doing imitations of Eric Bentley.

—He'd arrive with his blackamoors, she said.)

She had dinner down the street at the Epsteins' with Gore Vidal. She told me someone once asked Gore if the first person he slept with was a man or a woman. His answer:

—I thought at the time it would be rude to ask.

(That line of his has been making the rounds for years now.)

Elizabeth was asked at a lecture who was her favorite American woman novelist.

—Henry James.

No laughter in the audience, she said.

We talked about the fatalism of Leopardi and the beauty of *The Leopard*. She admired Updike and regarded my verdict against *Rabbit Run* as the wrong one, just because I didn't like the black invader of suburban quiet who ends up stealing Rabbit's wife. He was more than a device or a symbol, she argued.

She said she wanted to do something on Ruth in the Bible and the second marriage. Or Desdemona as a sort of hippie, taking up with Othello. (When did we have that talk about Berryman and his

character Mr. Bones?) Sigrid had sent her chapters of her novel and
after the Charles Rosen lecture, Elizabeth told Sigrid the truth, in
a nice way, very tough, yet fair, she thought. She wanted her to give
it up and try something more real. Susan told Elizabeth it was the
worst thing she'd ever read. Elizabeth said Susan would never sit
down with Sigrid and tell her why, because she wanted her to fail.

A THREE-PAGE LETTER from Mr. Silvers was waiting for me when I
got home. Elizabeth said she understood how irritating that could
be, and you wanted to say to them that they didn't write this, you
did, but she also suggested that making the asked-for revision
might be easier than I thought, or at least worth it.

There was never any drama in sitting beside Robert Silvers and
going over his changes in my manuscripts. It was disarming that he
was so thoroughly prepared when he talked to you, that he seemed
to know as much about your subject as you did. He was handsome,
always younger than I expected, and sounded like an Old Etonian.

An appointment would go by in a daze, he was so kind and
right about everything, and yet I knew he was capable of screaming
at assistants and slamming whatever was in his hands down on his
desk and putting on tiptoe everyone except Barbara and Sharon
DeLano, the assistant editor, seemingly always dressed in a flowing
black top and black trousers, who was so well informed concerning New York's cultural fronts, she was the person who told Susan
Sontag what performances to go to.

Elizabeth said she understood my irritation over the queries.

—You want to tell them that editing is not writing.

(But she'd always said writing included the ability to edit
yourself.)

I stomped around, resolved to put back the reference to, say,
Walter Benjamin that Mr. Silvers had deleted. I intended to stand
on my feeling that literature should be spoken of in a universal

voice and why shouldn't I approach black writers with concepts got from white critics. I didn't know how to say I felt I was being kept in a certain lane. Elizabeth warned against the practice of making overreaching comparisons.

—'James Jones, like Homer, is interested in war,' or 'Marcuse and Foucault are not as great philosophers as Aristotle or Plato.' This is the problem with academic criticism. It doesn't tell us anything.

To know that Susan Sontag freaked out at the sight of her marked-up manuscripts did not help. Still, Elizabeth thought that the additions had to come from me if it was important to me.

—Write criticism as carefully as you would poetry, she said.

(James gave me a doubtful look when I told him at lunch this afternoon that I'd found this line of hers. What has mattered to him most as a journalist and essayist has been to have an editor on his side, one who wants him to succeed.)

It was Sunday. She urged me to call Bob's office from her phone, not to be afraid. When I did, I was astonished to hear the piece had been set into galleys.

—I hate to ask for it.

She had in a drawer in the broad, dark desk in the living room an envelope with a few emergency twenty-dollar bills.

—I hate to give it. But you have to have money for taxis in New York or you have to leave.

TO WALK THE streets of Manhattan was a great consolation, getting back inside even more so. My doorbell rang before I put the needle down on the all-by-myself record. Robert Fleming, a young black journalist who hung out on weekends late in my old bookshop, introduced the poet Mbembe Milton Smith. I remember the gravity of Mbembe's handshake, his face a museum piece, dark angular planes, eyes solemn in deep sockets. Mbembe recited slowly, as if intent on haunting the room. He could make his jaw move sideways. He smoked a pipe of tobacco.

They tried to tell me up there on my high horse that poetry was a big world. I had never heard of Robert Hayden, closeted down at Fisk. It was a profound and humbling experience. Mbembe and Robert, in colorful, double-knit trousers, took turns speaking verses of Hayden's poem of the Underground Railroad, 'Runagate Runagate.' They both knew it by heart.

HALLOWEEN NIGHT WE divided up into three taxis. Alexis Adler, the biology major in the gang, said she first fell for New York when she was a child visiting from Seattle and realized you could get a candy bar on every corner. Our favorite place on White Street, over in Tribeca, the Molotov Cocktail Lounge, had been rechristened the Mudd Club. So much of our lives already took place there. We thought of it as the home of the B-52's, the gang's favorite band, or one of them.

Felice loved their Farfisa organ and the Vox amps, an old carnival sound pushed back at us through time. The band was catching on, but the audience still had the room to fling arms about in. The lead singer wore a lobster suit with claws and during guitar solos he jumped down to dance with the audience.

(The guitarist, Ricky Wilson, died of AIDS.)

—Their shit is excellent, Felice said, dressed in long white lace. Her piece in *Stranded* about feeling the vibe had caused a sensation in this new downtown scene.

We danced that mess around.

I woke sitting on the floor of the Mudd Club with my back against the wall, confused by the legs moving to and fro. Maybe this was the night a pretty black girl in a baby doll shift, with hair semi-Bride-of-Frankenstein style, pogoed down the steps behind Felice, making rhymes of our names. Jennifer skipped into all hearts, on the run from Swarthmore and a Westchester household of Antiguan women.

(She published her memoir of this period, *Spill Ink on It*, under the name Jennifer Jazz.)

From the Mudd Club music around the same time, Felice gathered up Samo, the name then used by Jean-Michel Basquiat, adding a moody tag artist, so I thought, to the strays crashing on her available mattress, couch, and floor.

THE U.S. GOVERNMENT was telling us that we needed the Shah; the British embassy in Tehran was sacked. To avoid anarchy, military rule was needed. The news screamed about Soviet access to the Indian Ocean. The Iranian government blamed the oil situation on left-wing students, but students didn't work in the oil fields.

We—*we*—were saying the conservative Muslim elements were grossly exaggerated.

Elizabeth rang the activist Rose Styron to start an ad in the newspaper.

She went to Boston, and from there to Dunbarton to see the headstone. She had to change her mind about staying in New Hampshire with eccentric friends of Cal's youth whom she loved, Peter and Esther Brooks. They could never quite get themselves together, she said, because no one in their families had needed to since before the Industrial Revolution. She went back to Boston, to her friend William Alfred. He could never quite get his plays right, she said. Faye Dunaway loved him.

While Elizabeth was away, Janet Flanner died. When I was a teenager trying to imagine New York sophistication, Janet Flanner appeared on *The Dick Cavett Show*, on Gore Vidal's side as he faced off with Norman Mailer. My sister informed me that the lady wearing gloves on a TV talk show was a hometown girl. She got away from Indianapolis on a train, got out of New York on a ship, and for fifty years wrote a 'Letter from Paris' for *The New Yorker*. 'Josephine Baker has arrived at the Théâtre des Champs-Élysées in *La Revue Nègre* and the result has been unanimous.'

The day Flanner died, I was lurking at a very queer dinner party beside Howard when Virgil Thomson piped up from the gossiping bowl,

—Of course, Lizzie doesn't approve of me. This wine should have been left open for two hours. Mind you, she once did. Well, I don't approve of her.

In those days, Virgil Thomson would fall asleep, suddenly. He woke just as abruptly.

—Now tell me what I was talking about.

He was in his mid-eighties then, the author of a clutch of autobiographies, and had been owl-like his whole life, or so said photographs of him in his young dream of Paris, student of the great teacher Nadia Boulanger, collaborator with the vainglorious admirer of doughboys Gertrude Stein. He said other people needed five-hundred-dollar stereos, because they had five-dollar ears. He, however, had five-hundred-dollar ears and therefore wasn't bothered by his five-dollar record player.

One of his operas had recently been revived. It didn't matter that I hadn't seen it. I'd heard the record and read him in *The New York Review*, a name on my old list of names to reckon with. He was pleased. He said Barbara was a bitch and not to be trusted.

It was Howard who roused himself to wonder where he'd heard that Elizabeth Hardwick and Barbara Epstein were such champions of Virgil Thomson.

—Yes, they have great friends, he said.

He told me that Nancy Cunard once went to a May Day rally in red rags

—designed by Chanel.

He said that Henry Crowder, Cunard's black lover, a jazz composer, complained to him:

—That woman is dragging me down.

His chin sank on his neck.

Howard and I came back from the bathroom.

Virgil opened his eyes and said to me never to ask someone what he did for a living; only what he was interested in. He said that some nice people came from Indiana. Janet Flanner wasn't one of the girls who liked girls, like Gertrude, he said.

—She got syphilis and then pregnant and decided that that was enough of men.

When Elizabeth was back and I was safely on West Sixty-seventh Street, I gave a filtered account of my candlelight encounter with the Homintern.

—Virgil has total self-confidence, Elizabeth said as she made her way to the red sofa. —He's fond of gossiping about the dead and can be very funny. But the living he doesn't get quite right. She said Virgil wrote the most entertaining reviews of concerts he'd slept through.

'To love intelligent women is the pleasure of pederasts,' Baudelaire said.

I said I thought it was funny: when first in New York, as a supposedly militant runaway, I put on a jacket and tie and the nerve of the hick posted me to the musty lobby of the Algonquin Hotel, where the Round Table of *The New Yorker* wits held court in the Jazz Age. My sister had given me *Paris Was Yesterday*, and in her introduction, Janet Flanner revised her 'Letter from Paris' about Josephine Baker in which she'd been, she felt, too timid: 'She was an unforgettable female ebony statue.' I tapped the bell on the little table, smoking Black Russians and drinking Black Russians, none of which I could afford. I didn't say to her that the hotel, unlikely hiding place for someone like me, was a spot where I could ignore the panic of being.

Elizabeth said my Round Table phase had been me being camp, like the Twenties themselves. *The Crack-Up* wasn't camp to me and Janet Flanner had had the sense to avoid Dorothy Parker. To me, the Harlem Renaissance was a part of Jazz Age expression. But

Elizabeth had a touch of her Depression generation's contempt
for the excesses of the Jazz Age. No, Hemingway, that writer who
taught American literature the value of the short sentence, brought
out the era-transcending worst in himself on his own, she laughed.

Flanner wrote the introduction to the translation Elizabeth
had of *The Pure and the Impure*, I reminded her.

She smiled broadly, hugged her shoulders, and inclined her
head and looked up at me, as though to concede to the student the
point. I wanted to say I went to the Algonquin because I hadn't yet
met her.

—Katherine Mansfield was nineteen when she wrote *In a German
Pension*.

Unlike Susan Sontag, Elizabeth Hardwick did not mind being
called a woman writer. Who would not be proud of intellectual
descent from George Eliot:

> She was melancholy, head-achy, with a slow, disciplined,
> hard-won, aching genius that bore down upon her with
> a wondrous and exhausting force, like a great love affair
> in middle age. Because she was driven, worn-out, dedi-
> cated, George Eliot needed unusual care and constant
> encouragement; indeed she could not even begin her
> great career until the great person appeared to help her.

Eliot was successful and her illicit union with George Henry
Lewes, the already married philosopher, was very respectable, after
all, so much so that Elizabeth was glad to find Eliot's 'irregularity
of temperament as an artist,' as she called it, on display in her marriage to a much younger man after Lewes's death. The young man
was boring and lived until 1924. 'A strange old coot for the Jazz Age.'

That essay made her laugh. It was from *A View of My Own*, her
first collection of essays, *Partisan Review* pieces, for the most part.
She still had that edition of George Eliot's *Letters*. I especially liked
her image of Eliot 'leading a literary life from morning to night.'

She worried when I said maybe she was saying that in not having feminine appeal, George Eliot managed to have the equivalent of a man's career. She thought she meant that Eliot's brilliance could not be denied and Lewes played his part in protecting her, offering her unhesitant devotion. She had come to think that Eliot as a serious linguist and student of philosophy acquired a knowledge of things and systems her time would have called masculine.

(She would one day say the same of Joan Didion, because of her interest in how systems worked, or her knowledge of how machines were put together, her 'precision of language' about details of the material world.)

—Had I read *Middlemarch* when I was sixteen my life would be so different now.

—Pray? she laughed.

(I did not say, terror of the Causabon in me.)

Elizabeth cared about Hawthorne's injustice to Margaret Fuller, early translator of *Conversations with Eckermann*. The three Brontë sisters were not beyond further interrogation. And even if Virginia Woolf was undetainable soliloquy, a special conversation could be had with Isak Dinesen, with Doris Lessing when still in her right mind in Africa, or with Christina Stead, out there deadly observant in Australia. She was interested in the books by women that made their way to her from Carmen Callil's Virago Press (with Ursula Owen and Alexandra Pringle), a good thing to come out of London, she said, with its list of new women writers and not always well-known women writers from the past.

Elizabeth said one had to read Stein when young, when one was most open to literary experiment, but she'd missed *The Making of the Americans*. During the Depression, Richard Wright read 'Melanctha,' Stein's story from 1913 about a black girl sitting on a fence and talking strangely, to his fellow black post office co-workers in Chicago, who loved it and laughed their heads off, he reported.

Elizabeth said *The Autobiography of Alice B. Toklas* was Stein's best book.

In the early Sixties, she went to a dinner in Paris for Alice B. Toklas, a tiny, dark woman with a mustache. Elizabeth said she felt a poke in her ribs. It was Katherine Anne Porter:

—Honey, if I looked like that I'd kill myself.

Elizabeth frowned when I said that I didn't like Porter's stories in *The Leaning Tower* that were set in the post–Civil War South of ruin. I was surprised she'd fallen for something so Southern myth. I preferred the title story, set in Berlin in 1931. A struggling artist from Texas was counting his pennies and

—He's a drip, she interrupted.

To her, Porter's interconnected stories about a woman and her former slave in their old age exposed the white person's fantasy that the black mammy had always loved that white person. I thought Katherine Anne Porter had had some unsavory political connections. Elizabeth had her number, but rather liked her, as in, How far would a girl go to reinvent herself and more power to you. Moreover, Katherine Anne was a mess, which made her temperamentally irresistible.

Unbroken cloud cover hid the rain as it came down. Elizabeth said the song 'Gloomy Sunday' had been adapted from a Romanian song about suicide.

I don't remember when she and Harriet stopped going up to New Hampshire for Thanksgiving at the home of rich relations known to me only as Aunt Sarah and Uncle Cott. She once said she had to keep after Harriet to write them a thank-you letter and was not above writing one for her. They must have died before Lowell did, because she was amused by her own thwarted calculations, like the comeuppance of a character in Balzac. In the end, they did not leave Lowell a penny. She was sure they thought Bobby was crazy and would just give it away. (Or maybe it was Harriet whom they overlooked, cursed because of her father.)

P. N. Furbank's prudish biography of E. M. Forster and then Fran Lebowitz's wicked *Metropolitan Life* nudged her out of the Gloomy Sunday feeling.

Children do not look good in evening clothes.

—Worth the price of the whole book, Elizabeth laughed.

I had her V. S. Pritchett to return, *The Living Novel*. I liked his idea that nineteenth-century Russian literature was about the isolated, lonely man or woman in his or her room. I was on the right track. It was the kind of book that added to my list of names to reckon with. She agreed that clearly for Ellison and Wright the Russian novelists were their antecedents in a way that nineteenth-century American literature was not. Russian novels had slavery and freedom, nationalism and suspicion of assimilation, but they did not have race, or black people as social scenery. Nevertheless, she thought Hemingway probably more important in Wright's and Ellison's development as writers.

I finished *Dead Souls* on the subway to West Sixty-seventh Street. Gogol burned Part 2 and then died nine days later. She said as soon as she opened the door that you wonder how he would have turned Chichikov around.

IT WAS EARLY December, freezing. The Nova Convention kicked off downtown, a festival of films, readings, and discussions organized by *Semiotext(e)* founder Sylvère Lotringer. I really did mean to get to the Merce Cunningham, the Philip Glass, and how did I miss John Cage.

Felice, Luc, Alexis, and I dropped acid. Felice said a dear friend of hers from Paris was probably dead at the bottom of the Mineshaft and since it was never cleaned Guillaume's body would never be found.

We were in a large old hall on Irving Place and in position, leaning on the stage at the feet of the B-52's.

—They caught fire, Felice said. They're smoking.

Photographers fighting to get the best shots muscled in on us.

They were impressed that Frank Zappa, Tom Verlaine, and Richard Lloyd had also turned out for the new dance band from Athens, Georgia. The opening band, the Stimulators, had had to start a scuffle at the stage to get paid. The haze was intense. White rabbits lined up for the johns. There were so many people from CBS Records bounding around Felice that Bud, Edward Kliment, our fellow English major, had to take her home.

The next day, Luc and I were having an uneasy lunch near the Strand. Then things were fine after we'd gone another round over Patti Smith. We'd been having knockdowns about Patti Smith since her tremendous show at the Vietnam Victory Day convocation in Central Park in 1975. I was dishonestly disputatious on the subject. She kept fucking Rimbaud. A woman claiming Rimbaud. I didn't like Rimbaud's later life in East Africa; I paid more attention to the betrayal in his heterosexual relationship there than I did to his slave trading, as some black writers were beginning to speculate he may have fallen into.

(Is it in Enid Starkie or Wallace Fowlie? I saw in a friend's study not long ago a copy of the old New Directions Louise Varèse translation and trembled to caress the cover, to remember my determination in class to understand, to get him for real.)

I usually finished one hundred miles from 'Rocking Rimbaud,' saying something against Gallic constructions in criticism written in English and that I wasn't ready to separate meaning from language. In this round, Luc countered that no technology of control existed for fantasies and by the way language was meaning. Luc didn't have to convince me that the aesthetic of 'antidisestablishment totalitarianism,' as one band called it, wasn't my path. But alternative reality was just my kind of party.

> *Voyager now, on a ship of night*
> *Off to a million midnights, black, black*
> *Into forever tomorrows, black . . .*

Luc and Eva, having patched things up, met Felice and me at the door on Irving Place. There were photographers and frenzy in the street. If *we* had to stand in line, then we were certainly going to nip brandy. Once inside, we tried to take up our positions, but we couldn't get anywhere near the front of the stage. Where had they come from, the white guys in down jackets gripping beer cans, blocking the view and not dancing. Blondie played. There were boys in yarmulkes and boys in drag to push them back, but they didn't look good, like they had plastic furniture covers over themselves. We were merely on speed. The B-52's were on top of things, as usual. A lesser band played next and everyone fled.

We were jammed together on an upper stairway landing. Hash made a coffle of smoke from Sid Vicious, to Eva, Luc, Felice, and me. Not so long before, Felice had tried to get a room at the Chelsea Hotel but the man on the desk told her they'd been booked solid since Sid Vicious had murdered his girlfriend. In private, everyone was mean about the victim. Then, out of nowhere, Rockets Redglare, standing opposite us, lost it, exploding, to who knows, that he was not a faggot. The cold stairway landing shook.

Doomed to meaning, Felice and I went to Kipling's Last Stand on University Place. There were crowds and the glare of white lights in the frozen black street. Felice's new motto was: never stand in line. Brad gave me a hug and a kiss. Howard was too excited from filming for three days to be ticked off I'd missed his calls. Burroughs was laughing and eating chicken. Jim said again that a certain poet I didn't like had been really good. I was too intimidated by their cool not to agree with Jim and Brad.

Kathy Acker was going to read at Kipling's Last Stand, Felice saw. She wasn't so sure about that, not after *Kathy Goes to Haiti* and Kathy the white chick narrator fucking every black man in her path. Some nights made Felice sensitive to the fact that of the, say, half-dozen black people in a given rock or new music club, she knew them, most likely had brought them. Race and the scene were not cool, she felt.

Felice was the first person I knew to wonder about the real Mardou Fox, the bebop black girl whom Kerouac leaves in *The Subterraneans* after being proud for Bird to clock her by his side in the club. Who was this girl and what had they said to her at home when she night after night was hanging out with a white guy, and a poor outlaw white guy at that. I hadn't realized she was a real affair.

Howard told me that that was Gore Vidal fucking Kerouac at the Chelsea Hotel in *The Subterraneans*. I thought he was made up.

—I thought you were hiding under the bed.

Howard said Kerouac may have been into Charlie Parker, but he'd always had crosses burning on the lawn in his head. Howard blinked at just how racist Missouri-born, upper-class William Burroughs probably was, too.

He got up, hunched his shoulders, and his hands hung like a puppet's, as Burroughs's did. But he didn't do the voice, not there. He cared about the film he was making and about Burroughs. We looked over at the neck-scalped white boys appreciating what Burroughs was saying.

—Socrates, Howard said low.

Howard had his routines, like making fun of lines from the black Beat poet Bob Kaufman's faucet of colorful psychedelic imagery.

—Tonto is dead, he whispered. Then, *a voce alta*: —TONTO IS DEAD.

Schizo-Culture celebrated a generation that considered itself a dissident culture. It was sullen youth, with Burroughs as a founding bishop of hard attitudes. He read from the Dr. Benway section of *Naked Lunch* and his performance told everybody how to read him. I'd see in Howard's documentary that Burroughs could be blackly hilarious, just as everybody said.

Nova hailed its own scene and New Wave's antecedents, pioneers. Women and the Beats was not yet a heard story. Baldwin had his own reasons for loathing the Beats, Mailer's white Negroes, and, later, hippies. It was not my scene, but what mattered to my friends were the inspirations of the open road, their freedom from inner borders, and making a difference, with words or film or music or photography or . . .

Felice hung out with the B-52's until dawn.

The next day I was early and Felice was late. Elizabeth had fronted her the extra money for the apartment on First Avenue and St. Marks, around the corner from Luc's. It was a walk-up, nice, we said, with abundant light and fairly new appliances, and was not the only place in the East Village that featured a slanting floor.

Elizabeth said she was giving us a real home-cooked meal. She had a new crockery pot and was trying out a meat loaf the way she'd seen her friend the novelist Robert Rushmore do it, with the bacon browned on top.

There was so much wine to get through. She took some whacks at Patti Smith and read Rimbaud at the table: 'I think of the history of France, eldest daughter of the Catholic Church.' Or: 'Everything I am I owe to the Declaration of the Rights of Man.' Or: 'I enter the true kingdom of Ham.'

She praised Felice's story in *Stranded*. Felice was working on another one, about a crash pad in London. She'd no idea until it was too late that she'd been invited to stay in a stash house under surveillance. Felice said she'd been thinking the whole time that if she got busted her mother would kill her.

—Good, Elizabeth said. She said that Felice's close relationship with her mother acted as a brake on her self-destructiveness, just as my alarming lack of self-confidence saved me, she went on to say.

Professor Hardwick did not mess around. I addressed her that way when we were in front of my friends. She had written for *Vogue* a short piece about women. I remembered it at the dining room table:

Accountability is what we have lost. Change is on the wind like a pestilence.

Somewhere in the piece she said that she used to think:

What if Mama and Papa *knew*.

—That's right.

She was not pleased to be quoted in front of someone else. She said back when she was our age it was not about drugs; it was about sex.

—You know, the doorman used to give you looks. And a man would be there, and I'd think, It's eleven o'clock. Get out.

She said that it was essential to be able to live out the down times, feeling bad, especially for writers, and for the young who liked too much to escape. She said Harriet's boyfriend got her high on Thai sticks in Castine that last summer and it took her fifteen minutes to get upstairs.

I washed the dishes and Felice found a joint of Harriet's in the silverware.

IT WAS A pleasure to come up from the subway onto Broadway at Lincoln Center in the worst of damp, greasy winter. I made a point of getting that mandatory Sunday phone call home out of the way. When I angled toward Sixty-seventh Street, I was happy, even when I knew I was in for it.

Elizabeth was not interested in the floral tributes I couldn't imagine ordering from the right places, but any book from a secondhand shop was received with amusement. I once brought her a novel by Josephine Herbst, a writer who'd influenced her in her radical youth. What she liked most for me to have in hand were cigarettes and magazines, journalism that might occupy her through the dregs of Sunday after we'd turned on the dishwasher and switched off the lights.

Nuits d'insomnie ô nuits de Manhattan!

The rewards of revision, my five contributor's copies of the December 21, 1978, issue of *The New York Review*, had been delivered to my door by messenger, nevertheless Elizabeth had one of hers on the chair by the door from habit.

—The problem with finishing anything is that you then just have to do it again, she said.

Hurston said that as the only black student at Barnard in 1926 if you had not had lunch with her then you had not shot from taw. Elizabeth appreciated the line, while explaining that taw is the big marble that you hit the others with.

It was a scream to us both that Fannie Hurst, the author of a Stone Age bestseller about a black girl who passes for white, had lived around the corner on West Sixty-sixth Street and that Zora Neale Hurston had ever tried to be her secretary. The bestseller had been a movie twice, the second directed by Douglas Sirk, the first starring Claudette Colbert, who at a great age would be in the revival of some dreadful play that Elizabeth walked out of, telling her row that her date could stay if he wanted but she was going.

(—I stand on never having seen a Neil Simon play, she once said. —I don't remember what I said about Malcolm Lowry, but I'll stand on whatever I said.)

She said it was a big deal that they'd had David Levine do a drawing of Hurston. In her gangster's girl's hat.

She thought I should continue to write about figures in black American literary history. She said that by writing for the *Review* you could compose a book that way. Because you could write at length for the *Review*, the pieces could add up, become chapters, she said. It made up for the hours of drudgery each piece represented.

No matter how much Bob and Barbara paid, it always seemed to work out to two cents an hour.

Elizabeth was having a Maria Callas festival. *Medea* had been broadcast on PBS the night before. Callas really hurled those severed heads from the back of the cart. I put on *Tosca* for dinner. We settled with our plates on the red sofa. Elizabeth swayed to 'Vissi d'arte.' It was in Florence, in 1951, that she first heard Callas. Cal was sick again, she said, and someone asked her out. There was a Mexican soprano she liked better: Oralia Dominguez? The great world ruined the voice of Maria Callas, she continued. Callas became thin and went into café society too much and lost Onassis anyway.

Why not sit through that bootlegged recording of *Aida* made in Mexico City in 1951 that I'd brought her on the five-finger discount from the bookstore where I used to work? She'd not listened to it and it had been more than a year since I'd given it to her. Callas hit a high E-flat in the triumphal scene and you could hear the audience roar. We took it off. Nor was she up to the bootlegged recording from La Scala in 1957 of Callas as Iphigenia. She had just enough stamina for her favorite aria, 'Casta diva.'

—Maria Callas changed the repertoire of the opera house with choices like *Norma*. No voice equals hers for drama.

(Queens devoted to Joan Sutherland would walk out of bars rather than debate further with the followers of Beverly Sills. I'd move away early, because there was nothing left to say after someone said, 'Leontyne Price.')

Louis, her Cuban elevator man, pulled at my silk scarf.

LUC WAS LISTENING to reggae and drinking Algerian wine. The Salon of the Rejected, he called us, including me, according to his mood, in the glare of his lamplight. He sat among piles of his books waiting to be put in order. Roaches scurried under notepaper and record covers. The wall he'd built himself in the hopeful period of having a new apartment remained half-painted. Outside, the cold and the stillness of the street waited.

Jean-Michel's graffiti along cement walls and up the sides of brick buildings marked our shadowy route to the Mudd Club.

Which institution has more power:

a) The Catholic Church
b) McDonald's
c) Samo

Felice had pull on the door at the Mudd Club she'd not known she had. Howard called from across the bar, but he was with Burroughs and Burroughs's tall, blond boyfriend, James Grauerholz. They went away and the B-52's didn't go on until midnight.

It was never too late for Isaiah's, the reggae club with the matchbooks that said 'Tuesday's.' The door said 'Bottom,' and in this week's version of itself, Isaiah's was to be found down a long, green, translucent hallway, up a flight of narrow steps, and behind a Caribbean woman chewing gum, taking money, pointing to a sheet of paper. Isaiah's moved so often, its managers in theory sent their patrons notice of their next location. A chain-link fence was sure to be involved, wherever it moved. That night it was in a very small and very dark place. A few Rastas leaned against walls, gangly white college couples stumbled around, a few older white couples weaved, a lot of black men were dancing with white women. Not many black women there with the hypnotic bass. Felice danced by herself and Luc also danced alone, both in the middle of the room, keeping each other company.

ELIZABETH WAS LEAVING Christmas night for Rome. The American Academy there had found her an apartment where she could get her lectures together. From Rome she would go on to Delhi, Bombay, Calcutta, Madras, Bangalore. She was not stopping over in London, after all.

She did not much want to see Caroline, who was suing Gaia Servadio over *Insider Outsider: A Personal View of Britain*, a stupid book, she said. Ostensibly, Caroline was furious over the way Servadio related her divorce from Israel Citkowitz, with him standing outside Sonia Orwell's, hoping to be asked up to the wedding party for Cal and Caroline. She said Sonia Orwell came off badly in the book, as someone who only took care of losers and the sick.

She said it may have been that Caroline hated the last paragraph of the section in which her marriage broke up.

—The most objectionable line is: 'And so he returned as a corpse, fooling everybody.'

She said that was a bit vulgar. Her name was misspelled throughout. She said she didn't mind the Rutgers book about Cal, Berryman, and Plath in which *Seduction and Betrayal* was quoted a lot.

—It's peculiar, about how they could not write lyric.

She said Steven Axelrod's book wasn't bad either.

—Except he likes *The Dolphin* and not *Day By Day*, I said.

She shrugged.

Lowell's coming back to America was also in it.

She said it made one wonder about Caroline's insistence on an official biography.

—She's usually more shrewd than that. She wants someone English, thinking it will be all England. And the amount of trouble. She hasn't a clue.

Elizabeth said she would not cooperate.

—I'd just say it's too close and complicated and painful. I'd feel like a fool giving my self-serving rap for the record.

I'd noticed in the bibliography of Axelrod's book that 'Summer Tides,' for Caroline, was listed as having been published in *The New Review*, while 'Loneliness,' for Elizabeth, was listed as unpublished.

—I'm not going to compete with Caroline for the corpse.

She was too busy, on the phone with airlines, shopping, then Alvarez, Voznesensky, National Book Critics Circle meetings, letters.

She was having trouble getting together some pages about George Gissing. His was a Victorian hard-luck literary story that fascinated her. His effortful failures. The torture of writing. That was what drew her to him. The scarcely paid labor in cold rooms, his catastrophic wives.

I never looked where I was going and hadn't paid attention to the marquee until I saw the large crowd on my own corner. Cecil Taylor and Sun Ra were playing at Symphony Space on the corner of West Ninety-fifth Street and Broadway. I was on my way to Sixty-seventh Street on a Saturday night. She was going soon. Another meat loaf huddled in her crockery pot and she'd fished out her Timothy Wilson record of carols from Winchester Cathedral.

On her notepad on the coffee table that she showed me:

'One is always a little scared.' Yeats.

She was feeling feverish after another cholera shot.

THE NEW YEAR began with violent denunciations of Susan Sontag. Sigrid had broken up with David for good.

(Sigrid Nunez's articles of indictment against her boyfriend's mother are forcefully given in her memoir, *Sempre Susan*.)

—Think of the sinking of the Austro-Hungarian battleship *Saint Stefan* and no orders to abandon ship. Some things make no sense, I heard someone say on the subway.

The Indianapolis Recorder, the black newspaper, was sending the *Review* its editorial from the previous year on Jim Jones. The white head of a cult of mostly black members, Jones took nearly a thousand believers from his temple in California to the jungles of Guyana to build a new world. Back in November, before Thanksgiving, a congressman had flown down to investigate Jonestown and was murdered along with two television journalists, a newspaper photographer, and a People's Temple member who was trying to escape Jones's compound. The next thing anyone knew, the majority of Jones's followers were dead, forced to drink juice laced with cyanide.

We woke up to aerial pictures of a campsite strewn with mud-colored bodies. It was hard to make sense of it at first. All the T-shirt colors and clothing heaps looked like a dump of some kind near tin-roofed sheds. What turned out to be hundreds of white paper cups littered picnic tables and the ground. I scrambled to turn off the television.

Diane Johnson, one of Barbara's girls, was writing on Jonestown for the *Review*. Barbara had never asked my help with anything before. It turned out that the Reverend Jones had had an Indianapolis phase in the early Sixties. My father didn't know anything, but he remembered Jones when he was head of the Metropolitan Housing Commission. He said black people trusted Jones, because he sent his children to black physicians, which at that time had been more than a gesture.

Barbara had not heard a word from Elizabeth. I phoned her when I got a postcard from Bombay that said when she'd be back.

Kissinger blamed Jimmy Carter's human rights policy for the downfall of the Pahlavis. The violence in Iran was getting worse.

And toward the end of January, Elizabeth phoned. She was back. She said six o'clock. She said of course she was sure.

But she was sick, wrapped in a shawl on the sofa, running a slight fever, her head congested. I didn't even sit down. She was near tears.

It took Elizabeth weeks to get over a frightening cough and then the rest of the bug or whatever it was she had. She complained daily of sinus trouble, but the beauty shop and the 1979 National Book Critics Circle Awards night were twin duties. By day, she had on her heavy coat, and stood shoulder-hunched, wreathed in woolen scarves, one a gift from Barbara, trying to remember what the last thing she said was and what she needed to have with her. She had new reddish-tan ankle-boot-like shoes with laces and a wedge heel sympathetic to her foot troubles, she said. They kind of matched the beanie-like hat she pulled down on her head.

She called to say that she had survived the first two days of jury selection. But for one case, a few people were questioned. When her name was called, the assistant DA whispered to the judge and she was excused without a word. She said her eyes were running a bit, her nose draining. Some things got to her more than they should have. She'd stopped talking about it, because there was nothing new to say, she claimed, but I did not forget that *Sleepless Nights* was coming out in a few months.

Naipaul was right about India, about its doom, she said. Calcutta was the worst. She said she thought she'd go mad: arriving at two in the morning, taken to a room with no windows, a cavernous hotel full of mildew. She was so crazy, she said, she sat up all night until it was time to be driven to a lecture the next morning.

—Sweepers on their haunches, everyone squatting like that, people crammed in small living quarters. She remembered little boys around a fetid puddle looking for fish.

—Children are everywhere, like roaches.

A small girl came up to her when she was waiting in front of a hotel, begging, moaning, pointing to her mouth. She gave her a rupee. A mass surrounded her, pulling at her clothes, moaning.

She talked of cars pushing slowly through the crowded streets and people everywhere, walking.

—It's as if every stone in New York were alive.

—Where are they going?

—I asked myself the same question. I don't know.

She said politics in India were a joke and had no relation to anything. A chess game.

—Desai is an idiot.

He wanted to get rid of English as the official language, further isolating the country, as she saw it. Bengali, Punjabi, and Hindu-stani were very separate, she said.

—Eight million were sterilized last year and it made no differ-ence. Think of all of New York not being told that the government had done this to them.

She was not very fond of the Brahmins she met. Europeans, Americans, and affluent Indians frowned on tipping waiters, driv-ers, and the like. Typical Elizabeth: she'd sneak behind when her hosts weren't looking and thrust something into their palms.

—It was all play money to me anyway.

One morning at the beautiful hotel in Bombay, she noticed a tent on the grounds. Some of the workers were on a hunger strike. She couldn't wait to get rid of her hosts. The next morning, she got up before everyone else and went over to talk to them. She was very moved and asked to leave something: a hundred rupees. There was only one other name in the pledge book, that of a minister from Australia. She signed and slipped back to the hotel.

Even the airports were a nightmare.

—What can one do? Where does one put the images of India af-ter one leaves? The enormity of the place and its unanswerableness.

She never wrote about India. She had contempt for people who praised the country's spirituality. They tended to be upper class, she noted. She never got over the suffering children she'd seen. She'd not talked about India when she first returned. She needed to wait and said so.

(Katherine Boo's *Behind the Beautiful Forevers: Life, Death, and Hope in a Mumbai Undercity* made me wish Lizzie was still alive to talk to about it.)

She was sleeping until nine o'clock and not lying about it.

She was answering mail and did not need any help. —I just have to get up and flop down at the typewriter.

She read in the newspaper about the murder case she'd been excused from hearing. Frankie Tucker, Dr. Sweetlove, he was

Wedding photograph of the author's parents,
Aurelius Dewey Pinckney, Jr., and Claragene Parks
Pinckney, Atlanta, Georgia, 1947

The author with family, 1969

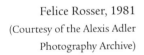 ABOVE: Lucy Sante (then
Luc Sante), Harvard, 1974
(Courtesy of Lisa Shea)

Felice Rosser, 1981
(Courtesy of the Alexis Adler
Photography Archive)

ABOVE: Alexis Adler, 1979
(Courtesy of the Alexis Adler
Photography Archive)

Jim Jarmusch performing
with the Del-Byzanteens
(Courtesy of the Alexis Adler
Photography Archive)

Jean-Michel Basquiat, 1979
(Courtesy of the Alexis Adler
Photography Archive)

Suzanne on the beach, Swampscott, MA, 1985 (© Nan Goldin)

Self-portrait on the train, Germany, 1992 (© Nan Goldin)

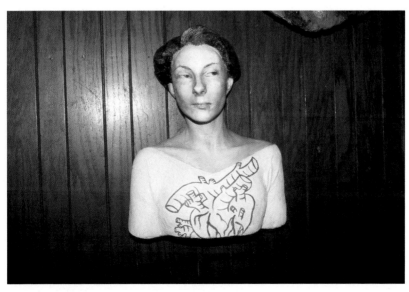

Bust of Maggie Smith at Tin Pan Alley by John Ahearn, New York (© Nan Godin)

Howard Brookner and William Burroughs
(Courtesy of the Estate of Howard Brookner)

Howard Brookner, Exeter, 1971

daryl and susan   berlin 1990

Susan Sontag and the author, Berlin, 1990 (© Annie Leibovitz)

Sterling Brown and the author, Washington, D.C., 1979
(Courtesy of the Estate of Thomas Victor)

once called, a singer or songwriter. A stabbing, some sort of tacky altercation.

—He looked like a lawyer. I'm crushed.

A drunkard from the BBC had been pressuring Elizabeth to appear in a documentary on Lowell. She didn't want to, told him she thought it unseemly, that poetry is one thing and the life another.

—I don't believe in wives, okay?

And Caroline was still pressing the official biography business.

—John Malcolm Brinnin or someone. You always hate it afterward.

Elizabeth was pleased when I told her about Flannery O'Connor's references in her letters to *The Simple Truth*, Elizabeth's second novel, her last novel, published more than twenty years before.

—I never thought Flannery liked my work.

ELIZABETH SOMETIMES CALLED at the last minute to say that I should just stop by on my way home from work. My new job was not like *Desk Set* after all. I'd failed the typing test at my interview. Fran never should have hired me; she should have fired me. The supply cabinet was a wonderland of free typing paper, pens, correctotape. I stopped dressing appropriately for a smoked-glass office. I was always late, because I had to walk across town from the nearest West Side subway station. Fran's authors adored her, several poets among them.

I brought Elizabeth the galleys of Robert Bly's Rilke translations. I said I was tempted to compare his to Spender's. She shot me a no-thank-you look. She'd come across Beckett's beautiful little book on Proust.

I had only a sketchy Scott Moncrieff sense of *Remembrance of Things Past*: the Swann bit and then the dirty bits.

'For every wound a scalpel,' she quoted from the Beckett.

I read *Dancer from the Dance* but was so jealous of Andrew Holle-ran's novel I said I found the promiscuity dull.

She noted that I had been fascinated enough with the men J. R. Ackerley picked up on trains in his memoir of discovering his Edwardian father's bigamous secret, *My Father and Myself.* She would not let go of my Bloomsbury thing, even unto the next generation, the *Enemies of Promise / Brideshead Revisited* sort of Anglophilia she didn't believe had subsided in me.

The ideal would be Elizabeth's and Barbara's friends Bobby and Arthur, the pianists.

—That's very rare, she said.

Elizabeth said the name of the game was to get through Saturday night. Her story about Holland, which she was calling 'The Faithful,' was in the anniversary issue of *The New Yorker.* She gave me a copy.

I rang her the next day to say how much I liked it. She was in bed, taking Dristan for her sinuses, eating eggs, determined to be okay when she went to the ballet with the girls.

She was reading a comic novel, *Sanjo,* narrated by a mentally impaired woman. She read out a line: 'I wonder if it's time to do nice-nice.' She said that was masturbation. Susan had told her about the book.

By the time she finished reading the novel, she wasn't feeling better. She passed on to me the ballet ticket Barbara had given her.

The girls agreed that Tomasson was quite good. Suzanne Farrell and Peter Martins were exquisite, they said. Barbara was, again, very different from the woman boss of *The New York Review of Books,* where she'd throw the women's room key at the wide horizontal window of the mailroom without looking to see whose face might be in it.

She also wasn't her unburdening self in Elizabeth's kitchen, exasperated and wise. I'd seen her dressed for parties. But this was as though she'd changed eyes for the evening as well. She didn't move once she'd dropped everything in the aisle, after she settled into the difficult continental seating of the old State Theater. Her eyes shone throughout *Midsummer Night's Dream*. It was what she and Elizabeth had most in common: to be pierced by beauty.

Barbara's true smile plumped her cheeks and made her younger. Her son Jacob would tell me that John Ashbery gave Barbara Zimmerman the nickname 'Bubsie' when they were students.

Barbara's girls, writers, editors, agents, painters, former dancers, single women, lesbians, wives, former wives, second wives, heiresses, and two widows, were everywhere in the middle rows of the theater. They were in ecstatic conversations as they left, women who knew what they were talking about.

Barbara and her girls scooted away from what they referred to as Those Chagalls.

It was a school night, but Luc's co-workers from the Strand were having a party an easy subway ride straight down to Vestry Street. Luc had been to six parties that weekend. He couldn't remember how he got to the last two or how he got home. His shower hadn't worked in two weeks. Tiles fell one night and clogged the drain. Another epic landlord battle. He'd just been going to films, one after the other: *Les maîtres fous, La chasse au lion a l'arc, Jaguar*, or *Babatu* by Jean Rouch, a French anthropological filmmaker who worked in West Africa.

Alexis helped Felice up the stairs. Felice was hobbling on a cane, having twisted her ankle in the Mudd Club, but we danced until well after two o'clock. Luc put on punk music; Eva put on Motown. Suddenly, I took myself away, not belonging, whether dancing with my friends or sitting in a chair and watching them. That part of town was abandoned. I found a taxi, miraculously. The snow poured down. The name of the game was to wake up in a few mean hours in time for Monday morning.

Elizabeth read me a bit she was writing. She was searching for another fiction project and was trying various scenes, to see if she could find entrance into any of them. One of them was about a young man, separated from his wife, waking, struggling to open his eyes, as someone would 'when resisting chloroform':

> This Saturday morning his apartment was as he had left it Friday night. Only it looked, to him, a great deal worse. He felt he had met with an accident. The accident he met with was seven glasses of Scotch, two packs of cigarettes, and a record playing over and over in a bar.

We laughed, knowing exactly where she got that from. My head hurt.

O sleepless nights, nights of Manhattan!

Town Bloody Hall, a documentary of the Town Hall panel 'A Dialogue on Women's Liberation,' held in 1971, had just been released. Elizabeth pronounced the film boring. It showed her just blithering, she sighed.

(In the film, Susan, smiling, goes after Mailer, in defense of Diana Trilling, saying she didn't think Diana would like being called 'the foremost lady literary critic.' It wasn't gallantry or a compliment, it was patronizing. He didn't mean it as a compliment, Mailer replies. Nevertheless, Trilling says she would allow it, like saying 'lady jumper.'

—I'm not going to sit here and let you harridans harangue me and say, Yessum, yessum, Mailer, author of *The Prisoner of Sex*, says at one point. Germaine Greer, author of *The Female Eunuch*, is as combative in return.

Lizzie reproaches Mailer from the audience, for contradicting onstage something that he'd said in an article in *Harper's*. Mailer tells her that as usual she doesn't know what he's talking about. Perhaps he remembered her writing in *Partisan Review* in 1965 that she abhorred his novel *An American Dream* for its 'callous copulations.'

No, her curls were not so tight back then, I see. Her hair was more flowy. The documentary shows her as I first knew her. There was nothing old about her.)

She was too tired to meet Beryl Bainbridge at Books & Co.

—What is it? She doesn't know me. It will be, Hi, and another restaurant.

She was trying not to take a drink so that she could press on with her thing on Patty Hearst and terrorist rhetoric.

THAT SPRING V. S. Naipaul was very unhappy with his career. He felt, apparently, that there was this filled shelf of his books and no one read them. Elizabeth was going to interview him for the *Times*. He was coming over.

—I feel I ought to do something for Naipaul, don't you? What are we in this business for anyway?

She liked Richard Locke, the young editor at the *Times Book Review*, and she felt sort of sorry for him having to be there, and wanted to help him, if having a conversation could be seen as aid. She'd still have to write it. But she didn't think Naipaul would ever be as popular as he wanted to be. His work was difficult, his own, his way of writing about societies and history.

Elizabeth was invited to the Signet Club up at Harvard. She wasn't going to be able to go to Lexington to get her Phi Beta Kappa key. Student manuscripts were piling up like bricks. She would push through them in her usual way and not miss anything.

—But then I forget who Frank is and have to trace back.

She knocked herself out for those classes and was obsessed with quitting. The students drove her crazy.

—They don't get anything sometimes.

(I remembered being that way and often still was.)

The girls and their gloomy heroines were themselves, she said, and then there were the boys and their attempts at humor.

—I'll say, You don't know anything about amnesia. You can't

have her wake up like that. Or I'll say, Think of S. J. Perelman. Get it right.

She cared. When I took her class, the student rating forms for the *Course Guide* sent her into fits. Often, she got high marks. But sometimes a dull class would flunk her, student vanity affronted because she wouldn't say everything was wonderful. She was willing to tell someone already on page 400 that his project was hopeless and he should start over.

Francine du Plessix Gray was interviewing her for *Vogue*; Gray's mouth made perfect circles when she spoke. Richard Locke was to send questions to which she would write the answers for the *Times*.

Elizabeth's 'interview' with Naipaul went well. It showed, she said, how complicated his ideas were, how difficult he was.

Shiva Naipaul's book on Africa was out, but had, she thought, too many easy put-downs of African fatuities. She wasn't sure Naipaul was too thrilled with his brother being a writer. She said Naipaul didn't like too many people, not even Conrad, to whom he was often compared. She and Lowell had met him once in Trinidad many years ago.

The jacket of Shiva Naipaul's book said that it was in the style of Greene, V. S. Naipaul, and Paul Theroux. She said V. S. Naipaul and Paul Theroux were good friends. Were Shiva Naipaul and Alexander Theroux?

She said V. S. Naipaul had no money. One night when I was there, he rang her to say he was thinking of moving to Connecticut. He was with a South American woman who had left two children. His wife, a First at Oxford sort, was devastated, having devoted her days to this peculiar, fastidious man. Bob Silvers had briefed Elizabeth enough. I could feel her pull back from him, leaving her huge admiration for his novels and reportage in the collection plate.

(She sussed out what people close to Naipaul learned the hard way: how shortsighted is the pride in being friends with an artist famously difficult, misanthropic.

—You think you're the exception, but he'll turn on you, too.)

When Elizabeth spoke to Naipaul for *The New York Times Book Review*, he'd written fourteen books. I'd not read him and started with *A Bend in the River*. She said the great one was *A House for Mr. Biswas*, but I read two impressive nonfiction works and then *Guerillas* instead, quickly, for me, putting off the fat one.

I said he was like Mann in being able to make his novels about large things and she gave a dry Maybe look, which, in Professor Hardwickese, meant, You can't say anything about Naipaul until you've read *A House for Mr. Biswas*.

> It has come about that this writer, who at the beginning might have appeared in unique occupation of a marginal and peripheral world, is instead writing from a historical vicissitude, utterly contemporary. His vision is fixed upon the brutal collision of cultures, the elaborate paralysis of 'areas of darkness' and 'wounded civilizations.'

(In a few years, she became skeptical of Naipaul's sweeping judgments. Was it the second book on India or his book on the South? When she was keen on his work, she told me she'd asked him what the red dot on the forehead means.

—It means my head is empty, she said he said.

Then, when she was less accepting of his vision, she said, —Vidiya's problem is that he is a little brown man.

And he didn't want to be, she meant.)

Maybe it was Hannah Arendt who said that the Third World did not exist.

(However, *The Enigma of Arrival* vindicated the admiration Lizzie had for Naipaul years before, she felt. She was intrigued that in his books he presents himself as traveling alone, when in fact the first wife and then the long-term girlfriend had been with him every step.

James said just now that that is a necessary strategy in travel writing: readers have to feel they have your full attention.)

Elizabeth's reflections on Naipaul appeared in the Sunday *Times* and Jean Rhys's death was announced the next day.

—Come down.

I remembered when I was a student how excited Professor Hardwick had been to discover what else the woman of such invention in *Wide Sargasso Sea* had written. The lost novels of Jean Rhys were coming back into print in the U.S. when the *Letters of Virginia Woolf* and *The Diaries of Virginia Woolf* and Woolf's fugitive essays were also appearing, one volume after another. *Good Morning, Midnight* was the best of Rhys's early work, Elizabeth said. She found the novel's main character chilling in her masochism.

—Masochists are the proudest people on earth.

> Let's say that you have this mystical right to cut my legs
> off. But the right to ridicule me afterwards for being a
> cripple—no, that I think you haven't got.

Elizabeth studied a photograph of Rhys in old age, tracing the lines in her face with her finger. She said you could see how beautiful she'd been and what a drinker she'd been as well.

I WAS LATE to lunch with Barbara at a French restaurant, our first as just us. She announced straight off that she was hungover from the party they had for *Sleepless Nights* the evening before at the World Trade Center.

I was terrified of boring her and sat damp with the understanding that we had a chatty friend in common, knew too much about each other, and yet were not intimate ourselves. Elizabeth had set us on our geodesic paths.

Barbara had been at the *Review* for years, every day, Saturdays and Sundays, after her kids entered their teens and went off to school. It was her identity, Elizabeth once said, invoking the clause that dignified her talking to me about Barbara as tender analysis of the absent person. Barbara had sort of seen and heard it all and wasn't moved by much, she said.

That didn't seem to be the case. She was interested in young people's education. Devie had taken me to see Baryshnikov early on in his New York career and Barbara said every time she saw him, she relived the wonder she experienced seeing him dance for the first time. We got onto that Met production of *Ariadne auf Naxos* with Pavarotti, Christa Ludwig, and Jessye Norman. She preferred to talk about Velázquez rather than Bacon. I didn't need Elizabeth's advice not to mention *Breaking Ranks*, Norman Podhoretz's memoir about how he came to be a bore, a neoconservative, that Fran told me was then making the rounds of publishing houses in manuscript.

The end of lunch was coming. I'd had too much coffee in order to keep from drinking but was sure, at last, I'd not said anything two-steps-backish with Barbara Epstein.

Barbara had been to Los Angeles to see Jacob. She hated L.A. Tans everywhere. She said when you heard while waiting at the luggage claim someone say, That's all right, Arnold. Let me get that for you, Arnold, you knew Arnold had had a heart attack recently.

—How are you, Barbara? she said to herself. —Fine, since my heart attack.

Elizabeth said they'd not had too much to drink at Windows on the World, but Barbara, usually proud and private, was so miserable that it showed.

As we left the restaurant, Barbara said she heard Bob in there, talking to some French person. She tried to explain that it had nothing to do with her affection, but she'd had it up to here seeing him everywhere, even in London. She was off Susan, too, which occupied us until the Fisk Building. She said she was sick to death of the article on the SALT talks that she was reading.

MY BOSS FRAN was hoping to publish Sterling Brown's *Collected Poems*. She sent me down to green Washington, in the company of Tom Victor.

I'd gone to the library. Sterling Brown invented his own folk idiom to express a rebellious sensibility. The son of a distinguished pastor and professor of religion, he grew up in a house of six school-teacher sisters, and then went in search of black life where there was not always electricity. He carefully observed the Joe Meekses, Bessies, Big Jesses, Luther Johnsons, young Freds, Johnnies, and Sams who abound in his poetry. He paid attention to their walks, their spare-ribbed yard dogs, bulldog brogans, landscapes of locusts, cotton, and flooding rivers, their habits of mind.

He believed in what he called 'the folk eloquence of everyday talk.' He said he understood how Ma Rainey could 'jes catch hold of us somekinddaway.'

I thought his work was telling us that his first duty was to the poem and not to his sympathies, because he trusted what his folk nation stood for: railroad men highballing through the country, trying to get 'de jack'; lowlifes playing checkers with deacons; nice girls unrecognizable under streetwalker paint; an itinerant guitar player singing his mother's favorite spiritual, his cigarette held by the strings; a disillusioned veteran buck dancing on the midnight air. Laughter is a vengeance, he'd said.

—He sounds spooky, Elizabeth said.

Sterling was sitting on his porch, with his pipes, waiting. Tom set up his lights and Sterling showed me his 'hellified' library and record collection. He talked the whole time while Tom photographed. Tom cajoled, flattered, persuaded, never stopped moving or answering, working rapidly, as if his subject's resistance or self-consciousness had to be overcome. Sterling was difficult. He teased Tom, an edge in his voice. Tom was able to roll with it. He thought

Sterling gave him heat just because he was white, whereas I was Edward and Lillian's grandson, had become somewhat acquainted with his work, and was myself trying to be a writer. Tom had trouble keeping Sterling's eye on the camera, because he was talking at me so much. Tom finally asked me to stand behind him.

Sterling was still tall and boxy. His thinned, white hair was straight, and his complexion a pinkish brown, like a rubbed-down eraser. He, like Zora Neale Hurston, had published his first book after the Harlem Renaissance had come to an end, supposedly. His reputation as a poet rested on a single volume from 1932, *Southern Road*.

(James said we have maybe only about thirty-three poems from George Herbert and maybe thirty-three poems are all we need, all he needed.)

Sterling was bitter, particularly against Harcourt Brace, the publishers who rejected his second book of poems. The blow made him stop writing poetry. He was thirty-three years old in 1934.

(*The Last Ride of Wild Bill*, a long ballad, was published by a small press in the mid-Seventies.)

He said he'd wanted Harcourt to bid on the *Collected Poems* as a kind of vindication. The volume was to include his previously unpublished second book, *No Hiding Place*. He said he was at work on his first poem in forty years.

He was one of the few black writers of his generation who did not want to be part of the Harlem Renaissance.

—There were no intellectuals in Harlem.

He spoke like Aunt Alvan, his cousin in New Jersey, like how I thought I remembered my grandmother sounded in Atlanta and her sister on the Georgia border with Alabama, as if they talked in measures, don't you know. My mother could imitate them, but she didn't sound like them.

(I sometimes thought that my father's father, when not in the pulpit or in front of white people, must have sounded like his own gun-carrying grandfather, he had such a hissing, nasty, seeing-in-the-dark way of speaking.)

None of the black intellectuals lived in Harlem, Sterling went on. Countee Cullen, the only one from New York, was the son of a prominent minister who would not let Countee associate with the people. —Count-*tay*, he pronounced the name. The real intellectuals were elsewhere, at Howard, or the University of Chicago. People only went to parties in Harlem. They didn't live there, or they didn't live there for long, he said, and I was not to take the ass-licking coterie around Carl Van Vechten seriously. He despised Van Vechten's Jazz Age bestseller about Harlem, *Nigger Heaven*.

—Zora Neale Hurston was the biggest liar in the world and I'm the second.

He meant tall tales. He told me one.

I said, thinking it for real, —Oh, really?

He gave me an odd look.

—That's something we, as a people, have lost. Son, you ought to know when I'm telling you a tale and appreciate it.

In the kitchen, while deciding whose gin to give me, his or Daisy's, he said, —Zora wanted me to love her, but she didn't like men, because of what they could get, just being men. He said something really rude, large face smiling.

I said Zora Neale Hurston was turning over in her unmarked grave, forgetting that Alice Walker had had a headstone made for her when she found where she was buried.

—If she is, it's with her legs wide open.

Not only did Sterling hate Allen Tate, he hated Pound, he hated Eliot.

—When I read *The Waste Land* at Harvard, I thought it was a lie. This is not a wasteland for blacks.

(Who said do not write essays that contain exclamation points?)

—Poetry. I want poetry. I like poetry to be simple, sensuous, and notice I didn't say sensual, not what some silly girl once wrote in a paper; simple, sensuous, that is, appealing to the senses, simple, serious, and impassioned.

> *It is late and still I am losing*
> *But still I am steady and unaccusing*

He interrupted himself:
—and the second 'still' is in the Elizabethan sense here.

He went on, and at the end the words 'dive' and 'five' were two syllables each.

He met Frost only once, he said. They talked of this poem and locked arms, he, the son of a former slave, and Frost, the son of an unregenerate Confederate, he called him.

Frost was the speaking voice of poetry when Sterling was a student. He had also been taken with the muckraking poetry of Carl Sandburg and the dramatic monologues of E. A. Robinson. Things American, of the people.

Sterling's first edition of Nancy Cunard's anthology from 1930, *Negro*, weighed eight pounds.

—Daisy was worried that something was going on with Nancy and me. Nancy came here to the house once. She was skinny and tall as that door. Daisy looked at her and knew she had nothing to worry about.

Sterling began to talk of his wife. She was in the hospital. They met on a tennis court, in 1923, when he was teaching at the Virginia Theological Seminary and College. He taught at Lincoln University in Jefferson City, Missouri, and at Fisk, before he settled in at Howard University in 1929.

—I have been hired, fired, rehired, retired, and hired again.

Whenever he opened his mouth he taught, the habit of more than fifty years in the classroom and receiving pilgrim scholars for almost as long. I was sure I'd read somewhere that he said he discovered realism at Williams College, when he was a freshman

in 1918, and departed for graduate studies at Harvard with the
knowledge that his colleagues in Phi Beta Kappa didn't dance. He
said he didn't mind being called a New Negro but he'd been an old
Negro for so long it was too late to do anything about it.

He spoke of his wife again, tried to say what she was like, and
came close to tears.

—Made a man out of me.

His hand shook as he tried to set down his glass.

He asked me to fetch his pipe and tobacco barrel from the
porch. He talked a little about Du Bois, living next door to him in
Atlanta, and dinners with my mother's family, and polite concerts
at Clark College and Morris Brown, the sort Hurston would have
made scenes about.

The thought of song made him go back to speaking of Daisy.
He never said what she was in the hospital for, what her operation
was for, but he said over and over that she was on the mend. He was
waiting for her to come home to put him in order, he said.

I said she would be all right and I said it weakly. I didn't know
what to say.

He warned me not to tell his sister and we had a second drink.
He changed his slippers and guided us to Daisy's rose garden. He
fed the birds, joking, talking off color. He went inside and got his
beret and sang as Tom photographed him.

—I'm a bo-diddly bitch. Hired, fired, rehired.

My mother had remembered an article in *Jet* that said he'd been
institutionalized for flipping out.

—Over this black thing. Something about being yellow.

Sterling brought up the episode out of nowhere. He claimed
he called the dean of the department a son of a bitch for hiring
or inviting some pig, and generally made a ruckus at the meeting
in question. The dean's wife called Daisy and told her everyone
thought he was out of control. Hence, the bin, he said.

He rang for his taxi driver, a man who fifteen years ago had become a friend. Helen came over. She wore her silver hair in a braid coiled high on her head. Her skin was smooth, her voice frail.

Before we left, Sterling showed us the basement where he worked. More walls of books and records, the overflow stacked on sofas, the desk behind another wall, the liquor.

—Too good to give to cats like you two.

It was an intimate gesture, showing us his hiding place. But he went too far. In his heartbreaking exuberance at life, he took us to the hospital to see Daisy. She was clearly embarrassed, though unable to speak. Her arms moved helplessly in the air. She tried to smile. We withdrew. A beautiful woman, fair, silver-and-white hair, deep, liquid eyes, and tubes everywhere. Against the white sheet, it was like viewing a captured ghost.

Daisy died two weeks later. Of a heart attack, Helen said. She said her brother was very upset. She said she knew that was an understatement, given how dependent Sterling had been on Daisy.

EVA WAS GOING to San Francisco. The party moved to the Mudd Club. There were too many chic people and European accents. We transferred quickly to Felice's, with Jennifer, the renegade, as the deejay.

The next day Luc called from Grand Central Station.

He sat down and wiped his eyes. When he could speak, he said Walter Benjamin had wanted to write a book that consisted entirely of his favorite sayings. Luc was twenty-four years old then, when five years was a long time. I'd known Eva for as long as I'd known him. He felt bad for their problems, for the times he walked out.

—I haven't cried since I was nine, he said after another long wait.

He said he felt bad about not being able to change his life. He felt guilty he couldn't pick up and leave the way Eva did.

—I feel like a piece of my body has been torn off.

(I may have to take this out.)

ELIZABETH HARDWICK'S EYES were everywhere. For weeks, all spring, rapturous reviews of *Sleepless Nights* had been appearing in serious journals, newsmagazines, newspaper book review sections, and the columns of glossy magazines, usually accompanied by one of Tom Victor's photographs, but sometimes by one of Jill Krementz's portraits of her. She had some mixed notices, as they say, but even these were respectful.

Daphne Merkin was an editorial assistant at Harper & Row, the office she worked at near Fran's. She kicked off her shoes and made me promise not to tell Professor Hardwick that she was reviewing *Sleepless Nights* for *The New Republic*. It was the kind of work that made reviewers want to write well themselves. They were drawing on their best selves, rising to the occasion.

John Leonard in *The New York Times*:

> In her splendid interview with Richard Locke in last Sunday's *New York Times Book Review*, Elizabeth Hardwick mentioned her admiration for Rainer Maria Rilke's *The Notebook of Malte Laurids Brigge*. She called it 'a miraculous, perfect work' . . .
>
> Elizabeth's city has no tourist attractions, no agreeable cafes overgrown with famous people, no Left Bank of Robert Lowell. Even the usual gates to the usual city of the self—father, mother, children—are for the most part missing. Or she chooses not to visit them. She stays, instead, in seedy hotels . . .
>
> This savage eye sees everything . . .
>
> What do they add up to, these episodes and sketches and fragments, these memories of 'lost things' that we take, 'down from the shelf like a can,' after Kentucky and Boston and West 67th Street and various men of bad

character and the bodies we have buried? What does it always add up to? We ask for freedom and are danger-ously alone, especially women . . .

Sleepless Nights, like Rilke's *Notebook*, is miraculous and almost perfect.

(What's with the 'almost,' I thought.)

Upper West Side dinner parties congratulated *The New York Times Book Review* for getting Joan Didion to review *Sleepless Nights*. Not for her Elizabeth Hardwick's disclaimer in interviews that the work was not as autobiographical as people might think. If the subject of the novel was memory, Didion said, then the 'I' to whom the memories belong is 'entirely and deliberately the author.' We recognize her life from her earlier work and from the poems of Robert Lowell. It is not the story of a life, or about a life, but a meditation on that life, on life.

> The author observes of her enigmatic narrative: 'It cer-tainly hasn't the drama of: I saw the old, white-bearded frigate master on the dock and signed up for the jour-ney. But after all, "I" am a woman.'

Didion said *Sleepless Nights* was as evocative and hard to place as Claude Lévi-Strauss's *Tristes Tropiques*, a work Elizabeth much ad-mired and had written about. Didion likened Hardwick's method to that of the anthropologist, the traveler on the watch for the re-vealing detail, for the precise observations of strangers. Most of the 'meticulously transcribed histories' offered in Hardwick's novel are of women, she said, the common thread being that in the cul-ture Hardwick writes of 'the freedom to live untied to others' is 'hardest on women.'

That part of Didion's reading of *Sleepless Nights* took me by surprise, what she calls Hardwick's 'radical distrust of romantic individualism.' The 'terrible point' of Hardwick's novel, that 'life ends badly,' was, for me, still a convention of Romanticism, the terrible destiny for Werther, or Kleist, or Jean Seberg, but still off in the misty future for me and the gang.

Lévi-Strauss had not been particularly on her mind when she was writing, she said, but then you write with all of your experience alive within you, and that includes your reading. Didion's approach to Elizabeth's 'fieldwork' moved her, another woman writer in command of what was concentrated in her own tonal qualities.

I let the romantic individualism question in my head go unasked, embarrassed I may have misunderstood as virtuous the lost, lonely clerk. Didn't he tend to murder, come to think of it.

Old Mrs. Lowell's lamps kept disappearing from the living room, replaced by incredibly chic creations from Ambiente. Elizabeth was tired of the dark, heavy furniture. She sent her old cocktail bar to the Salvation Army. A delicate piece of false bamboo took its place.

—Can't go wrong with tan and white, honey.

I just nodded my head in agreement. Had there been no brown window shades when I moved into West Ninety-fifth Street two years before, there would have been no shades on rollers still.

One of her sisters back in Kentucky used to make her furious by refusing to hang curtains.

—They'll only get dirty, she said she said.

Sleepless Nights kept her triumphantly in town until the end of June.

SUSAN SONTAG HAD been spotted dancing in the Cock Ring, a joint in the West Village down toward the river. The bulletin ran up the street, as if someone had thrown a switch. You could follow the current. The air was warm with anticipation and boys in full bloom, every man a bud, opening, in shorts, in black trousers, showing shoulders, necks, chests, everyone watching, and watching himself be watched.

Within hours of my telling her, Elizabeth in Maine enlisted the help of Barbara, still at the *Review*, and the sleuths fetched up the name of the person *with whom* Susan had been dancing: Fran Lebowitz.

I didn't tell Elizabeth too much, mostly because when in a mood she could go on about

—this relentless cruising.

Not giving her ammunition was a tested-on-parents, judgment-avoidance tactic.

She had an appointment in Bangor about a lump in her throat. Typically, she brooded on it and told no one. Then her take-hold mood came down on her and she was calling with reports. Somehow Bangor, or was it Bucksport, wasn't enough. She flew back to New York for super medicine, as she called it.

She had a battery of tests, consulted Susan's doctor, eventually got the shah's surgeon. I was to tell no one. Barbara was the only person I knew who knew and we couldn't bring ourselves to talk about it. I felt the lump, just under her jaw. Harriet called every day. Elizabeth and I found amusements in the afternoons.

—Oh, I have a blouse like that, she said in the middle of *La Cage aux Folles*. It's Italian. The audience turned and laughed. She was recognized more often.

—You are an actress? The veiny-armed French waiter in Dazzels was smiling above her.

—Yes, I have a supporting role in the continuing farce of my life.

On the day of the operation, the day I got a ticket for running into the subway with a cigarette, she was fixated on the cost, on insurance. I purchased stupid champagne truffles and put them in a box with a blue ribbon. New York Hospital. Fourth floor. Room at the end. A screen was pulled in front of her bed. There were other white women sharing the room. They stopped talking when I entered and took a seat beside Elizabeth's bed.

I looked at her a long time. Asleep, her face drawn, hand on her throat, hair dripping onto the pillow, a great gauze strip on her neck, brightly colored tubes running from her body to machines keeping sentry, her lids so intently closed. She stirred, woke, turned, looked at me from far away.

To speak pained her. A black nurse appeared to give her an injection. I took the box to West Sixty-seventh Street and left it inside on the wicker chair. Ben Shahn's widow lived just off the lobby by the front entrance. I heard her door open for the first time ever.

The tumor was benign. She was cheerful, with no memory of my visit or of Harriet's later. They ate the truffles.

She was indifferent to her scar, though she continually inspected it and asked was it too noticeable. Then she was gone, back to Maine, back to work, watching the sea at high tide.

— *Part 5* —

Elizabeth made fun of Mary McCarthy's new novel, *Cannibals and Missionaries*, which I'd not read. It was as though she was getting it all in before McCarthy arrived in Castine for the summer. She described the people on whom the characters were based. She said she would say something to Mary and not have to write anything to her.

(No one had a better understanding of *Sleepless Nights* than Mary McCarthy. She would write generously to Lizzie about it and praise the cool in her having left Cal out of the story. Lizzie cherished Mary's letter to her about her novel. However, Mary's appreciation did nothing to soften Lizzie's judgments about her old friend's late fiction.

She said it was interesting that Mary the brilliant essayist was such a conventional novelist, and after what had been promised by the sensation of her early short story collections, *The Company She Keeps* and *Cast a Cold Eye*. I couldn't believe Elizabeth had written an essay, published in *A View of My Own*, in which she said as much: that after her radical beginnings, Mary McCarthy turned into a rather straight novelist. It had something to do with Mary needing the autobiographical element and being a prisoner of a dutiful scheme otherwise. She rated *Memories of a Catholic Girlhood* highest of McCarthy's work. She was moved by how much of herself Mary had displayed. It was such an honest expression of herself as a writer, she thought.

McCarthy's novel *The Group* was a bestseller in 1963. In those days, there was a kind of snobbery about bestsellers, as if their popularity meant they could not be truly serious. But what else was every guy's ambition to write the Great American Novel? Elizabeth published a short parody of *The Group*'s sexual frankness, 'The Gang,' in the *Review*, under the pseudonym Xavier Prynne. Furthermore, in his review of *The Group* for the *Review*, Norman Mailer really ribbed McCarthy as 'our foremost lady novelist.' Bob Silvers explained decades later that Mary had been hurt, but eventually forgave them, and agreed to go to Hanoi to write on the war.

Elizabeth said something similar about Gore Vidal. He had so many qualities as an essayist and so few as a novelist. She didn't want to sound self-important, because he shouldn't care, but she felt he guessed what she thought of his fiction and rather held it against her. Nevertheless, his historical fiction was not to be believed. She never wanted to put Barbara on the spot about it, she and Gore were so close.)

I wasn't drinking and the reefer was easy. I was trying Proust again. I also had on Purcell.

—Not at the same time. One or the other, honey.

I WENT RUNNING in Riverside Park. I went to a grocery store. I wrote a clever parody, I thought, of *The Ghost Writer*, and sent it to Elizabeth in Maine. She'd read Philip Roth's new novel.

—It's a joke.

She ordered me not to repeat what she said.

(She would become a great admirer of Roth's Zuckerman novels. And she was astonished by the energy of his mature years.)

It was impossible to feel clean. The lunch-hour rivulet of sweat down my spine instantly chilled in the air-con of the office lobby. Phoning, making appointments, listening to excuses, hassling over contracts, and every book on Fran's list being behind schedule made walking through the humid park after work a chance to dream of getting lost. I seldom went into Central Park and whenever I did, I risked getting turned around. I went down paths at top speed, as if on the lam, worried about the office, my desk at home, people I might have disappointed or offended, everything I'd not done, not read, not experienced, never would.

—The coward is someone who does not realize how much one can get away with, Elizabeth once said.

Several writers were competing for Plath's biography. Or several publishers were aiming to battle over a single Plath biography. Olwyn Hughes, nagging agent for her brother, Ted Hughes, was holding out on the contract for Plath's *Collected Poems*.

(Someone asked A. Alvarez why Ted Hughes's second wife, also a poet, killed herself.

—Pure envy, he said in reply.)

People on the park benches who looked like they had their lives together could well have been secretly unhappy, hanging around at the hour when Central Park emptied out and got dangerous, but they were not, I was sure, sinking into a hole as dark as mine. I'd no idea what to do with misdelivered old-fashioned print rolls that had to be cut by hand. There were copyright pages that had to go upstairs, order forms for bound galleys, another form for the copyediting department, and still another for jacket copy. I went in on a Saturday to take care of messed-up shipping instructions and I went in on a Sunday to move the pots and clean the pans from the photography session for Mai Leung's *Chinese People's Cookbook*.

—So who's this Osip Mandelstam? Is he in town? I heard a big-shot editor bark one Monday.

I fought not to let down Fran completely. Floppy brown bangs and laughing young eyes and she sailed out of her office late as she hugged a jumble of papers against her colorful muumuu. Paul Bowles sent her the children's stories he was writing, and in addition to distinguished poets, she published offbeat cookbook authors and radical feminists; she supported the beleaguered biographers of Frida Kahlo and Jane Bowles; she protected the material for a biography of Billie Holiday left behind in a cabinet after the suicide of the author, Linda Kuehl.

However, there was more than a little something in running

downhill, letting everything get out of hand, until you bottom out, assuming there was another chance, wherever you landed. Repudiating one life freed you of the responsibilities incurred trying to live it. The second marriage, thinking it will be better. The new job. The paranoid person who drops friends and takes up with another crowd. Of course, it's not better. Starting over was real only for so long.

—I know, Elizabeth said. It's very hard to like yourself.

JUST ABOVE MY HEAD came out in September. James Baldwin had been to Harper & Row for a big powwow with the high-ups. His longtime publisher was weary of spooning dollars into him, the rumor went, and he was making pitches around town for the something next.

Word that he was in the building touched every corner of the editorial floor. Editors hung up and floated from their offices into the central aisle; we editorial assistants slowly raised our fantastic necks over plants and cubicle divides. The elevator doors opened onto what was an unnatural silence for a business and there were the unprecedented eyes, the famous man's short height, the authority of his dark skin. Someone must have been with him, but his gray suit seemed to be the only thing moving. Baldwin's outsized grin faced us and went by, like an entr'acte note across a stage.

My discovery as an undergraduate of Baldwin the essayist was a memory that went with autumn weather, with Salingeresque leaves blowing across the hatched brick paths of campus. Cool air had come in from the north. I had to stop when I got to College Walk and lean on the granite ledge. I had to finish 'Notes of a Native Son,' in which Baldwin told of his escape from Harlem and from his father's bitterness as a journey out of Egypt.

It was a moment that affirmed what reading was for and what writing could do. The campus moved around me.

I would have far too much to say about him. I couldn't help

it. I didn't want to. The politics of disillusionment inclined me to think of him as having reached the boundaries of his nature too soon. A previous novel, *If Beale Street Could Talk*, and an autobiography in the form of an essay on film, *The Devil Finds Work*, said the Sixties were over and he was going on, but it was *No Name in the Street*, his angry reproach to the nation for the political violence of the Sixties, that most informed my sense of him then.

I compared Baldwin's young eyes staring right up into the camera on the cover of the Beacon Press edition of *Notes of a Native Son* with the wounded, averted gaze twenty years later on the back of the Dial Press edition of *No Name in the Street*.

> *and the night cold and the night long and the river*
> *to cross and the jack-muh-lanterns beckoning beckoning*
> *and blackness ahead and when shall I reach that somewhere*

The poet June Jordan phoned to say I had to meet with her and what she called other media people to figure out how to respond to the police murder of Luis Baez.

He was a mentally disturbed youth with a pair of scissors. Five policemen shot at him more than twenty times. There had been a demonstration in Bedford-Stuyvesant at which Baez's coffin was carried past the police station. Tompkins Avenue got out of hand and the police themselves rioted against the demonstrators throwing bottles, cans. June said she and her friends the writer Alexis De Veaux and the actor Gwendolyn Hardwick had had to crawl to safety.

Shortly after Baez's murder, Elizabeth Mangum, a young woman fighting off eviction in Flatbush, slashed a policeman in the arm with a knife and was shot dead. She, too, had a psychiatric history and although she was black and the police involved were white, the fatal incident was judged not to have been racial in character. Grand juries found no criminality in the deaths and the police commissioner called for better training in handling disturbed persons.

IT WAS SUNDAY and Elizabeth said the next time someone followed me home it would not be Miss Dent, but someone with a pistol, if I was lucky. I did not get the reference to *The Stories of John Cheever*. She thought she had given me his stories. She had. She said not to get into the habit of mind to dislike a writer too quickly. That was not what she meant by the critical temperament.

She said she'd had a hard time deciding whether to vote to give the National Book Critics Circle prize for fiction to Updike or to Cheever.

Her sad anniversary had come and gone. To look at the window where she had waited for him. Walcott's tribute to Lowell seemed to me about a soul leaving a body. She said of course she'd read it, more than once, but for some reason couldn't get her feelings together about it yet. She'd not seen Margaret since the Walcotts divorced, but she liked his plays and enjoyed the memory of their children and Harriet in the swimming pool on St. Lucia.

Robert Silvers's office had called to reassure me, because he didn't want me on the edge of my seat about the Baldwin piece. He was away in London. I'd rewritten it, with Elizabeth's help. I told her my struggles, but did not ask her to read what I was writing for the *Review*, and she made a point of not consulting Bob and Barbara beyond the casual remark when she knew I'd handed in a draft. But this time was different. We sat on the red sofa and she went line by line, asking me again and again what I meant here, what I meant by this word, that notion. When I came up with a better way to say something or when I hit on what she considered a good line, she'd say

—Now you're writing.

What Pound could do for poetry in his reading, correcting, and criticism, she could do for prose. My school days would never end.

(She scoffed, that is the word, when I wrote down in a notebook what she said to us in class.)

She was suspending one of her rules again, because it bugged her, the meetings Bob, Jason, Barbara, and Whitney had been having that she got told about as an afterthought.

—They never tell me anything.

I'd been to the office to see Mr. Silvers some time before, but he was still in one of those meetings. She said it had nothing to do with respect for Karl Miller (a legendary literary editor of exacting taste, as James remembered him), but she was vehemently against *The New York Review of Books* starting up *The London Review of Books*. Her opposition had in it her Caroline-motivated anti-Englandness. She said when Bob and Barbara got back after the *Review*'s summer break, even Barbara had a British accent.

—Oh rally.

Elizabeth was having an awful time with a piece on Faulkner for another publication. Say what one would about the *Review*, the difference when writing for other periodicals was dramatic. She said she could not get her feeble pages together at all. Then, too, a cheap biography of the Lowell family was coming out, and she was having a problem with Lowell's estate, she didn't say what. She had an idea for a novel to be called *The Last Straw*. She went to stay with Lee Gardner in Newport.

My sister Donna was again in the hospital. She had broken off another engagement, this one unsuitable to begin with. She had ECT again, and there were tearful phone calls home, and an attempt at a cheerful phone call when I could at last speak to her.

—You sound like you need to get blasted, too, she said.

Howard and Brad took me to the Bar on Second Avenue and Fourth Street for the first time.

THE B-52'S WERE playing in the park, but it was raining. Howard and Brad got a large place together on Bleecker Street. It was a sublet, two apartments. We stepped through a hole in the wall to get from one to the other. A paranoid ex-yippie lived downstairs and fell to pieces when faucets leaked, Howard said. Jim was there with his crew, filming. Howard and I went out to buy vodka. He believed in ancient conspiracy theories, which told me he was deep into his Burroughs documentary.

Later, at Felice's, Luc and Jennifer took turns on the turntable. Jim brought pot, pizza, wine, and two musician friends of his, Cynthia Sley and Barbara Klar. I thought everyone was from Ohio, like Jim and Phil Kline. I thought they were from the town Rocky and Bullwinkle also came from, Cuyahoga Falls. Howard took the joint from me.

Luc explained the difference between high hustling and low hustling and how these days people needed to have a little Las Vegas in them just to stay in between.

Now that the Mudd Club was overrun, Tier 3 was the place to go, a dive off White Street, an obscure door easy to remember, because it was next to a white cube-like building with a textured façade and the name 'Teddy's' in large, unlit, cursive-like script on the front. I can't remember when Jean-Michel started to quarrel with the super of Felice's building. But at some point, he took a magic marker and began to publish his case against the man all over the wall going down Felice's stairs. A feature of arriving or leaving her place in one piece was being able to check if any fresh insults had been added.

Luc put on a strike benefit for the Strand Bookstore and his magazine. The staff strike ended the day of the party. Howard and I were very far gone by the time we got to the District 65 meeting hall and the old gang of everyone.

Mbembe Milton Smith appeared in the crowd, his pipe in his teeth. He was high and happy. I nearly said I liked his stories better than his poems, or I liked listening to him give his poems more than I actually liked his poems. I was so willing to be stupid that evening. I said I had read an essay on Shakespeare and the vernacular by John Crowe Ransom, of all people, and he made me want to stay on the side of the simple. Mbembe moved on.

ELIZABETH BISHOP DIED on a Saturday in October. The sky had that endless bone color.

—Are you coming down?

Ten years or so earlier Lota de Macedo Soares flew to New York against her doctors' advice and, once she made it to the apartment in the Village where Bishop was staying, took an overdose of Nembutal. She slipped into a coma and was taken to St. Vincent's Hospital, where she died. Elizabeth said she would never forget her elegance and wit. She said she didn't think Bishop ever got over what happened. Bishop had left Lota and that destroyed Lota maybe.

—And Elizabeth as well maybe.

How long a life sixty-eight years seemed to me then.

STERLING WOULD NEVER give us his telephone number. I had to call Helen and he'd call me back. But all summer long he had called me up at home at unpredictable times to tell me things: Machado de Assis wasn't white; I should have been in a black fraternity; Jean Toomer, his father's parishioner and his basketball teammate at Washington High School, was not, strictly speaking, trying to pass. He was always in the middle of a sentence attacking Agrarians. To what he said was Robert Penn Warren's

Nigger, your poetry isn't metaphysical

Sterling had answered

Cracker, your poetry ain't exegetical.

His temper came from his grief. His phone improvisations were unpleasant. He said:

—*Sartre ain't worth a fartre.*

Genet is gay.

Imagine a Negro appearing in The Blacks.

Something aggressive began to spoil the smile of his learning.

—Fran tells me you're entranced by a lady whose last name begins with the initial H and ends with K. Now what are you doing with that cracker?

—She's not a cracker, I said.

—She was married to one.

—Robert Lowell was not a cracker.

—He was a Yankee, but he wanted to be a cracker. He tries to be difficult, not that he is.

Sterling hated the New Criticism and 'Ode to the Confederate Dead.' He hung up before I could say I didn't know Allen Tate.

I had to go over Sterling's manuscript with the copy editor. That meant I had to call Helen. He was not phoning back. There were so many errors and illegible words in the copies of the poems we had. Finally, Sterling's manuscript went to the printer. He got carried away with the dedications. It was his last book, his summing up.

He called one more time before he gave up on me. There was to be a conference on African history in D.C. Sterling wanted me to come to a party and meet Sterling Stuckey, the historian named for him, and John Henrik Clarke. I said I couldn't leave work and, no, I also couldn't let him pay for it.

—Man, you are so influenced by those white intellectuals. You need to get away from them and be with some niggers.

THE SUNRISE DINER waited on the corner of West Fifty-seventh Street and Eighth Avenue, a few doors from the *Review*. All I had to do was make it up the subway stairs. Newspaper, coffee, and cigarettes guarded my surrender until the recovery pile of fried food arrived. This diner was a New York in no position to make judgments but did so anyway. I carried books, emblems of my guild. Public displays of book learning signified nothing, not insofar as the white woman with ethnically thick ankles in the booth opposite me was concerned. She put her bags on the other side of her, out of range of my snatch-and-run expertise.

That you could hear music when you pushed through the right side of the squawking white metal double doors told you that Bob and Barbara were out. The taste in music in the mailroom had gone experimental, Michael Johnson having moved to the necessary quiet of the subscriptions desk. His place in the mailroom had been taken by a classmate, Noah Shapiro, son of the *Review*'s business manager, Raymond Shapiro, who derived gentlemanly pleasure from paying writers.

Janet Noble in the large, motley production studio was maybe working on a play for her Irish theater group. Peter Anastos used to write the programs for his drag ballet troupe, Les Ballets Trockadero de Monte Carlo, in the studio, Prudence once said. On this quiet day, the corner of her mouth as she sat in profile at a typesetting machine in the studio said that S. J. Perleman had died not so long ago. They'd become close. I slipped by.

Mr. Silvers came back and begged off our appointment, saying he had another conference and then had to catch a train to see his sick father.

They said the other day the whole office had heard him shriek and then he tore out of his chair. Forgotten appointment. No one had reminded him, and he'd told everyone to remind him, and no, he did not forget, why would he forget, he would not be the one to have forgotten, all of them had, or one of them.

Sunday, out with Ian Hamilton, he was late. We tussled over every phrase and had a long back-and-forth over why Baldwin had not hit back at Eldridge Cleaver in *No Name in the Street* for his vicious attack on him in *Soul on Ice*,

—as he could have, devastatingly, Robert Silvers wanted to add for me. His view was that Baldwin was so into the Black Power movement in 1968 he was not to be diverted. I argued that Baldwin was intimidated by Cleaver's assault and had a fear of being thought a traitor.

We were saying the same thing, but I zapped up to Elizabeth's to tell her Robert Silvers didn't know what he was talking about and she agreed, remembering how impossible it had been for anyone to hit back against attacks from black militants.

Bob had sent Elizabeth to Memphis in the days following Martin Luther King, Jr.'s assassination on April 4, 1968, to cover a march in his honor held the day before his funeral in Atlanta:

> This love, if not always refused, was now seldom forthcoming in relations with the new black militants, who were set against dependency upon the checkbooks and cooperation of the guilty, longing, loving whites. Everything separated the old Civil Rights people from the new black militants; it could be said, and for once truly, that they did not speak the same language. A harsh, obscene style, unforgiving stares, posturings, insulting accusations and refusal to make distinction among those of the white world—this was humbling and perplexing. Many of the white people had created their very self-identity out of the issues and distinctions and they felt cast off, ill at ease, with the new street rhetoric of 'self-defense' and 'self-determination.'

She was surprised that I had continued to read in her bound volumes of back issues of the *Review*. I looked through them when I went in over the summers to get the mail to send to Maine. I'd touched the red-bound volumes and nothing else, I very much wanted to be able to say. Her essay on the aftermath of King's death was of a particular beauty and intensity, about the brilliance of his intellectual convictions and 'the pragmatic clarity' of his oratory when addressing his congregation, the masses. In the essay, she wondered if his death did not foretell a waning of black attachment to the Christian faith.

THE AYATOLLAH WAS a catastrophe. Elizabeth was having a party for Mary McCarthy. She didn't want to have it and Mary's guest list made her dread the whole thing. She said Mary and her husband, Jim West, did a lot for her in Maine. She was happy to do something for her oldest friend and her book. She said she just couldn't face all those couples from Bard. She said I would not understand what she meant by the change in Mary since they were young. In Paris, in Maine, there were these rather formal affairs.

The day before the party, we chipped away at the peeling paint in the dining room ceiling so that it wasn't noticeable. Her regular painter hadn't phoned back. She suspected he'd had a nervous breakdown. She had had chairs reupholstered in colorful fabrics. She wanted to lighten up her living room. I moved pieces around. She complained again about the office building that had gone up across the street. It was dark, but weirdly warm outside.

(She used to have an old wooden chest with metal corners as a second coffee table in the living room, but at some point replaced it. In the poem 'Off Central Park,' in *Day by Day*, Lowell noted her single wooden big square marked like a chessboard. It

stands laughing at us on the threshold.

We were looking through the poems and she glanced over at the cube in front of the wicker bench, where the chest used to be, and smiled to think he'd noticed it.)

Elizabeth had inherited from Mrs. Lowell a weird Thanksgiving centerpiece for the dining room table, a curved silver belt with silver cuffs and clamps on thin chains that held artificial eggplant and miniature pumpkins and another kind of squash. She worried that cookies, strawberries, and champagne would not be enough. The party was not to begin until nine o'clock, after Mary's reading. Elizabeth ordered quiches from a place Fran liked. I picked them up. I'd not thought of quiche as heavy.

Mary Gordon, a former student of Elizabeth's, came down-stairs. Her first novel, *Final Payments*, published by Jason, was a great success. Elizabeth found it interesting that in a time of liberated women, Mary Gordon's novel was about an unfree Catholic girl.

—Another disciple, Mary Gordon said in greeting.

(Mary Gordon published an angry account of her later falling-out with Lizzie in Elizabeth Benedict's anthology *Mentors, Muses, and Monsters*.)

Mary Gordon was to introduce Mary McCarthy at the Y. She hurried off.

I missed the reading and went home to change. I took my time. When I got back to West Sixty-seventh Street, it was odd to see Elizabeth's living room lit up in autumnal harvest blossom, and to hear it bounce with crowd acoustics.

Mary McCarthy's family dashed at one another: her husband; his beautiful daughter, studying art history, Alison West; Mary's brother, who'd starred in *The Day the Earth Stood Still*; his young pregnant wife; two older children also in film; Mary's gentle secretary from years before, Margo Viscusi; and her husband. Eugene McCarthy, no relation, was tall and knightly and Dwight Macdonald ossified, but not stupid. His wife fretted because she couldn't remember Sally Austin's name. Mary McCarthy kissed cheeks and clasped hands, accepting that to be the object of attention entailed a moral obligation to shine.

In photographs over the years, Mary McCarthy's style did not change. Her hair became white, but it was the same cut as on her book jacket from eight years before, and then eight years before that, the careful flip at chin level, just above her neck. The chin, the

smile, the eyes, it was Mary McCarthy in a really good suit, brack-
eted by pearls and pearl earrings.

(McCarthy's parents died in the Spanish flu epidemic of 1918.
It was to Elizabeth an almost unfair literary advantage for Mary to
have been an orphan, thrust into schools conceived in the Dicken-
sian mode.

Mary Gordon reviewed *Cannibals and Missionaries* in *The New
York Times Book Review* and, full of praise for McCarthy's novel,
said that maybe homely George Eliot had to become a writer, but
beauties like Colette and Woolf had options, implying that so had
Mary McCarthy in her Irish charm. Beauty, the younger Mary said,
freed a woman from apology and gave her safety.

This was maybe not what Lizzie had in mind when she spoke
of McCarthy's 'difficult feminine charm' that Gordon referred to.
Maybe Lizzie imagined it more as a weapon than an exemption.

Lizzie once said wives at those *Partisan Review* parties didn't like
her and Mary and their double act. They said challenging things,
wore bright red lipstick, and were pretty, unlike the dull Communist wives.)

For a party, the atmosphere was a little rigorous. *The Gnostic
Gospels* were over by the big window and *Gödel, Escher, Bach* in those
chairs pushed together in the corner under her surviving Goya
prints. The *Madame Rosa* film trio by the quiche in the dining room
remembered to lower their voices. ABC News vowed to continue
special nightly coverage of the hostage crisis. Nobody dreamed
how long the hostage crisis would go on. ABC eventually converted
its nightly hostage crisis coverage into a late-night newsmagazine.

Mary McCarthy's friends were solicitous, as though her novel
had foretold events: Arab terrorists hijack a group of liberals en
route to Iran to investigate atrocities under the shah. They demand celebrated works of art in the West as ransom.

Often Bob and Barbara were headed to the same place, but they
never left the office together, at the same time, or shared a taxi. It

was like a contest: who arrived at the party later than the other. Who had to leave the party first was another contest.

Harriet and I found a corner.

After the party, Elizabeth laughed to Sally Austin, her next-door neighbor in Maine, that I thought everyone was bohemian, like her.

We were recuperating on the red sofa. It felt like spring out.

Once at a party in the south of France F. Scott Fitzgerald mistook Claude McKay for the butler.

Felice fled Bud's party where everyone had given her a hard time about her fight with Alexis. They'd fallen out for good. Alexis was taking Jean-Michel with her. The insults he'd penned against Felice's super had moved at thick-tip strength down the stairwell. (One day people would regret letting Samo come back in a rage and wipe out what he'd painted on walls when he lived with them.) Felice said she couldn't afford the apartment on her own and would have to move out. Jennifer was sought-after and undecided. Eva was back, yes, but determined to break things off with Luc, which maybe explained why I'd not heard from him.

There was another party, this one at the Gotham Book Mart, where John Ashbery was reading from *As We Know*. He was a known mutterer, pulling on a Gauloise between phrases, letting out a gust of smoke as he continued. A reading style of zero affect was common among New York School poets. 'Litany' had been published not that long ago. He wrote more and more as the years continued, like someone much too relaxed with his shrink.

It was a very Ashbery party: wall-to-wall boys, every one of them handsome. The actor Richard Thomas seemed a new addition, but he was not one of them. Neither was the writer Harry Mathews, sometimes mistaken for gay because he carried a leather wallet on a loop, an American who had lived in France for some time, like Ashbery himself, and Maxine Groffsky, devotee of the arts, friend of painters and poets. Howard pointed out Derrida and the painter Jane Freilicher, Barbara Epstein's roommate downtown when she first moved to New York. I liked Freilicher's water tank rooftops and her portrait of Kenneth Koch, who also read in a monotone, even his comic poems. His former student, the baseball and Keats fanatic David Lehman, talking to Ashbery, sounded just like Koch when he read.

Brad had passed his orals with distinction. He was talking to Ashbery's boyfriend, David Kermani, our classmate Cheri Fein, and the artist Joe Brainard, whose shirt was unbuttoned to his navel, his signature look.

Everyone was so glamorous and at ease, I lost my nerve and had to let myself out into West Forty-seventh Street. Howard waved through the glass.

It was early enough to phone Elizabeth from Columbus Circle. She said she was going nuts trying to finish her Phi Beta Kappa lecture for Virginia, the same one she would give in Kentucky. She lent me D. H. Lawrence's stories, a volume she wanted back. I'd only read 'The Prussian Officer.' They were wonderfully educational, especially after my parents and then Pat called to say that Donna had been successfully snatched away from demon pain and come home from the hospital in a hopeful mood.

Lawrence describes men very well in the stories. Elizabeth's idea was that tuberculosis made him tired halfway through the later novels and he couldn't be bothered with getting them together. She liked the image of Lawrence being neat, living cheaply, doing a little cooking, struggling to make one hundred pounds sterling. Frieda was a slob.

—I can't forgive him for Frieda.

Another Monday came. We ate quickly. Elizabeth and Francine du Plessix Gray were reading at the Y. Elizabeth was manic. She dreaded doing it. She hated to go to readings herself. She paced; she changed her clothes.

We met Inge Morath in the lobby, a spectacular woman. Barbara arrived with Dominique Nabokov, the composer Nicolas Nabokov's smartly dressed young widow, and Rose Styron joined them. It was a large crowd, especially for a rainy night. Francine Gray read two dense chapters from a work in progress, a history of friends. Her beautifully accented, rapid, round, soft English was hard to follow.

I'd never seen one of Elizabeth's performances. She preferred to lecture, she said. She said when she gave John Cheever the gold medal at MacDowell, she was going around saying she had nothing to say, just six pages. John Leonard told her that she was the biggest liar. Her talk went on for forty-seven minutes. She didn't know how that happened.

At the Y she came out and told us the only thing she ever learned from a reading was the condition of the poet that night. She said she had hoped the idea of reading would make her write something. She wasn't able to and so read bits from notebooks, a lot about Gissing: 'They had three children, all happily buried.'

Then she read from *Sleepless Nights*, the part about cleaning women. As she went along, she began leaving more and more out, finally skipping whole sections until suddenly it was over. Afterward, she said it was a question of time.

—Was it all right? I just couldn't read the whole thing.

I gave her a cigarette and noticed that her hand was shaking.

Barbara said Gore told her that when he ran into Norman Podhoretz in California, he said to Podhoretz he thought the *Review* was going to do something on *Breaking Ranks*, after all. Podhoretz took the bait. He wanted to know who would be writing the review. Podhoretz guessed it was going to be Philip Roth. Gore asked Barbara to request a checking copy from Podhoretz's publisher to make it look good.

Podhoretz's publisher at Basic Books was his wife, Midge Decter. Her assistant was one of our classmates, Robert Richman, who was dating one of Bob's weekend assistants. He confided that he'd heard the *Review* was planning to do the Podhoretz. Like a mob hit, you had to let that one play out.

Barbara said Elizabeth's public image was as the Goody Two-Shoes of the *Review*. She was witty and friendly onstage, that Southern voice jumping out of nowhere, high pitched, loud.

—I can really get it out there. That's something I learned from Cal.

It was important that people be able to hear, she said.

(I'd gone to the Lilly Library in Bloomington, Indiana, to hear Plath recordings.

> *I may be a bit of a Jew . . .*
> *I have always been scared of you.*

I'd expected someone girlish. Instead, her voice was deep, her thespian's accent that of the American long resident in England.)

Elizabeth was glad it was over.

We sloshed downtown to the home of Grace Schulman, poet, director of the YMHA Poetry Center reading series, editor of Marianne Moore. Someone kept handing Elizabeth cheese.

She was still so keyed up after her reading, she was deliriously affectionate toward the important strangers giving us a ride in the wet back to West Sixty-seventh Street.

SHIITES COMMANDEERED MECCA and the Iranian Revolution was still occupying the U.S. embassy in Tehran.

I wrecked Thanksgiving in Indianapolis by refusing to attend on the grounds that it was so close to Christmas. The two holiday meals were identical in content anyway, what my mother had been taught nice girls had to know how to do. Otherwise, she had zero interest in preparing food beyond the obligation to provide her children with balanced meals. My mother said that there were enough black women out there who were known as good cooks; she didn't have to be one of them.

My parents treated their holiday rejection in Las Vegas, where they lost and had, my father said, a contest of wills because he wanted to go to the Hoover Dam. My mother was of the opinion that he'd seen it enough. He went. He did want to mention that Pat was going into the hospital to have an operation to have two cysts removed.

Elizabeth couldn't believe the ham had turned out as well as it did. Barbara was there. Ian Hamilton seemed nice, and Harriet had developed asthma. Elizabeth remembered what she wanted to say about Guy Davenport's stories, that they did not have much fictional drive, strenuous though they were designed to be, intellectually. Later, she called to say she was of course going out of her mind with worry, but didn't Harriet look beautiful. She felt sorry for my mother, who, she said, had just got one daughter back from the hospital.

Who were those people in the streets of Tehran?

The bright weather departed for real this time, overnight this time. Eva had been staying with Felice and that was a tense situation. Stanley Crouch, whose work I read in *The Village Voice* and *The New York Times*, introduced himself over the phone, saying right off the bat that Huey Newton was always a bully and that Cecil Taylor had always been competitive with Duke Ellington. He'd written something about Baldwin that I found shocking.

(What did he say? I won't leave my chair—the swivel chair broke—or click on anything to answer the question, but I do remember my sister Pat using her Brando-as-the-Godfather voice after she read Crouch's piece. Out there in Indiana with her DNA-thick glasses, she loved *The Village Voice*. My father would have read Baldwin in magazines, but there was no Baldwin volume in the house that had not been left there by me or my sisters. Those nearly disposable Dell paperbacks.

My father would have written off Baldwin for his support of the Black Panthers. He said anyone could have seen what was going to come of the Panthers from what had happened just a few years before to Robert F. Williams, head of the Monroe, North Carolina, NAACP chapter. The success of his protests to integrate public facilities turned many whites in his town violent. He organized a group of armed blacks to counter the KKK, arguing that the only way to stop lynching was with lynching. In 1961, he fled the country. To call for Negroes with guns was a one-way ticket to Cuba, at best, my father said.

My grandfather hated *The Fire Next Time* for what Baldwin said about religion, he said in letters to church publications, but what he really minded was Baldwin's fame as someone who escaped having to be a preacher.

About Baldwin, my mother would have used reformist Negro women's club language: he has his own problems.)

What Elizabeth said about my reflections on *Just Above My Head* in the latest issue of the *Review* made all the difference to me. She made light of the help she'd given me.

Meanwhile, she needed to be reassured about her piece on Faulkner's *Uncollected Stories* in *The New York Times Book Review*.

> His original union of high classical style and vocabulary with the most daring and unaccommodating experiments with form, fractured methods of narration, shifting, shadowy centers of memory and documentation makes an art that was very demanding in his lifetime and not less so now.

In the piece, she thought a great deal about the character of Popeye from *Sanctuary*, 'the criminal mind beyond interpretation,' she called him. I'd not read it, did not know Popeye had been abandoned to a pyromaniacal grandmother. She would not lend any of her Faulkner, fragile hardcover editions. I could get them in paperback.

(—Fish flakes, her friend Elliott Carter called the crumbling pages of his old books and scores.)

Had the pyromaniacal grandmother in *Sula* any relation to the grandmother in Faulkner?

—You have to read it and tell me.

She would not defend *Intruder in the Dust*; she would give Baldwin that one. Back in school, I'd taken a lashing from her for not looking with more imagination at what Faulkner was maybe up to in 'That Evening Sun,' and how he conveyed Nancy's terror of what lurked in the ditch. Nancy was no stereotype.

But I liked *As I Lay Dying* very much. Professor Hardwick was happy. She considered the end a scream, the new wife, the new teeth. 'Meet Miz Bundren.'

Faulkner could not be otherwise and be Faulkner, Elizabeth said. I understood his ambition was like that of Proust, to describe the end of an age. She gave that a maybe, though she said she could see what Sterling meant by saying that Faulkner burned down the plantation tradition in American literature when he set fire to the big house in *Absalom! Absalom!*

She confessed abruptly, and not without shame, that in her youth the expression white people used for an unattractive black man was Park Ape.

To start the Christmas season, the U.S. embassy in Tripoli was sacked. The temperature in New York yo-yoed all month, down to my final day as an editorial assistant at Harper & Row. I'd handed in my papers. One of my last tasks was to have Ted Hughes read to me the corrected verses of *Moortown*. Fran spoke of his magnetism of voice. Rick Kot, my tall, robotically perfect, but warm replacement, took the call. Her authors were not going to miss me. Eva gonged to say join her and Luc outgassing at Tier 3.

THE NEW YEAR began with me in Indianapolis, getting over appendicitis. Dr. George Rawls, a fellow bridge club member, with his wife, Lulu, told my parents afterward that I was red hot. I swore into the phone to Luc that Rousseau was pretty funny, as liars went, and Percodan a glorious truth serum. Eva had gone back to San Francisco. I'd missed Luc's party for her. Everyone had been there.

Elizabeth phoned me when I was released to tell me who'd won the NBCC awards. She said she was still cross-eyed from New Year's Eve, going from the Cerfs' to Mia Farrow's, where it was like intermission at the Met, people going up and down staircases in some place owned by the Harknesses. She was showing Felice's novel to an important editor at Simon & Schuster.

When I got away from weeks of tender care, back at last to New York, February was so cold I thought my face would break.

Samurai Mover, real name John Wade, moved Luc to an apartment on East Twelfth Street, across from a Catholic church and school with mesh screens over the large windows. Peter Orlovsky, Ginsburg's former but still cherished partner, lived on the next floor up. Luc's table was a door over the bathtub in the kitchen. The walls quickly acquired crypto-Leninist slogans here and visitors' art there, and by the front door in the kitchen somebody had been busy on his wall denouncing pity as a petty bourgeois reaction.

We hurried on foot, heads down, to a new club on Second Avenue, near Houston Street. Felice was in a band.

—You don't have to pay, the guy collecting money said to me.
—You do, he said to Luc from a vinyl chair. Earle refused.

(Lydia Lunch had an event with a guest list of five hundred.
—You just hoped you were one of the five hundred, Felice said. I wasn't.)

The poet-drummer Barbara Barg was in the band, as well as Barbara Klar, whose boyfriend hauled her Farfisa organ from Twenty-sixth Street. Maybe Jennifer was in it, too, in a reluctant, backup way. Charlie had dyed his hair jet black.

(Charlie had had an invitation-only birthday party for four hundred that I heard about afterward.)

Felice, all legs in black tights and boots, miniskirt and black leather jacket, hair in Rasta knots, jumping about, shouting into the microphone,

Bitch, behave yourself.

She could do it all, sing, dance, and rock and roll with the lead guitarist.

After Cargo, Felice's band, the other band gave me a headache. I sat on the steps. Howard came up. He was about to do a video thing at the Guggenheim. Felice told him she'd played and he left. Her band went somewhere to listen to the tape. We went to the Soul Party at Little Club 57 on St. Marks Place. Bad wine, muddy tapes of James Brown, and, apart from Felice and me, only one other black person. The chicken was long gone.

(Felice Rosser's band Faith has been going since 1988.)

Several people met up and nodded at Felice's place after devouring cheeseburgers. She was pleased to learn that Auden had lived right around the corner. I was spaced the next morning, not hungover, but experiencing ego disintegration.

The rock cried out no hiding place.

I got a summons for failure to appear in court, stemming from a ticket I'd got the previous summer for running into the subway with a cigarette. It came with a ten-dollar fine. When the police stopped me, I was carrying no identification. I gave them my real name and address.

SUSAN SONTAG ONCE told Elizabeth that some mornings she woke thinking she wasn't smart enough to write, to pull it all off.

I was trying to write about race in *Vile Bodies* and *Decline and Fall* for an anthology Henry Louis Gates, Jr., a scholar at Yale, was preparing. (I thought at first that Skip was white; it sounded like a white nickname.)

—It's easy to admire what you can't do yourself. Think of yourself as the author. You must hit on the very thing that worries the author, what he thinks doesn't really work, but maybe it's all right, he can get by with it, so-and-so liked it, the thing about which he is very ambivalent, but unable to give up or revise.

You have to learn to do it for yourself, she said, to stay ahead of the reader, to protect yourself when you write.

I gave up. I went to the *Review*. I could see one of Bob's assistants, Shelley Wanger, moving on water skis between his desk and hers in the back, facing the door. June Jordan was on tour and sent an essay on Whitman she wanted me to pass on to the *Review*. I was taken aback to a prissy degree. She said Whitman was her oral tradition. Then she said *The Star-Apple Kingdom* was proof that Derek Walcott had been taken over by whites.

(April Bernard told me a few years ago that a class of hers had refused to read 'The Schooner Flight,' because its form came from *Beowulf*.)

Whitney's door was closed. He and Bob and Barbara were in a meeting. It was not my place to report to Elizabeth that I'd heard they were meeting about *The London Review*, but I wanted to.

Elizabeth asked me to get a copy of Kate Chopin's *The Awakening*. She'd been approached by an independent producer to do a screenplay. I found R. P. Blackmur's *Form and Value in Modern Poetry* in Pomander Bookshop next door to me as well and read the essay on Hardy in the bank. I liked Hardy, as Elizabeth and other professors had wagered I would someday. The used stock at Pomander Bookshop was in mint condition, the framed postcards of writers tastefully Modernist to the point of predictability. The tiny shop was spotless, which was rare in the city's secondhand-shop culture, even a threat to it. Neighbors like the cultural historian Jervis Anderson or the poet Patricia Spears Jones chatted in its natural light. The genteel owners of the bookshop had been together forever.

(They gradually broke up, Carlos Goez and Tim Mawson, they who had met as young men in London in the hotel business. They went their own ways, and both died from AIDS.)

Elizabeth and I went down Broadway to see *Angi Vera*, by the Hungarian director Pai Gabor. It was about a nurse in 1948 in Hungary corrupted by her unintentional success in navigating the Communist state. Elizabeth thought it was wonderful, how it left the government nothing, yet the characters were very brooding and ambiguous. She said had it been an American film, the whole thing would have been unbearably sentimental.

She said even the Conrad stuff in *Apocalypse Now* was so meretricious and wrong she couldn't stand it.

—European films are so far advanced.

Elizabeth had been on a panel over the weekend about dissent and censorship, with Bob, Brodsky, Susan. Toni Morrison told them a bizarre story. A friend of Morrison's in Atlanta asked for a copy of *Song of Solomon* at a bookstore, then at the library. She asked the librarian why it had been removed, who gave the order. She was told that it wasn't an order exactly, but Coretta Scott King called and indicated she did not quite approve of the book.

I took Elizabeth's typewriter in for repair; I took mine in.

Mbembe called to say he was pissed off at me about something I'd said about Naipaul, but then he thought of some fool in Togo, appearing on television with wings. I couldn't follow what he was saying. Mbembe was hopeful of a job at Purchase. He'd bought a little car and he and his girlfriend, Lee, were headed upstate.

I never heard from him again.

> there was the startle of wings
> breaking from the closing cage
> of your body, your fist unclenching
> these pigeons circling serenely
> over the page . . .

That March, Elizabeth and I were early to the Elizabeth Bishop memorial at the Poetry Society of America on Gramercy Park. Naomi Lazard presided. Elizabeth spoke, but was not sure the audience got what she meant by Bishop's 'modest sophistication.'

I had the feeling that Jonathan Galassi, a young editor, took in Elizabeth Bishop completely, a Harvard square in a bow tie talking about his treasured professor. Howard Moss read from the poems, ending with 'One Art.' Kathleen Spivack read a poem about playing Ping-Pong with Bishop. It was a sestina and Elizabeth wondered if Spivack's choice of the word 'arthritis' didn't strain her lines. We observed a silence for Millen Brand, who had just died, and James Wright, and Robert Hayden, but they forgot Muriel Rukeyser.

It wasn't strictly a memorial. An awards ceremony followed. Elizabeth didn't want to stay for the reception. She fixed what she called a Depression meal: everything leftover in the refrigerator.

She'd seen a film about Cal, thought it very beautiful, except there was too much of his madness, too much talk about it. That bothered her because she felt it took away from how hard he worked. Anyone who saw his worksheets would know.

She had another Caroline thing, but wasn't up to discussing it. Caroline's raps upset her, she said, but then she would get over them and become reluctant to go on about anything. What a mercy to be someone who could translate experience into words, and not someone who just felt, someone who was burdened by feelings.

—Words are not a release, but they are a way of coping, of not being encircled.

On the first day of the transit strike, in the quiet where rush hour usually was, a tranquil city stepped from the bath and dried off in the sun. New Yorkers declined to take taxis. They walked to their midtown offices in a great solidarity of sneakers or strolled home in the opposite direction after a mentally rejuvenating night.

Elizabeth had been struggling all week with Blackmur's book on Henry Adams.

—I'm going out of my skull with boredom. I do not want to spend my old age writing term papers.

She said while you're working on one thing, you're so agitated by the six other things that you don't feel you're working at all. Her laundry hung on a small wooden rack in the room where I used to type lists. (A woman from Spain, Nicole, had been doing the housework since Harriet was a girl.) She had no dryer. We walked past her bras.

Felice laughed that the strike made no difference to the East Village, everyone there being on permanent vacation. (The first time I'd heard the phrase.) She was waiting for her check from Simon & Schuster to clear. We assumed Luc and Jim were trapped on Long Island, where they'd gone to work on a film.

Howard expected me to make it down to his and Brad's place anyway. He said cars were dangerous to French intellectuals born under the wrong sign. Camus, now Barthes.

ELIZABETH WAS LEAVING to lecture in Memphis. She was going to Lexington for her Phi Beta Kappa.

—You mustn't be afraid to call Bob.

I wanted to write about Jean Toomer.

The party was at Alexis's new place. Samurai Mover had deposited her on Twelfth Street, on the other side of First Avenue from Luc. Jennifer and Malu, the non-drinking Filipina Jordanian Christian classmate from Ohio with the cousin in the PLO, put bananas and rum into a blender. Phil, Jim, and Sara Driver were wiped, having come from a shoot. Jean-Michel had decorated the apartment: the television screen and the refrigerator door were abstract works; he'd turned the floor into a big continuous canvas. His sculptures hung from the wall; a vacuum cleaner piece blocked the bathroom door, which was also a piece, in gray and black, *Famous Negro Athletes*, with a Picabia-inspired torn heart.

It was Felice's birthday. She and Alexis and Jean-Michel were best friends again. It turned into a memorial for Jean-Paul Sartre, who died the day we were supposed to file our taxes. We raised our bottles and smoke.

June Jordan and her girlfriend had a ceremony, a kind of public announcement of their commitment. The mixed and white families were there. It was a beautiful day. There were lavender roses all over June's apartment. We were given empty wineglasses. We seated ourselves, some of us on the floor.

The two women appeared to the alto of Carmen McRae singing 'I'm Coming Home.' They took their places in facing rocking chairs. They recited a poem to each other, kissed, exchanged rings, and we filled our glasses for a toast. I was in the mood to cry.

Elizabeth was aghast at my weekend. June and her girlfriend were not being grown-up, she said.

—Ludicrous. Why repeat mass mistakes.

She said she objected to their having a wedding in the first place.

—Sounds like the Sixties. Not very oil-hostage Eighties of them. She said imitating straight behavior gave it too much credence.

—Commitment is just this: I'm sorry, May, I can't go home with you. I'm in love with July. That's it.

(No, that was not it, but in those days of Edmund White's previously unimaginable-as-aboveground *States of Desire: Travels in Gay America* and Guy Hocquenghem's essay in *Semiotext(e)* on Pasolini's murder by rough trade, marriage did not figure, or was actively denounced.

He died of AIDS, Hocquenghem, the curly-headed philosopher whose *Homosexual Desire* I ordered at the Oscar Wilde Memorial Bookshop on Christopher Street, sort of thinking my interest in it would make me interesting to the shop staff. It didn't.)

Elizabeth insisted the scene at June's was not very radical in its implications.

Moreover, adventures in heterosexuality on the part of any queer guy other than Bowden Broadwater, Mary McCarthy's third or fourth husband, was him just trying to be what she called an all-rightnik.

I recalled why Harriet did not tell her much, for the same reason that my sisters and I told our parents absolutely nothing.

Elizabeth was so snide when I first mentioned the Jane Austen-worshipping girl I met on my bookshop job that I'd refrained from relating any of our on-again, off-again comedy since then.

—Office romances are the lowest form of love.

My club life, when acne conditions permitted, only said to her,

—This relentless cruising.

Colette's phrase for the thin psychology behind Don Juan's desire: 'statistical fervor.'

Elizabeth had no respect for Henry Miller, not even for the clean hands of his *Quiet Days in Clichy*, and to her Anaïs Nin was trucking in the most tiresome exhibitionism. She said nothing ages as fast or as badly in fiction as descriptions of the sex act. She would not share Francine Gray's fascination with Sade. The French were also keen on Jerry Lewis and Bernard-Henri Lévy. And for her, Casanova was a mere type, perhaps a bore.

Sexuality had become political, she noted in an essay for the *Review* that had kicked off the Seventies for her, and in it she shook her head at the innocent who had yet to discover sad flesh. 'Pity the poor body,' she wrote.

> The nature of sexuality is repetition. Phallic compulsiveness is an exaltation of repetition and yet a reduction to routine of the most drastic kind.

In the essay, she touched on Andy Warhol's film *Trash*, which I remembered as disappointing because Joe Dallesandro was too smacked out to do anything drastic and which Elizabeth wanted to forget because Holly Woodlawn buggered herself with a beer bottle.

'Self-love is an idolatry. Self-hatred is a tragedy,' she wrote.

Elizabeth didn't care how ancient a philosophical matter it was, the mind-body problem in Gertrude Stein was a type of essay in *Signs* not on her avenue of approach. But she wrote for *Signs* a carefully admiring essay on Simone Weil, the inspired repudiator of the body. Elizabeth tried to account for Weil's identification with suffering that required her to take it on herself.

She noticed that Simone de Beauvoir was okay coming in second place in her class at the École Normale Supérieure, because in first place had been Simone Weil.

Beauvoir's going on about le Maître seemed to her like a back flip with twists onto the pyre.

> *I am afraid to own a Body—*
> *I am afraid to own a Soul—*

To hop off her griddle, I asked Elizabeth if she had finished her piece on R. P. Blackmur. She was interested that I'd read his poetry. She said it had her walking up and down.

The next day, she called. The editor at *The New York Times Book Review* had telephoned to say no one could make heads or tails of her piece on Blackmur's *Henry Adams*. She was scandalized.

I went down to the red sofa and read an *éloge*, beautiful, tender, honoring both Blackmur's work and *The Education of Henry Adams*. She wrote it the way she wrote it; she knew what Blackmur meant when he said one must have an 'internal intimacy' with a text. That was her critical approach as well. She could learn a book quickly and once she got Blackmur, she said, she loved it. The Henry Adams had always been one of her favorites. Old Campaigner. She decided she couldn't ruin the tone of her essay by going back to explain for a *Times* audience who Henry Adams was. She thought to expand it for the *Review*, making it more about Blackmur. The funny thing was she'd expected everyone to consider it slight. It was not; it was about Blackmur's way of thinking.

When Elizabeth came back from the trip home to Lexington that she claimed, suspiciously, was not worth talking about, she said Susan's pages on Roland Barthes were immediately interesting. Susan spoke of Barthes's 'amorous relationship' to reality and to writing, his 'elegant, exacting' voice, his 'unworldly, uncosmopolitan' temperament, his being an ingenious student of himself.

> His sense of ideas was dramaturgical: an idea was always in competition with another idea. . . .
>
> All his writings are polemical. But the deepest impulse of his temperament was not combative. It was celebratory . . .

The essay sounded like Elizabeth Hardwick. She said that Susan told her she had thought of her as she wrote it, of how she would do it, which Elizabeth said she found sweet. I did think from what I'd read of Susan Sontag's old and new work that knowing Elizabeth had improved her writing. Elizabeth said my recent things hadn't sounded like her at all.

I WAS WAITING for Luc. We were to have a drink to mark his last day with Tom Victor, the nut and enthusiast, as Elizabeth called him. Luc had been Tom's assistant. He challenged Luc's creed that all bosses were shits. But Luc had a new job in the mailroom at the *Review*, starting the next day. He arrived, announcing,

—This is the voice of Algeria.

Masses of people had been leaving Cuba by small vessels. The boat exodus had begun the day Sartre died and was still going on. Had Castro maybe made a mistake, Luc laughed. Wouldn't

Washington rather get rid of him than absorb thousands of Cubans. How many professionals could he let go without undermining the society. Criminals and the mentally impaired. Jamaica was a powder keg, the *Times* reported. The unbelievable saga of the Vietnamese boat people was still recent. The world's unhappiness climbed onto pitching plastic rafts.

Luc had cool plans. I did, too.

Out in Brooklyn, across from the Brooklyn Museum, the large apartment of Alexis De Veaux and Gwendolyn Hardwick was like a theater, objects and furniture spare and carefully placed. The lighting was dramatic, worthy of the animated crowd that had gathered to hear De Veaux read from her new book-length poem about Billie Holiday, *Don't Explain*.

She was forceful. The church answered back.

—I heard *that*.

It was a convocation of free women. Alice Walker had just edited *I Love Myself When I Am Laughing . . . and Then Again When I Am Looking Mean and Impressive: A Zora Neale Hurston Reader*: 'I think we are better off if we think of Zora Neale Hurston as an artist, period—rather than the artist/politician most black writers have been required to be.'

(Felice just told me that she once interviewed June and Alice Walker for *The Barnard Bulletin*. Afterward, Walker sent her one hundred dollars, telling her to use it to go home. She should always stay in touch with home, Walker said. Felice's grandmother was from Walker's hometown, Eatonton, Georgia. Felice took the bus to Detroit.)

June Jordan smiled. Born in Harlem, she grew up in Bedford-Stuyvesant, a Brooklyn where mothers carried pails of ashes up from basement furnaces. She went from her black life to a white prep school and asked Barnard to make the connection between what she called her black universe and her white education, but it failed her, those being the Eisenhower years. However, Barnard gave her analytical skills, she said, and the white boy from Columbia across the street, she said, soon to be her husband and the father of her son at Harvard.

Malcolm X had actually smiled at her. The riot in Harlem in 1964 called her to her activism. June's husband stayed away. She was the protest tradition of ridicule and sarcasm, telling Daniel Patrick Moynihan in one poem not to liberate her from her

black female pathology.

(The then Secretary of Labor Moynihan wrote a report in 1965 to President Johnson saying that liberty would not be enough, because the great obstacle to equality was the disintegration of the black family. The brutalities of ghetto life had created absent fathers and mothers with illegitimate children. Segregation was harder on black men than black women, Moynihan said, and kept black men from becoming strong father figures. Negro children without fathers floundered and failed.

To have female-headed households was a part of the disorganization of black family life. Not only did black women have more children than white women, they had them earlier. But matriarchy had defined the black family for generations and accounted for the poor performance of black students relative to white ones, he said. It was also maybe why most crimes of the body, such as assault, rape, and murder, were committed by Negroes.)

June had once written about the path to black identity as running through suicide and violence. Bigger Thomas was Fanon's truth, crazy but not paranoid. But I knew from my reading about Zora Neale Hurston that June had argued in an essay back in 1974 that we needn't choose between Wright's and Hurston's interpretations of the South. *Their Eyes Were Watching God* was the black novel of affirmation, the most exemplary novel of black love, she said. Yet Bigger Thomas had as much to teach us about the need for love as Janie Starks. We needed both; we needed to protest oppression, but also to keep faith in our resilience, what we were like when white people weren't around. I once told her I didn't believe in that kind of distinction anymore.

People were still talking about Herbert G. Gutman's *The Black Family in Slavery and Freedom, 1750–1925*, published in the year of the American Bicentennial. Gutman said that slavery had not destroyed the black family. Gutman maintained that more black families were headed by two parents than we would have thought.

I said that *Roots: The Saga of an American Family*, by Alex Haley, a bestseller of the Bicentennial year, was the popular version of Gutman's thesis. Haley traced his ancestry back to a character he called Kunta Kinte, a youth kidnapped in the Gambia in the late eighteenth century. The television series based on Haley's story gave black Americans the equivalent of a founding myth, a landing at Plymouth Rock. Haley had imagined an upbringing for his great-great-great-great-grandfather, making him a link to what had been previously a seemingly unknowable African past. I didn't know about Cudjoe, or somehow didn't take in who he was.

I said black people are the natural heirs of American Whigs, trying to introduce Eric Foner into the discussion of Eugene Genovese's *Roll, Jordan, Roll: The World the Slaves Made*. Someone brought up Albert Murray on the South, not a writer I understood.

June was hostile to anything that made black culture a pathology, as she called it. We had a duty in our work to combat the prevailing image of black culture that had mostly to do with poverty as the breeding ground of violence, antisocial behavior. The story that blackness was sickness, the heritage of a bondage that wiped out the African past, had to be overcome.

June also condemned what she viewed as divisive. *Black Macho and the Myth of the Superwoman*, Michelle Wallace's provocative polemic on male dominance in the civil rights movement and on the abuse supposedly in the culture between black men and black women, was divisive, June insisted. I got the feeling that Michelle Wallace, daughter of the artist Faith Ringgold, a formidable activist, could put black women on the defensive, as had *For Colored Girls* at first. How else could we quarrel with Wallace's contention that black men regarded the movement as mostly a story of black men vs. white men and that black women were expected to stay in the background, to be defended, essential though their participation had always been.

Maybe black women needed a movement. *The Autobiography of Malcolm X*, which Alex Haley had helped to shape, had never been out of print.

The black women laughed, as at a little brother, as if to say just because I'd not heard of something did not mean it did not exist.

I met Wesley Brown and couldn't hear what he was saying, but I think he was halfway through a novel about a minstrel performer. His debut novel, *Tragic Magic*, a tale of prison, Vietnam, and black men, was written with a verve, style, and intelligence to be envied. We talked about a wonderful oral history of black America, *Drylongso*.

We all loved Sewall's biography of Emily Dickinson. I said Dickinson should not be taught in high school. The woman from the Feminist Guild I was talking to thought Dickinson should be taught in schools as early as possible.

June introduced me to Marilyn Hacker, and we were lost in the satin blouses and gold earrings and bejeweled braids and feathers and whirling skirts and heels of black women in motion, one dyke more beautiful than the next, a new song by Mighty Sparrow at full blast.

It was an all-night affair.

Around eight o'clock in the morning, the remaining party of melted dots and spots that we'd become left the building, the Brooklyn Museum scowling at some very high people philosophizing about the Hegelian dialectic, whatever that meant, with no taxi in sight even to be not stopping for black us.

MR. SILVERS SENT *The Wayward and the Seeking*, Toni Morrison's edition of Jean Toomer's unpublished writings. Toomer came from one of those high-office black families brought by Reconstruction to Washington, D.C. He published *Cane* in 1923, an Expressionist mix of prose poem and lyric poetry about a South replete with the erotic. But then he turned to Gurdjieff and the mysticism that killed Katherine Mansfield. He decided that, being light-skinned and silent-film-star handsome, he contained racial multitudes, and in the four decades remaining to him, he never published another book. I read *Cane* a few times, like learning my lines. I took it with me to the Bar at East Fourth Street.

Jean Toomer was bonkers and maybe that was a precondition for his attempt to pole-vault over the color line and to exist mentally outside the jurisdiction of invented racial categories. Alas, there were good reasons, I discovered, why his unfinished autobiographies as philosophical treatise or Quaker pamphlet had been unpublished. A few pages in Georgia O'Keeffe's biography provided the most touching and convincing portrait of Toomer. I could make it harder for myself by adding 'The Negro Pattern of Life' from Kenneth Burke's *The Philosophy of Literary Form*, a work Ellison had relied on and that I'd spotted in Pomander Bookshop. Ellison talked somewhere of writing with one's blackness drawn up around one.

Jean-Michel was still covering every surface of Alexis Adler's apartment on East Twelfth Street with art: the radiator, the wall above Alexis's bed, the lamé coat Felice had given her as an apology for their fight. This was an artist too poor for most art supplies, they understood. Alexis and Luc collected Basquiat from the moment they met him: postcards, drawings, notebooks, sweatshirts. They never doubted he was the real thing. I saw a distracted street kid, ostentatiously quiet. His brown skin had the most beautiful undertone. I think he still had dreads when I first saw him, though he would shave half his head soon enough. Alexis said Jean was so enamored of a particular David Bowie album, he played it all day long, over and over. *Low.*

Mount St. Helens was erupting that late spring, sending ash

for miles over Washington State. Alexis's family had escaped from Germany to Vladivostock to Japan, and finally to Seattle.

The first duty of the revolutionary is not to go to jail.

How nice to sit with a little Che too playfully on our lips, watching volcano or boat news on TV on mute. Howard cleaned up his place by shoving debris against walls and clearing surfaces with his arm. He was gracious, whether set up in a villa or squatting in a rehearsal space, passing around glass plates of cocaine and hash-oil-coated smokes. His dining table had been my step-grandmother's. I still had his grandmother's.

Two of our classmates and three Belgian dancers discussed how Merce Cunningham's arthritis was influencing his choreography. Joe LeSueur had a life after Frank O'Hara, writing for a soap opera I liked, and John Giorno was off to a poetry festival in Brussels.

William Burroughs had just returned from a conference in Paris on 'Truth.' He did not believe in gun control. Criminals cannot be regulated therefore citizens should not be disarmed. He mentioned his new novel, *Cities of the Red Night*. Fran had had it under the table and I read it, seven hundred pages of time travel, germ warfare, lost reptilian civilizations, and apocalyptic ejaculations.

Howard and Burroughs recalled filming the Dr. Benway scene, with Jackie Curtis as the nurse covered in blood. Legendary barkeep Slugger Ann was her grandmother. Her bar was down Twelfth Street on the other side from Luc. Luc had told me Jackie was ill. Maybe that was why Burroughs turned pensive. Howard switched the subject to the latest Naropa Institute scandal. But Burroughs was suddenly doing his Pie Man routine.

After everyone left, Howard gave in to his bad mood. He diced up too many lines. Brad was working as a model in Milan. Howard planned a rendezvous with Brad at the elegant George V in Paris. However, out of nowhere, Brad was giving him this song and dance, saying that he had to stay in Milan, that he couldn't find an editing machine for him in Milan. Howard suspected that the upshot was, Don't come. He drove me mad, switching channels on the TV though his favorite Hitchcock was on.

We woke in time for the party for Mack, the dancer in the *Review* mailroom, who was moving his luxuriant mustache to San Francisco. Barbara's assistant, April, was also departing, to go to graduate school at Yale. Gathered in front of the filthy refrigerator, the discarded books tables, and a cleared-off side table of free food, Prudence, Shelley, Suzanne Merry, Chris, Michael, Noah, Luc, a new lesbian in the production studio with a white cowboy hat from the People's Republic of China, Barbara, Dominique Nabokov, with a camera, and Mr. Silvers, interested to learn that Jean Toomer knew the Imagist poets as well as Steichen and Mabel Dodge Luhan. It was clear who was drinking at lunch and who wasn't.

In the next sentence it was already Africa Day on WBAI. A woman's voice read dull parts of Cabral over the radio. Why not blow town.

Elizabeth was very upset when Vernon Jordan was shot in Fort Wayne, Indiana. She asked that I bring cigarettes and a small container of heavy cream. I called my parents, but they didn't know any more than the news. Someone with a high-powered rifle was waiting for him when he was out jogging with a friend, a white woman.

SHE WOULD BE going soon to Castine. I told her June Jordan had said earlier that day that she had to bathe, dress, and meditate before she went to *Mother Courage*, a hit for Ntozake Shange. A weak smile. It was hard to have ideas about Brecht, Elizabeth said, distracted.

Naipaul spoke of people who kept up with the revolution the way some people kept up with the theater, but we didn't get on to

Edward Said writing about Naipaul in *The Nation*. And Luc had just passed on to me from the office the first book by George Lamming I would read. But it was as though the lid had come off Elizabeth's smile.

She wasn't drinking. I stayed sober. She was worried, because of some trouble between Caroline Blackwood and Mary McCarthy.

During Cal's last summer in Maine, Mary wrote Caroline a letter intended to be consoling. There were some unfortunate remarks, but when Elizabeth read it to me, it didn't seem that bad.

(Where is the letter now? Has it been published?)

What Caroline probably didn't like was Mary saying that Cal's return to Castine would make the summer. Maybe she didn't much like either Mary's tone of rebuke about Caroline not having left a forwarding address when she moved from Redcliffe Square to Ireland. To tell her that it was typical of her was like scolding a child.

Not long ago, Elizabeth said, Caroline was in Paris. She visited Mary, drinks turned into dinner, and Caroline went off on one of her raps. She told Mary that Cal had been writing a poem against her and was sore at her. She said that Elizabeth sent telephone bills for calls from Castine to Ireland. Mostly, it was Caroline getting even with McCarthy for that letter.

Mary was taken in by Caroline's rap and wrote Elizabeth a horrible letter. Elizabeth, defending Cal, she said, answered that none of that was true, the poem Caroline referred to was just a few lines of something scratched on a piece of paper. Caroline had tried to have them typed up as a poem. It didn't work. Elizabeth told Mary that what Caroline was mad about was the letter. Mary said she didn't remember writing Caroline a letter. What letter? Mary was driven, planning on asking Sonia Orwell about it when Sonia came out of the hospital.

Neither in her letter to Mary nor in the phone conversation she'd had with her that morning had Elizabeth said to Mary that she had read the letter and, in fact, had it still. It had been among

Cal's things, and she just left it in the satchel he had with him in the taxi when he died. She told Mary that at the funeral, Caroline, in her drunken state, was obsessed with the letter, furious, going on and on about it. Elizabeth felt terrible about not saying she had it, and she decided she couldn't let Mary go around asking everybody about the letter she didn't recall, though everyone had seen it.

(How had they seen it? Who was everyone?)

She felt she should have returned it to Caroline or torn it up, but Caroline was such a troublemaker she just let it sit there. She was reluctant to send the letter back to Mary. It was tough enough admitting she had it, she said. She didn't want to embarrass Mary. Maybe that was Mary's problem, let her be confronted, I offered.

Elizabeth planned to give a précis of the letter and say she tore it up, but she realized that that would have been a disaster. The letter wasn't that bad, Mary would not be embarrassed, I said, whereas were it destroyed, Mary would worry what had been in it.

Elizabeth said she could not afford to tell anyone that she destroyed a letter to Caroline. It would get back to Caroline and she could then put it about that Elizabeth was destroying her property or suggest that who knew what else Elizabeth had done away with. Caroline had an infinite capacity for revision, Elizabeth said, the boldest falsifications. Not that she needed an incident for her twistings.

—Cal's last visit to Ireland, Caroline ran away to London, complaining that he refused to stay with her. Then, after his death, she insisted to the very same people that everything had been fine between them.

Caroline made a workroom of Lowell's for a film crew, though he never lived in Ireland. She was also saying that his last letter he left on a bed and she'd had to destroy it, because there was a robbery and something was poured on the letter.

—You don't destroy someone's last words because of a stain. You don't leave a last letter around. She wouldn't have destroyed it had it been anything to support one of her revisions or anything except I'm sorry, we can't go on.

She said Caroline would say anything and having, in all likelihood, destroyed her letters to Cal, then saying that Cal returned the *Dolphin* letters to her, whatever those were, Caroline would say Elizabeth was here ripping up things in Cal's papers.

She decided to let Mary have the letter back and maybe she would be satisfied to let it drop. Maybe she needed to tell Mary not to tell Caroline, which would have made matters worse. She said she had to cough up about the letter, having defended Cal by explaining to Mary what was behind Caroline's rap in Paris.

Elizabeth said these episodes showed that Caroline despised Cal, just as something in Mary's recklessness illustrated how she got herself pulled into trench warfare with Lillian Hellman.

(She didn't refer at this time to a letter she got from Mary when Cal first left her, saying that she had seen him with Caroline in London, and they seemed happy.

—I thought, Mary, drop dead.

'Happy' was what she said Mary said when she first told me about this letter from her old friend. She brought it up more than once.

Saskia Hamilton showed me the letter McCarthy wrote after seeing Lowell and Blackwood in London in 1970. They seemed 'calm and serious,' was what Mary had actually written, referring no doubt to Cal's pattern of taking up with someone when he was manic. She was assuring Lizzie that this wasn't like that. Maddening enough in its way.)

STERLING CALLED. He was pleased with the published book, *The Collected Poems of Sterling Brown*. But two of the Slim poems had been omitted as well as a crucial stanza of 'The Ballad of Joe Meeks.' His forbearance was heartbreaking, as though he'd known all along the curse would not be lifted.

Pomander Walk, New York City
(Courtesy of Dominique Nabokov)

Drawing of James Fenton by Don Bachardy, 1977
(© Don Bachardy)

James Fenton, Manila, 1983

Harriet Lowell and
Robert Lowell, West
Sixty-seventh Street (Henri
Cartier-Bresson © Fondation
Henri Cartier-Bresson /
Magnum Photos)

Harriet Lowell, 1973
(© Estate of Evelyn Hofer)

ABOVE AND BELOW: Robert Silvers, offices of *The New York Review of Books*
(Courtesy of Dominique Nabokov)

LEFT AND BELOW:
Barbara Epstein,
offices of *The New York
Review of Books* (Courtesy of
Dominique Nabokov)

Bob, Lizzie, and Barbara at Grace Dudley's
(Courtesy of Dominique Nabokov)

Lizzie and Barbara, 15 West Sixty-seventh Street
(Courtesy of Dominique Nabokov)

The author and Lizzie, 33 West Sixty-seventh Street
(Courtesy of Dominique Nabokov)

Mary McCarthy and Elizabeth Hardwick at McCarthy's house
in Castine, Maine (Susan Wood / Getty Images)

Elizabeth Hardwick (© Estate of Evelyn Hofer)

While making a movie, Richard Pryor took a break to freebase cocaine in his trailer. He set himself on fire. Howard found that hilarious and paid for my taxi downtown to whatever performance we were going to before we closed down the Bar. The after-hours transvestite bar across the street was expensive, but it had a good jukebox. Howard was leaving for Milan, or for Paris. One of his schemes, to fly for free as a messenger, with very little luggage. He could not bear to be separated from Brad, he said.

Elizabeth was once again energetic and melodious: to the theater on Thursday, the ballet on Friday, the next night dinner with the independent producer she no longer wished to adapt *The Awakening* for. Though she found it very deft.

—Nothing embarrassing in it.

My sister Donna said it was the kind of book she liked only after she'd finished it.

Elizabeth had Harriet on tap for Sunday and after her Anne Dunn, a dear friend of Barbara's who looked after troubled Jimmy Schuyler, Elizabeth explained, followed by Francine Gray the night after that. She'd seen David Kermani somewhere, liked him, thought he deserved credit for holding Ashbery together, and she'd seen Jayne Anne Phillips somewhere else, on the arm of the cutest black boy.

—She's a good writer.

We were to meet up, but she found a speech in her purse and remembered that she had to appear at Barnard.

When Elizabeth finally had a free evening, it was not to talk about Jean Toomer or Henry James and *The Awkward Age* as she'd said, but one of her home improvements.

—Yep.

She always threatened to put me on a scaffold to dust her chandelier. No, not yet, thank goodness. No, her plan was to replace the plain doors put in her bedroom after the fire with better doors stored downstairs from all the remodeled rooms in the building. And then there was the library, but it would take all summer to

get the books on the proper shelves. She'd sold her studio downstairs and I packed up books, divided boxes into what she wanted
and what could go, one of those jobs she left me to, because some
books excited something like an allergic reaction. They bothered
her sinuses.

I was glad not to be taking a red sofa and kitchen exam on *The
Awkward Age*. I'd not finished it and wouldn't. I was ready to say
Edmund Wilson hadn't liked that 'stage-play' of 'mouthfuls swal-
lowed imperceptibly.'

Harriet was feeling better. The doors looked awful.

—Don't be too critical.

She wanted to start over with primer and stain when she came
back for Jean vanden Heuvel's party the next week. I helped her to
put away the books she'd used for a review that had been printed
a while ago. Her work added to my reading list; the *Review* added
to my reading list, as did Luc, and I was falling behind, unable to
catch up, that being the whole point.

I'd not read Dickens's *Martin Chuzzlewit* or *Studies in Classic
American Literature* by D. H. Lawrence, books that figured in her
review of a book by an Oxford don that scolded America and its
English visitors, from Dickens and Trollope on into the twentieth
century, a book that really put down the English writers who remained here: Auden, Isherwood, Huxley. It had practically no index or footnotes, but she had me find in her shelves every book he
mentioned, and if it wasn't there, either I or Bob's office got it. She
likened the book's density to 'wandering around an arboretum.'

> No scruple deters Peter Conrad in the swift execution
> of W. H. Auden. He slices on, in his practiced, glinting
> way, gathering authority where he finds it, in yesterday's
> garbage pail, in policemanlike sifting of texts, in the
> scene of the crime, New York City, in bad associates, cash
> in the drawers. Poems are evidence and he investigates

them in the sense that a handwriting expert investigates a ransom note . . .

'Lay your sleeping head, my love, human on my faithless arm,' a beautiful poem in the classical English lyric mode, is intolerably chastised in a governessy aside of great foolishness . . .

The lyric that Elizabeth defended sounded to her like Wyatt, she said.

> *But in my arms till break of day*
> *Let the living creature lie*

(James said that Auden's most famous lyric would maybe land him in jail today; the poem was about a youth who was fifteen years old at the time.

In *The Table Talk of W. H. Auden*, Alan Ansen remembered Auden saying that he was happy to leave his first teaching post at a boys' school, because the students kept trying to seduce him. Ansen said that Auden let the administration at the University of Michigan in Ann Arbor know before he was hired that he was queer. His bravery was in his matter of-factness about it, in 1941.

When James was a student at Repton, Isherwood's boarding school, he organized a reading on Auden's name day. The local church was St. Wystan's.

—He had that name because of the place.

His grandfather had been vicar nearby at Burton-on-Trent. Auden received a letter from this young scholar and thereafter took an interest in his work.

Auden came back to England after the war with an American accent, people said. But James said Auden's accent was invented, a sort of 1920s British.

There was a memorial for Auden down the street from Columbia at St. John the Divine in the fall of 1973, but I was too nervous to enter the cathedral. I knew he'd been Isherwood's great friend and early peer influence.)

The thick Lawrence study didn't fit back into the shelf. Elizabeth said she would probably never use it again and told me to put it on the chair by the door and remember to take it with me.

She was vigorous with contentment. The flight to Bangor took only an hour; then into a rented car for the hour's drive to Castine.

—The drive is very nostalgia creating.

She first went to Castine in 1954. They stayed with Cousin Harriet. She'd spent every summer there since 1957, when Harriet was a baby. Cousin Harriet was ill, unable to leave Washington.

—To the store, and then I'll dash into the liquor store, drive around, then to the house to see if any disasters have occurred.

She was fond of Link and Margaret, the local couple who looked after things, closed and opened the house every year. Margaret came at seven once a week to clean. She left at nine o'clock.

—Anything else you want me to do, Miz Lowell? Nope. Fifteen dollars change hands.

She said she was still hauling buckets and sponges after Margaret had gone. The cleaning women in *Sleepless Nights* were a composite.

She thought she'd go ahead with that film script of Kate Chopin. She said she nearly forgot she was due to get on a plane to appear at Berkeley before she went to Maine for the rest of the summer.

Elizabeth said, offhand, that she was going to get a will. She couldn't understand why she needed a literary executor, there were no papers. She needed what Lowell had, since their stuff was, somehow, joined. She remembered how surprised she had been to learn that the University of Kentucky had the manuscript of *The Simple Truth*.

Texas had not come through on Lowell's estate. They felt that, ultimately, they were competing with Harvard. It gave her pause about what she had. It wasn't much but it was much more valuable than worksheets. Hundreds of letters from Lowell, none from her.

—People will say he didn't keep them.

I told her not to be ridiculous.

—That's right. The bitch tore them up.

There was something in her old contract with Harvard about everything found later belonging to them.

—He gave them to you.

—Yes. I'll say that. Some he did anyway. Oh, Cal, I think I'd like to keep that. He'd say, Here. For the rest, I'll say that, too. Like Madame Stravinsky. Igor *gave* me the score of *Firebird*.

DOWNTOWN CAME UP and passed out in front of *The Times Square Show*, taking place in an old movie theater on West Forty-first Street and Seventh Avenue. It was an early summer night of blue hair, Buddy Holly glasses, rum bottles in paper sacks, and a voluptuous moon keeping watch over Nan Goldin and Kiki Smith. We were to think of the Armory Show, and Linton Kwesi Johnson's *Dread Inna England*, screened as a part of the show, was a very heavy film, and back outside best friends were unable to stand up much longer, a version of 'the aesthetic headache.'

—It's hard to put all your living in a weekend, Felice said. It takes more than three days to change your life.

Felice's subletter paid up in black hash and when it was gone, we zipped up her duffel bag and carried it with tears to the airport bus. She was off to finish her novel in Paris. It was June.

We took sandwiches back to the *Review*. Luc put on a tape of Poet and the Roots. He said the first chance he got he was going to take down all the posters and postcards and yellowed newspaper front pages on the mailroom walls, years of collage and tradition.

—Just to be contrary, to be negative, to be me.

He was already calling himself the Pete Best of the Del-Byzanteens,

the band that Jim, Phil, and Suzanne's boyfriend had got together, and for which Luc would write lyrics and liner notes. He
had to pick up a book from the Society Library and take it to John
Richardson.

I could not begin to explain the psychodrama of him and Eva,
her sister, their boyfriends, their crazy parents' house on the Jersey
Shore, someone's roommate back in San Francisco, Luc's relationship with said roommate. But he was writing. He read to me a piece
I've never forgotten, 'History Is Made at Night.'

(The piece is given the title 'I Was Spanking and Freaking at a
Disco Place' in Sante's *My Life in Poetry: 1970–1981*.)

Luc read at April Bernard's writing workshop; and Elizabeth,
fed up with planes and graduate students, having been overworked
at Berkeley, observed that Luc would find more freedom of expression away from downtown than he thought. There were no writers
to compete against downtown, he would say, and the environment
of the *Review* had a freeing effect. Of course there were writers
downtown.

Catharine R. Stimpson was leaving Barnard. We were packing up her office, some copies of her novel, *Class Notes*, back issues
of her journal, *Signs*, presents from her family, objects from Liz
Wood's children, from former students. She was a popular professor. We referred to her as Catharine R. Her favorite student, Leslie
J. Calman, Professor Stimpson addressed as Leslie J.

Why not leave town. It could all happen in a paragraph.

Luc had given me the new *Semiotext(e)*. Foucault, Guy Hocquenghem, Kate Millett, and others rapped about Boy Love, cross-
generational relations, and lowering the age of consent. Catharine
R. predicted it would split intellectual feminists and radical gays
forever.

How did one's name get on weird mailing lists in New York, we
wondered, careful as one had to be when asked to sign petitions.
Pamphlets from an organization calling itself 'Black and White

Men Together' were one thing for my elderly upstairs neighbor to see dropped through our shared front-door mail slot, but literature from a group called 'The North American Man-Boy Love Association' unsettled me. No Auden there.

I woke in the Mudd Club at five in the morning and went to find a taxi, but couldn't decide where I was headed.

From Gertrude Stein's *How to Write*: 'A sentence is not emotional a paragraph is.'

THE NEW YORK REVIEW OF BOOKS divorced *The London Review of Books*. Karl Miller was furious with them; Bob and Barbara were furious with him. It had been too much of a drain. The *Review*, as Elizabeth called *The New York Review of Books*, had lost something like $145,000. The Paper, as Barbara usually referred to one of the leading intellectual journals in English, which she had helped to found, was on unsteady ground because of the losses incurred. (James said Susannah Clapp had been something like Miller's editorial secret weapon at *The London Review*, devoted though its contributors already were to him.)

—All we've accomplished is to set up a competitor, Elizabeth said.

ELIZABETH SAID SHE wasn't smoking; Mary McCarthy didn't seem well.

—I feel she's not in good shape.

Bob had sent Elizabeth a galley of Robert Towers's awful review of Lillian Hellman's *Maybe* in the forthcoming issue of the *Review*. She said it was very ordinary, not altogether favorable, but Towers bought Hellman's image of herself. Barbara told her she liked the piece, that it put the book down, but wasn't mean.

—Why wasn't it mean, Elizabeth said she said.

Hellman had a huge party for the book: drinks at Regine's; dinner at Griselde's. Elizabeth said Hellman should have taken out an ad. She said Hellman probably liked the attention she was getting from her lawsuit against Mary McCarthy, even though some of the attention was mixed.

I'd missed it, but my sister had seen the episode of *The Dick Cavett Show* the winter before during which Mary McCarthy said that Lillian Hellman was an overrated and dishonest writer. McCarthy said:

—Every word she writes is a lie including 'and' and 'the.'

Elizabeth said Mary would say she'd said it before, it was such a good line.

—And, but, and the.

Elizabeth said that although Mary and Lillian both had been on *The Dick Cavett Show* before, Hellman would have considered Cavett as hers. She was the playwright in the black fur coat ad, wrinkles and incisors in Avedon profile. She had a ton of money and had the nerve to be suing everybody. It had already cost Mary a fortune.

Norman Mailer had published in *The New York Times* an obnoxious letter addressed to McCarthy and Hellman, 'the giraffe' and 'the anteater' who detested one another, he said. The awfulness of McCarthy's barbaric attack had been matched by the recklessness of Hellman's defamation suit, he said. McCarthy had accused Hellman of what every writer was guilty of, while Hellman would be fostering self-censorship were her action to be successful, he said.

Richard Poirier, editor of *Raritan*, defended Hellman. And in response, Norman Mailer wrote an even more objectionable letter to Richard Poirier.

—Why a stupid fag-baiting letter, Elizabeth said.

Mailer had called Poirier 'an orotund asshole.' She said Mailer's rant was more libelous than what Mary said about Hellman, because it was about Poirier's qualities as a person and not a response to questions about the worth of writers. It was also not private; Mailer sent copies of his letter all over town. Luc gave me a copy, along with a xerox of John Cheever's Rolex ad.

Elizabeth wondered if it was wise of Mary to say nothing. She could not have her friends writing silly letters. Diana Trilling may have been right about *Scoundrel Time*, but. She said 'but' as though to say she of course could not make common cause with her. Trilling's publisher had even canceled Trilling's contract for a book of essays a couple of years earlier, because she wouldn't delete the unpleasant references in them to Lillian Hellman.

(In 1945, Diana Trilling gave Elizabeth Hardwick's first novel a nonsensical review in *The Nation*. Elizabeth never mentioned it, but it was also not the kind of thing she would have hung on to.)

As a leftist, Hellman had been a *Watch on the Rhine* ally of Moscow. Hellman was furious, Elizabeth heard, back when Lionel Trilling chose to trust Whittaker Chambers, the witness against Alger Hiss. Some people said the reason Chambers's encounters with Hiss were so detailed was because the conversations took place in surreptitiously gay bars.

(I asked Jason Epstein a few holidays ago if he had known Whittaker Chambers.

—No, but I also never met Hitler.)

Elizabeth was on the phone after she read an interview that a popular woman columnist had done with Hellman. It was, she pronounced,

—Cloying.

She said people had done less to earn an invitation to the Vineyard.

Then Mary was in the hospital.

—Shingles.

Elizabeth felt guilty she hadn't defended Mary. She had to wait to see what happened, wait for a dramatic moment, if it looked as though she were going to be fed to the lions.

She painted the barn door in Maine. Keeping house was a

bother; she said she seemed to be always cleaning. The script of *The Awakening* was going more slowly than she had expected.

In another phone call, Mary McCarthy was out of the hospital, but not cured. Elizabeth said she had an idea for an oblique comment on the lawsuit, something on the awful things writers have said of other writers, especially Dr. Johnson.

—If Cal were here, he could give you thirty thousand examples going back to the Greek generals.

She said she was working on something else, something too silly to explain. She didn't want to write a mere story; she wanted an advance.

—I wish you were coming up for the evening so we could talk about it.

I was still very much for *Ideas*.

She didn't want to use the third person, and the omniscient narrator made for something very conventional. She didn't want to give up the first person, since she could employ it to such a radical advantage.

—You can think with it, she said.

She'd begun her new novel like this, I think (if I am identifying correctly these loose pages Harriet and Saskia found):

> What sort of plot would contain the subject of the city? The bookstore is plundered. A cigarette fell into a basket, but fortunately it had been emptied of paper and so the burning cigarette lay there on only one piece of paper that covered the bottom so that ashes would not seep through to the floor and that piece burned quickly, and the straw was seared black. That was all. Good news, good news, Henry said. Very good news . . .
>
> What is wonderful in New York is that nothing is hidden. There are no secrets, no mysteries, only imaginative and yet banal fantasies that transform so confidently the obvious.

I noted how much she wrote about New York when she was in Maine and how much she wrote about Maine when at her dining room table in the city with the typewriter she'd lugged into place herself. There was a correlation between geography, or distance, and reflection.

—Don't get drunk unless you have a good reason, she said.

'WE FIND THAT most Negroes in that collaboration end up being collaborated right on out of the pie.' When black people did not participate, they knew what they were doing. I read the late speeches of Malcolm X during the two-hour flight delay on a sweltering runway. A Russian ballerina had a tantrum. Some Cuban passengers who needed urgently to reach Miami lost it next.

Hannah Arendt noted in *Crises of the Republic* that black people were not part of the original consensus universalis and were therefore distrustful of efforts to include them. Were Malcolm X and Arendt not in agreement?

For my sister Pat, Lenny Bruce concluded most debates nicely:

—Yada yada, warden.

My mother was not in the mood and we got to our feet in the banquet hall for President Carter's entrance, for 'The Star-Spangled Banner,' and for 'Lift Ev'ry Voice and Sing,' the Negro National Anthem heard at every annual convention of the National Association for the Advancement of Colored People. My mother and my sister were lightly holding hands, as though each glad the other was there.

I met Warren Marr, the editor of *The Crisis*, the NAACP's journal, who said as soon as we were alone that he was close to Bruce Nugent, the provocatively barefoot pretty boy of the Harlem Renaissance. Nugent was from light-skinned, upper-class Washington, D.C., and it showed in how dated his notion of literary decadence seemed to be, a mood taken from Beardsley and *The Yellow Book*. But I judged him based on a single story, 'Smoke, Lilies, and Jade,' in Nathan Huggins's anthology, *Voices from the Harlem Renaissance*.

Nugent was alive and well in Hoboken, Marr reported. He said that when Countee Cullen and Yolande Du Bois got married, Cullen's best friend, Harold Jackman, a dandy, as they used to say, went on the honeymoon with them. Mr. Marr had my number, Upper West Side local of the Homintern. Queer history was also an oral history, and it was sometimes a surprise who could contribute to it and was willing to. Mr. Marr had published Nugent's only book and Nugent had also been married to his sister.

I closed my mouth and we were joined at the hotel bar by my father and his esteemed professor from Howard University, W. Montague Cobb. Dr. Cobb's anatomy class had been one of my father's favorites. He may have been an amateur, but Dr. Cobb could really play the violin, my mother said. Dr. Cobb had practically built the Howard University Medical School, in my father's worshipful version.

Dr. Cobb instructed me to pick either Rabelais or Shakespeare. I chose the latter and he said we had grounds for a discussion. *Julius Caesar*. He leaned on the giant, circular lobby bar, ready to begin the lesson. He asked a question. My father gave me a look. I didn't light up.

Embodiment of Du Bois's Talented Tenth, the light-skinned Washington, D.C., chapter that would have kicked out Bruce Nugent in his day. Dr. Cobb's diction had right edges when addressing the young. He and his cohort had never doubted for whom they fought. I felt sheepish, because he was paying my father a courtesy in giving me any of his time. I was not meant to know about sacrifice, that was the point, but in return I was certainly supposed to know more than my father's fidgeting and Dr. Cobb's waiting smile said I did.

(Decades later, James supplied the answer to Dr. Cobb's query: the central problem of *Julius Caesar* is who will strike the first blow.)

Back in May, a terrible riot had broken out in the black neighborhood of Liberty City, across the bay from the Fontainebleau.
The Miami Beach hotel was buzzing with NAACP committee
meetings on the upcoming election, on the thousands of acres
of agricultural land black people were losing every year in the
South. What good were they doing, delegates asked themselves at
their after-dinner windows, angered by the demand they tour the
charred wreckage of Liberty City or else, like they didn't come from
such places themselves. Althea Simmons, stalwart head of the
Washington office, was already calling it the Miami Riot of 1980,
noting that there had not been disturbances on such a scale since
the 1960s. I escaped through the palm leaves, under a profusion of
stars, stealing away to embrace one of South Beach's finest.

Otherwise, I was a bartender back at the Columbia Medical
School Faculty Club.

> *Poetry*
>> *is like mining radium.*
> *For every gram*
>> *you work a year.*
> *For the sake of a single word*
>> *you waste*
> *a thousand tons*
>> *of verbal ore.*

On the way to the subway, I came across the John Brown Group
selling 'Death to the Klan/Smash White Supremacy' buttons, pro-
moting the *Clark v. Nixon* lawsuit, hawking battered paperbacks,
Reader's Digest condensed editions, and frayed dictionaries. Middle-
aged white women with cropped hair manned the table of Assata
Shakur leaflets and Black Republic newspapers.

I asked one of the women if their efforts were related to the
massacre in Greensboro, North Carolina, last fall. The Commu-

nist Workers' Party, a Maoist breakaway group, had given up on New York City and gone to North Carolina to find workers to organize. White workers ignored them, but black textile workers began to listen. The Klan attacked, leaving half a dozen demonstrators dead. She wasn't CWP, she said. I could tell that she didn't want to give a rival faction too much credit for having been killed.

— Part 6 —

She asked me to get her a copy of *Lolita*. Shadows vanished from the hot September pavement. First a few drops. They hit me as I walked next door. It was going to be a relief from the humidity. As soon as I stepped from the bookshop, the sky broke. The wind swept the rain down West Ninety-fifth Street in Boxer Rebellion waves, hundreds of thousands of drops attacking my shoes. I didn't go back for an umbrella. It was fun to have to make a run for the subway. People were squealing.

Sleepless Nights was on the trade paperback bestseller list. Elizabeth said she found it bewildering. She was accustomed to the attention of her small circle. She sometimes laughed that the *Review* was one of those publications that not many bought but everyone seemed to have read. The possibility, the reality, of a larger audience made her retreat into herself.

—Your work has a life separate from yours.

She showed me a story she'd written over the summer, 'The Bookseller,' which I found marvelous, subtle, sweet, unusual. Roger is the owner of a small, narrow secondhand bookstore, 'and he and his shop are rooted like cabbages in the mixed sod of Columbus Avenue.'

He loves books, but he doesn't read them. Yet he takes them in somehow. He knows the first line of everything, the first page of everything. He is a friend of literature, sensitive enough to reputations to prefer 'Crocodiles' to 'Sanatorium.' She imagines him large, benign, crumpled, wellborn, faded, pleasantly anarchic, passive.

> The byways of life have captured him, even *captivated* his
> mind, and it is possible to think that his contentment

comes from never having to set out the dishes, watch
the oven, make drinks, freeze ice, have coffee cups ready
and table chairs assembled.

She makes her bookseller somewhat comic as a presence on the
street, a topic of conversation among loyal customers and friends,
a cheerful writer of unwanted, hopeless manuscripts, inhabitant
of a junk-filled upstairs apartment. He is the prize silently fought
over by three women who have attached themselves to his store.

It is a love of the city that Elizabeth as the writer shares with
her character, the flow of audiences after film and opera, the Chinese restaurant and all-night Puerto Rican grocery, 'the palmist's
storefront broom closet,' 'the Saturday-night rubbish.' 'And the
sluggish waters at the curb stir under the tidal moon.'

Elizabeth was particularly pleased to have found a place for a
graduate school experience at Columbia that to her was a sort of
firsthand witnessing of a change in taste, reputation.

> Roger. I can see again his large head bowed, as if in
> grief, in the Milton seminar some years ago. He brought
> to graduate studies his pen and his notebook and the
> steady downward tug of his dilatory, procrastinating
> nature. It was the modernist T. S. Eliot and his resur-
> rection of the metaphysical poets that had led Roger
> disastrously to the seventeenth century. By the perverse
> authority of institutions, he was brutally dragged by
> his light curls into the study of Milton, a poet not even
> very high in the regard of Eliot at the time.

Barbara loved the story, Elizabeth reported. *The New Yorker* did,
too, she admitted. She was encouraged, because it was to her the
start of a new novel, which for a long time she referred to as 'The
Bookseller.'

The weather went back to steamy as soon as the downpour stopped. It was too hot for anything other than salads and a strange Polish dish of cranberry and boiled egg.

—I feel as though I've had a stroke, Elizabeth said, wiping perspiration from her forehead and pulling her hair back.

It had been three years since Lowell's death. We didn't say much about that. After a while, one couldn't.

As it was, Elizabeth had had to face down a book about the Lowell family by C. David Heymann. She said it was cheap, like stealing jewelry. The letter from Lowell that Heymann cited in his notes was probably a forgery. The date had been moved to five days before Lowell's death, as if he would have paid attention to Heymann in the drama of his visit to Ireland. The quote from Lowell about Heymann's Pound book was probably a forgery, too.

When the galleys of Heymann's book were sent around, Richard Eberhart wrote a long note in praise of the book. Elizabeth said Eberhart was probably pleased with how he was portrayed. Elizabeth had written him a letter, which he had not answered. She had seen him at the Academy, but he didn't mention it.

—He has no moral sense.

She noted that the letter from Eberhart was not printed on Heymann's jacket.

Heymann came once to see her when Lowell was in England.

—Without tape recorder, pencil, or pad.

He wanted to know when Lowell was returning to America, and if he would see him when he did. Elizabeth told him she didn't know. He stayed twenty minutes. Later, Lowell said not to help him; he didn't like the Pound book; he didn't like Heymann.

Heymann wrote two letters in which he asked very perfunctory questions. She didn't answer. They were about dates. She thought he could look them up himself. In his acknowledgments, Heymann said Elizabeth had endured a lengthy interview. He sought to imply that she participated in the project, that there was an intimacy between them. He took remarks she'd made in interviews elsewhere and pretended she'd spoken to him. He rewrites information from *Sleepless Nights*; he distorts '91 Revere Street.'

—Cousin Billy is made up. Cal was just being funny.

Heymann had them married in the wrong place; had them go to weekends in the Hamptons. He put Lowell at Quo Vadis and 21, nightclubs where he'd never been, she said. Heymann had Lowell washing his face with lye, one of the falsehoods Caroline told her editor. Jean Stafford supposedly snuffed out a cigarette in the palm of her hand. Elizabeth said she'd no idea where that came from, but it wasn't true. Heymann claimed to have a letter from Stafford, but then withdrew the claim when challenged.

Harvard and the estate refused him permission to quote from Lowell's letters. The Heymann book upset her, had caused her weeks of agitation. Nothing in the Amy Lowell or James Russell Lowell sections of his book couldn't be found in Martin Duberman's biography of James Russell Lowell.

Her aim was to expose the corruption of Heymann's scholarship, so that no one would regard it as a serious source. One of her summer projects was to write a memoir in answer to Heymann, a deliberate document, in a finished, literary style, to be deposited with Lowell's papers. She was the only one alive who knew what was what, she said. She read me the beginning and it was very beautiful.

(Saskia Hamilton appends to *The Dolphin Letters* 'Cal Working, Etc.,' which she identifies as excerpts from notes and a letter Lizzie wrote to Ian Hamilton, around 1981 or 1982. There are phrases in the two and a half pages that sound like what she read to me in the sweltering autumn of 1980, but they have to do with what she talked a lot about, so I could have read or heard the phrases somewhere else: how the emphasis on his madness, his breakdowns that she likens to 'brain fever' in nineteenth-century fiction, distracted from or obscured his dedication to work.

Strange, what I have written about the working habits, the coming out of the hospital is not new. It is what I wrote in the 'notebook' I tore up, which did not seem to have a proper context for such reflections. It turns out that one has very few ideas finally and I have written more or less these same things to friends over the years in letters that also contained my distress over Cal's actions . . .

I thought she made for posterity a careful going-through of the facts and the poems. I have not yet begun to look back through some boxes of my own.)

BARBARA CALLED. She was eating with Helen, her daughter, who was going back to Berkeley the next day. Elizabeth loved to stock up leftovers. She shoved the chicken back in the refrigerator and we went down the street to Dazzels.

Helen wasn't the little girl in sneakers with frizzy hair, hating Spence. She said she didn't like Berkeley, either.

Elizabeth was doing the Nabokov lectures for the *Times*. She and Barbara discussed the Nabokov–Edmund Wilson letters.

Elizabeth said that Wilson appreciated Nabokov as a cultured European, but he didn't really get Nabokov's work, didn't quite like the books.

Barbara said Wilson teased the writers he liked and would have nothing to do with writers who weren't worth such a correspondence.

Elizabeth said Wilson was troubled by Nabokov's perverse ideas about literature, Dostoevsky being sloppy, for instance. Wilson didn't like puns, and he had this notion that Nabokov's English was somehow not right, going on about usage. He didn't like *Lolita*, which Elizabeth considered scandalous of him.

—Elena did, Barbara countered.

Wilson's widow. She edited his *Lectures and Writings on Literature*, a book I remembered on the table when Lowell was alive.

The really troubling issue of Karlinsky's edition of their letters was Wilson correcting Nabokov's Russian.

—Nabokov was very polite about that, Elizabeth said, laughing.

Jason tried to get his company to take *Lolita*. However, a real greaseball, Barbara said, some paperback guy with a name like Simon Hook, came to meet Nabokov and asked him a lot of smutty questions about how he found out such and such about schoolgirls. Véra Nabokov, very refined, explained that every day Nabokov rode the buses with note cards, observing.

In *Pnin*, there was a reference to a book called *A B* or something like that, written by a schoolmaster. When Elizabeth met Nabokov, she asked him about it. Trunks of books used to come to his father's house in St. Petersburg. One such book was *Antony Brade, A Story of Schoolboy Life,* by Robert Traill Spence Lowell.

Mary McCarthy didn't much like *Lolita* at first. Barbara remembered that the footnote of her letter said Bowden thought the nymphet was America.

(I thought she praised it in *Partisan Review*.)

Clive James said Wilson was easy to underestimate, Barbara said.

I glanced between them, recognizing the name of a *New York Review* writer equally at home in *The London Review*. I also thought I sensed that Barbara didn't mind, if she was not relieved, that Elizabeth was writing on the lectures for someplace else.

Wilson was shocked by *Lolita*, Elizabeth noted.

Barbara said that Edmund didn't mind writing that goo about working-class women, but not about a young girl.

She, the editor, seized the check, adding that the Toomer revisions she asked for would take no more than an hour. I'd been at work on the piece forever.

We dropped off mother and daughter at their door, the street deranged with mugginess.

Some couple in Talcottville had written about Edmund Wilson, a book full of silly remarks, Elizabeth said, ringing her bell. She thought Barbara was insisting on some points out of loyalty.

—You've come through. She meant that I had won a measure of acceptance from Barbara. Jacob was staying in Elizabeth's house in Castine, then going to Yaddo. He and I had become friends. He said they had a dog named Smoky who committed suicide. Smoky ran into the traffic of Columbus Avenue, sat down, and looked back at them. Harriet's large brown cat, Summer, disapeared early in my knowing them.

Elizabeth was heading to Maine to close up the house. She said I should get a copy of *Lolita*, too, so we could talk about it, the work of a stateless European who became a great novelist in English, she added. I'd see that line in print much later.

—You don't know *Speak, Memory*? Come *again*. What have you and Luc been doing.

I MET LUC at his favorite Ukrainian restaurant, on the corner of Ninth Street and Second Avenue. I sat at the counter, reading a version of Tsvetaeva. The world's literature could only come to me as English translation.

To drink of pleasures as they ever flow

Luc arrived in his usual crumpled corduroys, a venerable jacket over his T-shirt in spite of the Apache weather, the look completed by solemn black shoes. He didn't ask why I myself was in my grandfather's soggy dark jacket and trousers with the unusable right pocket. He nodded at the frayed tie, one of Lowell's that Elizabeth had given me. He understood it as code for me having a meeting with adults. He had a side gig helping Gore's boyfriend, Howard Austen, to pack.

He had sat through a five-and-a-half-hour film shot in Nice in 1919. He loved it. He was interested in B. Traven again, in the books coming out identifying him. He said John Berger's essay on the Kertesz photograph of a red hussar leaving his wife and child taught him how he himself could reflect on history.

Luc always placed his desk so that he wrote facing a wall. He had a way of usually looking fresh faced, but at that moment was looking a little rough, like his dream filterless cigarette brand. In the psychodrama of him and Eva, sister, roommate, guitarist, and San Francisco, I worried that the person most likely to get hurt was the most innocent of them.

We moved on to Nightbirds, a small bar across the street with a front door of frosted cocktails etched into the glass. He agreed that Susan's essay on Canetti in the new issue of the *Review* was good and I said the Updike on Nabokov was only okay, but Luc hadn't tried it.

Jim was back from Mannheim, where *Permanent Vacation* was a success. It was selected for the Australian and Berlin festivals, and also for German television, the lifeline of independent film, Luc said. Sara's film would be next, he said.

Summer's soundtrack was still playing from boom boxes. 'Computer Love' by Kraftwerk escorted us from corner to corner. I kept to myself, after all, the ten-minute teatime interview I'd had with George Plimpton at *The Paris Review*. Impressed though he was that my reference came from Elizabeth Hardwick, he said up front that they weren't looking for anyone aggressive or ambitious. Luc was going to Maine with a former roommate from West 101st Street. No one had heard from Felice in a while.

The odors, the streets of New York, the litter, the crumbling buildings, the threatened taxes against winnings at legal numbers parlors.

—How are you?

—A little bit sick.

—I couldn't get you all last night.

—Yeah.

—I've been sick that way, too.

Elizabeth was in Castine. Jacob was gone. He'd got someone in to clean so there was little for her to do to close up the house, she said. Some drunk had plowed through the alders between her and Sally Austin. She said she should begin staying in Castine later than Labor Day.

—I'm as cozy as I can be. Coffee and electric heat.

My sister Donna had gone back into the hospital, but was on weekend leave. She and my father blamed the Dexedrine in her diet pills. My mother proposed a visit to Mrs. Roney, the beautician with the basement shop in her house back in the old neighborhood. Every black woman my mother knew had been going to Mrs. Roney all my life. Then came the Afro, and the battles mothers lost to daughters, fathers to sons, but everyone kept returning to the ministrations in the old neighborhood.

(Where are the Afro picks of yesterday, combs with long prongs and a handle in the form of a clinched fist?)

Indianapolis was not called Naptown because it was the sleepy crossroads of America, Donna said. Indianapolis was the headquarters of Madam C. J. Walker's company, founded before World War I. She manufactured products for nappy hair, Donna concluded.

(Mike Ransom, who had succeeded his father as the general manager of the Madam C. J. Walker Manufacturing Company, the writer Jill Nelson's uncle, was a hero to Donna because she loved White Castle hamburgers and in the early 1960s he led the sit-in against the restaurant, locally. Judge Ransom, as he was known, took to reading *The New York Review of Books* and my father said now there was a friend.

Madam C. J. Walker's great-granddaughter and future biographer, A'Lelia Bundles, had won every prize at the sprawling New Frontier high school I went to, and she never let school administrations use her exceptionalism against other black students. Her family had been among the first to storm across the red line into the highest-rated school district in the state. These Walker families did not go to the long-segregated summer resorts of the Great Lakes region. They went east, to Martha's Vineyard, to the big leagues.)

Now my sister was being taken to get the latest thing in black hair.

The Jheri Curl relaxed the tight coils of Afro sponginess into terrier silkiness. My father said every black postman or black human resources director was now walking around looking like Lionel Richie, their hair treated by the traditional scalp sauce mixed with something he called TGA.

He said it acted like lye and I could hear my mother in the background say emphatically that it was not lye. I listened on my end as my father said they would never have let me get a conk had I wanted one and that was what a Jheri Curl was, processed hair, straightened black hair, so why were they encouraging Donna to do that to her head. She had his mother's hair.

After her hair got waxed and looped, my tearful sister said she was glad I wasn't there to see her and that she couldn't wait to go back inside.

They took her back early.

Pat was going in for tests in another wing of the same hospital the next day.

My parents said there was nothing I could do. I didn't keep them long.

The telephone booth on the corner of West Seventy-seventh Street and Columbus Avenue was infamous to patrons of the several gay bars in the area, ringing wildly at four o'clock in the morning, growling with the voices of guys into S&M.

ELIZABETH, KNOCKED OUT from her weekend in Castine closing up the house, said she had tried to stay clear of the whole thing between Mary and Lillian at first.

—Iraq and Iran, blowing up each other's pipelines.

She still wasn't smoking. She wrung her hands. We'd done her doors again. They looked like oak, sort of.

—I can imagine being the queen of England but I can't imagine being Lillian Hellman.

She said that Barbara cut her dead on the street after her piece on *The Little Foxes* appeared. And it had been in their own Paper. Why, indeed, Barbara had never been taken in by Lillian's act, particularly. One of Lowell's translations in *Near the Ocean* was dedicated to Hellman.

—Lillian's memory is very self-serving. She just can't tell the truth. All she is saying is, Look I'm an awful person, but I'm tough and courageous.

We were eating in the kitchen. She was still pretty much just back. I didn't mind not schlepping everything to the dining room, did I.

(—One of the kitchen people, Ada Long, Lizzie's close friend of many years from the University of Alabama, would call herself.)

Mary was injudicious and she also spoke true. Yet Lillian Hellman had, indeed, defied the House Committee on Un-American Activities, refusing to testify, to name names.

In 1952, Hellman said to the committee that she was not willing, then or in the future, to get in trouble people who had not been disloyal, or to save herself by accusing the innocent. Hellman said she'd answer questions about herself, not about anyone else. Her famous retort to McCarthyism:

> I cannot and will not cut my conscience to fit this year's
> fashions, even though I long ago came to the conclu-
> sion that I was not a political person and could have no
> comfortable place in any political group.

Murray Kempton's review of *Scoundrel Time* in the June 10, 1976, issue of the *Review* was the first writing of his that I was aware of as being by him, this hero journalist:

I have never quite understood upon what altar Miss Hellman's moral authority was consecrated; but that authority is there, was there even before the apotheosis of her
risky yet grand appearance before the Committee on Un-
American Activities . . .

When we consider the general practice of using memory so earnestly as an instrument for mendacity, it is a
sufficient miracle for Miss Hellman to be so honest a
witness; and our admiration for her integrity cannot
grow smaller for a final impression that *Scoundrel Time* is
not quite true. Honesty and truth are not just the same
thing, since the first has to do with character and the
second with self-understanding of a cruder kind than
hers.

The year before Hellman's congressional appearance, Dashiell
Hammett had gone to jail for refusing to divulge the names of do-
nors to a bail fund that aided Communists. Hammett was a Communist, but his stand had mostly to do with a feeling that he had
to keep his word, as he said. Hellman had been closer to the party
than she wanted to say in *Scoundrel Time*, but it was maybe to Hammett that she had to prove herself worthy, by sticking to a simple
idea. In other words, her motives were as romantic as they were
political. The best points are always domestic, Kempton says.

(Hellman's previous memoir, *Pentimento*, would turn out to be
the undoing of her reputation as a hostage to principles, in spite of
Scoundrel Time. In *Pentimento*, Hellman remembered the wartime
heroism of a friend, 'Julia.' The Austrian authorities had knowledge of only one American woman who had been in the resistance
in Vienna during World War II. The story Hellman told mirrored
that of a woman she did not know, a friend of Stephen Spender's,
alive in Princeton. The suspicion that 'Julia' was a fabrication, a
rip-off, figured largely in McCarthy's dossier on Hellman.)

Elizabeth imitated the scene in the film of *Julia* when Jane Fonda as Lillian Hellman types and then holds her head, types and seizes her head. She said it was the absurdity of trying to show the creative process on the screen, like Kirk Douglas as van Gogh, shiny and croaking.

She said the terrible thing was that William Jovanovich, Mary's publisher, hated the *Review* so much he wouldn't let any of the essays from her forthcoming collection appear in it. To print any of Mary's wonderful essays in the *Review* would let everyone know where they stood on the lawsuit. Barbara was of the opinion that the Paper should take no specific stand, not even a letter from Elizabeth. It was too bad, Elizabeth went on, because a serious essay would put Mary above the conflict. Jovanovich wasn't doing her a favor. She suspected Mary felt he'd been so nice to her she couldn't offend him.

Then, too, an essay appearing in the *Review* could make a collection, establish a climate for a book. That was true of *Seduction and Betrayal*, it was true of Susan's essays. The *Review* created discussion, anticipation, publicity worth a thousand advertisements. It put a book in the air. She said Mary desperately needed a serious book after the last few novels.

ELIZABETH HAD ADMIRED Susan's piece on Canetti and thought more of the Updike on Nabokov than I did. Susan and David were in Japan, she said. Gore was funny in his review of Edmund Wilson's diary *The Thirties: From Notebooks and Diaries of the Period*, reading it as the musings of a citizen in good standing in 'The Alcoholic Republic of Letters.'

Mary was appalled at Wilson's diary, Elizabeth said, because of the sex. That was ironic, considering how proud Wilson was when Mary McCarthy was his, when he felt in possession of her. He betrayed the dumpy guy's disbelief that he had won a pretty girl. For

Wilson, education was seduction. There were stories about him locking Mary McCarthy in a room in order to force her to write.

(Several years in the future was Lizzie's review of a biography of Edmund Wilson by one of those, to her, absurd professional biographers who had also written one of Lowell. The review was an occasion to knock biography and to do something with her long-held thoughts on Wilson.

She praises him for his 'many volumes on an astonishing range of subjects,' his wonderful clarity, his 'capacity of mind,' but, throughout, the piece is flecked with her amusement at his confidence as both a fornicator and a diarist.

She remembers what Mary had to say about her life as Mrs. Wilson, a marriage that was ending just as Lizzie was getting to know her. By the time of Lizzie's essay on Wilson, McCarthy had written in her memoirs of

> her detestation of Wilson's body and soul, information provided by her decision to become his wife. She had disguised him in satirical portraits in her fiction, a disguise on the order of sunglasses.

Lizzie observes that they had a son and that although Mary 'added' two more husbands after she and Wilson divorced, that marriage, 'successfully escaped,' still rankled.

> She had much in common with Wilson, especially in the need to instruct. Some persons are not content to have a deep aversion to another but feel the command to have others share the documented distaste.

Mary wanted to instruct Wilson's subsequent wife, the 'cosmopolitan' Elena Thornton, in 'the true nature of her husband.'

We had a good time with *The Triple Thinkers*, from that canvas bag of works by Wilson that she'd forced on me a few years before. The nerve to say as Wilson did that Byron's achievement was to have 'raised the drunken monologue to a literary form.' He should talk, I thought at the time, sitting in the West End. But Wilson conveyed the excitement of his encounter with Pushkin's *Evgeni Onegin*. 'He throws himself at her feet.'

Wilson felt himself knowledgeable about Russian and Pushkin, she'd write, and she praised his prose translation of 'The Bronze Horseman.'

She agreed with Wilson about Nabokov's translation of *Onegin*,

> a folly of . . . earnest magnitude . . . attacked by Slavicists for its wild, peculiar vocabulary in English and for its 'original' dissertations on matters of prosody. Wilson was critically dismayed and moved without hesitation to say as much.

She wrote that Wilson's criticisms of Nabokov's book on Gogol, 'one of the most exhilarating, engaging, and original works ever written by one writer about another,' for what he saw as Nabokov's 'poses, perversities and vanities,' revealed the 'irreconcilable difference' in their styles of composition.

Wilson's complex, speculative chapter on Dickens in his collection *The Wound and the Bow* showed his method as a critic: to find the relationship between suffering and creativity. Meanwhile, Nabokov's lectures on *Bleak House* 'seize the novel as it is flying off the page, seize it with delight.'

In *Patriotic Gore*, she noted, Wilson's idea was that American prose fell into deplorable exaggeration in the first half of the nineteenth century, because of the influence of the sermon and public oratory. His 'shocking appraisal' of *The Scarlet Letter* as 'sluggish' and *Moby-Dick* as 'clottedly dense' told us why he could not find beauty in Nabokov's language. The Civil War, for Wilson, broke through the fabric of false eloquence in American prose. The Gettysburg Address was among his models.)

Nabokov's *Bleak House* lecture: '5. The sociological side, brilliantly stressed for example by Edmund Wilson in his collection of essays *The Wound and the Bow*, is neither interesting nor important.'

Back on the night we were talking about Wilson's diaries, I told Elizabeth that Nabokov's verdict against social context unsettled me, given that black literature constituted for me an ongoing work of history.

Nabokov also said in his lecture that the most important thing about a work was the tingle it sent down your spine. She said that was the judgment that haunted her.

I had to admit I'd learned from *To the Finland Station* (a book Susan dismissed) and I was wide awake throughout *Patriotic Gore*. Wilson on *Uncle Tom's Cabin* was more impressive to me than Baldwin on the book he read so repeatedly as a kid that his mother took it from him, he said. The intention of their essays was not the same, Elizabeth pointed out.

I was, I thought, indebted to Wilson for my introduction to Charlotte Forten. She came from a Philadelphia family of rich free black abolitionists. She kept an altogether vivid journal as a young woman in the 1850s, describing Massachusetts plant life, or the George Eliot novels that her Salem sewing circle was reading. Forten wrote in her journal in 1854:

> The character of Margaret Fuller interested me greatly; there is a charm even in reading of a nature so earnest and impassioned, combined with the richest mental endowments and possessing with all its defects so many qualities that were truly lovable, and worthy of the highest praise.

Forten made translations from Latin and French, grateful for her learning, not overly proud of it. I was the one who was snobbish in retrospect on her behalf. In 1862, she went to teach freed black people in South Carolina, bright and beautiful.

—How interesting.

(Forten's poetry was not yet available in book form, only an edition of her journal that I hunted out in the New York Public Library. Benjamin Quarles talked about the Forten family in *The Black Abolitionists*, but this morning I can't find the book I got from my father's swaybacked shelves. I'm embarrassed I felt so beholden to Wilson. It wasn't until I read *The Journals of Charlotte Forten Grimké*, edited by Brenda Stevenson, in Henry Louis Gates, Jr.'s series, the Schomburg Library of Nineteenth-Century Black Women Writers, that I got annoyed with Wilson for saying that she was just a colored girl yearning for culture. Her pride could handle it, Wilson's assumption of superiority that was actually a failure of imagination on the part of the Princeton boy from 'the minor gentry' who himself never stopped reading.)

However, *The Thirties* to me was not just the record of hangovers or of Wilson's success at making cunts throb. He knows what Scottsboro is about, but even so his pages crackle with the nigger caretaker at the shooting lodge, the niggers playing on combs, the niggers in houseboats in down-at-heel Virginia, where there are nigger cabins among the light green corn and the blue-gray cabbage, and nigger baseball in an open field, and one enthusiastic Negro with round shoulders and blue overalls at a coal-miners-union meeting. Up in Tennessee, he saw a nigger woman by a crooked cypress log, and her indifference to him and his party bothered Wilson a little. He saw more niggers beading stems in a tobacco barn and visited an old house with a cypress alley and was told that the place had been looted by niggers when the owners died.

I didn't have to ignore such passages with Elizabeth and she did not downplay the racism of local color in American literature as peripheral rather than integral to much of it. (Is this when we talked about Berryman and Mr. Bones?) But history could be neither denied nor rewritten. It couldn't be escaped, and I had to accept who

Edmund Wilson was, meaning his limitations, especially since every writer has beliefs or reflects them, a mind in its time, and his was a superior one in critical matters, certainly not all of them but some of them important. Not all journals and notebooks are preserved or are known to us for the same reasons, but Wilson's did seem to her intended for publication, we're all so fascinated with ourselves.

She was prepared to lend me more Hawthorne, which I didn't recall having expressed an interest in. I faked a reason and said my problem was how to want to read Hawthorne after high school classes in *The Scarlet Letter* and *The House of the Seven Gables*. She left me to scrape the dishes and went into her living room. Quickly, she returned to the kitchen table with Henry James's *American Essays*.

He was touched by Hawthorne's inability to respond to Paris or Italy in his travel notebooks. His protective Yankee detachment. She liked what he said about Hawthorne's 'excessively natural mind.' That was not what she was looking for. I wasn't going to turn on her dishwasher for two plates and so faced the sink. 'Never was a man of literary genius less a man of letters.' Well, that wasn't so great and not what she was looking for, either. She thanked me as I wiped my hands, because she hated unloading the dishwasher in the morning.

—Sit down. 'It is the story as old as the custom of marriage, the story of the husband, the wife, and the lover, but bathed in a misty moonshiny light . . .'

She read from James's remembrance of Hawthorne the two long passages about *The Scarlet Letter* and *The House of the Seven Gables*, 'the ancient virgin Hepzibah with her turban,' all the way until Hawthorne had wearied of Lenox, Massachusetts. She said *The Blithedale Romance* was the one about Brook Farm. I put her hint away in the refrigerator with other stuff.

It wasn't as late as we had thought. We'd started so early. We watched *The MacNeil/Lehrer Report.* Carter refused to debate John Anderson and someone was talking about Anderson's candidacy as a creation of the journalists.

—That's something Nixon would say, she said.

She loved Gogol's word *poshlost.*

ELIZABETH ENJOYED SUSAN'S party at NYU for *Under the Sign of Saturn.* Then there was dinner with the Epsteins; the Pritchetts were in town. She walked to *The New Yorker,* went shopping, walked to Blair Clark's, rode the bus home. She had a new hairdresser, no longer Kenneth's, but Bella's, on Seventy-second Street. She was going ahead with *The Awakening* script. She went to see the musical *42nd Street* with Corliss Lamont. He didn't bother her as much he used to. She liked him.

I found Kate Chopin's stories, *Bayou Folk,* in the library, and all those mammies forced me to resign from her fan club. Donna laughed when I told her.

Sterling was to read at the Y. I wasn't going. He was more than I knew what to do with. One time he said he was coming to town with the photographs and could I make a reservation for him at the Statler Hilton. I did. He never appeared. (I don't remember what photographs he was supposed to bring.)

Then he was in town again, reading at the Guggenheim. I had dinner with Elizabeth and was late, arriving in the middle of his rap. He was proud that he had never shaken hands with Carl Van Vechten, who, he said, had done more than bad liquor to corrupt the Negro. The Harlem Renaissance was a publishers' gimmick. It didn't last long enough to be called a renaissance and very few Harlemites were in it. Then again, he was in New York, so why not denounce the Harlem Renaissance, so annoyingly of interest everywhere.

—Harlem was the show window, the cashier's till.

He got so caught up in his grievances that he read only four poems in the end. He seemed bitter, starved for attention. I remembered that the first time I heard him read he charmed the audience with his digressions about stride piano, the shrewdness of the blues, A. E. Housman, Lena Horne. He was very short with me afterward. He said he was coming to see Fran the next day, but he did not appear.

> And so home, passing a nigger gentleman, perfectly fitted out in swallow tail and bowler and gold headed cane and what were his thoughts? Of the degradation stamped on him, every time he raised his hand and saw it black as a monkey's outside, tinged with flesh color within?

Virginia Woolf in her diary, volume five, in 1925, the kind of thing that would have cracked up me and Howard.

Howard came by the next night, glassy from a visit to Canon West at the Cathedral of St. John the Divine. The canon, high church, black, and queer, had given him advice on how to work things out with Brad, and every step required a lot of cocaine for me to understand, Aunt-Jemima-on-the-pancake-box amounts of it. We watched the Yankees bite the dust.

He remembered how into Bloomsbury we were when volume one of Woolf's diaries came out. With his serious expression, his mouth a straight line and his eyes aimed at you from deep woods, he said that we were young then. What were we now? Brad was giving up teaching to take a full-time modeling job back in Paris.

SHE WAS STILL combing out the tight curls courtesy of her new hairdresser. She said she was making a real New England dinner, boiling vegetables, the brisket of beef, cursing the slowness of it all.

I brought Elizabeth the slender galleys of McCarthy's *Ideas and the Novel*. She was going to see her at Princeton.

—Mary always says she doesn't believe in bound galleys.

I wanted to start with Mary McCarthy's assessment of *Jacob's Room*, Woolf's novel from 1922, as a 'position-paper for a Modernism that was Henry James's legacy,' he having 'scrubbed his sacred texts clean of the material factor.'

She liked the Mary who spoke of the 'wonderful reticence' of Henry James.

I hadn't read all of the James that McCarthy went into.

—I don't find him so difficult, Elizabeth said.

I had just finished *The Princess Casamassima*.

—*Premier temps*?

McCarthy talked about what Henry James had closed off for novelists who followed him. She talked about how hard discussion novels are, with history looming above the pages of the huge *Cancer Ward* and the huge *The Magic Mountain*. Her references were broad, from the expected to the forgotten to the always had been obscure. The novel of ideas was sometimes mistaken for the missionary novel, like Stowe's, but she meant works such as *Women in Love*, those novels of Lawrence's 'where reasoning occupies a large part of the narrative.'

Elizabeth recognized her old friend Mary in the passages on Stendhal, on Julien Sorel, who acted out his life according to ideas he got from books, even his lovemaking. Or she heard her true Mary in her wondering if mouthpieces like Levin could be done that way anymore, or was there too much disintegration and irony in life.

Elizabeth said she'd suggested to Bob and Barbara that Gore write on Mary's book for the *Review*.

—They both believe they are writing novels of ideas.

She put a halt to my summary of her two essays in the *Review* on the state of fiction.

(In one of the essays, 'Reflections on Fiction,' written in 1969, the novel is 'a long and complex creation':

> The parts bear a mysterious and clouded relation to the whole. The pages turn, one after another, and it is a distinguishing aspect of the novel that, around the next corner, almost anything can happen. We hardly know which to treasure most: expectation confounded or satisfied. A new chapter is a psychological shift and the interesting dislocations afforded by a flashback make great demands on the imagination.

And yet for all the detail, she goes on to say, it is hard to remember them, even to say what happened. You come away with a general impression. 'Exhilaration of the mind,' 'pleasure of the senses.' You were fascinated, you were convinced.

The novel asks time of the writer and the reader, she noted in the essay, what contemporary existence is determined to shorten. For the novels of the past, tranquility was a first condition, curiosity about human activities the second. New fiction will be written by altered psyches, she prophesized, seduction and sexual longing becoming the stuff of irony and satire.

In the large productions of Dickens, Thackeray, George Eliot, James, Conrad, or Proust, it was as though the energy of the readers went out to meet the inspiration of the writers. It wasn't plot that made these works so strong. After all, Victorian plot was pretty bad. The Russian novel was a critique of the English novel because it kept the exuberance and got rid of heavy plots.

Freud was the last great believer in plots, she says. Classical fiction had the coherence of crime and punishment, cause and effect. The mood of the contemporary writer was to admit 'manipulation and design,' a whispering from the wings that McCarthy called 'ventriloquism.'

In 'The Fiction Break-Up,' published in the *Review* in 1976, and later reprinted as 'The Sense of the Present,' she takes off from the novel that gave her such a vivid sense of what was happening in fiction, Renata Adler's *Speedboat*. I wondered why she gave Adler's novel so much attention. Elizabeth was full of praise for Grace Paley and she said Ann Beattie was one of the most influential writers since Salinger. She liked Tess Gallagher, and joked that Raymond Carver probably liked Gallagher more. But what was Adler? She said the woman in *Speedboat* felt no guilt paying attention only to herself and that contained a useful lesson for women.)

In 'Writing a Novel,' the narrator says that the only description in fiction she could remember was Princess Bolkonskaya's mustache in the opening pages of *War and Peace*. Elizabeth didn't remember that line at all, but it was true, she said.

Tentative, leaning back on the red sofa, saying it was her sinuses again, Elizabeth brought up something that she said had been bothering her for months. She was still hurt, distressed, that when she was last in Lexington, her one surviving sister said she really minded her description of Elizabeth's family in *Sleepless Nights* as poor. She'd been carrying that arrow in her side since the novel came out.

MY PARENTS WERE in Las Vegas, for my mother's postponed annual birthday junket. They were having a horrible time.

My father wanted to tell me his troubles. I was never ready for him to pull back the curtain.

being colored is an existential crisis I ain't solved yet

Pat, when I called her, asked me softly to keep in mind that everything that happened to us, our parents thought their fault.

Elizabeth phoned. Harriet had pneumonia. Her asthma meant that every time she got a cold it turned into this viral thing.

er.ly

—I feel so sorry for her. There is nothing I can do for her.

Elizabeth was upset, not easy to console, in something of a state.

She phoned again. She felt better when Harriet went into NYU hospital for tests. Their upstairs neighbor, Joan Brown, mother of Harriet's Dalton classmate Melissa, told her it was like the Hilton. She said Harriet was so appalled at what was happening to her she went to the library to look things up. In the hospital, she was in control, leading Elizabeth around, insisting they stop in to say hello to Dr. Brown. They asked her about mental illness in the family and Elizabeth heard her laugh. To get moving with a doctor made Elizabeth feel better.

Susan told her,

—You just hate bad medicine.

She said Susan told her that she was going to be outraged if they'd done nothing and just sent her home. She said Susan said she had a big *Wilson's Medical Dictionary*. Everyone in the Village came to her to talk about their illnesses. Elizabeth said Susan told her,

—What do you think these doctors are doing while you're getting dressed? Looking it up.

Elizabeth had her bourbon; I finished off the Margaux she had for Susan. Elizabeth was on the phone with Angela Carter, canceling the party for her. She thought Carter's essay on Colette in *The London Review* very odd. She'd calmed down enough to keep her date with Robert Rushmore to go to the ballet. Mary McCarthy and Jim West would be in town that weekend.

She thought Susan a little depressed, that she probably missed having Sharon around.

(Where had Sharon gone? Had they some break? Sharon was still at the *Review*. Prudence, romping away at the typesetting machine, like Bach's daughter, said Sharon and Barbara went after ballet tickets the way mob bosses scored season passes. Susan wouldn't know how without Sharon.)

Elizabeth said Susan was also annoyed at the Frank Kermode review in the November 6, 1980, issue. I said I didn't know why the *Review* chose him, a mind so distant from what she does. Kermode knew structuralism, but that was not the point, not what Susan did.

(James, before he closed my study door so he wouldn't have to field my questions anymore, remembered Kermode as a great critic, a polymath whose interest in narrative, for instance, resulted in a great tome on the Bible.

His introduction to the old Arden edition of *The Tempest* took me to a new way of looking at Shakespeare, to studies about the merchant companies trading in the Caribbean whose meetings and minutes Shakespeare clearly knew about.)

Elizabeth said Susan wouldn't like the Walter Kendrick review, either. He didn't get her at all. She said she was put out, much as she herself could knock Susan.

The next time she phoned, she said that Harriet was holding up well, though it was too early for her test results. Harriet was having her lungs looked at. Elizabeth was planning to be in recovery with her when Harriet woke. She said she loved the hospital, the experiment of family attendants, the efficiency of the place, the view of the Chrysler Building from Harriet's room.

Later, she reported that they'd put Harriet on powerful antibiotics. Elizabeth was due to lecture in St. Louis again in a few days and said she wouldn't mind seeing her friend Sally Higginbotham.

I WAS WASHING the dishes; Elizabeth and Barbara were at the kitchen table. Barbara had a secret. I was made to swear an oath and Barbara went to the wall phone and left a message with her doorman. Murray Kempton came over, pale, courtly, and thin. He had carefully combed white hair, a booming bass voice, and a bicycle clip still on one trouser leg.

We talked sports the whole time, the World Series and how cruel boxing is. He drank the Heinekens Elizabeth had left over from the summer. 'An alarming eminence,' someone said of someone.

ELIZABETH AND I watched the candidates' last television appearances, alternating between laughter and despair. A sort of soap opera set for terrifying Reagan and Bush, with a fake fireplace, and plenty of close-ups, long shots, dark suits, socks, Duke Wayne, Warren at Bunker Hill. Elizabeth noticed how much Reagan wanted 'to share' with us. Carter was filmed in a black church, with a children's choir singing 'Nothing but Blue Skies Do I See.' John Anderson posed in front of a bookcase.

—Wrong move, Elizabeth said. —Like the Fords getting off Air Force One and Betty was wrapped in a big fur while Jimmy Carter was out there in shirtsleeves.

We watched *The MacNeil/Lehrer Report*. Arthur Schlesinger, Jr., in a bow tie, was for Anderson.

—He hates Carter, Elizabeth said. —I like Arthur.

(When did we start to know about the Trail of Tears?)

Elizabeth missed the elegant Charlayne Hunter-Gault when she wasn't the host of the news analysis show.

Angela Davis was running for vice president on the Communist Party ticket.

—Gus Hall? That's like voting for Brezhnev. Is Gus still alive? Isn't he dead yet?

(Lucy remembered Gus Hall having breakfast with Alice Neel in a diner on Fourteenth Street some time back when.)

Elizabeth was suspicious of Angela Davis as an intellectual, because of the CP, but admired her consistency through the years. She made sense, never harangued. Maybe Davis felt she owed the party, given how the Communists had campaigned for her when she was imprisoned, as had the party for the Scottsboro Boys. She said she understood why black people remained in the party even after Budapest, but the party wasn't a serious place anymore.

Murray Kempton was fluent in Paul Robeson's grotesque moments as a Moscow loyalist. But wasn't Robeson beautiful.

She was not the fan my family was of Barbara Jordan, whose speech patterns didn't have enough echo of plain folk truth for her maybe. Jesse Jackson, Andrew Young, and Julian Bond were more her thing.

(Bond was from a family prominent in the history of black education and was head of the Southern Poverty Law Center. His wild side hadn't yet derailed his political fortunes. Ambassador Young backed the most militant choice in Zimbabwe, while Bayard Rustin didn't, a hero behind the times, I thought, so wrong. As for folked-out Jesse Jackson, who wore his bloodied dashiki a little too long, even for reasons of rebuke, he was the arsonist in the cellar just then for having called at the last midterm election for black people to support the Republican Party in order to teach the Democrats that black voters had alternatives.)

But she wouldn't want Harriet to marry a black man, because of the problems the children would have.

I said miscegenation didn't bother white America when black women were not given a choice.

She said I was more of a racist than she was, because I only liked white boys.

I would have let her put the dagger away, but she said white women with black men were inferior Desdemona types and black men with white women weren't serious.

No more William Styron for her, with his poor white girl from the South taking a beating in Harlem and jumping off the roof in his first novel. She'd never heard of Dorothy West's novel about a rich white woman with a big car and a black lover in it to show off or Paule Marshall's huge island novel of an interracial couple's intellectual romance, the one with the really awful title of *The Chosen*

Place, the Timeless People. What did she think Chester Himes was all about and, by the way, Vivaldo in Baldwin's *Another Country* was the sexiest white man in black American literature.

—Color me Flo. She waved an imaginary flag of surrender.

We followed the exploits of Florynce Kennedy, the black attorney and feminist always sporting a cowboy hat around town. Kennedy scared white women's groups and black women's groups alike. Kennedy said in her opinion oppression did not improve people.

But it wasn't really funny. Percy Sutton's research firm concluded half of blacks wouldn't vote. My parents were in mourning for the courts already.

Elizabeth was trying to diet and not smoke and drink so much, forgoing bourbon and wine. She turned chicken, stirred broccoli. We argued over Felix Rohatyn's article on the election. I disliked it; she thought it was good, not aimed to please either side.

She was going to watch the election returns with Barbara. Kempton would be in Washington. Murdoch didn't give him much to do, because he was not for Reagan.

She said Barbara and Murray went everywhere together, holding hands at Charles Rosen's concert, at dinner with Irene Worth and Stephen Spender. We laughed about the joy of meeting someone who likes you after years of thinking nothing would ever happen.

They sounded so out and about to me, I was amazed their romance was still regarded as a secret.

—There's a double standard.

Ian Hamilton was writing the biography of Lowell. The *Review* sent over Hamilton's piece on C. David Heymann.

—It's worse than *nothing.*

She was adamant that the piece as it stood could not be printed.

—One is never satisfied. Think of Madame Stravinsky off to London to exhibit her paintings, Elizabeth said.

Barbara had her girls and then she had elders she paid her

respects to, like Dorothea Tanning or Vera Stravinsky. She was devoted, but the Stravinsky household and mad and maybe brilliant Robert Craft as the keeper of the flame had its irresistible elements of comedy. Stravinsky's children had sued Madame.

—I don't know why people say I am unkind to the children, Elizabeth said in imitation of Barbara imitating Madame: —They are not children. They are all over sixty years old.

And a friend could find herself in the position of not being able to explain to her best friend why the great connection she had imagined with Craft had also been on offer to other women at the same time. The old friend would have to explain how she knew that that was not just passing on gossip.

I WAS READING Gayl Jones's novellas for Fran, *The Vampire Diaries* and *The Rainbow Hunter*. In the longer of the two, a brilliant sculptor is always trying to kill her husband and the traveling writer narrator doesn't hide her vanity at her own strangeness. But I really had no job, no place to go, and the Toomer got longer. Barbara said to give her a couple of days. I was still being outgunned by Bob Silvers. He studied up on everything that came in.

Prudence had given her notice, though the only thing she could bring herself to say on her résumé was that she could operate a GE coffeemaker.

Then Barbara had to cancel our appointment. She said she had been on the phone all day to her sister in Boston, because their old mother was going into McLean, the mental hospital. She was worked up about it, she said, and her sister more so.

Barbara screamed back at someone that the essay on the Polish writer who had just been awarded the Nobel Prize that had been on Bob's desk for ages was probably still on his desk, thank you.

—She's always been a bully, she said of her mother into the phone.

Elizabeth was worried what the *Times* would make of her Nabokov rap. It was much on her mind. She read me the opening, which was excellent. She phoned again to say she was hysterical, realizing she had to start over to get in the lectures, to conform to the *Times* way. The Blackmur incident made her hesitant about what the *Times* thought of her approach to books.

VIDAL WAS AWFUL on Mary McCarthy's *Ideas and the Novel*, she said. He scarcely mentioned Mary's book, except for what she says about humanity having found in film 'a narrative medium that is incapable of thought,' on the grounds that the camera was inarticulate. But he was not that gripping on Thomas Love Peacock. She did not agree with Vidal's positive assessment of Dawn Powell. I dumped my grandfather's frayed coat on the banister by her front door.

—And he has this boring idea about novels written just to be taught at universities.

'The serious novel,' Vidal called it. Mostly about 'the doings and feelings, often erotic, of white middle-class Americans,' the tone 'solemn' and 'vatic.' The serious novel required no invention, just sincerity. 'The Serious Novel is of no actual interest to anyone, including the sort of people who write them.' He is as contemptuous of the low, what he calls 'the conglomerate-publishers,' the commercial enterprise that relied on precedent in the search for what would sell. He was not the satirist he thought he was, she said. 'Posterity is a permanent darkness where no whistle sounds.'

—It was less than nothing, Elizabeth said.

Walter Cronkite presented the news and we got upset again over Reagan's big win, the hit list of liberal senators, including Birch Bayh, my parents' favorite, the long-serving liberal representing Indiana. We watched *The MacNeil/Lehrer Report*.

—Carter has a lot to answer for, she said.

She read aloud from *A Tomb for Boris Davidovich* by Danilo Kiš and told me to take it with me. Brodsky called the contents 'cautionary tales.' I got from the book something about form and use of history. Elizabeth was off to meet Russians in L.A. for the weekend.

Being broke let me stay home with Kiš, and with novels by Alejo Carpentier, a Cuban writer who grew up in France, and Cyprian Ekwensi, the Nigerian writer of Baldwin's generation who was a fascinating introduction to urban realism in African literature.

I was scavenging in my grandfather's time-thinned cashmere overcoat for coins fallen in the lining. I was reading when Elizabeth telephoned to say she was back and would I go to a bookshop on my lunch hour and check *The Charterhouse of Parma* for '*cavaliere servente*.' She was going over proofs of 'The Bookseller' from *The New Yorker* and that was not in *The New Yorker*'s Scott Moncrieff translation, only '*cicisbeo*.' But both were in Margaret Shaw's translation, in a Penguin paperback.

I copied out the phrase and went back to phone Elizabeth from my temp job working for Irene Skolnick, the subsidiary rights director of Harcourt Brace Jovanovich and a friend of Fran's. Elizabeth was pleased she'd been right that '*cavaliere servente*' was in it, something she gives the character Roger to say from his acquaintance with page 1 of another classic.

IT WAS A beautiful Saturday, clear, crisp, not too cold. I returned books for Elizabeth to the Society Library. Central Park was crowded with families of cyclists, people walking dogs, boys playing frisbee, joggers with thick thighs, super white people on horseback, the whir of racing cyclists, groups dancing on skates to disco, tracing figures and doing patterns, lovers embracing near the rowboats, mothers carrying infants, kids flat out on skateboards, people reading in Sheep Meadow, the leaves crunching under us tan, yellow, orange, red, and brown, the wind trying to run around.

The Nigerian exhibition at the Metropolitan Museum was

beautiful, if small. I wanted the brass and zinc heads, and the mudfish stool. I had to check the dates, the faces and urns looked so contemporary, not hundreds of years old, and Stanley Crouch arrived with several of his friends.

I walked back across the park to West Sixty-seventh Street. Elizabeth was trying to compose a letter to someone she'd taught whose new book was going to make a fortune.

—Paperback sale. Literary Guild. Motion picture sale. The works.

She said that if you're writing a story, a narrative, you can write every day, book after book, a flow of scenes and dialogue and character. And if one book is a bestseller, the others tend to be bestsellers as well.

—That's the way it goes, unless something awful happens. I think the worst thing that ever happened to you was meeting me, Elizabeth said.

We laughed. But a new drill was beginning: Make your book available. Make your book salable. Don't be too literary all your life.

I dared that there was nothing in her life but reading, really.

—Cal was the same way, she said, but he was able to write poems on subjects that concern common experience.

She said his work was full of rip-offs. 'Mother Marie Therese' has a last line taken from Baudelaire's 'The Old Servant,' though one wouldn't know it from Edna St. Vincent Millay's ludicrous translation. She said she didn't believe poetry could be written that way. Poetry was not all allusion and reference, she said, in a criticism of Lowell's poetry that for once wasn't about his choice of material.

—It just means that Baudelaire's last line was better than yours.

She said she felt that Lowell's reputation had declined since his death, that no one cared about him anymore.

She said again that I mustn't be too literary, that I must try to earn money. However, choice was not all there was to it. It was also a way of looking at things and your relationship with words.

You can't help the way things come to you, how you interpret life. I knew when she was goading me, and why.

Some people indicated how clever they were in their ability to dramatize things, like Barthelme, she said. Others in what they could put into a work, like Berger.

(Luc really looked down on autobiography as boring and beneath him. He claimed that the very abstract Walter Abish's new book was a masterpiece.

I'd not yet heard of Henry Dumas, the short-story writer who drew on the eeriest in black folk feelings. Dumas was in anthologies. How could I have missed him in those secondhand bookstore days? He was killed by police in a subway in 1968.

'What's your beef with me, Bo Schmo,' the young black journalist back in my secondhand bookstore career liked to quote. Ishmael Reed was king: 'So what if I am a crazy dada nigger.'

Charles Wright was whacked out enough to make the list of non-realist black novelists that Robert Fleming and I once came up with near closing hour in the bookstore over Scotch in suspect coffee mugs. There was Fran Ross's twisted Greek odyssey and the very Firbankian fictions of Henry Van Dyke. I didn't know at the time how much Eastern philosophy animated the peculiar work of Charles Johnson. John Edgar Wideman would describe the history of black literature as a story about a literature attempting to break free of its frame.)

Have a theme, Elizabeth said. And I mustn't retreat from my point, but be more strong about it, the generations of education in a black family, ministers and teachers at these black church schools, and then beyond, and how racism made all of that nothing. I shouldn't worry that it seemed snobbish or like bragging.

—If you worry what your friends think, then you can't write.

Besides, society thought no more of these ministers and professionals than they did of any other black person, she said.

(My father warned me that his father's slender memoir was

unreliable for reasons of snobbishness and race shame. As if a bachelor's degree from Brown and two desperate years in graduate school in economics at Harvard at a time when it would now allow black undergraduates to live in its dorms had not been enough, my grandfather added the University of Chicago to his résumé as a pastor. —Those were correspondence classes, my father laughed. He had inherited two unwanted boxes of his father's church-published pamphlet.

'The family was always kind and considerate of its slaves,' my grandfather had his grandfather saying in 1908.

—How can that be true, my father said.

In the digital age my father did not live to see, I can discover names my grandfather never mentioned, such as his uncle, Pee W. Pinckney.

—Short for Wee, I hope, Lucy Sante said.

Grandfather's uncle, born in 1878, was honorably discharged from the military in Manila in 1902 after only three years. When he died in Chicago in 1937, his occupation was listed as 'peddler.'

These hidden lives.)

Elizabeth was worried that I was headed for deliberate obscurity and poverty. It was she who was about to lend me Mikhail Saltykov-Shchedrin's *The Golovlyov Family.*

—If I die right away, Harriet will be rich, pretty set up.

She said as she looked back, she felt she hadn't written enough. But how could she?

—You're much more expansive than I am. Thank God. Don't lose that.

I was loading her dishwasher. Plates had accumulated in the dish rack, waiting for faithful Nicole. I said she had her own idea of things, her vision.

She hunched her shoulders as she sat on the chair by the wall phone. She said she despised *The Simple Truth.* She couldn't bring herself to write something so ordinary again. What was the point?

Though they were storybooks, as she was calling them in the kitchen, that did not mean that they were bad books. She said she couldn't do plot and character.

She could, but that was not the sort of contemporary writing that interested her. It was dark outside; her kitchen windows showed our reflections; the mirror on the counter beside the window showed hers.

She followed me out as I turned off the lights and she said she understood why people went to graduate school. That was a complete reversal. She'd always said that graduate school was for dogs.

She was advocating for the second career as I put on my coat. I found that worrying, the implied meaning that this was it, I was never going to grow as a writer. Either you had it or you didn't.

—Films, she said. I could write scripts like Gore and Isherwood and Max Apple. Fred Seidel was writing one for Bertolucci.

—I'll send a résumé to Motown.

No, she said, as she rang for the elevator, someone sees your story, wants it, asks you to try a script. No, she was not getting paid for the script she said she was still hard at work on. It annoyed her to have made herself dependent on a producer's luck in coming up with money. She was dying to replace her kitchen wallpaper.

Broadway in the night smelled strongly of dog piss and fish. The freshness of the day had been used up. Leaflets glued on the dark bus shelters I knew said, 'Liberal Upper West Side: Fight White Supremacy.'

My radiators whistled. It sounded like a civil defense test.

STANLEY CROUCH ACCOSTED me in the offices of *The Village Voice*, red-eyed and abrasive, explaining why he did not like Richard Wright. I was rescued by Thulani Davis offering to put me on the list for her newsletter of the Third World Writers Association.

I picked up John Boswell's *Christianity, Social Tolerance, and*

Homosexuality, from the Oscar Wilde Memorial Bookshop on Christopher Street, smarting every time I went in there that I aroused no curiosity as a presence, while Brad Gooch's first book of poetry, *Daily News*, faced the room from an upper shelf. Howard was in Paris.

I walked with the Boswell study under my arm to the East Village, where I guessed some regular at the Bar was already hip to gay sexuality rampant in the Christian society of fourth-century Antioch. Sure enough, by 'the long hairy arm of Coincidence,' an older painter I liked was teaching our favorite bartender 'Character and Anal Eroticism,' from Freud's *Three Theories of Sexuality*, he informed me,

 laughing with the cool waters

The reviews of Boswell's study had been rather grudging. I asked Elizabeth if she didn't think Keith Thomas in the December 4 issue had done the Boswell for the *Review* in a state of shock.

She complained of how silly the word 'gay' was in a serious text. —Socrates was 'gay'? I'm not going to say that. She said it offended her ear. —You can't call a whole group of people throughout time 'gay.'

Of course you could, just as the nineteenth century invented the term 'homosexuality.'

—Now you can't use the word, she went on. —I'm not going to call Frederick the Great gay.

His soldier-king father hadn't needed the word to throw young Frederick's intimate out of a window. Or was it a firing squad? A beheading? Or was that the story of another homo monarch? I was uncertain about the historical origins of the term, how it came to be the word for same-sex passions. *My Secret Life* referred to loose women as 'gay.' Hocquenghem lamented that 'gai' had not caught on in Paris. I said maybe we were having one of those historical modifications of the language. But I understood that Boswell was saying 'gay people' because it was what gay people were calling themselves.

Elizabeth said Richard Poirier, who had become 'an aggressive queer,' wondered if Boswell hadn't taken contemporary attitudes and placed them back in history.

Boswell wasn't being anachronistic, I didn't think. He was careful about documents, sources, the Roman literature of the time. The footnotes were difficult, like Hannah Arendt's. Then we argued over what were love letters and what were the conventions of male friendship back when.

And for that matter, I thought Gore's alternative term, 'homosexualist,' ridiculous in the extreme.

I put Rahv's *Freud and the Literary Imagination* by her door to borrow. I'd already spotted a good line, something about how Jung and Adler caught overtones from the symphony of life but missed its main themes. I told her I was reading Marcuse on Freud. She asked how much of Freud had I read.

Not enough, revolted by the last issue of *Semiotext(e)* that I finally got around to when I got home. After reading Hocquenghem's essay 'To Destroy Sexuality,' I got over my fascination with Hocquenghem the theorist.

'The Bookseller' was in *The New Yorker*. I called to tell her it was on the stands; I called her back to say her story was more than fine.

Harriet was better, but Elizabeth grieved to think of her sick ten days of every month. She said I couldn't know what my parents were going through.

I SKIPPED GOING by the pot store near Luc, a slot in a plain blue door, in order to be on time at the Public to hear June Jordan and Thulani Davis read.

Davis, from a family of black educators. Her grandfather, Arthur P. Davis, Columbia's first doctoral candidate in English, edited, with Ulysses Lee and Sterling Brown, *The Negro Caravan*, a classic anthology of black literature, published in 1941. She read, with very low affect, free verse poems about music or tap, and in between poems was witty, tentative, young-librarian-like.

June kept her hair short, white and gray. She could go elfin, with her pointy ears and burstful laughter. Her subject matter was very political, her style declamatory, heavily ironic, her poems constructed to end in punch lines. I sat there thinking she probably never rewrote anything.

The reading over, a crowd blew across the street to the Colonnade.

Ntozake Shange didn't really remember me, but she had good manners. A couple of years before, she'd directed June chanting and the anthropologist of black song, Bernice Reagon, rocking a cappella in a piece at the Public Theater about Sojourner Truth. Felice and I ambled around the garden party afterward, sipping at what we called our disaffection from the black cultural scene. It went away as soon as Shange turned up a transistor radio and pulled guests toward her to dance.

the lady in orange came lit up with love and night blueness

Felice had an orange stripe in her hair. She said she always checked out a black woman's hairstyle, because it said a lot about her socioeconomic group. Braids and jewels took a lot of time.

Shange said she knew the streets. Her thick braids had silver strands woven into them. She spoke with a slight drawl. She was what my mother and her friends called 'still a nice girl.' After some really bad life decisions, she was still a nice girl, they'd say. She could drop out of school, decide to become a single mom, move to the wrong city, for the wrong reason, i.e., a man, but she was still a nice girl, even with one of those African names she'd given herself.

I'd not yet seen *For Colored Girls Who Have Considered Suicide When the Rainbow Is Enuf.* I'd read it and it was one of those things you could think you knew everything about just from how often it had been talked about. She'd inspired a style of truth-telling in black women's poetry, but few had her poetic feeling. Ed Bullins was at the end of the long table, a playwright whose caustic work such as

The Electronic Nigger, about a creative writing class gone berserk, I'd read but had never seen staged. He was engrossed with Baraka.

The evening had been a tremendous success. We were loud, at least one of us completely stewed, and dapper Larry Neal, co-editor with Baraka of *Fire*, one of the most influential anthologies of the Black Arts Movement, stopped by my end. Whatever he was actually saying, I thought he was whispering to me a warning about why I did not want to be known as just another George Schuyler, a black journalist whose pride in his critical independence when writing for H. L. Mencken in the 1920s turned him into a right-wing hack columnist decades later. I got a chump feeling. Contemporary black literature was moving on the barge downriver while I waved from the plantation jetty.

A waitress turned on the television. The party deflated as news passed along the table that John Lennon had been gunned down outside his home, the Dakota, at Seventy-second Street and the park, right in front of Yoko Ono. A customer brought in the December 9, 1980, morning edition of the *Post*. It was hard to take in. Details of the story didn't make it more real.

SHE WHO ONCE told me to make my way as a writer by reviewing now bawled me out.

—Why are you writing ten pieces for seven hundred and fifty dollars when you could have had an advance of seventy-five hundred dollars for twenty pages?

She was wrong. I'd worked, which changed the tone of Elizabeth's reminder that these were my most energetic years.

When someone in our class insisted to her that she meant for her main character to be boring, Professor Hardwick said that to make a bore live on the page one would have to have the gift of Molière.

I like to remember the evenings she read to me something she was trying out or thinking about. I leave out her patient attention to the unsuccessful pages of the novel I'd been trying to write.

My novel had a new ending, I hoped, in the diabetic coma into which my grandfather had sunk. He was in Indianapolis, in the same black nursing home on the highway where my other grandfather had sat, partially paralyzed, limbs ugly as roots, as his few remaining years dripped away.

New York City police had called my father to say his stepmother was found dead and his father no longer knew where he was, who he was.

I left my father wheeling my grandfather around LaGuardia. By the time I got back to West Ninety-fifth Street, my father was calling to say that when their flight was delayed, his father made a run for it, and had to be chased down by airport security. The airline refused to take him on board for the next flight. I told my father to leave it to me and the next morning I drugged my grandfather's tea. I walked him onto the airplane and he thanked me, the redcap.

I thought my father would cry and I rushed off the airplane.

—Poor old darky, Elizabeth said when I told her the story. She meant to be funny.

I took offense.

Instead of telling her so, I argued with her about politics, always a bad idea with us. I'd whine that she wasn't listening, and she'd shriek that I was not making any sense, the knuckles of her open hand hitting the red cushion beside her in exasperation.

Without need for transition, she went after me again for the unreality of having agreed to write so many book reviews.

I'd heard of black psychiatrists who felt too messed up themselves to help lost ones cope with the black anthropologist and mental health pioneer Allison Davis's race achiever syndrome.

I remembered reading *Black Rage* when I was in high school, anxious to convince myself that whatever racial neuroses the two authors were talking about did not apply to me.

Elizabeth laughed down the phone that had we been as drunk at a party as we'd been the night before,

—You'd be wondering if you could ever show your face there again. There, take that.

I learned from books that that in which we were to find so much of ourselves also excluded so much of the selves we most cared for.

I FILLED IN for Barbara's assistant. I made an index of the current issue. I typed letters, read bad poems, arranged couriers to Gore Vidal at the Connaught in London. His piece on the U.S. Constitution. It was not the kind of office that made you aware of its windows.

Murray Kempton, the roaming reporter, rang often.

—Murray lives on the streets, Barbara said. The city was his beat.

Barbara had a new hairstyle. She'd seen her mother in Boston. Jacob drove to McLean while she sang, 'Over the river and through the woods, to Grandmother's house we go . . .'

Bob's three assistants sat in a large office facing his desk; Barbara's one assistant sat outside her small office, in the hall, as it were, shielded by not much, a wall that hid you when you typed. Whitney kept his door shut, but next to him I could hear into Bob's office; his door was always open.

The phone rang all morning. Dominique Nabokov would call, then float into Barbara's office and was still talking in English and French in the same sentence on her way out, adjusting her headband.

Once Barbara didn't want phone calls anymore and started to read, I took messages. She was going to sit there, all afternoon, into the evening, reading.

—Could you pass this on to Bob, puhleeze.

I read volume three of Henry James's *Letters*, at my usual slow speed. But I was ready for Elizabeth. Yes, there was something unshakable in Henry James. He was not easily distracted, to put it mildly. Belonging nowhere; at home everywhere. Worried about his brother and particularly about Alice, he was unexpectedly accepting of their deaths, as if it would relieve his siblings not only of physical suffering, but also of their failure. Was he weird about his brother Wilkie being willing to die for 'negroes' in the assault on Fort Wagner?

Barbara and Elizabeth were impressed by Jean Strouse's *Alice James*.

Henry James was a writer Elizabeth had all of, old hardcovers and old paperbacks, five dozen volumes by him and about him. Next to Henry James she had the dark volumes with faded lettering on the spines of intimidating works by William James. Elizabeth had edited *The Selected Letters of William James* in 1956. His grandson was still alive then.

It took her a moment to retrieve the name of the Van Doren brother responsible for the Columbia Curriculum in English after World War I. He condemned James as a tempest in a teapot. American patriotism did not forgive him his renunciation of his U.S. citizenship and retirement to Rye in England. Or was that Van Wyck Brooks.

—Shoot.

(James just told me when Churchill came to lunch at Lamb House he was insulting to James, who, after Churchill left, said that it was strange 'how with such an uneven hand nature distributes its riches, but it does rather buck one.')

She found it interesting that the rediscovery of Henry James came after World War II, when Americans were going back to Europe. Leon Edel had given himself fully to the publication of James's work and letters, but it was F. O. Matthiessen at Harvard who got things going with a book on the James family and then *Henry James: The Major Phase.*

She said Matthiessen had a big influence on Barbara, who was at Radcliffe in the late Forties, Matthiessen's time. And Harry Levin's and Daniel Aaron's. But it was Matthiessen and the James thing. That's where Baldwin got it from.

Giovanni's Room was the one Baldwin novel that to me showed most directly James's influence on him, because it followed the seasons, like *The Ambassadors*, and David's being American was as much an impediment to him as it was to Lambert. She said she could maybe see that.

She said it was revealing that Matthiessen, a queer, had brought back Henry James, a non-practicing queer, just as Newton Arvin, a queer, had led the revival of the work of Herman Melville, who was queer inside and on the page. And both Arvin and Matthiessen had paid the price.

Barbara loved *Krazy Kat*.

—Ignatz!

I thought it was German Jewish.

—You don't get it at all.

Galleys arrived like loaves of supermarket bread. Barbara came back from shopping and saw me with a copy of a pamphlet the *Review* published in 1968, *The Fruits of the MLA*, by Edmund Wilson, his impenetrable denunciation of academic editions of Melville, among others.

—What are you doing?

It was not the time of year for too much stomping in and out of other people's territory. The Christmas issue had been put to bed and it was as though the whole office was hoarse, saving its voice, slipping off, while Whitney and Bob rushed by me with puzzled smiles. Where was what's-her-name.

Elizabeth said her advisory role took the form of her suggesting someone review such and such and Barbara having to tell her,

—We've had ten thousand words on that already.

And when my few days of sitting at the desk outside Barbara's office were up, I could afford to buy small Christmas presents to go with stolen books, *Loon Lake*, Calvino, the history of the NAACP's crusade against lynching, and to pay to hear the Bush Tetras, Cynthia Sley's incredible band, at Club 57 on Irving Place.

Elizabeth said when she went back home to Kentucky on the Pennsylvania or Southern or whichever black-and-white-film-sounding railway, with an efficient black porter, her family, not quite understanding what she was up to, left her alone.

I DIDN'T HIDE in my room that holiday season. There were too many guests and there was too much pain in the house. The television in the family room ran loudly all day and all night, a luckier family pet than the bewildered sheepdog cooped up in the garage after dark, whimpering and pawing the door to the family room.

When by ourselves, we sat together in the garishly lit family room, including my brother-in-law, used to us by now, each in his or her own private spot, ignoring the terrible sounds of Christmas television and a penned-up large dog, reading *Loon Lake* or a history of the NAACP's crusade against lynching or *Newsweek* or *Italian Folktales*; Pat, my mother, and I with a drink of some kind nearby, Donna and my father not. My mother, my sisters, and me, we smoked away, apologetic to my father, because of his asthma, but lighting another menthol cigarette nevertheless. He'd try to open the door to the garage; my mother felt the chill easily. He'd have to go to his messy den with the green pile carpet of dust and a blues record that was just background for a long-distance conversation with his brother.

He wore a surgical mask in the mornings when he pushed the dog into its outdoor prison. He had also developed an allergy to the crabby old cat that had been carefully bred by a classmate of my mother's in Detroit. It had been banished to the cinder-block basement of appliances.

—Ming should give up the ghost, my heartless mother said.

I thought I'd get through loads of Pat's Kurt Vonnegut paper-backs during the holiday of having to behave, with the TV roaring, everybody keeping a head down over the printed page when not escaping on an errand. I got books out of my luggage and sat with our desperate holiday tree and the almighty television.

(I wish I'd talked to my sister about *Cat's Cradle*.)

I couldn't work on anything.

—You feel watched, Elizabeth said.

My sister Donna wrote poetry. She told me she never took an English class in college. She already had the necessary requirement. She liked to draw, figures only, a mix of shapes inspired by Giacometti's sculpture and John Lennon's drawings from *In His Own Write*. She read fantasy novels and found Toni Cade Bambara's latest so difficult she didn't want to try anything else. She said she didn't want to be freaked out when she read. She liked Louise Meriwether.

Donna washed her Jheri Curl again and my mother took up her station outside the bathroom door. My sister herself said she looked like a documentary on a rare bird's nest. Her laughter got rid of the Christmas that was blocking our way.

HENRY LOUIS GATES, JR., gave Sterling Brown's *Collected Poems* a glowing review in *The New York Times*. Others followed.

Baraka had written an article, with his usual cunning, retracting his anti-Semitism: I didn't mean Jews, I meant Zionism. I was misled into nationalism. Now that I am the only black revolutionary in America, I see the black light of Hugo's death.

It was Larry Neal who had died, of a heart attack, at age forty-three. I remembered June saying he kept very much to himself.

Pat would be convalescent for some time after the operation. Cysts, ovaries, it sounded scary. My brother-in-law and Donna insisted they could take care of her. There was no reason for my parents to miss the board meeting in New York.

I went with my parents to Jersey City. Aunt Alvan was my mother's much older first cousin. Her tongue was as quick as ever, she who experienced Harlem as a slum in the 1920s while getting her master's degree from Teachers College. She had always been on Sterling's side when it came to the inflated reputation of the Harlem Renaissance. She said her two sons were her Ph.D.

Some of my mother's Tuskegee cousins were defensive about being light-skinned, but Aunt Alvan's husband was white enough to be a white man. My memory can't turn up the volume on conversations that had to do with realty offices visited first by him. My ears filtered at a gathering years before Uncle Dick laughing that no one worried about leaving his girl with George Washington Carver, the wizard of the race who turned peanuts into milk and prayed for farm boys.

Uncle Dick had had a heart attack; Aunt Alvan had had a foot amputated. The pair looked battered, spotty, darker, as if recovering from an awful vehicular collision. My parents were silent as we traveled through the dirty snow back to Manhattan. I'd heard often enough how much Uncle Dick and Aunt Alvan meant to them, how my father and mother had stayed with these urbane cousins when they came to New York in 1947 for their honeymoon.

My mother complained that I never told them anything of my life, so she was delighted to meet my friends again. Eva they appreciated for being 'kooky.' My father said he would get the book Luc recommended, *The Gangs of New York*. He said he wished I wrote essays in the manner of Emerson instead of mere book reviews.

Downtown in the Bar, Eva and Luc were fighting and feeling sick. I went alone to the Mudd Club, which was out of it, like a campus hangout. That made the Del-Byzanteens look a bit like English majors, white boys hiding behind the security of their guitars. But they were very good. '*My hands are yellow from the job that I do*,' they sang. Sara and I danced and shouted. She said RCA was there, so we had to act up. I spoke to Suzanne, but I left when I began to feel too talkative for the hip crowd collecting in the greenroom.

Back at the Bar, no one had moved. It was still packed. Alexis pointed out her friend Keith Haring. I'd always wondered where they came from, the radioactive babies stenciled on the sidewalks and the Looney Tune–like eyes and the colorful radioactive Gumby shapes plastered on the tiles of subway stations.

(AIDS would kill Keith Haring a decade later.)

Evan Lurie, the keyboard player from the Lounge Lizards, told us what he said was a story of being young in New York: happening upon Cecil Taylor, his idol, and feverishly thinking of a way to speak to him, and then realizing that his idol was cruising him. At closing, when the owner shouted, 'Gentlemen, go home,' no one moved.

I HADN'T SEEN Elizabeth in almost a month. When we sat with our plates, she said that she'd been at the Academy all day with Virgil Thomson. Richard Rodgers left a fund, an award to produce or set up new musicals.

Mrs. Rodgers now thought she was head of a foundation, like Henry Ford. She didn't understand that she was the donor and that was all. To select the winning musical was difficult, a lengthy process. The board had asked Stephen Sondheim to act as an adviser and he agreed, which she thought said a lot for the Academy. But Mrs. Rodgers was enraged: Rodgers and Sondheim hated each other. The board answered that they had no way of knowing that, could not therefore have been either tactful or tactless.

They had a big meeting with Mrs. Rodgers, her daughter and son-in-law, the Guettels, their lawyer, and the Academy's lawyer, who was also defending PBS against Hellman.

—A real showbiz story.

Elizabeth said she and Esther Brooks couldn't get Bill Alfred to enter his musical in the competition. He was too lost in the fantasy of Broadway producers, which was very self-destructive, she said.

—Turning down a 'nut' of sixty thousand.

Every play got to Broadway after being produced off-Broadway. Elizabeth said his book for the musical was just beautiful.

She had two big lectures coming up. Her subject was New York City. The city was also the subject of her novel. She worried about putting all her ideas in the essays and being too dry for the novel. She hoped to print the lectures in the *Review*. But she wrote essays on Maine and was able to put Maine in *Sleepless Nights*.

She had to give them the title of her lecture by Monday. I suggested 'New York, Capital of the Twentieth Century,' which she loved.

(Frank Harris alert.)

Jane Austen's character John Thorpe was truly hateful, we started after dinner, but Elizabeth was having one of her comic fits. She railed against the accumulation of things, the oppression of too many possessions. She attacked a row of records, sailing duplicates and scratched recordings across the floor. I came back in the morning to pick up books and Mexican Christmas songs and Elisabeth Schwarzkopf from the floor.

Shelley Wanger was out with flu and I substituted for her at the *Review* for a week. I typed through the evenings a numbing article by Rohatyn. Mr. Silvers was having dental work and the painkillers made him nearly incoherent.

Paycheck cashed, I was bundled inside a Christmas present from my mother, a long, padded, down-quilted blue coat.

—You look like a mailbox, Howard said.

Fortunately for me, he said, and for him, who had to be seen with federal property, the Bar was closed. It had become so popular, the owner refused to pay protection. The Mafia shut it down.

The Homintern was quiet anyway, playing Samuel Barber's Concerto for Violin and Orchestra here, excerpts from *Vanessa* there, to mark his death. Howard had stories WNCN didn't, about the composer listening to a radio broadcast of his opera and being in such pain he begged the nurse for painkillers at the moment

Cleopatra asks for the viper. The cold windows the neighbors could hear *Knoxville: Summer of 1915* from were mine.

—Are you awake? Just barely?

Elizabeth had been sick, but her temperature was down to ninety-nine that morning. She was always taking her temperature. She'd invited me to the National Book Critics Circle Awards a few days before.

—I always feel there is nothing wrong with me. I'm just being lazy. We found chairs behind the bar. —Stay here. I'm too old and distinguished to mingle. But then she decided she really couldn't stand up. She'd gone home and slept. She was well enough to see Harriet, who was more than okay. Brodsky on Mme Mandelstam was what we cared about in the new issue of the *Review*, and Milosz's Nobel lecture, I added, but she said she admired my essay on Toomer, in print after so long. I never doubted she told me what she really thought. At all times.

Barbara said it was okay, but not one of my best. Elizabeth said that was

—Barbara's wallpaper quirk. If she notices the room is blue now instead of green, she'll say, How divine. I never liked that green anyway. If the walls are green the next year, she says, Fabulous. The blue didn't work.

Baldwin was really camp in the PBS documentary on Harlem, and high. He claimed he'd read all of the books in the Schomburg by the time he was thirteen. I'd missed the recent episode of Robert Hughes's series, *The Shock of the New*. Elizabeth said it was fascinating and gave her ideas for her lectures. She wanted to go on her own to the Urban Bookshop at Helmsley Palace, a shocking structure, even if the slab of a tower incorporated the august Villard Houses, once the offices of Random House.

When I hung up, Howard's head was in my refrigerator. He told me to get a new bed and some food. I believed I was practiced in the art of choosing clothes that were not clean but did not smell. I put on my puffy mailbox-blue coat and Howard placed an envelope between my lips.

ROBERT SILVERS'S OFFICE asked me to fill in for Shelley Wanger again.

—Don't write your memoirs, Barbara said.

Bob had been carrying on all day, acting willful. Barbara and I exchanged looks whenever we passed each other in the hall. Once, while discussing with Bob an essay by Tom J. Farer on Latin America and Jeane Kirkpatrick's position paper on how the Reagan administration planned to deal with non-democratic governments, Barbara turned to me and rolled her eyes.

—It's long, she said. —About one hundred and sixty inches, I'd say.

Bob took out the parts defending revolutionary governments, saying the parts about how bad authoritarian governments are were left in.

—In case anybody didn't know that, Barbara mumbled, tapping the door with a finely sharpened pencil.

Gérard Chaliand came in to talk about his report on Afghanistan. His son was sent to Luc in the mailroom, because he did not speak English.

Bob said he had to go see his old father in the country. His father lived in Rockville Center, just on the other side of Queens.

—You want to say, How is Sussex, Bob? Elizabeth said.

On low-key days, Bob would come in late, read the *Times*, *Le Nouvel Observateur*, clipping two articles for Chaliand, for someone. Then he got frantic about contacting Christopher Hill. The porter at Balliol said I'd have to wait and call the college secretary to get his new number, if there was in fact a new one.

—O fuck, Bob said.

He dictated a cable. It was so cute when the telex hammered

letters back at me. Bob wanted Hill to do *The Lisle Letters*, volumes of correspondence concerning the business affairs of an illegitimate Plantagenet and his ambitious wife in the murderous times of Henry VIII.

Bernard Bailyn at Princeton wouldn't do the Kissinger. Bob's file on Kissinger was enormous. Among the papers was something that got into William Shawcross's hands: Kissinger's own changes in a manuscript where he lies about nearly everything.

—Keep this in an especially safe place. If this is lost, so is a chapter of, of history.

He threw up his hands. My finger couldn't make space in the file cabinet. I didn't know where to go with it and just laid the file on a shelf behind his head.

Kissinger once wrote to Bob about the review of his memoirs. Bob invited Kissinger to respond at length. Kissinger did, but wrote on every page 'not for publication.' Six months later, Kissinger called Bob to ask why he hadn't heard from him about his letter. Bob told the former secretary of state he'd been busy.

In shirtsleeves and tie, Bob rejected an article on Louis Althusser, E. P. Thompson, and Perry Anderson of the *New Left Review*. I didn't follow the explanation in the piece as to why Althusser loathed Thompson's Marxism or the arguments that led Thompson to write *The Poverty of Theory*. Thompson began as a novelist, but he had so much research on the working class he wrote a history instead.

The newspapers said Althusser had done it at home and called the police himself, but we joked: 'I, Louis Althusser, having strangled my wife in the student café of the École des Hautes Études . . .'

Althusser was in the nuthouse, Bob said.

—We want to know just what *is* the pathology of this kind of theory, the sympathy for Stalin.

He ran to the men's room to shave before meeting Lady Dudley. He called her 'Kiddo.'

Alison Lurie entered, crooked smile and all, and took Barbara away.

Sharon DeLano wore a different pair of cowboy boots every day. The boot book she'd done with David Rieff was coming out in the spring.

—An expensive coffee table book, she answered.

She was in Bob's office looking for vitamin C, but found instead the nausea medicine Susan had given him for his dying mother, and he'd forgotten it, so it seemed.

Prudence's replacements were still with the fluorescent hum and galley-printing clunk in the studio. I rushed to tidy up and mark clearly the latest items on Mr. Silvers's desk. John Willett, of the Old British Left, arrived, carrying a Zabar's bag of cheese and books. He wore a thick, hardened coat, like a costume from some Brecht piece he'd translated. He asked directions to the Gotham Book Mart, certain that real bookshops in a metropolis stayed open late on Friday nights.

(James said that Willett, the Stalinist, probably did well out of Brecht's plays, but he made a nonsense of the Brecht estate in general, publishing volumes of the plays, poems, and essays haphazardly. When he appeared at the *Review* out of the past of black-and-white photographs, Willett was in my mind for his *Art & Politics in the Weimar Period*. Willett's study and Peter Gay's *Weimar Culture* were manuals to us.)

Dinner wasn't going to be anything. She couldn't be bothered to get things together.

When the *Review* started, Elizabeth explained, Bob would take care of the ideas and Barbara was the stylist. Many editors thought they were smart,

—but Bob and Barbara happen to be as smart as they think they are.

However, she believed Barbara to be exhausted by the *Review* and Bob, having taken, like the first Francis Bacon, all knowledge as his province, had himself become exhausting.

—Bob wants to tell these people how to write.

She said William Gass's essay on Emerson had been on Bob's desk for two years. Gass told her when she was in St. Louis that Bob hadn't written to him about it. She said she called Bob about it, but she bet Gass still hadn't heard.

—Who knows what it takes to put out a magazine like that. I must say Bob and Barbara are an unbeatable team.

Mrs. Astor sold her stock to Whitney when she got nervous about the *Review*'s politics. When Cal went to England, Elizabeth said, she made him give Bob and Barbara his stock.

—You're going to England. You shouldn't have *Review* shares. I made him sign the papers. He was rather sore.

Lowell was always very complicated about her and the *Review*, she said. He was very annoyed at her Frost piece in the first issue. He didn't much like the *Review* ever, she felt.

—He thought I was going to knock all his friends.

She said Robert Frost was envious of T. S. Eliot; he kept tabs on every prize Eliot won that he hadn't.

The *Review* had invested in a rug company and Grace had another grandchild.

Elizabeth was working on her lectures, but was frustrated, she said, because she didn't really know how to write them. She could get two lectures for California, if she just wanted to work up novels. But she wanted something arresting for publication. The subject, New York, was too large.

—It would be easier as a foreigner. Everything one has to say as a resident seems commonplace.

She complained that there wasn't enough textual impetus. Edith Wharton, Henry James. The rest wasn't any good.

I WENT TO Barbara's to help a chic friend of hers move her furniture around. To this European friend, I was, indeed, the help.

I wanted to say: I hear you're a whore.

Not even Barbara's help was 'the help.' Dorcas, the Ichabod-tall, bespectacled black housekeeper there at random hours, it seemed to me, examined arrivals from the top of the stairs. If one didn't interest her, she went coldly about her business. She had a majestic stride.

(Dorcas had to go when it was discovered she'd been running crates of untaxed cigarettes up from North Carolina. She had several sidelines going and had made a great deal of money.)

The layout of Barbara's place was the same as Elizabeth's, only reversed. Her stairs by the front door started on the right; Elizabeth's on the left. Elizabeth was competitive with Barbara about who was further ahead in decoration, while Barbara did not think about things in that way. Both apartments looked genuine and patchily got together. Both were mostly walls of books. Barbara had her group of Daumiers, a still life by Maurice Grosser, Virgil's friend, and that gray horizontal painting was by Leonid Berman, whoever he was, and that very small painting of a wonderful lighthouse was by Helen Wilson, Edmund's daughter, who had his forehead, and there was a framed piece of yellow legal pad with a coffee stain on it that was a poem by Auden he'd written out for them. Jason was Auden's publisher.

He rang the bell and came in and asked for his six-o'clock-on-the-dot martini, Barbara once said. He had been talking for some time before he realized he was in the wrong apartment. The Epsteins' downstairs neighbors had recognized Auden and were happy to serve him cocktails.

Subletters of Auden's and Kallman's unclean apartment on St. Marks Place had been utterly astonished when they opened the cupboard above the bed and found in it only a jar of Vaseline and a pair of castanets. Neither gossip nor anecdote, but oral history.

(Suddenly it comes to mind, Thekla Clark's beautiful memoir of her friends, *Wystan and Chester*.)

I moved Barbara's furniture as instructed by Barbara's friend, who, when Barbara got home, wouldn't let her put back her knick-knacks of rather a high order. The new look showed the shabbiness of the furniture, to Barbara, and her spirits began to sag. I cleaned out files, Jason's notes on the Chicago trial.

It was true back then that to have stayed at home for days on end felt like an accomplishment to us who were always out. Then there was a young *Review* party and Prudence brought down the house reading Frank Sullivan's 'The Night the Old Nostalgia Burned Down.' Felice was back, Howard and Brad were planning to leave again, and the Bar had reopened. It was filling up with lesbians and gay-friendly straight couples.

I made it to Elizabeth's, who was watching McEnroe and Vilas, and we had an argument, because she loved McEnroe as a hand-some, brilliant player. She was trying to make an effort, with blue-fish and a little lime juice and ginger, as suggested by her friend Lee Gardner. We had another argument over police shootings of youths.

—You're not as radical as I am, she said.

She said these police were scared, with wives and families at home, and that the victims were armed and violent and that more policemen were killed.

—Bullshit.

The ghettos were insane, but so was filling someone with twenty-four bullets.

Elizabeth's third glass of vodka, for which I was to blame, had her rolling about *The Shock of the New*. She hated Jackson Pollock; she loved Rothko and Motherwell. She said she didn't like nature; it was 'too vast.' She was too urbanized to know what to think of the Grand Canyon. Mayakovsky had something of the same reaction. She said Rothko would die if he saw the dummies meditating before his paintings in the de Menil temple in Texas.

—That's what you get.

There were so many provocative phrases in Hughes's script,

though he could never cover everyone, but she couldn't use any of it, felt there was no textual equivalent to the visual.

THE VILLAGE VOICE published a piece by Vivian Gornick on Elizabeth Hardwick, Joan Didion, Diane Johnson, and Rosellen Brown. Barbara told Elizabeth she was now more famous than Jean Harris, but according to Vivian Gornick, Jean Harris was a better writer.

(Murray Kempton had been going up to Westchester to cover a sensational murder trial. Jean Harris, a Virginia girl's school head, stood accused of shooting her lover, the Scarsdale diet doctor. For some reason, or many, several notable women writers, such as Diana Trilling, were observers in the courtroom. Murray was predicting Harris would get 'Man II.' Elizabeth liked the ring of that expression.)

Elizabeth Hardwick's photo was on the cover, 'The mother of them all.' What Gornick seemed to object to was how indeterminate or indefinite these women writers were.

Susan made her first phone call to me, and was brutally dismissive of Gornick.

My sister Pat called, saying she knew some violent offenders who owed her favors.

Elizabeth was annoyed at first, but then decided that that was a part of writing books, you became a subject. Mary had had a big put-down in the *Voice* the week before and Susan got chopped up in the *Voice* some time before that. Harriet said she saw it on the newsstand and ran the other way.

I told her not to go to her A&P. Elizabeth was once recognized in her grocery store by someone who had seen her on *The Dick Cavett Show*. She was sometimes stopped on Columbus Avenue. She minded that her picture would be on the newsstands all week.

—I certainly won't go on Columbus Avenue. I'll be cut.

(Margo Jefferson just alerted me to a piece in *The New Republic* in which Gornick reexamines her animosity toward Lizzie's work and says she misread Hardwick's essays and *Sleepless Nights*.)

Elizabeth talked about Koolhaas's *Delirious New York* and her frustration at not really knowing architecture. She said the poor of the American city had become like the outcasts of Bombay, untouchables. Society had given up on them; all problems seemed insoluble.

As she worked on her New York lectures, her phone calls found her more entertained. Twain summed up what the city was about: 'Last year I didn't have a penny. Now I owe you a million dollars.' Or she was drawn to 'the pranks of Krishna,' and re-creating the deities every day.

I curved down Broadway all the way through the snow flurries to West Sixty-seventh Street.

She complained of a rash, which she thought at first had come from the tetracycline the dentist gave her, but she decided it was the wool against her skin. She'd lost her hearing aid and had to buy a new one.

Elizabeth said even the cost of Harriet's shrink made her panic.

She did an imitation of T. S. Eliot describing a visit with the Empsons.

—Maug was on the potty as we arrived.

She spoke of Ivor and Dorothy Richards and their

—wonderful, goofy purity. Their kind will never come again.

They were interested in saving the world, in bringing literacy to all. She said she and Cal used to roar with laughter at the record of basic English and the huge thorn needle Richards would leave for them to listen to. At dinner, he would pull poems out of his pocket and recite them. (I can't remember the opening line she bawled out.)

—He had a Yorkshire accent. I don't know anything about English accents, as you know.

Elizabeth patted the hamburger and suddenly remembered Richards's 'Mobile.'

(What is that?)

—I wish I could remember more about it. President Pusey asked Cal, Why would such a smart man want to do a thing so silly? Good question, Cal said. I wish Cal were here. He remembers all this.

Dorothy used to break out in a sweat when Eliot came, Elizabeth said. What should she do, who should she invite. She was not at all domestic.

—Usually tuna.

But she gave these cocktail parties for Eliot.

—She adored him, it was impersonal, because he was this great poet.

She said Dorothy was an enthusiastic alpinist. Even after breaking her hip or being in a car accident she would go at it again. She said they traveled constantly, even to China.

She said that if you told Empson that he was eccentric he wouldn't know what you were talking about. Once he asked them for 'lodgings.' They offered their house. She said when he and Hetta turned up, Clarence, the doorman then, was so shocked by their appearance he told them he must have the wrong place. I loved the Kenyon story she told me back when of Empson putting chewing gum in his ears to block out the noise of the students.

—Empson was very conscious of what he thought of you as a poet. That gum is probably still in his ears.

She got up to put the hamburger in the broiler.

Ecco was to reissue her two previous novels and *A View of My Own*. When Daniel Halpern called her to tell her she said,

—You haven't read them.

The Godine edition of her *Selected Letters of William James* was on the coffee table.

(I'd almost missed in *The American Scene*, which she lent me, Henry James's backhanded compliment to Du Bois: that the South had so degenerated, the best book of the year 1903 was by a black man, *The Souls of Black Folk*. Bars of the a cappella sorrow songs head each chapter while Du Bois's own prose is toccata. His essays sail toward painful clarity. He had the humility and the imagination to know what he beheld in a people's survival. He had a genius for the concrete.)

To see all her work in print had to have meant something.

We talked of the child killings in Atlanta.

—They'll blame it on the kids, you wait and see.

I decided to wear a green ribbon, though I couldn't stand to read about it. The victims were all black children.

FRANCINE GRAY CALLED the office.

—Is Barbara there? Do you have a radio? Turn it on, someone tried to kill Reagan.

We crowded into Bob's office around his television. Luc's theory was that General Haig was staging a coup.

—How come everyone else wins the sweepstakes? I fuck with my emotions the way a stunt driver fucks with his body, Luc said.

He said his heart got broken

—Over and over and into smaller and smaller pieces.

Luc read me 'The Fifth Wheel.' He'd copied out Brecht's poem on his door. And in thinking of El Salvador and General Haig, he said he remembered 'On the Wall in Chalk Is Written.'

Luc had seen the Del-Byzanteens when they opened for the Four Tops at Private's. He heard Lee Perry, 'the Beethoven of dub,' he called him, at Irving Plaza. He'd been running around with Jack Smith, whom he described as the crazy visionary predecessor whose aesthetic influenced everyone, from Warhol to punk to Nan Goldin. Luc had quaaludes and cocaine, and the whole time he said he was suffering from what Elizabeth called 'coupledom.'

Everyone was with someone and you weren't.

I was forever crossing paths with the Australian doctor and his musicologist and their boyfriends.

—I know, I know. I can't even speak of it, Elizabeth said.

Someone had been phoning and not saying anything when she picked up. She lifted her goblet of vodka and began talking of 'Bartleby, the Scrivener.'

Luc and Felice arrived in black leather. She wore a red scarf and turquoise tights.

—It's Merce Cuningham, Professor Hardwick said of Felice's costume. —How's your mother?

—Fine. She frosted her hair.

In the kitchen, Elizabeth said Felice's conversation was pure dialogue. Felice had finished her novel; we were celebrating.

Elizabeth said when she was young and wanted to send out a story she sat and sat until it was finished.

—You'll never finish your novel, she said to me.

She and Luc were avid fans of Abish's *How German Is It*. So, too, was William Gass, who had real independence of mind, she said, but he liked the new Shirley Hazzard and she thought it had been written to win prizes. She was trying to get Abish the Faulkner Prize.

Violently prejudiced against the English novel after 1840, Luc described that whole body of literature as 'a matter of taxidermy.' He was working on his manifesto, a gospel of literature.

—You're as Dada as they come, aren't you.

—Situationist. *Sous les pavés, la plage.*

There were more dead in Atlanta.

BOYS WEEK AT *The New York Review of Books*, we said. Stephen and Natasha Spender came in to see Bob on Monday. Virgil was also in that day, shuffling, piping, —No books in here. Must be business.

Tuesday, Bruce Chatwin appeared, beautiful in his Saint Martin tan.

—And he knows it, Barbara said.

Hiking boots slung on his shoulder.

(He died from AIDS. Susannah Clapp's memoir, *With Chatwin: Portrait of a Writer*, is so refined.)

Wednesday, Harry Mathews arrived.

Thursday, Jean Hannon Douglas, a painter, had cottage cheese and Perrier with Barbara behind closed doors.

Thursday, Bob stomped in as usual. We joked about buying him sneakers.

—Getaway shoes, Luc said they were called uptown.

Right away Bob started chewing out Shelley. She shook her head as she rushed off. Then Bob swept into Barbara's office and demanded to know where the Washburn galleys were.

—Don't talk to me like that. I put them on your desk.

—I *will* talk to you like that. Bob slammed the door and continued to shriek like a madman. He stormed out. The galleys were on his desk.

The worse thing was having to pretend not to have noticed, for Barbara's sake.

FELICE CAME INTO the *Review* the next day. She'd been working long hours at Xerox and sometimes hung out in the mailroom at lunch with Luc and a Fela Kuti or Kraftwerk soundtrack turned down low.

—You could feel it on the subway. Another prisoner on hunger strike dies in Ireland, another body found in Atlanta, Bob Marley, and now a holy man, the pope. I wanted to tell Him, hey, it's getting a little tense down here.

She almost wept. Felice also wondered if calling a guy to wish his band well at a performance in Jersey made it seem like she was chasing him. She was dressed for work, in black leather and ruby-red heels. She and Luc called England. Malu wasn't coming back. She'd married Andy Cox, the lead guitarist from the fierce band the English Beat. She'd edited *The Barnard Bulletin* with Felice.

Bob was out with Caroline, who looked awful.

Barbara jumped up and away. Murray was going to Rome to cover the pope and she was taking him to the airport, sprinkling perfume on her neck, checking to see if she had enough money for a taxi. Good for him, she said, since he had had nothing to do but sit in the courtroom with Jean Harris, she accused of well-bred murder up in Westchester.

Sunday, Elizabeth said Bob had given a dinner the night before for Naipaul. She and Renata and Naipaul's girlfriend Margaret sat whispering about how nothing changes with a married man. Barbara came with Murray.

—She feels she's a couple now. I said, No, you're not. Barbara said, Yes, I am. Here I am with my ball and chain.

The Newhouse family's Advance Publications, the corporation that had bought Random House, wanted to revive *Vanity Fair.* They offered Bob a lucrative editorship, which was what all the trouble and secret meetings at Jason's new digs in the Hampshire House were all about.

(The legend is that Gore Vidal advised Barbara to move out first, and then Jason would have to go.)

The offer was very tempting for Bob, who had nothing for the future. He told them Grace was rich, but he was not a kept man.

Elizabeth said she told Bob to demand first that the name *Vanity Fair* not be used. It wasn't a distinguished magazine.

—So there'll be Victor Pritchett in the middle of two hundred ads. Big deal.

Bob turned it down. Bob and Barbara got a salary increase. He made the *Review,* but the Paper gave him clout, she said.

Qaddafi was being interviewed via satellite on *The MacNeil/Lehrer Report.*

—Born charisma, Elizabeth said and went to the kitchen to check on dinner.

The mob hadn't shut the Bar down; they'd closed to fix the plumbing. Bob Johns, the chesty bartender, asked me how frequently I wrote for the *Review*. His classmate Polly Scarvalone worked in the business side of the office. He sometimes came up to have lunch with her. Bob and Barbara had been relieved to have something about Toni Morrison's *Tar Baby* from me that was quick and not in need of babysitting. Bob Johns said my review made him laugh.

(His boyfriend collected him at the end of his shift, early or late. One day in the future, Bob's fans would notice that after he served a customer he'd step back from the bar, arms folded, not making eye contact. One day without warning he and his thick chestnut hair weren't there anymore. One day in the future, Polly was in tears in the office: AIDS. Her friend was gone.)

I CALLED BARBARA to tell her I'd be late. My bathroom ceiling had come down and it smelled like a frog pond. She said her night with Lizzie wasn't à deux like in the old days. Terry Kilmartin came, then Murray. Barbara said she got tight and when she came downstairs in the morning, she discovered that Lizzie had done the dishes.

Elizabeth laughed that Barbara wouldn't take hold, as she liked to say, wouldn't get the washing machine fixed or buy a new one. Elizabeth knew perfectly well that she herself had ignored a leak from her dishwasher and eventually it flooded her downstairs neighbor. She'd only recently settled the insurance. Elizabeth was having people for the weekend. Sally Austin and Harriet were coming.

'But I did not in the least wish to carry justice around in my clothes.' Luc gave me Maurice Blanchot's *The Madness of the Day*, saying it blew his mind.

—There's no known photograph of him.

Jim Jarmusch's film *Permanent Vacation* was getting unpredictable responses, but Veronica Geng, very much one of Barbara's girls, liked it. Luc introduced the Del-Byzanteens at the Ritz. In his suspenders, he looked like a Bolshevik haranguing the crowd.

—Sometimes they're sad, sometimes they're mad, and all the time they're bad, bad, bad.

Sara had finished her film, *You Are Not I*, and was looking for a lab. She talked to the band to calm them. The gang was there, except Howard and Brad, and Nan and Suzanne, who were in the Yucatán. And it was beautiful Jennifer's turn not to come back from London.

The greenroom airlocked with prohibitive cool. There were a lot of people I knew only by sight.

Luc had a fit of fifthwheelitis on the way to Negril's, kicking over trash cans. Big Youth was onstage. White *Voice* types sat impassively. Jamaican women swayed; men with beards and large knit caps called 'Do it, do it, do it' fast and low through the ganja dark. Big Youth pranced through his famous toasts. *Natty dread in Babylon.* He shook his locks wildly at the audience, fell to the floor, flinging his head, jumped up and down, threw the microphone and ran offstage. He came back, the jewels in his teeth and his eyes aglow.

The pharmaceutical shelf in the xerox room at the *Review* was bare. People like me had cleaned it out, stuffed their pockets with vitamins C, B, E, multiples, aspirins, throat lozenges, antibiotics, bandages, sinus medications, eyedrops, rubbing alcohol.

Barbara had been out with Jean Douglas. Her niece, Susan Minot, was Barbara's new assistant.

I'd read *The Simple Truth* and assured Elizabeth she had no need to fear the Ecco reprint. (It's such a smart book, and an angular one.) I wondered why Parks's wife was crying at the end.

—Don't ask me. I haven't read it since. It took me a week to get that tear.

She decided she'd write the new novel in the third person. She didn't want it to be at all like *Sleepless Nights*. She pulled out the yellowed sheets from her drawer, the bits and pieces she'd written, beginnings and endings. She worried.

—I got so scared. I'm so scared. What am I doing? Don't be like me.

THE NAACP INDIANAPOLIS chapter threw a banquet in my father's honor. He ignored the lesson of his father's life: when your congregation organizes a tribute to you it means you're finished, on the way out. Someone remembered that the day they were to study venereal diseases my father came to class in surgical gloves. Reverend Benjamin Hooks, the new NAACP executive director, struck me as a man condemned to say the same thing over and over. My father had been on the side of those who helped Hooks to ease out his predecessor, Roy Wilkins, dazed and shrunken, from the directorship a few years before. The audience rose, some to applaud, most to escape the heat.

Ming, our cat, had not given up the ghost. How would I explain to Howard everything that happened after my mother tried to go after my nappy hair. The Australian doctor's expression in our West Ninety-sixth Street Red Apple supermarket when he saw my Jheri Curl said it would be best for me not to try. I looked like a bad verse of the Negro National Anthem.

Broken rules. *La Source, Divertimento,* with Farrell and Martins; *Vienna Waltzes,* with McBride, Farrell, Martins, Tomasson; and audible gasps from the audience. I met Elizabeth, who, like me, had just decided to go. I went once in a while, Elizabeth more often, Barbara, Sharon, Susan, Jean and Gordon Douglas, fanatically. We were included upstairs in the magic kingdom of Lincoln Kirstein and Arlene Croce, Elizabeth Kendall and Margo Jefferson, Maxine Groffsky and Win Knowlton, Maxine's publisher husband, and

David Kalstone, who was at the center of the terrifyingly precious circle around James Merrill.

(Kalstone died of AIDS.)

Kalstone escorted us to the corner and I walked Elizabeth to her door.

(I forgot that James Merrill also died of AIDS until James just reminded me.)

The next day the editorial assistants' network was busy and I soon heard the network report that an editor at Random House went into another editor's office and talked about her embarrassment at seeing Lizzie Hardwick the night before at the ballet. I was told the editor, a white woman, said that there was Lizzie Hardwick, this old white Southern woman, with a black boy in his twenties, and she wanted to take her aside and ask her, What did she think she was doing.

I should have kept my mouth shut, but the moral high ground beckoned, a mountain meadow of attention. Barbara said some people are afraid to be the last to know something and so jump out there with wrong conclusions. I should have kept my mouth shut. Elizabeth and I were not insulted in the same way. She threatened to make threatening phone calls to the editor in question. It was not difficult to get her to let it drop.

The same talk would go on in Castine, she lamented.

—Maine is very nineteen thirty-nine.

She confessed she worried that the doormen who didn't know us well might think we were having an affair.

(Back when Harriet was still at Dalton, we went to a former child star's party and elected to play hooky the next day and were sitting on the red sofa. Professor Hardwick came back to town earlier than Harriet had been expecting her mother. What was I doing there? She said later she hadn't known what to think; maybe we were sleeping together.)

Not long after the ballet matter, a letter for me came in care of West Sixty-seventh Street. Elizabeth was angry. Why did Edmund White think that I lived there? Then why would he send me a letter in care of Elizabeth Hardwick? I'd no idea. Now that was embarrassing.

A white youth would have made her a rotating-headed predator, whereas a black youth announced a breakdown of identity. Thanks a bunch, world.

(There is a photograph online that gives me the creeps: I am posed on the arm of the red sofa and I have my hand geekily around Elizabeth. My mother during one of her maneuvers asked if Elizabeth was my girlfriend. Well, how would we know. You don't tell us anything. My mother's postgraduate classes in child psychology prepared me for a style of female interrogation that followed the logic of a trap: You killed five people in that bank robbery. No I didn't, I only killed three.)

She was a white woman of distinction and I the mugger on an episode of *Hill Street Blues*; she had position and I none. Yet the vulnerability was hers, not mine. Henry James's expression 'social death' had a real meaning for Elizabeth. She wasn't a radical girl anymore; she was a heroine. She was sixty-five years old, a woman of a certain age, the shoreline of insouciant life and of not caring what anybody thought much eroded.

—You think every old white lady is like me.

No, that wasn't it. I was pretty sure there was no other writer like her.

(Years later, Lizzie disclosed to me that in the 1940s she had affairs with both J. Saunders Redding, the literary critic, and Roi Ottley, the journalist, two extremely handsome black men.)

Her doors looked great. She said she'd learned at last how to do it right. She'd done the staining on her own.

Going downtown on the IRT, I encountered the Lions of Israel, stern, silent, tall black men in military caps and heavy scarves pulled up to their noses that made me think of the chador look.

Black vinyl or leather jackets, studded wristbands, chains, elaborate black slippers, a huge placard proclaiming the dispersed were wrongly named: Haitians were the children of Benjamin, Panamanians were the children of Levi, Seminole were descended from Reuben . . . They were so solemn and quiet, which freaked out the passengers more than their message did.

Stanley Crouch, wobbly on a bicycle on Second Avenue, explained that I knew these white women because I was not a sexual threat to their husbands and therefore socially acceptable.

And Shine swam on . . .

—— *Part 7* ——

Elizabeth thought Angela Carter had a black boyfriend. She didn't. Her boyfriend was a potter, she'd been with him for seven years, since he was nineteen, she explained when she came to stay with Elizabeth for the weekend. Angela Carter was tall, and it would be just writing on my part to add a red face behind glasses. I do remember a head of fluffy white hair, though she was probably only in her forties then, and she was easy to imagine always in a big sweater. Carter was teaching at Brown. She volunteered to make dinner and produced a heavy concoction of beef and pasta.

Angela Carter: from Battersea, working class, red brick, bohemian, not one of the British bluestockings who filled Elizabeth with impatience. She noted that Carter had no interest in going out for newspapers and even less interest in clothes. They went to see Louis Malle's *Atlantic City* and had a good time. It interested Elizabeth that such a daring style came from such a shy person. Carter was prolific.

Men resented a woman they could not charm, Carter said. She didn't think her current publisher cared whether she lived or died. She didn't talk much about her work. She said that her first four books were awful. She'd begun something at Brown, but hadn't made much progress with it, she said.

Another hunger striker at Maze Prison had died. There was sporadic burning in Belfast. Carter didn't think there should have been a vote in 1916 or that the Brits should have gone over in 1969, but since Northern Ireland was what it was, in Parliament, and so on, that was that. She threw up her hands, not knowing what to think.

Carter showed more confidence about the hazards of birth control, why society was reluctant to develop a pill for men. She knew all about IUDs, having used one for ten years. Maybe she was thinking of children. I said children would be a nice thing. Elizabeth interrupted to say queers could not have children unless they were prepared to give up living as queers. Carter, too, was against the whole lesbian-gay parent rap.

—You can't have children unilaterally, Carter said.

Elizabeth's cigarette was burning down between her fingers, and she was gesticulating with her glass before she began to speak, a sign of impending argumentativeness. Her voice rocketing around the room, Professor Hardwick, as I was calling her that evening, declared,

—Dr. Arendt was against birth control. She said it was a fundamental interference with the body.

My left foot jerked, as if a nail had pressed against it. I bounded to the toilet tucked under the stairs and tore off my sneaker. Inside it, a huge water bug waved at me. The women could hear me, mocked and banging my shoe on enamel edges.

I'd been about to bring up Arendt's warning to Baldwin after she read *The Fire Next Time*: that the lovely qualities we attribute to the oppressed don't survive liberation, 'not even for five minutes.'

BACKSTAGE AT THE 92nd Street Y on Lexington Avenue, Elizabeth said Barbara had been against having Susan in the *Review* in the beginning, because she didn't think she was a good enough writer.

—I had to fight for her.

Susan sat at her typewriter with her enormous subjects, in furious effort, an outpouring of words. She worked up her essays in a marathon of typing, smoking, and speed, rumor had it. She had help with research. She liked helpers. Her ideas were brilliant; she just had no ear, Elizabeth said.

(—It was just this big blob of snot, Sharon, one of Susan's most devoted readers, would say of the first draft of her essay on Sartre.)

Elizabeth's introduction of Susan was good. She spoke of her as 'a peculiar monument.'

(And yet Elizabeth would never reprint her introduction to *The Sontag Reader*, and Susan would never stop asking me why that was.)

After fretting about what to read, Susan chose paragraphs from the end of *Death Kit* and all of 'The Dummy' from her collection of short stories, *I, etc.* In between her first novel and that story, she had identified what she could not do as a fiction writer.

Elizabeth and I were by ourselves in the greenroom of makeup lights and a covered baby grand. We could hear, a ways off, the thrum of book signing and book lovers having wine. Susan's stage laughter approached. People filed in behind her and formed little squads of talk. Tom Victor snapped pictures. Grace Dudley, a black fortress of empire bodice and puffed sleeves, glared. Tom backed off. Dominique had already slung her camera into the as-you-were position. I'd had my head shaved at Astor Place, on Howard's advice.

Susan wandered around, blitzed out. Just back from Shanghai, she'd taught classes at the New School that morning. She looked awful, large, in black trousers that made her rear seem enormous. Elizabeth did not like her jazz shoes. Susan had amended her dyed hair. The salt and pepper gone to jet black, like a coat, with just a touch of white over the ear.

Susan drew me aside to ask, How was Lizzie, really. Lizzie seemed fragile to her, she said. I was a little too charmed to have been in her confidence.

—Never talk about someone you know very well to someone you know less well, Barbara said.

I'd heard Barbara when journalists and graduate students came to her office to ask about Vidal or Roth. She answered every question without revealing anything or lying.

—The open smile and the shut mouth.

The day after Susan's reading, I returned *The Portable Faulkner*, a paperback almost as old as the several non-lend Faulkner volumes in Elizabeth's library, and said I wish I'd never read 'Percy Grimm,' or 'A Justice,' or 'Wedding in the Rain,' or 'Delta Autumn,' they were so great. Elizabeth didn't mind my talking to Susan about her. She was amused, trusting me more than she did Susan.

—She treated you like a member of the club.

Susan had embraced me and asked what I was writing. She looked beautiful after that, not too large at all.

Elizabeth and I went to the ballet (was it the incredible *Mozartiana*?) and on the way back to West Sixty-seventh Street, talking about being both encouraged and defeated by Faulkner, she said one must decide on a literary audience.

—That means don't be boring.

Be one step ahead of the reader, don't repeat what the reader already knows, be ironic or fanciful, she said. She'd laid down these laws before, as if waiting for me to get it, now maybe uncertain I could. That her strictures could be contradictory was reassuring.

She said she sometimes tried to remember the West Sixties in their run-down state before Lincoln Center was built. Delmore Schwartz lived in the neighborhood. I told her I would bring her *Blueschild Baby* by George Cain, a drug novel set in a pre–Lincoln Center West Side. It was always fun that *West Side Story* was about those streets.

She said everyone reads 'In Dreams Begin Responsibility' and nothing else by him, not his poetry, but Delmore Schwartz had been a good critic. When he was in his steep, drunken decline, she saw him someplace and avoided him. (Sitting on a bench? Or is that an image I have of him from a photograph?) She said she felt guilty.

—He was impossible to help.

The news we turned on was a shock: the black body found in

the Chattahoochee River in Atlanta on May 27, 1981, was not that of a child.

I WAS SUBSTITUTING for Shelley again. I picked up the phone:

—This is Abbie Hoffman. Are you going to do a review of Jack Abbott's book?

Norman Mailer had published a piece in the *Review* the year before about how he came to know Jack Henry Abbott, an inmate with an interest in literature. Abbott was doing time for forgery when he killed a fellow inmate. Decades got added onto his sentence. When Mailer was working on *The Executioner's Song*, his novel about the white murderer in Utah who in 1977 demanded that he be executed by firing squad, Abbott wrote to him, saying he shouldn't believe everything he got from Gary Gilmore. He offered to tell him what prison was really like. His letters to Mailer formed the basis of his book *In the Belly of the Beast*. Mailer was instrumental in getting Abbott paroled; he wrote the preface to Abbott's book.

Reform-school raised, solitary-confinement survivor Abbott was out on parole, getting ripped off at his ex-convict's boardinghouse, being taken to Macy's by Erroll McDonald, getting into trouble for smoking in the library, chewing Bob's ear off about Heidegger.

—It could be worse, Bob said.

The *Review* wasn't going to do Abbott's book. They'd done so much of it already. A story was going around that he squashed his cigarette in the palm of a librarian who asked him to put it out.

Though Abbott had been serving a long sentence, he seemed frivolous to me and Mailer deluded in his quest for a real white Negro. Abbott was certainly no political prisoner, as almost any incarcerated black person seemed to be, even Eldridge Cleaver in his gold-medallion, semen-spraying letters from prison, reprinted in *Soul on Ice*. George Jackson was another matter.

Jean Genet was Howard's thing. (When she came back from a special trip to Cuba, Harriet said she trusted Genet when he claimed that Raul Castro, Fidel's brother, was gay.) Chester Himes was mine. Elizabeth had a vague memory of Himes's novels from the 1940s about blacks falling out with the Communist Party. She didn't know *Cast the First Stone*, Himes's novel based on his experiences in the Ohio penitentiary in the late 1920s and early 1930s. A college dropout, he'd been convicted of armed robbery.

(How much of a gay novel he'd written ahead of his time was made evident when the original version of his novel was published as *Yesterday Will Make You Cry*.)

Himes's autobiography was pretty nuts, wildly bitter. Luc had read it. Chester Himes's detective novels were very much Luc's thing. He knew them in French translation.

Barbara was not into the whole Jack Abbott thing, that was for sure. She hadn't been able to hold out against the *Review* publishing him.

—Barbara's tough, Elizabeth said after I got out of Bob's office for the night.

Once, while watching Menachem Begin on TV after the terrible bombing in Iraq, Barbara remembered what Auden said of Podhoretz: 'God's gift to anti-Semitism.'

Elizabeth had a theory that Barbara in her battles with Bob used what Elizabeth considered not exactly a woman's strategy, but one not unrelated to the temperament of someone in the opposition, if not in the resistance, someone in a weaker position, ostensibly: Barbara obstructed. She held things up, shrugged, said she was looking at this, still thinking before she passed a manuscript to the production studio.

They were like a married couple, only worse. Elizabeth speculated that Grace probably minded how much time Barbara spent with Bob in the office, which was why Grace didn't really like Barbara.

Bob would rush back to his office and, crying for all hands, pro-

duce a memo backing up his argument, with xeroxes of encyclope-
dia entries or of articles from learned journals attached. They took
turns ambushing each other in his or her office, one always standing, the other dug in behind the books and papers on the desk.
They flung galleys, they slammed books, but nothing was printed
unless they had both agreed to it in the end.

They sat together in Barbara's office after lunch to decide what
would go in the next issue and again to determine the order of
the pieces. In those days, Barbara chose all the illustrations that
weren't by David Levine, and she showed Bob everything she had
in mind.

Bob had delayed his departure for Lausanne, but Shelley didn't
change her plans. Bob couldn't understand why she didn't. (Elizabeth once said pretty girls had a hard time getting credit for being intelligent.) He called Wednesday morning. I asked for more
money. He agreed. I worked until Jonathan Lieberson and Charles
Rosen arrived, competitively entertaining, their brilliant riffs far
over my head.

'Oh really?' I kept repeating, like they were Sterling Brown telling me a tall tale.

(Jonathan Lieberson, who wrote about philosophy but also
liked fashion, would succumb to AIDS. He had had radical treat-
ments for the time, total body transfusions of blood.)

Bob let me slink off. After they left, he was in the office until six
in the morning, he said the next day.

He was editing Jacobo Timerman's Amnesty address, hoping to
publish a 'calmer' version of it. I was sorry about that, the original
was searing. He denounced 'semantic adventurers.' Timerman had
been imprisoned and tortured by the Argentine military regime he
opposed.

Bob was happy. Barbara was out of the office. I worked still
later. I asked him if he didn't want to go home and help the housekeeper pack. He laughed. He laughed at everything I said. I referred

to his assistants, myself included, as the elves. He laughed when I told him not to go abroad without mad money.

I made mistakes that would have gotten a regular assistant told off, but Mr. Silvers patiently explained to me how things were done. Liberal conscience was not the only reason he could not bring himself to yell at me. He loved Elizabeth Hardwick.

In those days of no hierarchy at *The New York Review of Books*, only Bob and Barbara had the power to commission essays, open to suggestions though they liked to be. The two assistant editors were managing editors. It was a theater of secrets and American intellectual history. There may have been no place to go at the *Review*, no editorial ladder to climb, but the vibe was that if one survived Bob and Barbara then one could walk out of there and get a big job anywhere in publishing or journalism or get into a prestigious graduate school.

They themselves weren't writers, but they understood them. It couldn't be taught: to love writers, their works, their ideas.

I typed up a list of books by month from the mound of catalogs Bob had marked. And his notes about possible reviewers.

—O I have done another one, he sighed with satisfaction.

It happened to be a day he'd promised his father he'd meet him, and that meant I would be done by seven o'clock.

—O good, we have crackers, he said, attacking a box of saltines.

'There is no resolution but in death' in Max Hayward's translation of *Doctor Zhivago* that I was reading between batches of manuscript pages to decipher and retype. Finally, Bob left, brown cheroot in mouth. He left me the galleys of a Harlem history that he and Barbara had in mind for my next piece.

FREE OF BOSSES at last, Earle and I left the office and, after nostalgic French fries at the West End Café, we found the garage doors pulled down over the shops along 125th Street, revealing murals painted in a sort of local Zhdanovism. Near the spanking plate doors of the Freedom National Bank, the fast-food joints were open, and so were the bars where what went on went on softly behind the glow of pink, blue, green neon. 'Positively no dust smoking. Positively no guns. Positively no loitering in the restroom. Positively everyone will be searched.' The armada of churches was quiet, the storefront dwellings of the Holy Spirit as well as the flagships guarding the Haussmann-like boulevards. Brilliant mosaics of broken glass formed under the amber lamps.

Blight had made Harlem monotonous in appearance. The tower of the State Office Building stuck out like an insertion brought from Brasília. Not that far away, a blue Palladian façade waited. The avenues had a grim sameness. Many structures were husks, their windows like the sockets of skulls. No graffiti, though one lonely wall had painted on it 'Support the Freedom Fighters.'

Eighth Avenue starting at 110th Street and some of the tenements leaning toward St. Nicholas Avenue were nervous bazaars for heroin with names like Circle B, Sure Shot, Three Hearts Ready to Kill, and Blue Magic. The glassine packets were slipped through peepholes by children too young to be prosecuted. Much of the dope on the street was stepped on, we heard, cut with quinine. As a tourist I was not afraid of the junkie scratching his flesh off, one of those whom the Darwinism of using had not taken away. The working addict was not a new phenomenon, the one who held down a job to support a habit. He wanted no trouble, especially not with the police.

Five black youths came by, slapping five and one carrying a third-world briefcase, Luc said it was called, the radio turned up to gospel level. The five black youths weren't interested in us, but their haughty indifference was like them saying the well-meaning tourist of our student days wasn't welcome anymore. But like the professional druggies, the aggressive, defensive black youth were not what we needed to be afraid of, not the actual ones far down the street by now. It was the fear of macho blackness in my homo head I should have mistrusted. The boarded-up, empty feeling of most of the streets added to my unease and could get too easily filled in by what I'd read. A bottle from somewhere broke across our path. We retreated.

I first saw the streets of Harlem when I was a child, shortly after the riot in the summer of 1964. There was broken glass everywhere. My parents were speechless and would not stop anywhere, but we drove slowly, as if in farewell. Since then, Harlem had become a password for danger. My father said I must have some kind of death wish. They were just waiting for someone like me, he said. I was going to write about histories of Harlem, I said. Sterling could say what he liked, Harlem had been the capital of black America. He told me not to tell my mother.

My mother's foot was still in a cast. She'd broken her ankle trying to go en pointe. She was in her late fifties. She sewed the laces into her shoes herself. She said she could not forgive her bones. It was because her favorite ballet, *The Tempest*, had been on channel 20. Crutches did not suit her as accessories, and she refused to use them, hobbling down the hall, my sisters said, making my father carry her to the car and from the car downstairs to Mrs. Roney's basement chair for an appointment she did not want to cancel. She'd called me the night before to remind me to call on Father's Day.

—If your handbag is black / How come your shoes are brown. Donna said it was a Delta Sigma Theta song, our mother's Negro sorority. Donna had betrayed her and gone AKA in school.

My brother-in-law and I saluted the nationwide heat wave.

Kafka's *Letters* Pat said were hard going, but *Amerika* cheered her up. She said ease with weirdness was a side effect of her specialty in juvenile law. She said that meant she seldom got paid and was once asked at gunpoint by a grandmother to pray with her on her knees for her grandson's release. My sister kept her files in brown paper bags in the trunk of her car.

The arrest in Atlanta had shocked many with the possibility that a black man could be a serial killer, that a black man could commit a white man's crime.

(Including Baldwin. The last book of his life would be the worst book of his life: *The Evidence of Things Not Seen*. If not an exoneration of Wayne Williams, convicted of two of the murders, then it was an attempt to be skeptical about the evidence against him. Or have I misremembered the book, one I have not reread?)

THE FIRST WEEK Elizabeth was in Maine, she was coming from Bucksport with groceries and booze. She swerved to avoid a deer and the car went out of control. Apparently, she jammed her foot on the accelerator and there she was spinning in the road. She crashed into a tree.

—I saw this tree and thought, Good. It's over. Poor Harriet will have to come get my bones.

Boom. Car on its side. Not a scratch, except for a sore arm from trying to pull and wriggle out the door to hail a passing car. It was a miracle she emerged uninjured. But there was damage of another sort; she was depressed and shaken for two weeks afterward. She just didn't feel like doing anything, didn't feel up to anything. She felt guilty, though everyone in town told her of having smashed into a deer. She told me she called Harriet in hysterics.

It took her a while to get herself together. But she even recovered her groceries. Mary McCarthy and Jim West took her to pick up a new car. Her wreck was stored in the same garage. Mary and Jim got her to look at it: a few dents. She thought she had totaled it.

—Totaled.

She liked to repeat stories that ended with someone recounting to her, 'I totaled it.'

The visit to the garage soothed her anguish about the car. Mary drove her off in a new Buick.

Elizabeth was working on a piece she called 'Back Issues,' for the autobiography number of *Antaeus*. She thought maybe she could put it in her book. She did not speak well of it.

—It's stupid.

It came from her idea that what is one's life, one's autobiography, other than what one has read.

She'd finished a draft and hoped to have the whole thing ready by the time Harriet came up at the end of the month.

She'd been reading, of course.

—I start *War and Peace* in the morning and I'm finished by five o'clock.

Mary's seventieth-birthday party got to her. She left early. Everyone in town was there, gardeners included. Champagne fountains.

—I thought the lawsuit would have put an end to these parties and put us out of our misery. If you ever repeat that I'll kill you.

She hadn't been in the mood for Castine social life. One evening alone with Mary she'd really enjoyed. They started talking about *Jane Eyre*.

—Mary says she doesn't believe her. Neither do I, I said. And we just went on talking about how interesting Rochester is.

Belfast, Beirut, Elizabeth sprained her thumb. She couldn't type. Fortunately, it was the thumb of her left hand.

—I feel I've turned into some hideous hypochondriac. Before the thumb it was the virus; before the virus it was the accident.

That deer.

BOB WAS OUT in the late afternoon. Norman Mailer called, said it was urgent, and left his Cape Cod number. Jason, impatient, called twice from Sag Harbor. He wanted to know where Bob had gone. I thought Lillian Hellman had kicked the bucket.

Jack Abbott was wanted for questioning. Jack Abbott was suspected of having killed a man the day before. In a restaurant on

Second Avenue, the Bini Bon, near the Bar, at five o'clock on Saturday morning.

Abbott had been with a rich French girl and a rich Filipina, a student at Barnard. Apparently, he got into an argument with a waiter, Richard Adan, twenty-two years old, about the bathroom. The one for customers was occupied and Adan wouldn't permit Abbott to use the one reserved for employees. Abbott asked Adan to step outside and there Adan was stabbed to death.

The first reports would turn out to be inaccurate.

The *Post* claimed Abbott 'panicked,' ran back inside, and asked the two girls to 'dash away with him.' They refused. He hadn't been seen since.

When Bob returned, Norris Church answered the telephone. Mailer was too out of it to talk. Then Bob called Jason. He called Mrs. Mailer again. He paced, from desk to absent assistant's desk, tapping papers, making noises.

I kept tabs on him between stacks of books. He came near. I asked him stupidly if he regretted helping Abbott.

—Yes.

Almost shouted.

The *Times* reported, incorrectly, that Jason had signed the parole letters. Jason refused all along, which had angered Bob. It was only him and Mailer, exposed, responsible.

—He has a short fuse, Bob repeated.

He had had lunch with Abbott Friday. Abbott complained that the city was getting to him. He had until the end of the month before he could leave. After lunch, Abbott was at Random House. He was said to have been down, morose, but didn't say anything.

—He said he was on codeine, Bob said.

Codeine? Cocaine?

—Yes, that's it.

Street cocaine was usually cut with speed. That could have easily lit his fuse. The girl from the Philippines lived near Abbott's halfway house on the Bowery. They met at a party Erroll had taken Abbott to. As for the French girl, there were a lot of rich French girls downtown.

Mailer got a call from Abbott on Saturday morning at six o'clock. Mailer said it was too early and couldn't he call back. Abbott usually spent the weekends with the Mailers. He got on with Norris Church better than anyone. Mailer had done a lot for Abbott, guaranteed him a job, and so forth, but he wasn't prepared to adopt Abbott. He had problems of his own: his former wife Beverly was suing him.

There was a knock on Erroll's door Saturday night. He didn't answer; he wasn't expecting anyone. Erroll went out later, to dance at Xenon's. (Soon he'd be checking behind his curtains for Abbott, then not sleeping at home.)

At first, Bob thought Abbott had a lot of cash from his agent, Scott Meredith, but Erroll said he didn't have more than one hundred dollars. Bob said Abbott knew the PATH subway system and from Newark a bus could go anywhere. But not without money.

Bob went to Barbara's at nine o'clock.

Elizabeth called.

—One hates for the predictable to happen.

She said self-destructive was not suicidal. She didn't think he was dead, but a confrontation with police would end it all. They were scared men who didn't want any trouble with a dangerous con. They were perfectly willing to shoot him.

I thought he must have been hiding out downtown.

In the Belly of the Beast had been well reviewed, mostly, and Abbott had an idea for a novel about prison. He got money for a play he wrote while in jail, never having seen a play, after reading the Shaw and Strindberg that Mailer sent.

He should not have been left alone, should have been in an AA for people addicted to rage, Elizabeth said. He was obviously someone who couldn't bear any sort of authority or interference.

Crossed was crossed. A life in prison. But a chicken was just another way to make an egg.

Pat was relieved I'd never met Jack Abbott. She said unfortunately, much like Gary Gilmore, Abbott helped those who wanted to justify the Supreme Court's renewal of the death penalty.

My father said he bet *The New York Review of Books* was upset to learn they were pushovers.

Felice said Richard Adan had just landed his first paying role, in a play written by her friend Nathan. Everybody knew the Bini Bon had no bathroom and that you had to go to Nightbirds across the street and that was what Adan, the nice, helpful waiter, she said, had been trying to explain.

Governess of floods, she was wearing her white lace gown and white knit gloves, perched shoeless on a step on St. Marks in front of Little Club 57 with Jean-Michel, who said he was on mescaline. The red queens were off their heads, but very, very quiet.

HOWARD AND BRAD moved into the Chelsea Hotel. Howard bought a television, a stereo, and two air conditioners, and took Brad to East Hampton. He left me the keys to their new place. The Chelsea was expensive, some of it nice, but a lot of it was squalid. Howard said he would not have been surprised to come across Bani-Sadr sneaking up the stairs.

I thought I could live without adjectives, but heartbreakers were in control, slightly contemptuous of affection. Richard Howard lamented that the French have a word for the hair on top of the head and another word for the hair on the rest of the body.

> *There was no prince in Seville*
> *Who could compare with him*

The great thing about the Bar, raucous, smoky, jukeboxed, was that nobody played dumb. A petition against nuclear weapons circulated around the pool table, between pinball machines, among poets, composers, merchant seamen, painters, musicians, art critics, roadies, photographers, actors, performance artists, curators, sound engineers, script doctors, translators, set designers, filmmakers, waiters, models, theater directors, bartenders from other places, assistants, dancers, liggers, novelists, future fashion designers and future novelists, the unclassifiable, the sweating, the unknowable, the many not yet, a cartoonist, a sex bomb of a cartographer, and a pleasant editor of the Gertrude Stein–Carl Van Vechten *Letters*.

> *Nor sword like his sword*
> *Nor heart so true*

Who showed up was a surprise, like the way Xenophon could look at the soldiers of the Persian expedition up close.

—Don't ever touch me.

—What do you know of symbolic illumination?

—No one reads the *Eclogues* but queers.

—I heard there was a magazine in San Francisco for queens into mysticism.

—I have bad news. I may have the clap.

—There's always a rival.

—Virgil said J.J. is going to the dogs like a gentleman.

—Sylvia Miles would go to the opening of a refrigerator.

—I was letting myself out in humorous rodomontade.

—We walked out of *Cave Girls* by the East Side Faction at No Rio.

—He made waffles and played Greek music.

—My coffee is buffalo blood.

—Somerset Maugham fucked me from behind.

—Then what happened.

The Bar was flying, headquarters for one objective narcissist after another, Weimar-minded guys reacting to Frank Moore's painting *For Sex I Like to . . .* , in the Porn Show at Little Club 57, an exhibition censored by priests, Frank said.

(A decade later, gorgeous and bold Frank Moore died of AIDS, one of that cohort that started to live longer on drugs. His paintings are beautiful, as I remember them.)

It was going to be the summer that did not quit. It was the last summer before we believed in the plague.

> *I was Pharaoh*
> *He the Hebrews*

The Reinaldo Arenas reading (he would die of AIDS) at the Bowery Poetry Project had already happened, but I didn't read the flyer correctly until halfway there.

> *May these brick waves clatter down*
> *If I did not love you well.*

To recall faces in the Bar before AIDS changed the lives it did not end is to cover the page with parenthetical asides.

> *(Betcha by golly wow*
> *You're the one that I've been waiting for forever)*

Voyager II blacked out for a while after sending back photographs of Saturn's rings and seven moons.

(JAMES WAS LYING on his back in the sitting room, reading Logan Pearsall Smith's memoir. He said Pearsall Smith was writing it in his room on Edith Wharton's yacht, while she was above him in her room writing her memoir. Pearsall Smith remembered that when he was a child his Quaker parents were ambivalent about taking the children to the circus. They didn't mind them seeing animals but feared the temptations of the acrobats. The compromise was that the children would cover their eyes when the acrobats appeared. Pearsall Smith said he looked through his fingers.)

ELIZABETH HAD SUSAN all weekend. At first Susan canceled, then when Ada Long from the University of Alabama was with Elizabeth, she changed her mind. Elizabeth was tired and wrote to Susan not to come, everyone was sick. Susan told her not to be silly. She told her she was coming in order to prevent Lizzie from turning into a recluse.

It was just like Susan, Barbara said, to cancel and then insist on coming.

—Susan can't go there. She's too big for that house.

I told Elizabeth I didn't get *Fathers and Sons*, though Bazarov's mother and father ripped at my heart. She said she chose not to believe me. I had *Pale Fire* on deck.

—A silly book, Elizabeth said.

She said she had this conversation with a woman in Maine about her newlywed daughter:

—'Doug comes home to lunch every day. He don't want nothing. He just pushes me right down on that bed, Ma.'

—Well, at least she won't have to sweat over a hot stove, Elizabeth said she answered.

Castine had a blackout. Elizabeth said she was going around saying,

—If this goes on half an hour longer, I'm going to go down to the drugstore and loot it. What else are they for?

She didn't think anyone in Castine got her urban jokes.

She sent me her new story, the vibrant, lyrical 'Back Issues.'

It celebrates the New York Public Library, the aristocratic monument on Fifth Avenue, a couple of blocks across town from the indignities of Times Square. (She doesn't say so in the story, but Bryant Park behind the library was rather unsafe and abandoned in those days.) But the library, 'a hallowed spot,' has its readers, scholars, and 'the others, the others,' lost and seeking New Yorkers of various descriptions that Elizabeth in her late work delights in wondering about.

> In the library are our Back Issues, old copies of our literary magazines. Quarterlies they were for the most part, inspirations of the vernal equinox and the winter solstice. Long and short memorials to the thoughts of many therein. More hours of these lives were spent on book reviews than on lovemaking or even on making a living.

Elizabeth's nameless narrator re-creates the contents and intensities of the small journals and quarterlies of another time. She is carrying a notebook for her research. She notices a beautiful black-eyed, black-haired man waiting for his book to come up from the stacks and when they sit, coincidentally near one another, she is interested in the medical book he is reading. She speculates that he is Armenian. 'The beautiful man from the race of martyrs was dressed well enough in the style of modest indoor occupation.'

The handsome foreigner is Greek, 'another *ethnic*,' a waiter in a restaurant, and he extends the moment they had in the rain under his umbrella on the library steps. He gets her information from her library slip and calls her up. She'd said to him that she was a teacher, and he, a teacher back in Greece, feels no social awkwardness in pursuing her. He reveals himself over the phone, telling her all about his family and emphasizing how ordinary and disappointing to himself he is. 'No need to imagine harassment from such an abyss of self-examination.' The narrator hears from the 'Greek exile' one last time around Easter, and they have an amusing exchange about his bride-to-be, an older divorcée.

The narrator does not say she is in Maine, but the Back Issues have piled up, one of which takes her mind off having crashed into a tree to avoid a deer the day before. She 'totaled' her car.

'Back Issues': rapid musings on New York, its 'defiant calendar of merchandise,' or 'the honorable suicide of old buildings.' Here, as always, her economy of expression, the gift for the striking image, the resonant detail. Subversive feeling is her woman's freedom, as when the narrator first sees the flirtatious Greek: 'Write it down just as male authors write of the haunting face across the room of a beautiful woman.' She reads a translation from the French in a Back Issue, 'But novels are written *by* men *for* men.' It's not true for her narrator, the ironic 'she.' After all, her subject is reading.

The narrator says her jottings about George Gissing are for an article on him that she never wrote. Elizabeth got to use up the Gissing quotes she copied out into notebooks. She also deployed or deposited in a safe place a memory, that of John Berryman in that postwar culture thick with earnest literary quarterlies.

> No one in the public library today brings to mind the early John B., peering over his large, glinting eyeglasses from the stage of the YMHA, the temple of poetry readings. There he was then, quite intense, and learned; there he was in a smart tweed jacket, there before the faithful girls of New York. High-style infatuation. In the vestibule where white wine completed the evening, the poet could be seen skating as if on one toe over the oil slick of questions, diverting away from his own lines to *The Winter's Tale* and gorgeous Perdita, left to the wind and the waves, and the parenthetical paranoias of Leontes.

(I should look up the letter in which Lizzie's tone with Lowell in *The Dolphin Letters* changes. I think it happened after he was forced to say that he and Blackwood had deceived her as to how far along Caroline had been in her pregnancy when they first told Lizzie about it. Lizzie reacts as if she had been made a fool of all over again. I don't remember how the name of John Berryman comes up, but she throws out in this letter that she knew him rather better than she has ever said.

Trying to get her pride back. My sense is that she knew him before she met Lowell, that she was remembering herself in Berryman's audience, not one of the faithful girls, rather more to the side, because he would have known from reading *Partisan Review* who Elizabeth Hardwick was.)

BY SEPTEMBER, Jack Abbott was phoning from Mexico. He called Scott Meredith to ask for money. He wrote to his sister also. Meanwhile, M. A. Farber of the *Times* dug up the dirt: Abbott cooperating with officials or not, threatened by both sides. Some letter saying he wasn't beaten when in fact he had been beaten, presumably by another inmate.

Bob said he realized why Abbott had been taken from the prison at Marion, Illinois, so quickly. He'd turned snitch.

Bob was haunted by the crime and the man. Abbott wrote to him every day. I could imagine Bob alone at night, rereading Abbott's letters, looking for some clue, trying to understand.

When she first met Abbott, Barbara said she thought he was wrapped too tight and Bob naïve in an odd way.

Bob thought it possible Abbott could get to El Salvador as a mercenary or something that strange.

I sat at Shelley's desk with her small vials of perfume samples and Venedikt Erofeev's *Moscow to the End of the Line*. Joseph Brodsky appeared and said the real title of Erofeev's novel was 'Moscow to Little Russia,' the subway station at the end of that line. He was wandering around, waiting for Bob. The translation I had was by

H. W. Tjalsma, but I said by mistake that it had been done by Vera Dunham. Brodsky went off.

—That's unfortunate. Do you want me to be blunt? She sits between two chairs, ja? Whenever she goes there, she kisses . . . It's a good book and she wants to do that . . . (He made more kissy faces.) She believes she is a grande dame and she is not, ja?

He scratched his chin and said that Dunham curried favor, that she was part of the Yevtushenko wave. The Erofeev novel was not as anti-Soviet as it seems, he warned.

—It is very satirical, but not so anti, you know?

Dunham wrote the introduction, I corrected myself apologetically.

(Beloved by his friends, Brodsky at the rostrum tended toward the arrogant, perhaps as a force field. His performances could make one understand why society had mixed feelings about intellectuals as unproductive entertainment.

When Brodsky and Bob appeared onstage with Czeslaw Milosz, Bob concentrated on *The Captive Mind*; Brodsky concentrated on himself. He was so rude, the gentlemanly Milosz stepped forward:

—We have a saying: between Poland and China lies a small nation.

—He is a grown-up, Dominique Nabokov said, the highest praise Barbara's girls had for a man.)

Bob had the crazy idea that I should work for Jerzy Kosinski. He and Brodsky left.

Sharon said it was a well-known scandal that Kosinski didn't write his own novels. He got suckers to edit them, as it was called.

Dunham was much more left than Brodsky, Barbara explained. She was in good spirits. The new issue of the *Review* was terrific.

—I was Jason's first office romance, Barbara said.

She was going to have dinner with Elizabeth at Des Artistes.

—Another year.

On another day, Elizabeth said she enjoyed being surprised

that the fact-checkers at *The New Yorker* let stand in a piece on Marguerite Yourcenar the description of Northeast Harbor in Maine as 'remote.' To me, Yourcenar's novel *Coup de Grâce* was a big letdown, while the film of it had been perfect. Her novel *Memoirs of Hadrian* was also less than I'd expected, dry and not romantic.

Roy Wilkins died. My father still felt a little guilty. Bob knew his nephew, Roger Wilkins, a good journalist who should write more, he said.

My parents arrived from a terrible time in Atlantic City. I wouldn't let my father visit the *Review*. He was known to sell NAACP memberships with Nation of Islam zeal, hitting up black guys, white guys, Asian guys, in airport men's rooms.

—Are you afraid I'll embarrass you?

(My parents came to adore Barbara and Murray.)

They didn't know that Aunt Alvan and Uncle Dick had been taken away by their sons until they went over to Jersey City and found a large family moving into their house on Atlantic Avenue.

—YOU'D THINK MARY had never read Sartre's *Les mots* or even Simone de Beauvoir, Elizabeth was saying in her kitchen.

—*Memoirs of a Dutiful Daughter*, I began.

—Yes. Mary is supposed to be writing an intellectual biography. It was appalling.

Elizabeth stood rigid and imitated Mary McCarthy:

—In Cincinnati, basketball, women's basketball was very important. Period. Or: At Garland High School, grades were not important. Period. Then she'd stand aside and say something like, I believe Latin should be taught, but to everyone. Oh, I am so upset about it. Please don't tell anyone I said anything. It was just awful.

She pressed her head with her hands and checked the pesto.

—I can just see it. She whirled around. —She gives this stuff to Jim. So Jim would read something from *Cannibals* and come

to Mary and say, Dear, well, I think this might be somewhat con-
fusing to the reader. Elizabeth struck her Mary McCarthy pose
again. —Oh shoot, Jimmy. That's the best part. Back to Mr. West
pose: —You're right, dear.

As Elizabeth stirred the sauce, she said,

—That's what happens to couples. Cal used to read some of
my things. Some seventeen sweated-out pages. He'd read them
and look up and look around and say, Very good. Have you ever
thought of writing about Keats? It was maddening. I'd say, Drop
dead. Always something so remote. Have you ever thought of writing about (she paused as he would have) d'Annunzio? Oh. Here we
go. For once there's enough sauce, not too much spaghetti and not
enough sauce. I want to use this up. I've been freezing it all summer. Every time someone brought me some basil, I'd run to the
kitchen and get this thing out and dump it in there. Have you ever
seen so much goo? Okay. Here we go.

We had too much on our plates.

—But Cal used to tease me all the time. When we were in Italy,
he said, You mean you've never read *The Wonders and Horrors of the
Vatican*? He was making up an art book. And I'd say, No, I'd like to
read it. Can you believe it?

Is whispering nothing?

She'd told me this before. I never stopped her when she repeated
herself. The anniversary of his death was upon her, but she seemed
more together about it, not as thrown back in time.

—It's not a crime to fall in love with someone else, she'd said.

NYU BEGAN A conference on Hannah Arendt's work. I got there as
Mary McCarthy was describing Arendt's dramatic, theatrical personality. She recalled Arendt's solution to the Berlin crisis: move
the city stone by stone. That was, to her, a matter of engineering,

not impossible, and not a matter of politics. The problem of the schools, McCarthy remembered Arendt saying, was that too many went without hot morning meals and therefore could not learn. Again, a problem of administration, distinct from politics.

I liked McCarthy's phrase about public acts coming from the darkness of private lives.

Bernard Crick, donnishly unattractive, said the linguistic school at Oxford didn't like Arendt and he did a stupid imitation of deep-voiced, thick-tongued Isaiah Berlin putting her down:

—It's just, pop, metaphysical free association, your, pop, Arendt.

I noticed that Crick promoted his own work and that of his friends based on his claim that he wanted something more substantive.

He conceded that Arendt was brilliant at describing freedom, but she wasn't so good at defining the public life, the responsibilities of the polis. He disagreed with what he thought was the importance she gave to 'hopeless resistance' in *Eichmann*, pointing to her using Cicero's dramatic line about the wisdom of the slave's committing suicide before his freedom was defiled. He said her imprudence was one of her charms. Crick tossed off some comments that pleased him concerning Kant's influence on Arendt's work.

(Angela Davis made Kant and Hegel necessary equipment for black militants, Marxist and nationalist. Her 'Lectures on Liberation,' a pamphlet with a picture of her and her alluring Afro on the cover, her UCLA lectures from 1969 before Reagan fired her, were passed around on campus almost like samizdat. She read Frederick Douglass in the light of Kant's analysis of violence. Kant's observations of Africans in his anthropological writings were unknown to us in the days of finding out that those who would be masters were the truly dependent ones.)

McCarthy stepped on Crick for being a poor listener. She said she was talking about Kant's influence on Arendt's ideas concerning aesthetics. She said she had not described Hannah as imprudent. She had not said that there was no extant tape of Arendt's voice. She said Arendt didn't like radio or TV programs and there were probably very few recordings.

Someone had brought an interview done with Arendt in France, we were told, but the magnetic tape had been erased when he went through customs.

Elizabeth once said that Arendt told her she didn't like being on TV because she was afraid of being recognized in someplace like the grocery store.

The questions from the audience were a torment. In answer to a question about 'women's lib,' McCarthy quoted Arendt as saying, 'What will we win if we lose.'

Elizabeth didn't like Mary saying that. —It's too conventional.

We were filing out behind Barbara, Elie Duvivier, and Frances FitzGerald.

—Hannah could say conventional things, Elizabeth went on. —I remember she said, Oh, that's nonsense. Women of my mother's generation could do whatever they wanted.

—I've been meaning to call you, Bob said.

I made as if to run.

Alison & Busby had reissued three novels by George Lamming and had published two new novels by Roy A. K. Heath. Alison was the white guy and Busby the black woman, the only black woman in publishing in England, and the secret of their success was that they were not married, we joked.

The problems with the piece I'd handed in to Bob were several. Heath was from Guyana, which was not Lamming's Barbados, and I wanted to argue with Naipaul. Moreover, Mr. Silvers thought my anti-Thatcherism gratuitous.

Where in England had there not been riots that summer. Alison & Busby had also reprinted Colin MacInnes's 1957 novel *City of Spades*, about the tension in London between black youth and teddy boys, everybody crazy a little. Unsentimental, it stood out against its period. Luc and I fought over it in the office.

I wrote instead about two writers I admired, Ralph de Boissière and Austin Clarke, the first piece of mine that Barbara read before Bob had. She took me over after that and said she preferred I write about what I liked and it didn't have to be books by black writers, only what I was interested in, don't worry about timeliness, that was never going to be my thing.

(In those days, physical effort went with the mental strain. We could end up typing each page several times, crossing out, whiting out letter by missed letter, striving not only to finish, but to achieve a copy clean enough to hand in. Luc was meticulous. I rather admired the state of Felice's pages. She sometimes fell asleep on top of them.)

Daphne Merkin and Leon Wieseltier entered the conference reception. Bob said that Wieseltier's bombshell in *The New Republic* was not too distressing. He'd written it for the *Review*, but they had to say no. To attack Arendt because, in Wieseltier's argument, she blamed the Jews for what had happened to them in Europe was going too far.

Daphne had been at Yaddo, not finishing her novel, she said.

(Barbara didn't like Daphne asking to take off the High Holy Days when she worked at the *Review*.)

Bob's manner gave away nothing. Jack Abbott had been arrested, in Louisiana, working in an oil field. Authorities were tipped off by a prostitute. He'd been to New Hampshire, then Guatemala or Mexico. He came back to New Orleans, no one knew why. Jason said Abbott's best friend in New York was a Puerto Rican transsexual. Abbott said he wanted to write something for the op-ed page of the *Times*. I heard Bob no longer read his letters, but just had them filed.

THE HUNGER STRIKE at Maze Prison in Ireland ended. Luc and Eva started at each other. The Jersey shore had been cold, in summer. Luc was in a mood. Eva could always get to him.

Yes, I being
the terrible puppet of my dreams, shall
lavish this on you.

She was in town on a very Eva scam: Her old aunt on Fifth Avenue was giving her a powder-blue 1965 Cadillac. She expected her to drive it across the country, back to Frisco. Eva, however, was trying to sell it in New Jersey. She and Luc were planning to take pictures of it in front of nondescript diners and filling stations so she could mail them with letters to her aunt when she was back out west. She planned to use the money to fly to Greece to rescue her mother.

('E.S.P.,' in Sante's collection of essays *Maybe the People Would Be the Times*, is a beautiful portrait of her and American youth. I am sorry Eva is not alive to read it.)

Felice wondered if she could ask her agent or her editor to pay for a typist. We met Sara Driver at Tin Pan Alley, a dive bar on Forty-ninth Street, just off Broadway, that had become the Times Square outpost of the downtown scene, complementary to Rafik's O.P. Screening Room not far away. The woman who ran the bar, Maggie Smith, was making something unusual, an artists' space, a performance venue, a gallery, in an obscure, unlikely joint down a few steps from the sleaze on the other side of the sidewalk. It was a crazy downtown scene up there on the small stage, while the Tin Pan Alley regulars at the long bar, street people, working addicts, and disability check aristocrats, stuck their tongues and chins into their booze. Maggie was very political. She denounced even Emma Goldman.

The muscle protecting the liquor license was conspicuous at the bar. Realistic busts by John Ahearn jutted out from the reddish wood walls like patron saints fixed on the prows of ships. Tin Pan Alley was popular with the Colab crowd, artists like Cara Perlman, who showed her finger paintings. Maggie hired only women, as waiters and in the kitchen: April Andres, Janet Stein, Ulli Rimkus,

Andrea Clarke, Cynthia Sley, Nan Goldin, actors, artists, musicians. Women's bands; women filmmakers. Mostly.

On the little stage at Tin Pan Alley, Felice read some of her chapters about Detroit, clutching her pages to her stomach as she ran back to her table in the middle of her last line, hiding from the explosion of applause. Alexis De Veaux returned from Zimbabwe and read from her new play that was getting good reviews. Lise le Compte upstaged her husband. Spoken-word poet Hattie Gossett knew how to make herself heard. And Linda Yablonsky. Nan photographed the writer Cookie Mueller, who often came to see her in Tin Pan Alley. (Not only gay men would die of AIDS. Nan photographed Cookie in her coffin.)

(Luc and Richard Boes, Vietnam vet turned actor, were supposed to give a reading, but they didn't show up. Lucy said she still has the poster from that night.)

And Nan's slideshow of her photographs with a soundtrack, then in its earliest incarnation, called *If My Body Turns Up*, got everyone's attention, most of the ruckus being people talking to or about her slides as they clicked by on equipment that did and then maybe didn't function. Soon, Nan wouldn't know everyone in her audience; the audiences for *The Ballad of Sexual Dependency* would no longer be made up mostly of the people she had photographed.

Nan's birthday shindig down on the Bowery was a going-away party for our apprentice selves. It started at three in the afternoon. Her loft of brick that she shared with the artist Greer Lankton, maker of bizarre sculpture, didn't seem to have any windows. *The Man with the Horn* hopped or blew softly. The party was quiet at first, and I thought it would be one of those nervous-making gatherings of ultra-cool scene stars. Some people watched Björn lose again to McEnroe. Other people played board games in another room. Most hovered around the table heaped with food.

Drinks made in blenders are lethal. It was as though an alarm had gone off, and people were completely bananas all at once. Phil led off, complaining about Jim's leaving the band.

Suzanne took care of him, listened to him, as she used to at school. She who never drank had a drink and was instantly bombed. George was describing his book on cults. Felice was wild, coming in and out, doing who knows what. Luc didn't remember passing out on Greer's bed, beer in hand. One moment he was dancing, then he was asleep, then he was up and dancing again. He said he dated the end of his youth from the time when Eva moved to San Francisco.

—I must have been resting, I never pass out.

We flew around, burning, fire catapulted from a launch during a medieval siege. Nan's neighbors finally complained. On the Bowery of all places. We were in the hall, on the steps. Felice was lying facedown in the hall; Suzanne was throwing up tidily under a ceramic lid; Phil was bleating with his head between his knees; Luc and I were trying to push, throw, pitch, or shove each other over the banister. It was November, but it could have been summer. A couple began to have sex on the extra mattress in Nan's living room.

People thought they were in control. We were already running out of time, losing altitude, but we didn't realize it. Felice said she collapsed on St. Marks and had to depend on the kindness of a stranger to get to her door.

—I'm among the missing today, Nan said the next day and hung up.

People hadn't only been drinking. There had been those murky corners of the loft, and drug debris among bottles, paper plates, *Bomb*. It wasn't supposed to be clean living, but people swore, firstly to themselves, that they were in control of not being in control.

—Don't let nobody tell you you play better stoned, Charlie Parker said.

When one of the gang or someone one of the gang knew had a screening, we showed up. Bette Gordon, Vivienne Dick, James Nares. We met up for performances of the Del-Byzanteens, the Bush Tetras, Chemicals Made from Dirt, Volte, Fab 5 Freddy,

Funky Four Plus One, the Sequins, Grandmaster Flash, the Sugar Hill Gang, Liquid Liquid, Richard Lloyd, the Revlons, Television, Burning Spear, or V at the Peppermint Lounge, Hurrah's, Bond's, the Pyramid, Berlin, Tier 3, Chase Park, AM/PM, the Bowling Alley, Danceteria, A7, the Ritz, Tin Pan Alley, and, may the king live, the Mudd Club. Or was that CBGB's.

Felice said New Wave that had been five white dudes in leather jackets at the counter in Dave's Luncheonette at five in the morning had turned into fifty white dudes in leather jackets in Dave's Luncheonette. The Happy Few thing was gone. She said five hundred black leather jackets were pushing up to that counter.

Diego Cortez's No Wave show at PS1 back in February was a turning point in the mood of what was happening downtown. Several of Nan's guests had, like her, been in it. The music of the scene had taken off first; then the films were having surprising reach. Art from downtown was next. It would take the writing from downtown longer to migrate, nevertheless the stakes were going up rapidly.

If I only have one life, let me live it as a lie.

I was the fellow traveler, hanging out in an aesthetic that interested me, because they were my best friends, but it was not mine; I was just on the train downtown or having a reluctant time-out from the Bar to meet the gang at, say, the funky French restaurant on East Sixth Street where Felice was working. She took the job chopping and washing and waitressing because she'd had too many speeches at Xerox. Her bosses there said they knew she liked to write poetry and songs, but she had to become serious. The drawback was that her new boss was a sort of dealer.

He soon fired a relieved Felice; Maggie gave her work. Then Felice fled home to Detroit to make the revisions her publisher suggested that Professor Hardwick worried might be unnecessary. She was reluctant to interfere.

Of the completed draft of the novel I had under contract, she said, —This defeats even me.

The corridor threatened to be long, never knowing where one belonged, to which scene, which community, or even to oneself. Family and friends kept one's best self in the love locker.

I belonged to every writer I read, at least for a while, until I took myself back, aware of those writers who would not let me get away without first lodging a piece of themselves in me, and then aware which of those writers saw me as they were pushing it under the skin and which did not.

MADISON AVENUE WAS closed up. The American Writers Congress at the Roosevelt Hotel. To register was a pain. By the time I got my name tag, it was so crowded they weren't letting any more people into the ballroom. Harassed staff chanted, 'The fire marshal won't allow us to let in any more people.' Angry milling about. Victor Navasky of *The Nation* was in charge.

On my way, I'd stopped by West Sixty-seventh Street, because she said maybe she'd change her mind.

Bob had complained that the *Review* was listed as a sponsoring organization. But there were so many magazines listed, why make a stink to get out of it. Nothing would be asked of the *Review*; the conference just wanted its name. Barbara was listed as a panelist and called them.

—I've never worn a name tag in my life. At St. Bernard's, they gave you name tags. Mrs. Jason Epstein, mother of Jacob. I took it off.

Mary McCarthy had a fit and got a *Nation* secretary on the telephone. She wanted it announced to the congress that she was never asked, had never agreed, never given permission. She practically threatened to sue.

Elizabeth said she turned to Jim West and said in a whisper

that that was not the way to do it, that it was too self-important, and West said something like you're not kidding.

—We don't need any more of that, she said he said about Mary wanting to sue.

(I had asked the previous summer what Mary McCarthy was going to read at a benefit in Maine with Elizabeth to save Ram Island. Barbara said:

—Her deposition.)

Elizabeth said Mary hadn't seemed well at the Arendt conference. She ate and drank too much at lunch. They got out of a taxi some distance from the auditorium and she was shocked by what an effort walking was for Mary. She heard in Castine that Jim went to Blue Hill to purchase gourmet meals, which he and Mary then ate in the hotel in Bangor, where she was writer in residence.

Mark Danner, the new kid from Harvard in Bob's office, said there had been a flurry of letters between Bob and Mary because he didn't want to print her talk on Arendt. Elizabeth warned Bob not to ask for it. But he did at their lunch; he hadn't heard it. No, he was there, I reminded her. She said she guessed the *Review* couldn't print something on Hannah Arendt claiming she was not political. Elizabeth hadn't liked the talk as much as I had.

Barbara hadn't told Elizabeth that Mary's talk had been turned down. Elizabeth wondered why.

I was mortified she hadn't known. I'd just assumed.

She was agitated about a big dinner she was having for Mary and Jim, with Barbara, Murray, Bob, Grace, Renata. Nicole was coming to help. She said she would ask Harriet to come down to see her old nurse.

—It's an old and valuable friendship. She might not come.

She meant Mary, hurt again by her friends at *The New York Review of Books*.

Elizabeth said Barbara was always telling her,

—You like Susan, but I like Mary better.

Elizabeth said it wasn't that she liked Susan more, but she found her real and interesting at the moment. She didn't like Mary's life, the dinners, the old couples, her old friend's high-handedness.

I wasn't sure Elizabeth and Barbara noticed how much they squabbled over Susan.

I'd heard Barbara complain that Lizzie was mad not to think Susan self-important, but Susan played up to Lizzie and for some reason that really galled Barbara.

Like Elizabeth needed to be protected; or that she could be taken in. I believed Susan cared very much for Elizabeth's work. And she wanted Elizabeth to care for hers, of course, with a needy, insecure, throbbing hope.

Elizabeth said with a sad shake of the head that Mary didn't show her anything anymore. *The New Yorker* turned down the first chapter of Mary's intellectual autobiography and she only knew that because Mary had asked her casually if six weeks was a long time. Elizabeth said it was awful of them to have kept someone like her waiting. And Bowden Broadwater had married the hot air heiress, as columnists were calling his South American girlfriend, Elizabeth noted.

(Lizzie wrote a beautiful foreword to *Intellectual Memoirs: 1936–1938*, McCarthy's second volume of autobiographical reflection, which was published posthumously.)

She wasn't going to the conference. We were always signing up and then not going. The previous spring, I'd stopped by to pick her up for the Sex and Language conference at the Plaza and she went back to the red sofa and laughed that she knew too much about one and not enough about the other to attend, though Lina Wertmüller, the conference head, was a scream.

She had saved copies of *The New Yorker* for me, saying she knew I could get my own, but she still liked pointing out things in it to me.

Jamaica Kincaid was publishing in *The New Yorker* odd, original stories about the West Indies. She was a close friend of David

Rieff's and wore white pajamas to the Knickerbocker Club. I'd no idea she was Mr. Shawn's daughter-in-law. *The New Yorker* had been running sections from a new book, *Russian Journal*, by a girl from Harvard, Andrea Lee, and Elizabeth had heard she was black, but her book wasn't about that.

—I'm so sick of Harvard, aren't you?

(Years later, Jamaica was amused that there we both were, running around New York, and yet we never met. Science fiction writer Samuel R. Delany's memoir *The Motion of Light in Water* is set in the same time period and on the same East Village and West Village streets as the poet Hettie Jones's *How I Became Hettie Jones*, and they never crossed paths. Delany was going into a folk club, and Jones into the jazz club a few doors down, worlds that do not intersect in these memorable books.)

Toni Morrison gave the keynote address of the packed congress, calling for writers to get up from their desks and to form a movement, to stop being solitary and to unite as a heroic, engaged, and militant body. She was denouncing deracinated clerks, that state to aspire to, I still believed. My former boss, Fran McCullough, and her husband, David, a Book-of-the-Month Club senior figure, saw me and pointed, laughing.

The Roosevelt was as crowded as a Shriners' convention, a weekend of Wendell Berry on the natural world imperiled, Mary Lee Settle, June Jordan making fur fly, Andrea Dworkin on pornography, and Arthur Miller on the *Times'* power; sessions of stern resolutions calling for a Literature Defense Network, for support of the air traffic controllers, and a resolution calling for peace in the world, I guess. Drink tickets were $3.50 apiece; Tom Victor wheeled, snapping pictures, and Dominique Nabokov was finding shots on the edges of crowds; photographers were all over the place. Wesley Brown had finished his novel on the man Jim Crow, an imagined dancer born into slavery who became a minstrel performer.

Murray Kempton was having second thoughts about having agreed to participate on a panel. Once he'd done it, he was elated.

Barbara called it his Ham Side. He wanted to know about Mary
Helen Washington, the feminist scholar and editor of *Midnight
Birds*, a slender but already influential anthology of writing by African American women. When I listened to Washington's history
of black literacy, I wondered if I sounded like her, congratulating
myself on having grandparents.

All summer I eyed the volumes in the office of *The Image of the
Black in Western Art*. Sharon spirited them away for Susan. I raved
about David Brion Davis's review.

—See, you have to know something, Barbara said, tapping the
air with a finger.

I knew she wouldn't want me to mention the death of Frances
Yates, to make her speak of something so private for her.

The best thing about the first session of the congress was leaving it. I sat out Oriana Fallaci's appearance, because of a *Playboy*
interview in which she said she couldn't stand homosexuals. I
watched the Yankees lose.

IT ALWAYS RAINED or threatened to on Election Day. David Din-
kins, I think that was, spoke from a parked truck on my corner,
mentioning that he'd been a mathematics major. I went to Books &
Co. to hear Elizabeth in discussion with Hortense Calisher about
the short story. Walter Abish, relentlessly experimental, added some
flip to the occasion. One panelist at Books & Co. said that he agreed
with Hemingway, that a writer must know his subject, otherwise
there's a hole in the writing.

—Like Hemingway's knowledge of Spain, Elizabeth shot out.

The panel talked about writing classes and Elizabeth, playing
with her amber necklace, said,

—The purpose of writing classes is to employ writers.

Books & Co. was very hot. I could sense her beginning to lose
it as the panel examined what it was calling 'the creative process.'

—I'm reaching for my gun. Why not talk about the mystery of talent.

Elizabeth wanted to skip the party and scoot by bus back across town to West Sixty-seventh Street to watch the returns. The black candidate lost.

—You're probably the only black in the city who voted, she said, going for the ice.

She said that when she attended a *Daedalus* conference in Washington, Thomas Sowell, the conservative black sociologist, was late to everything.

—He wasn't like an academic. Academics like to be at all these things. But he was getting calls, had to go here and there, and always late. I thought, At least you're black in that. Like Jimmy. Jimmy's overscheduled himself. You get this phone call.

I said I couldn't write about Sowell. His rap.

—Right. Need help, won't get it, never will, never have.

Adrienne Rich's new volume was having a hard time, but Elizabeth said she found some of the poems surprisingly aggressive. Of one about her mother-in-law:

—To whom is it addressed? Her old mother-in-law is supposed to shape up?

It was Elias Canetti. The Nobel Prize in Literature for 1981. She said they never gave it to queers or mad people.

—You miss it, it misses you, you miss each other.

Where had she heard that. No, she had no interest in *The Flight from the Enchanter*, Iris Murdoch's novel about her affair with Canetti, it was said.

The day before, Luc missed the twenty-fifth-anniversary reading of 'Howl.' Ginsberg was also going to read unpublished love poems to Neal Cassady.

—Crammed with fools, Elizabeth said.

Luc had come uptown with a copy of Mezz Mezzrow's *Really the Blues*, for the Harlem essay I was determined to get together.

He said he had two new favorite writers, Marthe Robert, a French critic who questioned the idea of bohemia, and Janet Malcolm, who had written what he called a moving and oddly constructed book on psychoanalysis.

He talked about Irving Stettner, a funny guy who was very poor but kept on with his life, publishing Bowles and Dubuffet, hanging sketches in restaurants. Luc said he respected him for living out the avant-garde life; the man was not a joke. Ted Berrigan's poverty wasn't funny. He and his wife, Alice Notley, the better poet, many said, with kids and no money, lived from poetry.

Maybe that kind of life was getting harder to sustain in New York City. In front of Pomander Bookshop, we stopped to see what Tintin titles were in the window. Early Scorsese had left the Thalia; Fellini's *City of Women* was next.

Luc's first piece in the *Review*, about Elvis Presley, in the issue dated December 17, 1981, was about to come out. He wrote it and put it on Barbara's desk. I was in the office, to go over troubles about my own piece, and I read his, flawless and brilliant, in the mailroom. I kept my mouth shut with Barbara about it; I didn't say anything until press week was almost over. 'Back Issues' was in the new issue as well.

—Now the poor baby will have to write another one.

Elizabeth meant Luc writing another piece. That was what writing came down to, she said. But in Luc's case, Elizabeth was excited to feel that *The New York Review* had discovered him, certainly enlarged his possibilities.

We'd been talking about why she did not underline in books and how much she used to mind when Cal, usually so careful, scrawled in theirs, though sometimes of course he couldn't help it. Sometimes she found evidence in a volume of his mind breaking down. Notorious names written in pencil in block letters. There was no denying how into dictators he was when he was going off.

Elizabeth said Luc's piece was very good.

She'd read 'Back Issues' the night before, about one o'clock in the morning.

—One isn't very happy.

She said by the time she took the galleys herself back to the office, it was much changed from what I'd seen.

—I removed these, these pimples.

Not her kind of word.

—It's better than the way it was. I said, What are these prancing banalities. You think it has the freedom of the sketch but once these constructions are framed they seem too tight.

When she said she hoped to put it into a book, she made it sound like a collection of short stories, not a novel in which this would be a part, the deer not the last thing, but a part of something spun out.

Elizabeth began her readings thusly (her kind of word):

—People often start by announcing that what they are about to read comes from a larger work. Well, I'm telling you this is from a much smaller work.

Kenneth Koch told her he loved that so much he stole it.

I told her that Luc loved 'Back Issues.'

—I was afraid to ask you.

She was happy.

BARBARA HAD A large Thanksgiving party. Europe was marching against the Russian and American nuclear presence. Barbara said it had been more like a meeting of the Council on Foreign Relations than Thanksgiving. Autumn had given up trying, like a taxi driver who said he would wait but then didn't. It was winter when we stepped down into Sixty-seventh Street, shivering and in a hurry.

Elizabeth was irate that I'd hinted to Barbara that were I she I would not trust a certain person she knew at Random House.

—You can't protect Barbara from an old friend.

I was still telling someone that someone had been talking. I was as thoughtless as ever. As for publishing big shots in general:

—You should never like your job that much.

I returned Elizabeth's copy of Fowler's *Modern English Usage*, ready to invest in a copy of my own. We went to the thrilling Constructivist exhibition at the Guggenheim. Her favorite was Popova's *Green Stripes*. She was still high on Modernism after her talk onstage with Susan at the Columbia School of Architecture. Harriet, Devie, and I were impressed; Elizabeth seemed more knowledgeable than Susan.

She framed a work on paper, done in chalk maybe, by Helen Frankenthaler, a Dalton girl, and hung it by her front door, over the white rotary telephone and the wicker chair. It was a red gesture, a forceful diagonal. I said it reminded me of the Popova. She looked at it a long time and said she didn't see it.

Red diaper baby and Weather Underground fugitive Kathy Boudin had surfaced after eleven years. Elizabeth said they all got into this dyke stuff because it was a big deal for women to rush about with guns. I. F. Stone, the noblest loser ever, was Boudin's uncle. Murray went to the arraignment. Elizabeth had saved the issue of the *Review* with Murray's piece on the sentencing of John Lennon's killer, Mark David Chapman. Lennon was Chapman's 'substitute suicide,' Murray speculated. She said she'd never get used to me having a subscription.

I read Jane Alpert's *Growing Up Underground* with Maggie in Tin Pan Alley and then when I dropped off something caught a glimpse of Murray writing about the book at Barbara's kitchen table, football game on the radio as he typed and tapped his pipe and talked to himself.

—Departs with his own honesty.

I could not imagine Elizabeth in a building without a doorman and a janitor. She made much of her physical ineptitude. She was that New Yorker who struggled with a trash bag in a sudden loss of common sense and awareness of a physical relation to the world. Yet she'd been a keen tennis player in her time, she once told me. She didn't smoke for years, just to be able to play. She said her sinuses and her lungs had always been problems.

She told me she'd suffered terrible burns when she was a child, modeling her new frilly dress too close to the fireplace. Her family despaired of her life. She lay in an agony for six months. She was six years old. She said Harriet told her not so long ago that one could hardly see anymore where she'd been burned. But she'd felt discolored, a freak, all her life. Self-consciousness made her physically shy.

She said when she told Barbara this story, Barbara looked at her and said,

—I was raised in a paper bag.

(Saskia Hamilton said this story reminded her to take seriously things that made her pause when she was doing research. She had always wondered why Lizzie didn't seem to react sufficiently in her letters to the news that one of Caroline's children had been very badly burned. It was so unlike Lizzie in her abundant sympathies.)

Elizabeth said she was getting deep into Melville. She found the character of Bartleby impossible to explain. What had Melville meant by him and what was his hold over us? Something in us wants to save him from himself. Is it that he has no life? Does Melville really mean to say he lives nowhere else, or is alive nowhere else other than the office in which he declines to perform any task?

She first picked up 'Bartleby, the Scrivener' as part of her reading for the essay on New York, but Melville was not Whitman, not in this story. She thought someone ages ago had written on the novelist and the poet and their days in Brooklyn, but who was that? She had sort of expected a great business scandal, on the order of the railroad fraud in *Chapters of Erie* by Charles Francis Adams, Jr., because 'Bartleby' carried the subtitle, 'A Story of Wall Street.'

She said she was getting more interested in Bartleby and less in her generalities about New York, though she was very pleased with the concept of 'Manhattanism,' and rolled it around, the mouse at her mercy.

She'd made shrimp and spinach, saying she couldn't face giving me another hamburger.

(She read Melville, she read him again, and thought about him, and broke out fresh notebooks. Something really lifted her in her dealings with Melville. Her interrogation of Melville's opaque character in the essay 'Bartleby in Manhattan' led to a full study, *Herman Melville*, her last book, in James Atlas's wonderful Penguin Lives series, published in 2000, when she was eighty-four years old.

I like to think she had in mind Nabokov's passionate aloneness with Gogol. In her study, Melville's work is as mysterious and beautiful as cave painting. She got what she said was a very dumb review from some girl at the *Times* who obviously had never read *Moby-Dick* and afterward she lost any ambition to publish another book, especially not a collection of her late stories everyone had been urging her to consider. She said she hated to publish books anyway. It was such a nightmare; it wasn't worth it. Melville's bitterness was convincing.)

—Give it a whirl, girl, she said Barbara had said to her when she was talking about writing something on Bartleby.

Why she thought Barbara in any way cool about her work. She said Barbara was harder to please than Bob. It was something else. She was more sensitive to what Barbara thought.

Everything about Barbara was complicated, but she cohered into a magnificence of concentration as audience, reader, she who left so little trace of her importance to American letters.

Style is more than personality, Professor Hardwick used to say in class. It is your character.

I never asked Elizabeth for whom she wrote. Bob, the future, her audience, herself. Barbara got it; she knew the answer: Elizabeth Hardwick wrote to honor the literature she cared for.

Abandoned Canal Street at first light was beautiful. I was touched by every street, thinking how marvelous each building was. I bought *The New York Times* at Fourteenth Street after sunrise and sat in a coffee shop until nine o'clock.

I HAD THE last standing-room ticket. Between me and the stage, phalanxes of guys in black tie. The set for *Le Rossignol* was beautiful; that for *Sacre* less so. But there it was, masks like chefs' hats for *Oedipus Rex*. Howard and satin-collared Brad said at intermission that you could tell who was there for Hockney and Bournonville and Ashton and who for Stravinsky.

I walked Elizabeth to her door. She'd expected Barbara, but where was she. Elizabeth thought the production too conscious of a period primitivism and not up to Natalia Makarova, who was like some creature from space. Elizabeth was too cold to stand there on the street talking about all that beautiful music, each piece so different in character, Russian, then Latin.

The Upper West Side was a comfort; some corner place was always open and in sight, even one of the Korean delis bankrolled by the Moonies and resented by black people. It felt too late to call her by the time I got home.

Elizabeth had been calling. It was my turn to read aloud, but not in order to share beauty. She once said I confused historical tone with fictional tone:

> Grandcourt held that the Jamaican negro was a beastly sort of Baptist Caliban; Deronda said he always felt a little with Caliban, who naturally had his own point of view and could sing a good song; Mrs. Davilov observed that her father had an estate in Barbados, but that she herself had never been in the West Indies; Mrs. Torrington was sure she should never sleep in her bed if she lived among blacks; her husband corrected

her by saying that the blacks would be manageable
enough if it were not for the half-breeds; and Deronda
remarked that the whites had to thank themselves for
the half-breeds.

I got comfortable in my relationship with Eliot as everybody's
narrator. It was like a tour of her story: she talks to herself, then
remembers us, but who is speaking, 'Perhaps it is not quite mythi-
cal that a slave has been proud to be bought first.' And I wanted to
say that was nothing compared to Eliot's weird rap on 'the Jews.'
Elizabeth said she couldn't think of anything else in Virginia
Woolf on Eliot, apart from the essay in *The Common Reader* where
she started that whole thing about George Eliot not being charming or feminine enough. I had a couple of Woolf's *Nation* pieces on
Eliot and Woolf mentions Eliot in her general essays on aspects of
women and fiction, but there was little on her in the diaries. She
admired Eliot, but the Brontës and Austen struck a deeper note of
feeling and kinship perhaps.

Woolf's father, Leslie Stephen, had been among the great men
who sniffed at Eliot's reputation and late novels. I'd been aiming a
can of poison at critters during our call. I swept up the bodies with
a sponge. The shelves were quiet again. A fine dust, like a powdered
spice, had settled on my tables and books from the construction
going on one block away. Fumes from it lingered into the night.

Eliot didn't seem to think anyone could be redeemed. But
there was something wrong with *Daniel Deronda*, maybe in its cru-
elty. Deronda becomes a Zionist, the quixotic thing he'd been longing for.

Elizabeth said she found it curious that after criticizing Eliot
for her girls, for making everyone talk too much, Woolf should
place romance, girlhood, memory, and nostalgia at the center of
these huge novels. Nostalgia is the thing that inspired Woolf, she
said, a point she'd made in her writings on her.

—Jesus and Virginia Woolf are the most maligned in our culture, Elizabeth said. The evangelical preachers and the feminists.
Poor radical Jesus. Poor elitist Virginia, Elizabeth said.

Her serious undertone was there.

—I had the most disgraceful dream. I've never dreamt about
anyone I know. I'm such a nervous person all I ever have are Freud-
ian nightmares. But this morning, Virginia Woolf said to me, Ah,
my dear. You've had it rather easy and that is very dangerous. I
woke up, of course. I wish I'd said if I've had it so easy why isn't
there more. Pity I didn't have it easier.

ONE SUNDAY, I went for our usual dinner. Elizabeth was in the
living room, on her red sofa. She gathered up the pages of a manuscript she was reading. She was almost finished. Eileen Simpson's
memoir, Berryman's first wife.

I was surprised the publisher had sent it to her. I heard there was
a line in it that said Elizabeth laughed at Cal when he was mad.

Elizabeth said she couldn't understand why Simpson wrote it.
Four hundred pages.

—What is her intention?

The whole gang, Berryman, Cal, Jean Stafford, Blackmur, his
wife, Randall Jarrell, Delmore Schwartz. Elizabeth said it was the
same thing over again: suicides, madness. It's a re-creation, conversations, summers. The book wasn't exactly mean, but she didn't see
the point of it.

Rather than write to Simpson, Elizabeth phoned her the next
morning and asked her what was her intention. The same old story
was all there. Simpson said she thought she was giving a picture
of them. The title, *Poets in Their Youth*, annoyed Elizabeth. The
Yaddo thing was in there. Elizabeth reminded Simpson that she
was not there, so why bother to repeat it. She said the Bollingen
Prize for Pound was in it and all the phone calls. There was some

line in which Elizabeth is quoted as saying she thought someone was 'right.'

—Eileen, I said, I have never in my life thought anyone was totally right about anything.

She said that evening to come over, after I'd written off another long day of reading, trying to write, trying not to take a drink yet.

A sad tale's best for winter.

She pointed out to Simpson that everyone was dead, meaning no one could defend himself. There wasn't that much about her in it, but in regard to the line that has her laughing at Cal, she told Simpson that these people, for all their suffering, were quite beguiling and amusing as well. She didn't care what Simpson said about her.

In some place, Simpson said Caroline Gordon wasn't as cool about her divorce from Allen Tate as Simpson was about her divorce from Berryman. Elizabeth told Simpson that wasn't the way she remembered it.

—You left out quite a few provocations, Eileen. That stopped her cold.

Simpson left Berryman, but said nothing about the many girl-friends, the countless nights Berryman did not come home, how she wept on Elizabeth's shoulder, her hysteria.

Elizabeth finally told Simpson that Simpson must be the better writer, because she felt that in order to get how volatile and complex these people were, she would have to be as great as Dostoevsky.

(Eventually, Simpson sent her a somewhat cool card saying that she'd followed some suggestions and made changes on pages such and such, ending with, 'Yours truly.')

The more Elizabeth thought about it, the more irritated she became.

—I'm on the warpath, she declared, seizing a cigarette.

Simpson, in the memoir, said Berryman didn't want to have children. He had a son by his second wife, and two daughters by his third, Kate. She was a nurse, rather nice, Elizabeth said, and had commissioned a biography by an English guy and reportedly didn't like it. Berryman's most important work was written after his divorce from Simpson. Elizabeth said she didn't like the suicide stuff, the stuff about his father being a suicide as well.

Elizabeth felt that Berryman was an obsession with Simpson. It was her second book about him. He was the only thing she'd ever done. She wanted to be a writer; Berryman was her experience; but she knew where her story was, which was why the suicides and drinking and madness were there. Same cliché picture. There must have been something of the wife's lingering resentment, the way Stafford could, after Cal's death, publish that story. The obsession of it.

('The Interior Castle,' about a wife's disfigurement in an automobile accident and the husband who had been at the wheel, is thought by some critics to be based on Lowell.)

She was a sweet, sentimental woman, Elizabeth said of Simpson, and not really a writer. After she left Berryman she went to New Orleans. Simpson married a nice man and was very happy. When he died of cancer, she was so grief-stricken, she could barely speak for a year.

—I have always wanted to preserve my memory of John as a donnish, finely dressed, oh.

She said she put it in 'Back Issues,' the young Berryman talking about *The Winter's Tale*. He was a Shakespeare scholar and that was very far from the general idea of him drinking and raving in *Delusions, Etc.*

—He'd call at five in the morning, drunk, and Cal would get on and say, John, why are you doing this to yourself?

The first time she told me about the phone calls from Berryman, Lowell didn't seem to have been around.

When Lowell was back and they were in Maine, Peter Taylor phoned, and Elizabeth heard him say, —It's *The Winter's Tale, The Winter's Tale.*

Irrational jealousy out of nowhere; the king wrecks things, no one can stop him; the queen is forgiving in the end.

—Not really. It's just one of those things one says.

Either Lowell or Berryman had a poem about *The Winter's Tale.* She wondered if she should take it out of 'Back Issues.' She decided to leave it because she liked the idea of Berryman quoting a relatively obscure play.

She objected to a lot in Simpson's memoir.

—I was much nicer to her than I am now talking to you.

She said she was going to review it.

I said why bother. She was deep into thinking about John Reed and Louise Bryant. We'd gone to a screening of *Reds* in the windowless Huntington Hartford building on Columbus Circle, Man Ray's *The Kiss*, or a copy of it, large red lips, facing the elevator on the top floor. Warren Beatty told Bob Silvers he loved *Sleepless Nights.* I thought the Simpson an unnecessary distraction.

—It's my period and I'm not going to let her get away with it.

She said she would never try a portrait of those poets. She wouldn't, because she liked them too much, felt they were better than what she had to offer them.

I said she could do them quite well.

—Maybe you're right, she said, turning aside praise in her usual way.

(*Poets in Their Youth*, Simpson's memoir, James would find interesting. And it irritated Lizzie that he did. And then much later James wrote a review of Lowell's *Collected Poems* that infuriated her. Bob and Barbara felt they had to print it, but the hard feelings on all sides never went away.)

As I was leaving, she asked me where I was going. Home she did not believe and answered the question herself:

> *Then wander forth the sons*
> *Of Belial, flown with insolence and wine.*

She pulled a twenty-dollar bill from the drawer, not for the first time. I said, not for the first time:

—I hate to take it. But night darkens the streets.

—I hate to give it. For once we're even.

She cracked up.

I meant to pay her a high compliment. I said she could go through any manuscript with diagnostic wonder. I said she was the Nadia Boulanger of American literature.

The pause was immense. Air got sucked out of the room and then blew back in when she spoke loudly.

—Oh. That is such a put-down.

She went to the red sofa. She walked somewhat stooped, escaping a blow.

I had no idea why the comparison wounded her and I was alarmed.

—I am not a teacher. I am a writer.

She fixed her eyes on me. Their color deepened, like turning up the blue gas flame on the stove. As if to prove what she'd just said, she said:

—There was no deer.

—— Part 8 ——

I can't tell crickets from cicadas. Fast forward, fast forward.

This is the wind, the wind in a field of corn.
Great crowds are fleeing from a major disaster.

In the early eighties, my father started to lose his mind. He was used to being audited by the IRS; civil rights people and antiwar people learned to expect harassment, he said. One of the Indianapolis papers reported that he was under investigation for mishandling NAACP funds; no retraction ever. He knew what was up with the phones, with suspicious vans parked in someone else's driveway. Everyone was against him, everyone worked for someone, no one could be trusted. Maybe his paranoia had been there always, one of segregation's buried antipersonnel devices waiting to be stepped on.

My mother had to surrender her own reason in order to remain loyal to a crazy man. She found her favorite poem, 'The Death of Arthur.' My mother's look said she knew that I was abandoning her and my sisters. My sister Pat, together with her silent husband, had no life outside of my father's demands and her declining health; my sister Donna suffered yet more psychotic episodes, once found wandering naked in Baltimore, Maryland. The story would get sadder still, endings that held no beginnings.

(*The New York Review* not only paid for the rehab, they did not tell my parents, who thought I was in a phoneless upstate cabin for a month and had to go to a general store to call them on those dreadful Sundays.)

James Baldwin died and I made up my mind. Fran said Baldwin

had two heart attacks and then the stomach cancer took over. My
father came to New York with the sales contract for my apartment
wrapped up in tape around his undershirt. I'd not been allowed to
say the word 'broker' on the phone. He was sure his enemies would
find out. That my father had been my landlord made possible the
way I had lived from one day to the next.

There's not a breathing of the common wind . . .

On that gray afternoon in December of 1987, down the street
from Columbia, St. John the Divine heaved with organ prelude,
rows and rafters of Henry Louis Gates, Jr., Caryl Phillips, Maxine
de la Falaise, Jules Feiffer, and then the pounding of drums. Following the cross came Maya Angelou, Toni Morrison, Amiri Baraka,
Eartha Kitt, so small, Quincy Troupe, with dreadlocks, and others.
The drums got louder and Baldwin's old mother, buried in a hand-
kerchief and a big fur coat, was wheeled up the nave, and his brothers, who bore an eerie resemblance to him, and more family, Ossie
Davis and Ruby Dee said to be with them, and friends of every age
and hue, old men on canes, babies in blue blankets. So many walked
toward the transept, I thought, That's the whole story right there.

Odetta sang a medley of songs. *Let us break bread together on our
knees.* Songs of early promise, movement days, purity and hope. A
niece said a prayer. Maya Angelou sounded like a Hallmark card.
Toni Morrison spoke mostly about herself. Baraka ranted about
white people. The relief of a choir. More prayer. Then a recording
of Baldwin singing 'Precious Lord' in a smoky baritone I'd not
expected. A jazz trumpet. Then the drums again. Up came the
dignitaries, the ambassador from France. I thought of Warhol's
photograph of Baldwin in black tie at Deauville. The coffin covered
with a black pall. So narrow and small, the casket, this little bird.
Barbara seized my hand. The rims of her eyes were wet. Behind
the wheeled casket, which people reached out to touch, came his
mother's chair and the stream of chief mourners.

Outside, the strange scene under gray cloud. His mother lost in mounds of flowers and thickets of people. Cameras perched above the hearse. His brothers cried and hugged people. Photographers snapped away at the mahogany coffin in the back of the Cadillac. I pushed through people to stare at it. That was my first funeral. I don't know why I didn't think the poor man's body would be there. My alma mater was up the street, but it seemed as if we were down in the Harlem valley, at the kind of storefront grief someone from the 1930s would have photographed. Erroll McDonald passed by and tapped my hand.

I found Barbara with Claire Bloom and Philip Roth. It was odd to be back on Broadway, surrounded by schoolchildren. Roth remembered 'Sonny's Blues' in *The Evergreen Review* and that he once shared a platform in California with Baldwin, who arrived late and already talking. Barbara forgot that I wrote about *Just Above My Head*. They were expecting something from Lizzie. Mailer's secretary told Bob's office that he was in the middle of a novel and would write something if he found the time. Barbara remembered when Baldwin used to show up late, after promising to be right over, with an entourage that sat in the background as he talked. 'Poor Jimmy,' she said. Barbara went back to the office. I took off my blazer. Baldwin was buried near the Robesons. Lizzie said she decided she was an old white woman who knew him only slightly years ago. 'How's Robert,' she said he'd say. She said the year before at the Public Library he had with him the most beautiful black boy she'd ever seen. Just before he died, his books, because they weren't selling, were taken out of print, the stock ground into pulp.

So flash'd and fell the brand Excalibur

Gayl Jones had been on the run in Germany since the early eighties. She met the wrong man while teaching at the University of Michigan. He said he was God, AIDS his divine punishment, and he brought a shotgun to a gay rights rally. Jones took off with him when he fled the U.S. She'd published a novel in German, but who was I on the dotted line.

Rick drove me to the airport on New Year's Eve.

—New York is intimidating, but you must not think of staying away too long, Lizzie said.

—The *Review* isn't a bad thing to have, Barbara said.

—Whatever you do, don't come back, Susan said.

—Hail Hail Rock and Roll, Luc said.

My father secured a letter of introduction for me from our congressman: To Whom It May Concern.

—See you in the funny papers, my mother said.

FROM A BOX of letters; from a shelf of old journals:

November 5, 1988

Dear little protégé of yore: Barbara tells me you will be coming home, yes, Lord, in December and how I look forward to your crossing the old river and coming to dine in the kitchen once more. That is if you can get into my stately home, since I've undertaken a 'major' renovation and am marooned not on the water but in a six-weeks desert of dust. There is a new window, very dramatic in the living room, and more dramatic I undertook a painting, bookshelves and all and many books on the top shelves disposed of and the floors scraped and so on. But the walls of the room were so bad it has taken them weeks to get in shape. And, oh, yes, I had a huge air-conditioner put through the back wall of the room, next to the big window.

Sleepless Nights is a 'book of the month' in Germany, my darling publisher called to tell me. And alas German TV is coming for an interview, which I despise and worse having to be photographed and all that, but I didn't think I could refuse. The publisher is bringing out the Complete Virginia Woolf and I said I would come to Frankfurt to do a few programs or something. I do mean to do it and go on to Berlin to prowl about a bit with you, posing as your grandmother on the Southern connection. I do feel like One Last Trip somehow, at least at the moment.

Love ever,

E.

Tuesday 12 April 1989

Lizzie finished the Updike. On *Self-Consciousness*, his memoir. It doesn't track, Barbara said, but it didn't matter, there were so many wonderful things in it. She had to fix a part on Vietnam. Updike is very conservative and Barbara feels Lizzie went off on the Vietnam stuff because she felt it was an attack on Cal. I wonder if Updike isn't such an Anglo conservative because in his day Jewish writers like Mailer and Roth were laying down the laws.

I went out in a drizzle to fetch the mail. One from Lizzie, too short, who is coming to Frankfurt in May. I liked *Dangerous Liaisons*, and so home, with worries about Ishmael Reed and money. I hope the shop downstairs can fix my computer. I don't understand what Skip Gates is saying about Ishmael Reed, but there are gripping discoveries in *The Signifying Monkey*. Reed writes out of his experience as a reader. Barbara sent Janet Malcolm's attack on journalists; Murray's columns; the new issue with Luc's great piece on hobos and Murray's beautiful meditation on Paul Robeson. Barbara also sent Susan Minot stories, April's book, as well as the issue of *Interview* that has a short thing on her. In the same issue, Luc has a very good movie review and there's a photograph of a Dutch dancer that almost made me jump out of the window. Barbara saw Klara and Erroll at Joan Buck's. They're getting married. No news about Patricia, la Storace. I went to the Berlin city library and the only translation I could find of *Götz von Berlichingen* was Walter Scott's, from 1799. Wordsworth said later generations would wonder what the Goethe worship had been for.

Monday 16 May 1989

Fassbinder called Frankfurt 'hell on earth.' I found Lizzie in the hotel restaurant downstairs. She checked me in, and for the rest of my brief visit we talked mostly about her cold, poor thing, which the next morning, Friday, she was certain was pneumonia. Her chest hurt, she coughed, she looked clammy, stairs were a problem.

She was happy her piece on Updike made something of a splash. Gottlieb called her. Maybe it's done something for Updike; she feels that no one really reads him anymore, though he has made a fortune. She handed it in while Bob was away and Barbara, Lizzie said, laughed, 'Good, I can throw my weight around.' But Barbara's reaction to the piece threw her into such a depression she said she started to write me a letter, but tore it up because it was incoherent. Best not to have these seizures on record. She said what got to her was that Barbara wasn't specific, all she would say was, 'It doesn't work.' Lizzie had some lines from the Neil Sheehan book about the ARVN being afraid to fight. With Bob, as when he came bouncing back to take up the Updike, it's easier because he tries to rewrite something and she just says, 'I'll work on that.' The awful thing about him is his pretending to know everything. 'I know Jimmy very well.' What Lizzie felt is that on first reading Barbara didn't like the piece. I said she does very much. 'She does now.' Lizzie said it was because they're both girls. Girls do that to one another. I guess she meant one goes into a depression anyway after the completion of something, desperate for a reaction, for the relief of a well-done. Lizzie's things come already edited. That's more and more what her writing is about. Down to the point, with little else, nothing wasted. She said she wanted to write to me because she understood my problem all those years: Barbara's negativity. It drove her crazy whenever she asked Barbara about a piece of mine and she'd said, 'It will be all right.' Well, she said, it wasn't serious, nothing like what she's heard from others who complain that when they get their galleys the piece has been rewritten. Immediately, Susan comes to mind, with everyone laughing in the office about what a mess her pieces are and she very petulant about them marking up her manuscripts so.

At least you can tell Barbara things. What held me up all those years were my late nights, not Barbara. She works hard to make me make sense, although I do sometimes get irritated that because when I'm writing about Afro-American literature, I have to explain everything, place the writers in context, and they don't when it's Waugh. (But, in all fairness, they do when it's Prokosch or Bruno Schulz.) And my things are always too long. The doom from Barbara's mouth is usually a remark like 'It doesn't track.' She said that about Lizzie's Updike. I read the Updike in galleys and it is not my favorite, but that may be because it's about Updike. But I understood what Lizzie meant. I rushed off the Reed piece Wednesday before I left and not hearing from Barbara makes me feel as though I am in the deepest disgrace.

Lizzie liked Murray's piece on Martin Duberman's huge biography of Paul Robeson, sort of. For the first time with him she thought it was overwritten, too polished. Harriet is fine. There wasn't that much money from Aunt Sarah, and it had to be divided between eleven cousins, $10,000 a year, so she doesn't mind that Harriet wasn't included. The real money, Uncle Cott's, was left to Harvard and dumber places; the Currier and Ives to the Salem museum, things she didn't like. What she liked were the Tiffany plates. Mary McCarthy is better. That's the Maine news. She wondered how McCarthy does it. 'I'm big and can hardly walk and my stomach's out to here, but I'm Mary McCarthy. I don't feel that way.'

So Lizzie went to her room to rest and look over her talk and I went to mine, with repairmen hammering at the door, 'I told them the cheapest,' she said, to clean up. Lizzie said the Frankfurter Hof was one of the great hotels of Europe, but I don't believe it. I arrived with a plastic bag of carrots and apples and felt rather grubby in the eyes of old women in black veils who shuffled with great dignity through the lobby. But Lizzie told me not to worry, she'd seen quite a few women in sneakers and pantsuits and men in horrible clothes and many heads topped by yarmulkes. There was a darling bellhop who fixed on me as a chance to speak a lot of English.

Her German publishers picked her up in a big new Ford. Arnulf Conradi is the translator of *Sleepless Nights* and Elisabeth Ruge interests Lizzie as the granddaughter of one of the generals killed after the July plot to blow up Hitler. The room at Fischer Verlag was packed. Lizzie I think surprised an audience accustomed to the serious and heavy, talking about Bloomsbury as an extension of Cambridge, very homosexual, and Woolf more English than the English. Sentences that are classical, but taken together what do they mean. *The Waves* has these speeches in quotation marks but the dialogues are not really exchanges. *Mrs. Dalloway* is a perfect book. Jokes about the Hogarth Press, jokes about Henry James, Woolf's imitation of his locutions in her diary. Her genius is that she is not to be imitated, but after her nothing is the same. That's genius. (She was once sitting around with Mary McCarthy and when they were thinking about who was really a genius they came up with the same two names: Lowell and Arendt.) So the talk went over well. Then an academic, a man Lizzie said was charming, did his thing: on and on about translation. Old ladies, girls, men with fuzzy hair around bald spots, boys with long wrists and big watches. So many sick-making rosy faces in the TV lights. People crowding into another room for wine. A girl I met five years before, 'the kitchen people,' the girl remembered to call our kind of fan, Ingrid Heinrich-Jost, is now writing for the *Frankfurter Allgemeine*. Too many people crowded around a table in an Italian restaurant. Conradi introduced an elderly woman with black watery eyes as Germany's greatest poetess. The woman smiled, very pleased, and said, 'Do you know I'm translated in Chinese?' Then she talked into Conradi's ear the rest of the night. Ingrid whispered that of course the woman was a rotten poet. Lizzie said if someone had introduced the great Marianne Moore like that she would have made some quiet, devastating remark. Lizzie was freaking out at that crowded table and asked Conradi to drive her back to her hotel. In the doorway she said, 'I've never been so happy to be sick.'

The next day was even less fun. At breakfast we read the papers and then we sat here and there. Say Eudora Welty and Lizzie will say that she does not compare to Flannery O'Connor. She dislikes the emphasis on the religious aspect of Flannery's work, a reading imposed by Robert and Sally Fitzgerald and Caroline Gordon. A photographer came, and we sat around some more. She had nothing to read on the plane and I went out in the rain and found the British Bookshop and got her more magazines and some Dickens I thought maybe she hadn't read since the day before yesterday. The rain stopped and I found myself pleased to be walking around and pleased that I'd found books she'd want. Two places had only Monica Dickens. I didn't want her to feel she had to entertain me and so fetched my bag and said goodbye. Too bad Lizzie was so sick. I couldn't find the hotel doctor, she didn't want to bother with calls. At least she enjoyed herself up until then: the opera, the reading, a dinner with much grappa afterward, she said. I took a late train and next morning woke up in Berlin.

Barbara called to say she's sending money, is worried about my not having any, and that it's press week and she hasn't really 'focused' on the Reed yet, but am I interested in A. Philip Randolph? I feel much better, called Lizzie, and Barbara called again and now as I start something for an anthology, I find in my notebook from Herzen: 'The desire to see one's name in print is one of the strongest artificial passions in a man who has been corrupted by his bookish age.'

Friday 9 June 1989

This morning I went to the library at JFK Institut to return those Reed books, take out others. Barbara said the Reed was fine, Bob said not fine, Barbara read it again and spent an hour telling me what was wrong with it, and so there's that to put through the grinder again. I went to the library to find some general, useless book on black fiction since 1960 and maybe it moved when it saw my fingers; it's not checked out, so it's scooting around the stacks somewhere. And to read again Hurston on Voodoo. Professor Klaus Krippendorff was in the lobby, very solicitous, but when I came back with nine books on black labor and A. Philip Randolph, one girl started asking me how and why and by whose say-so I was able to take books out, and I explained, and she said okay, it's just that we don't know you, and I said well I don't know you either and two girls checking out *The Sontag Reader* and playfully hitting each other over the head with it laughed and so the desk girl said yes, but they're our books, and kept stamping, so I thought I'd better be nice and produced a barrel of documents and they put the books under my own name now, that kraut love of tidiness, regularity, to keep Krippendorff from having to be responsible, such a thing could get expensive, one woman said, thinking I wouldn't understand her, and also to remove me from the professor's protection, 'all equal before the desk,' their smiles said when I left.

I phoned Lizzie, who goes to Maine tomorrow. For days I have been homesick for television. On the newspaper stands, the students were conducting themselves along the most brave and innocent lines in Tiananmen Square, and then one morning it all changed. I had to read about the footage of the one student pleading with a tank. To think of those poor people, workers and students, in Beijing.

> *It is superb in the air.*
> *Suffering is everywhere*

Saturday 26 August 1989
I didn't like Murray's piece on *Do the Right Thing.* Barbara said one day Philip Roth felt funny and the next he was having a quadruple

bypass at age 56. Lizzie seems fine, she said, but she won't write on V. S. Pritchett, who will be 90, maybe because he's so old-fashioned, but Barbara said that now, at his age, his stories have become very sexy. Shows the kind of life that can be built, but one has to do nothing else, only write. You have to be able to write in the first place, there's always that problem.

~

Friday 9 June 1989

I read about the Alaskans at the salmon plant losing their discrimination suit before the U.S. Supreme Court, another blow to affirmative action. Pat called the other day and joked about leaving the NAACP convention in Detroit and asking for asylum in Canada. She was very funny about Ishmael Reed. Legba, that voodoo god, she said, was antithetical to her traditions. Legba didn't keep anybody from slavery. Tell Ishmael Reed that, she said. Legba was having a cool time and we were the hors d'oeuvres. Lots of us were enslaved by Christians for that matter. She said she wrote Laura Nyro a fan letter at last, twenty years after that concert in Bloomington. She said she'd send the ayatollah a telegram about Salman Rushdie but she didn't know how to translate Lenny Bruce's yada yada warden. Donna wants to be seen with her copy of *The Satanic Verses*. 'I love fantasy.' Mama asked, 'Is your money pitiful?' Daddy asked, 'How are you fixed for funds?' He said the *Review* didn't have to put Nicholas Lemann in touch with him, because he'd have to tell him that black people have always been the underclass, nothing new in that.

Tuesday 29 August 1989

They all went to Washington over the weekend, Mama, Daddy, Pat, Wayne, Donna, Betty Heeter, and forty others from Indianapolis, on the traditional bus, for a Silent March, the women in white, the men in black, to protest, among many things, the Supreme Court decision on affirmative action.

Daddy doesn't sound persecuted when they're at the convention. To keep things to himself is strategy. Don't let them know that you know. Or is it the excitement of the genuine. He said Dr. King was eloquent, but he was sorry we never got to hear Dr. Mays of Morehouse speak. He doubts that there is even a recording of Dr. Mays in chapel. 'Not even reel to reel,' I could hear Mama somewhere in their room. Daddy said they didn't have equipment like that. 'Not on our level,' he laughed. The powers that be tried to get President Mays to cancel Henry A. Wallace's appearance. Dr. Mays refused. Wallace, who ran for president of the United States in 1948, scared people. But Dr. Mays said he would let the students hear him speak and they could decide for themselves, because that was what he was teaching them to do. 'A lot of important people fell through chapel,' I could hear Mama second.

Last night I meant to turn to the Randolph. It was so dark and quiet and lonely, but just around my desk. Life was less sad in bed, on my mattress, where I fell asleep over *Jacques the Fatalist and His Master*.

~

April 12, 1988

Dearest Darryl:

Susan and I appeared at the Y last night in an 'essay' program. I suppose it was as useful as those things can be. I do not understand why people attend and on this night missing the Oscars as well, although Sharon, Susan and I saw most of it over take-out Chinese at Barbara's. Susan was somewhat chagrined I think and didn't want to smudge her record on 'never having looked at TV.' She seems well enough and is finishing her long AIDS essay, but somehow I feel she is not to be called less embittered as the days pass. The struggle to make a living will never seem to her to be a proper burden. She does work hard indeed, but will not pay the price for the 'high seriousness' without complaint. There's so much money floating around in New York it must seem that a faithful servant ought to have more of it. I don't quite know how to sort out her tangle of feelings: she does play a rather romantic role of the great dedication. But here in New York all 'great artists' are rich as well as famous. It's a problem, old dear, wouldn't you say?

Always,

Elizabeth

Monday 16 May 1989

Susan hasn't written or anything. Her picture is everywhere these days. With her it's out of sight, out of mind. Lizzie said that at a big PEN dinner Susan practically cut her. And she hasn't asked Lizzie to sign any of the Rushdie petitions. Barbara told Lizzie that Susan was a bit cool toward her at Sharon's birthday party. They laugh about Susan, but notice it when she's distant. I'm the same way, but it's different. I thought I was a friend from below, like the little pals she went to movies with when she's not scheduled to see the truly great. She used to complain so much about the money Barbara and Lizzie got from the *Review* I wondered if Wylie's doing all right by her doesn't have something to do with it. Susan isn't one to be embarrassed. I think it's probably having become even more of a celebrity. It seems that at the PEN thing Wolfe was annoyed at something Susan said about his book not being any good. Lizzie brought that up as if to excuse Susan, to say maybe she had things on her mind. But Lizzie rallied and said Susan shouldn't talk about anyone's fiction not being any good. The AIDS book she described as 'not much of an effort.' She said when she used to sit on panels with Susan who was going on about 'those of us who are serious' she'd think 'that's not how I see myself.' Susan meant those of us who are poor.

Wednesday 30th August 1989

I had dinner with Susan last night and saw her again this morning. Barbara called before I went out last night, to say that the Reed was, at last, fine, and that Susan was so big and out of twenty things could say ten that were interesting and later Susan said Barbara and Lizzie made her feel like a kid because nothing more is going to happen in their lives whereas she still felt she had the freedom to chuck it all.

The DAAD has given her a large, bare apartment on Mommsenstrasse. Susan likes the streets being named after historians and poets. She slept after she got off the plane and I woke her in her panties and she walked around trying to put clothes away. She brought a few books: *A Passage to India* for the cave scene; a Thomas Bernhard (the autobiographies are dull, she said). That cave scene is only two paragraphs, but in memory it seems as big as a whole chapter. Susan plans to have Sir William Hamilton look into the volcano, like the lady having the revelation in the cave. She said she brought her notes and intends to do nothing but write all day and then we can play all night.

I have been thinking about this mysterious thing, why having an idea is sometimes not enough. She says she wants to tell a story, doesn't want to get into so-called Modernism, and is going to pretend that it will be published under a pseudonym, just to defeat that sense of 'Modernism' people expect from Susan Sontag, 'this monster I've unleashed on the world.' I told her to pretend she was in retirement and writing about something that interests her, like I. F. Stone on the Greeks. I know what she means about not wanting all those Modernist devices, whatever they are, and yet a novel about a historical figure, when you don't want to pretend. 'He didn't know what I know about him,' she said, or something like that, and it sounded to me like a first line, but the first line of something she doesn't want to write. I find her wish to tell a story, to write fiction, very touching.

He is most famous for having married Emma and been cuckolded by Nelson, who doesn't interest Susan. Sir William was an avid collector and he was also obsessed with Vesuvius, climbed it some two hundred fifty times alone or with a one-eyed Neapolitan guide. Susan is interested in the minds of collectors, knows what they're like, on collecting in general, but doesn't know why she fell in love with Hamilton, a figure in Naples over a hundred years ago, and not with someone like Micky Wolfson, or something like that, a very rich Jewish boy in Florida who has a private train which he uses to go around collecting and has bought a palace in Genoa to house them. She hasn't met him, he's gay, according to her, and he's not known, but she says he will be one day, as one of the bizarre Americans of the century. Why Hamilton and not him? Because of Vesuvius maybe. This person in love with collecting also in love with a symbol of destruction. She's not going to try to re-create the way Hamilton's time spoke, but at the same time no one is going to say 'okay' or be 'mesmerized.' Has she ever seen a volcano? No. Does she know Naples? Not really. It will be hard to make pages on lava interesting.

She showed me a letter from Rea Hederman, about Bob's sixtieth birthday, asking a few contributors to write some words about what Bob meant to them, for a book to be privately circulated. A funereal idea, and many to whom he means a great deal are ambivalent about him these days. Lizzie told Susan that Bob wasn't available to anyone anymore. 'The mask sinks into the face,' Susan said, and Bob doesn't care about literature or the arts anymore.

On opera or painting you don't get any more than what you get from Grace Dudley: 'great' or 'no, we didn't like that.' He's on de la Renta's plane, or Getty's plane, going down to Santo Domingo.

We went out to get something to eat, and to acquaint her with one or two streets and places. She said now that she knows Nadine Gordimer she doesn't like her. 'She's not a nice person.' But Gordimer is a great fan of Susan's, she said, and gave her her house near Nice for a month, and Susan liked having nothing to do but work, turning her back on New York, and thinks of this as something similar. There was nothing to do in that village at night, except make a big production of dinner. She knew no one.

She knows the Paris Bar, so we went there. On Kantstrasse, Susan said I had to get an apartment, that I mustn't wake up at forty and see that I have lived as less than a graduate student all through my twenties and thirties. I have this suspicion that should I even make it to forty I'll wake with regrets way beyond having or not having an apartment. She said a friend of hers from Buenos Aires tried to live in New York, moved from sublet to sublet, shed or gained possessions depending on the size of the place, and is now stuck in Buenos Aires.

Annie Leibovitz drove Susan to the airport in New York and there ran into her ex-boyfriend and blushed. She's very direct, Susan said, 'cuts right to the subtext,' and asked if Susan had a fling here would she tell her. No. What she doesn't know won't hurt her. Would Leibovitz tell Susan? Yes. Would she mind? Only if it were going to go on, 'but I told her I would never forgive her.' They see each other every night when Leibovitz is in town. Often she's off, as far as Hong Kong, to photograph 'the rich and the wicked.' She liked *The Color Purple* and *Bonfire of the Vanities* and didn't understand why Susan didn't. 'If *The Color Purple* were the only book on earth it would be a great book. But I have in mind something better. I know something better.' She tried to explain that if she showed Leibovitz a postcard of a setting sun in the West and said it was a brilliant photograph, Leibovitz would have in mind something better, and would not agree. I didn't say Lizzie admired *The Color Purple* as an epistolary novel and she didn't care about the film but thought I was hard on Walker. I didn't tell her about the call from Stanley. If Stanley praises you, then maybe you have messed up. But the main thing, Susan said, after Jasper Johns, Joseph Brodsky, Lucinda Childs (Bob Wilson loves her), is that Leibovitz is one of the nicest people she's ever met. 'She's like you' (I said I didn't know what love was because I'd never been loved back) and is surprised by affection because her affairs with the rich and the wicked were when-they-were-in-town things, with the other person in control. Goes to baby showers with friends from high school. 'I don't know anyone who goes to showers and she doesn't know anyone who doesn't.' She doesn't think of herself as a lesbian, doesn't want it to be known in her world that she is having a fling with Susan. Susan imagines her having dinner with the ex-boyfriend they ran into at the airport. An intimate thing, seeing someone off, and Leibovitz admitted she was afraid he'd think there was something going on, but added that she could deal with it.

I told her I saw *Measure for Measure* in rehearsal. She said it was not a great play. I told her about the Burroughs-Waits project in New York, which doesn't sound like *Der Freischütz* anymore. She said she thought I was going to tell her they decided to do Wilhelm Tell, the story of Burroughs's life. In the late Fifties, when Ginsberg, Burroughs, et al. were living in one room in a seedy hotel in Paris, she was living with someone in a seedy place around the corner and got to know them fairly well. 'Kaddish' is Ginsberg's best poem, otherwise you'd go to the real thing, Whitman, and she said she didn't like 'Howl,' because she had trouble with '*I've seen the best minds of my generation*' in 1954, that there was no way those guys were the best minds, nothing like Paul Goodman, who had a real mind. I said I have a soft spot for 'A Supermarket in California.'

She remembered the West End Café when it was an empty joint where losers got busted for heroin or picked up on morals charges. Susan, the great universalist, but I remembered walking toward the Berlin Wall with her last summer and she was saying what was different about her reasoning from Reagan's concerning the Wall, because we were on Mariannenplatz, with the real church visible on the east side, behind the Wall, and the porch painted on the part of the Wall that the Wall blocks of the church. She walked right smack into it. Susan walked into the Wall. Her head snapped, but it was her toe that did it.

The food came and she skipped around. Saw Berlin in 1958, 'before there was a Wall.' Used to come here when she was looking for films to show at the New York Film Festival in the 1960s and the Kempinski was the best hotel she'd ever been in up until that time. She said, yes, she should show her films at the Arsenal, but couldn't deal with bringing prints, but she'll do it one day, come back, she'll call Alf Bold, whom she likes. It takes a long time to die of AIDS these days. Bob Wilson said someone should tape Alf, for the history of avant-garde cinema in his head. One of the most important curators of film, Bob and Susan have both said.

This morning she said she hadn't slept. She read, smoked, thought about her novel. We had breakfast on Giesebrechtstrasse, a clear, blue day was unwrapping itself. One day Donald Barthelme felt funny and went to the doctor. The cancer was so far advanced the doctor thought he'd be dead in a week. He went quickly enough, in a matter of a few months. Susan saw him in February. He said he was 'oh fine fine' and he was dead by July. Then Susan was eating an omelette and talking about the fear when you think people will criticize you for writing about something you know nothing about, something she said I said when I was trying to write on Döblin. (I wrote a letter to Barbara, to thank her for our trip to Leningrad. For some insane reason she showed it to Jason. He said the letter was fine on Poland, but gets tangled up on Spike Lee, and so her new thing is I should get away from black stuff. She asked if I wanted to review the new Peter Handke.)

Susan said after Lieberson's service, at the Hedermans', Lizzie was sitting next to his mother and Lizzie said something like oh isn't it awful, these people with AIDS, and Jonathan having it, and Susan said his mother's face fell, and Lizzie went off to Caroline, and what upset Lieberson's mother is that he swore her to secrecy and she sat on herself and when Lizzie said that she wondered if he hadn't been going around telling everyone after she'd been instructed never to talk about it. Susan said people say Lizzie gets out of hand because she's drunk or deaf, but she thinks there's something punitive in Lizzie's character. Something aggressive, yes, and too much freely thinking out loud, or not enough. She asked if Barbara complained about Lizzie and I said no.

She said she calls Lizzie, but Lizzie never calls her back, and that one I can't explain because for a long time Lizzie was almost maddeningly keen on Susan. I think she feels dropped, the way Barbara says that Susan has 'dropped' her, and when Susan goes on about how vulgar Bob is in his social pursuits, she forgets her own campaigns or doesn't see them that way. Barbara keeps quiet when people talk like that.

I walked Susan to Wertheim's so she could get paper supplies. She told me about Giorgio Strehler and how Peter Stein comes out of that. Before a furniture store on Kantstrasse she said all Bob Wilson's chairs are derived from Charles Rennie Mackintosh. We went through a second store, arranged so that the different recordings can be compared. She recommended a dozen or so to me. Said the interesting thing about Jessye Norman is that she does German and French, but won't touch the Italian repertoire. 'I haven't slept in two days.' In one store, she was looking for Kleenex and was shocked to see that she was holding a box.

Friday 1 September 1989
The newspapers are bordered in black to mark the fiftieth anniversary of the German invasion of Poland. I can't forget the face of the

man in the photograph last week when he was turned back at the East German border with Hungary.

Susan called, in need of erasers. I had only one. (I also gave her the little clock I had from Eric, but I hope to get it back when she leaves. Eric Ashworth is the kind of agent who knows which client doesn't own a clock. How he and Rick are managing to live together, they're both so bossy.) I found Susan working on the French translation of *AIDS as Metaphor*. She complained that she wasted all of August, doing it or not being able to do it, because she was writing a long letter to the translator, telling him why this word and not that one, instead of correcting the manuscript and writing notes in the margin. She realized that day that such a letter was crazy, and saw it as one of the problems of working in isolation, that she had no one to tell her she was wasting her time, that creating another manuscript about changes would not help the translator. It's the problem of wanting to beat up the translator who doesn't get why she says 'infected' instead of 'contaminated.' Depending on them taking the changes from a letter and finding them in the manuscript leaves too much room for error or omission. 'Well, I know a way to self-sabotage and you know a few ways to self-sabotage, so we have that in common.'

Lizzie used to say that Nicole Stéphane taught Susan how to dress, but I think Susan has forgotten, or to wear what's comfortable she doesn't care what her sneakers and jeans and denim jacket look like. She goes out dressed up in her fame, in that recognizable patch of white in a fantastic hood of jet black hair. On the street she was talking about people and their incredible apartments and blond twins and literary libraries and how nice in Europe that cultivated people have power, but they didn't interest her. She said she was interested in intimacy, not sociableness, that she and Philip Rieff in the nine years they were married never had anyone to dinner. She likes blond adults, not blond children.

Susan was surprised I didn't know Arvo Pärt, who lives in Berlin and is all the rage in New York. Susan said Nicole calls her all the time, how awful her life is, no one wants to see her, her life is filled with humiliations, she wants to die. Susan told her she and I were both depressed so maybe it was just the change of season. The alcoholic character remains, and she may have stopped drinking on a dime, Susan said, not even vinegar in her salad, but some hole is still there. Susan said Nicole said she felt like Susan was 'becoming a myth,' because she doesn't get to Paris much anymore. Nicole was the one who said I don't want to sleep with you anymore and Susan said she didn't understand but they became close after that, confidantes, and talk every day. Melville's *Silence de la mer* was Nicole's great film, not the Cocteau, and one day people would learn of Nicole's quiet heroism during the Algerian War. We went to *Do the Right Thing*, third time around for me, and Susan said she had fantasies of being black the way she's had fantasies of being left-handed or AB negative, just not to be 'white bread,' and she felt that way about homosexuality. We were at the door of the Paris Bar, but she had to finish about Luc Bondy's testicular cancer and Gombrowicz, who liked boys.

> *Defenceless under the night*
> *Our world in stupor lies*

Tables of French soldiers were singing at the top of their lungs, and afterward I thought if Susan left today I'd be relieved. She asked me the other night if I wrote every day and I said no because journal writing didn't count. I wish I hadn't told her I kept a journal. She said she felt like a kid and there is something extremely childlike about Susan, but not entirely in the free and innocent way she means. She said she would write the thing for Bob Silvers's birthday, but, alas, couldn't print two-thirds of what she thinks of him. She envied writers who have a certain 'slyness' and could write something witty, maybe with a dig in there somewhere. I said

I never thought of her writing as ceremonial, but she sort of had to do something because of his importance to her work. She said that ultimately Bob wasn't the best thing for her work. 'Not ultimately. I'm much more daring as a writer than Bob will allow,' and mentioned Gass on Emerson, a wonderful essay that Bob turned down which seemed like such a scandal at the time. But I didn't think that was a terribly generous thing to say about the man without whom she might not have been able to make *On Photography* and *Illness as Metaphor* so good, never mind Barbara's part. She said she'd do the birthday thing because she didn't want to be left out of the party, but would have a hard time because of course she's only interested in the truth and apologized for what she was about to say, but said it anyway: 'I guess I'm too virtuous.' She asked Lizzie if she really liked Updike's autobiography and Lizzie said of course not and Susan said the persona of it was more shocking than Céline. About jerking off a woman in the back seat with his wife up front. Silly, male boasting, but Céline? Now Susan. I said maybe Lizzie wanted to honor his talent and Susan said, well, yes, she admired his sentences, but hinted that Lizzie didn't uphold a certain standard in not beating up Updike as a pig.

She asked me what I thought would become of Lizzie as a writer and the only answer is that she'll write less if she finds it too physically demanding. In this case, writing less means not writing at all, and it's too bad about the Brazil novel she'll never do, and Susan said Lizzie said she didn't know enough about it, and clearly Susan has the same worry about Naples. But there are those wonderful New York stories: 'Back Issues,' 'The Bookseller,' 'On the Eve,' so why not another New York book, held together by her 'I.' What Lizzie cannot bring herself to do, to write, her roving obsession with form, is not exactly a block. About her own reputation, she is shrewd, and sometimes I think of her line about Billie Holiday and the genius doomed to repeat heights of inspiration. Susan said one only had to write one book to gain immortality and she was sure that I like her think *Sleepless Nights* the best American novel of the last fifteen years (she used to say twenty), but because of what is left out, well, we know (no, I don't know), that it was barely a book and Lizzie can write pieces but not a book. Naipaul told her a long time ago: 'Write books, not pieces.'

I was talking about *Life Studies* being a very Lizzie book, *Near the Ocean*, too, and Allen Tate saying she'd ruined him, and she talks about how much she got from Cal, but he got a lot, too, and that idea of living with a poet getting into your prose, like the Mandelstams, I said. It was late and the waiters were at their end, stacking chairs, refusing drinks. Susan paid, again. On Kant-strasse, Susan said: 'I don't know if I ever told you this story, I will now. They took me up in the early sixties, 1962, and I saw them a lot. I mean a lot. I went to dinner at Cal and Lizzie's all the time. I met Hannah Arendt, well if I didn't meet her there I saw her most often there.' Lowell got a Rockefeller grant, $5,000, which back then was like $40,000. She'd just quit Columbia, and one night after she'd been there for the fortieth time he said he'd walk her down and put her in a taxi and there came the inevitable pass. 'But, Cal, I said squeakily. I was all of twenty-nine or something. Very virginal. No matter what I've done, I'm a chronic virgin. But Cal, you're married. He said, yes, I love Lizzie, and he didn't say but she doesn't understand me or we have an agreement. He said something much worse. But she's such a good writer. One can't have one's wife writing *Madame Bovary* in the kitchen. And I hated him. I think I said something like Why can't you? Or Why not? Very squeakily.'

She said it was interesting that he only married writers. Who else, I said, would put up with him, he was so crazy, and Susan said she knows how crazy he was, knew them well, saw him go mad, say *Mein Kampf* was his favorite book, talk about Hitler and Caligula, and she's sure they'll discover that manic-depressiveness is physical, otherwise it couldn't be treated with chemicals, but imagine

him saying that, she said, his jealousy of Lizzie, and it's true he
never liked the *Review* and teased her about reading *Partisan Review*
all the time, and she said she wasn't quoting him exactly, but the
last line was verbatim: 'One,' and he said 'one,' 'one can't have one's
wife writing *Madame Bovary* in the kitchen.' First off, she wasn't in
the kitchen. They had a maid, these dinners were served by a maid.
She was in her study.

There is this idea that Lizzie didn't write because of him, and
once she told me maybe, but there was Harriet to take care of. I
do think she couldn't finish *Sleepless Nights* until he was gone, and
he's in it, though he's not. Susan said she's never told anyone that
story, but since I kept a diary it seemed like the right time to tell
someone.

Poor Sainte-Beuve. Poor Taine. Renan shows the wisdom of
reticence in front of men of letters. But just when I was used to
their fits, the Magny gossip, and the facial expressions of Princess
Mathilde, the end comes so swiftly and painfully. Poor Edmund's
irritation and remorse.

~

Monday 16 January 1989
Sterling died. Mama said it made her remember the Bunche girls
and how jealous she was of them. One summer afternoon in 1984
I dropped by Sterling's house in Washington unannounced. He
was bravely holding forth on his side porch. Gin, red wine, and a
bucket of ice stood on a table. He was waiting in an old T-shirt for
a group from the University of Maryland. Stubble rolled across
a face that looked as though he was melting. He seemed to live
most of his life on that porch. ('I found me a cranny of perpet-
ual dusk.') Records were scattered across the living-room rug and
I said it looked as though he needed some help cataloging. The
heavens broke. I heard him say in no uncertain terms that he nei-

ther needed nor wanted any help. He stormed off to his basement retreat, returned to tell me that I was not to follow him down there, then blew back upstairs to tell me to get out of his house. I went next door to his sister's. Helen had broken her hip and was confined to a couch. 'I know,' she said. 'I didn't mean to upset him this morning when I told him to take his medicine.' She gave me a copy of their father's book *Bible Mastery* as a consolation. I heard Sterling calling and I hurried across the lawn. He wanted to make sure I knew that he meant *nevah* come back. He slammed the door so hard my glasses shifted. Some time afterward Helen died and Mama didn't hear any more about Sterling.

I did try to see Sterling again after he threw me out. When I was in Washington last summer. August was burning and Jesse Jackson had just been passed over for the vice-presidential nomination. 'I understand,' he told a baking, aroused NAACP audience. 'I wasn't always on television.' Because I didn't live in the U.S. anymore, I, clown, thought that I would get a soldier's welcome and be forgiven for wanting to take from Sterling more of his anecdotes.

Sterling's door was still slammed shut. I knocked at what used to be Helen's. The white guy in jogging shorts who'd bought both houses couldn't tell me to which nursing home Sterling had been taken, but he offered to let me see the garden.

They have forgotten, they have never known,
Long days beneath the torrid Dixie sun
In miasma'd rice swamps;
The chopping of dried grass, on the third go round
In strangling cotton;
Wintry nights in mud-daubed makeshift huts,
With these songs, sole comfort

They have forgotten
What had to be endured . . .

Thursday 27 April 1989

Barbara called. Howard died today. She said when she saw Brad, Sunday, he said he'd asked Howard if he was in pain and he blinked, to signal yes. His parents and his brother and Brad were with him. I called Brad, at Howard's apartment. Howard is still there, 'in the bedroom,' Brad said, and started to cry. Howard's gone. His suffering. I couldn't think of anything to say. We hung up. Howard. I wish I could cry, too, now. Right now. Brad said there were so many people to call. I'm trying to reach Bob Wilson in Amsterdam. Howard. Where are you? The last time I talked to him I had to do all the talking. He got out that he loved Italy, too.

Monday 1st May 1989

Howard was buried yesterday. 'You're all my children now,' Mrs. Brookner said when I called. And, yes, she'd like for me to write to her, there is so much she doesn't know about Howard, 'this smart alecky kid.' Barbara said Mrs. Brookner told a friend of Jacob's that it was wonderful, for her, as a mother, to see how many people cared. After you send your children out into the world you don't know much about them, and she was glad to find out how many people loved him. She doesn't want to come back to New York soon, 'it's been a long, long' and the missing word could be struggle, process, wait, or death. I also spoke to Brad who said the service at Riverside was nice, he read a poem, and amazed himself by speaking about Howard, too. Bob Wilson came. Brad said Howard wanted him to burn his papers. I said I was never for that. He said he wasn't either, but Howard had been so clear about it. So they carried the casket, 'shoveled dirt on the grave, you know,' Brad said, and 'that's that.' He wrote the obit for the *Times*, though it's under Steven Holden's name, 'and if you thought death was some other-worldly thing, to get an obit in the *Times* you have to pull strings.'

All the things we did back then not knowing what they could lead to. I think Howard got hooked around the time of the Burroughs film, and I don't know when he kicked, or if he ever really kicked it. After I came out of the rehab he said he'd been in one himself, which was news to me. But Bob Wilson and Brad told me that when his parents were coming up, the first time he was really sick, they had to rush through Bob's place on Vestry, to get rid of all the needles, so that his parents wouldn't see them. Howard was pretty cagey about that. When he and Brad moved out of the Chelsea, into separate quarters, he said that they were still together, just seeing other people, but I think Howard just told me that because he was very possessive. As for the secondary characters, like Alan and Donny, they underestimated at their peril the depth of the relationship between Howard and Brad. Heroin and Brad were doors to the sides of Howard I didn't know, didn't see, and, with my own secret drug life, there was a time when we were out of touch, although he called from the strangest places from time to time. All this weekend I have been remembering scenes; and then once his work on the documentary *Robert Wilson and the Civil Wars* started, the scenes in my head are fewer, and have mostly to do with the Chelsea Hotel, and the copy shop he ran with Brad. He was often out of town, which drove Brad crazy, maybe avoiding debts, and now I remember a night in the Michael Todd Room when both Brad and Sara Driver were pissed off at the groupies around both Howard and Jim. I remember two dinners Howard gave in Bob Wilson's place, one where April Bernard got drunk and let Duncan Stalker have it, another, Brad's birthday, with Frank Moore looking fat. When we were really in touch again, he was in California, I could call him from the *Review*, and he couldn't believe the film was happening. He was still obsessed with Alan, wanted to drive to the East Coast with him. I remember Howard on the street in New York before I left when he didn't tell me, because I'd rushed to tell him I was negative. He told me a story he'd told me before, about meeting Isherwood just before he died. Last year, when I left for Berlin, he was shooting in New Jersey, couldn't come to the party the Hedermans threw for me. Bob Wilson called me last spring and asked me if I knew where Howard was. In Paris, editing, I assumed. No. He and Brad had gone to Mexico and Howard had caught amoebas or something and it didn't look good, he said. Not good. When I was in New York I could go to St. Vincent's. Sit with Mrs. Brookner. Salute Brad. And almost forget it was a sickbed, Howard had so much humor and life going on around him.

We said goodbye over the telephone, and I didn't know when I called after getting back from Florence that we were saying goodbye for the last time. His nurse Tony didn't go to the funeral. He told Brad, 'I don't feel like a funeral today.' He has to protect himself from his cases, otherwise he couldn't work, couldn't do that kind of work. I cried so much at an AA meeting last spring when I tried to talk about his illness, woke up crying, that now all I can do is put his picture out, the one he gave me of him at Exeter, playing the guitar. Now I want the film to be released. It doesn't matter if it's good or bad, I want it as a memorial to him. There's no career, 'or life,' Barbara said, depending on a marvelous critical or commercial reception. I must ask Bob Wilson to tell me the story again of his visit to Burroughs in Lawrence, Kansas. Burroughs pointed to a box and said, 'That's Howard.' Something having to do with mysticism, with his spirit in a box. I'm insane myself. Howard's suffering. I can't remember Howard's favorite book. I think of Henry Bibb, whose narrative is one of the most beautiful things I have ever read, going to someone to get a chicken bone to rub on a girl he wanted to make like him.

(Brad writes about their love and friends, their work, and the poem he read at Howard's grave in *Smash Cut: A Memoir of Howard & Art & the '70s & the '80s*. It was for him a long journey. Decades went by in weeks, he says of Howard's illness. Sara and Jim left a note with their flowers at the grave: Where are you? Brad says that Howard didn't go on AZT, because he wanted to be as alert as possible while shooting his first feature film, *Bloodhounds of Broadway*, based on four Damon Runyon stories. He gambled, but he also sacrificed himself.

I remember a party where Howard was clearly straight, for the benefit of film producers, the voice from his bi/closet days at school. It was a big deal for him, to be in the major leagues after just two documentaries. But he didn't have final cut. The studio took away *Bloodhounds of Broadway* and gave it to an editor.

The winter following Howard's death, *Bloodhounds of Broadway* was playing at the cinema behind the Plaza. Two friends, Catherine Temerson, Israel Rosenfield, and I sat in the front row. Behind us were Howard's brother, his sister-in-law, and his little nephew. No, it was not so much Howard's film, not his clever, sly, spot-on way of telling stories. The little nephew, Aaron Brookner, grew up and made a beautiful documentary, *Uncle Howard*, that brings back the days when Howard was filming Burroughs and his circle. He lives again, in so much footage, but he's on the other side of a window you can't climb through.)

> *Brightness falls from the air;*
> *Queens have died young and fair;*
> *Dust hath closed Helen's eye.*
> *I am sick, I must die.*
>   *Lord, have mercy on us!*

Tuesday 21 June 1989
Jonathan Lieberson died Thursday night, Rick told me Sunday. Lizzie said Bob was devastated and when I got through to Barbara

last night she sounded depressed. Lizzie always liked him, she said. I remember when there were times Barbara didn't, but none of that matters anymore.

Friday 14 July 1989
Barbara said that Jonathan's memorial was quite something, that of course Bob was great and Jason (she'd say that), but Lizzie not. Her famous ambivalence didn't work. They all went to the Hedermans' afterward and Barbara said Lizzie made a beeline for Caroline, who looked like a bag lady, and spent the night with her in the kitchen.

29 September 1989
Virgil Thomson died, at the age of ninety-two. On the phone with Barbara, laughing tearfully about all-gay dinners of distinguished men and hopeful boys, a thing of the past. Virgil tried, but what could I learn about bouillabaisse. It was even funny-seeming to us that Maurice Grosser had managed to die of AIDS at the age of eighty-three. What of Maurice's boyfriend, Paul Sefacan? What must Virgil's last three years in the Chelsea without Grosser have been like. Staying on alone. Barbara assured me Virgil was well looked after, and then some. Much loved. I said I respect the history of his music but I like the music of Aaron Copland better. She said, okay, that left her Stravinsky. Did Virgil review *Troubled Island*?

　　She talked about Bruce Chatwin, almost the first time with me since he died back in January. His denial about what he had. A virus picked up in China. His manias, purchasing on impulse sculpture by Giambologna. He'd call Barbara in a state of euphoria. She said if you were going to go crazy then it might as well be over love for the world.

———

You understand terror, know how to deal
with pent-up emotion, a ballad, witchcraft.
I don't. O Zeus and O Destiny!

Jan. 8, 1988

Dearest Dee:

It's snowing and snowing here, called the Siberian Express on TV and very beautiful until it all becomes slush up to the knees. I hope it is as warm in Berlin as Mary McCarthy told me yesterday by phone it was in Paris. She's somewhat better off on the cancer tragedy; will not have an operation, deemed unnecessary, but only some weeks of radiation. The dear old warrior is not well otherwise, she said; the previous trouble that has tormented her for so long. I do feel very sad for what she has to go through and I miss her gallant eccentricity and worry for her future. Otherwise not much news from this front, except missing you and hoping you are if not content, at least much interested in the knowledge that you are where you are.

Much love, ever,

E.

Saturday 28 Oct. 1989

I didn't know Mary McCarthy died until I saw the obit in the *Tribune* yesterday. I rushed home on the dinner break at the theater to call Lizzie. 'I miss her already.' She called me back late. She was exhausted, having gone to the hospital every night, the last time Tuesday night at eleven. They said it would be her last chance to see her, that she wouldn't live another day, 'which turned out to be true.' She was going to get Jim and Alison's ticket, 'and wondering if I am doing the right thing.' They're going up to Maine today, the funeral is Tuesday. It was McCarthy's wish to be buried in Maine. Lizzie has known her for some forty years, and then there's every summer in Maine, but it's too soon to think about that. I think being tired is one of the ways to get through these things, like Mama going through Mrs. Young's things. I asked how Mr. West was. 'Oh, he's a pain in the ass,' Lizzie shot back. Having depended on McCarthy all these years, 'or Mary having been in control all these years, he's become a real sergeant.' She said Luc was adorable at the Whitings. She said that Harriet was wonderful, called late the night before just to see how she was.

Sometimes people like to see a tough person helpless. McCarthy had one of those tubes in her and couldn't talk, though she was lucid, took in everything, and knew at every moment what was happening to her. Barbara said it was hard to talk, not knowing what to say. She didn't like the obituary, thought it rather cold and grudging and judgmental. Barbara said Kakutani knew Mary and therefore one would not have expected such one-upmanship. Regardless of what one thinks of the later novels, or of her being over her head editing Arendt's *Life of the Mind*, an unborn, unfinished work anyway, or of her intellectual autobiography, one has to place her somewhere in American letters, the early stories, *Partisan Review*, Vietnam, and what these positions stood for. The theater put-downs were not just put-downs, she put Burroughs on the map. (Bob Wilson said Burroughs had muttered some unkind things about her.) And not only was she anti-Stalinist, she was anti–the anti-Stalinists. Barbara said when she was a student, McCarthy was the ideal. She didn't know her well, wasn't close to her, but was crazy about her, which makes her more direct and expressive about her grief. She could have the surface sadness and the anger at the hospital for putting her on the respirator too late, whereas Lizzie is more complicated about it, and can draw on several emotions within a twenty-minute period. Barbara said that Lizzie is more interested in Jim, that she had Andy Dupee on the phone for an hour to complain. I laughed and Barbara said she did not even want to talk about that. I can't take her fed-up-with-Lizzie mode seriously. She complains about Lizzie's obsessive raps, but that is her own obsessive rap, to obsess about Lizzie's obsessiveness.

When Lillian Hellman died five years ago, she took her lawsuit against McCarthy with her. Barbara said she admired Mary but was also sure Mary would not have acknowledged that she minded Lizzie marrying the crown prince back then, because she could never admit to having a low thought.

Lizzie said that that time years ago it was a scream when I said thank you for introducing me to Mary McCarthy but that wasn't the Mary McCarthy I'd been expecting. Lizzie had me down for dinner with Mary, but just that one time. Mary greatly relieved when Elizabeth came back to the dining room and she and I were no longer alone. Why is this boy trying to talk to me about Gramsci's prison letters, her anxious social smile said. Lizzie wouldn't let me help serve and said even after McCarthy had departed to leave the dishes for Nicole.

In *The New York Review* last spring, McCarthy had the most tender appreciation of Baldwin. She went back to the postwar years before either had moved to Paris. She'd never read anything by James Baldwin when they met at a *Partisan Review* lunch. She remembers his voice as breathy and soft, like Delmore Schwartz's. What stunned her was that Baldwin was so literary, unusual in black intellectuals of this period, she thought. He'd read everything and his reading was not determined by color. 'Olympian recognitions that were free of prejudice.' But she stopped reading him after *The Fire Next Time*, because she said she was afraid to and she found homosexual novels distasteful. Unlike homosexual husbands, I said to Lizzie. She laughed that as Firbankian as Bowden was, he was famously priapic, ready for anything at all times. 'Homosexuality, like gout, seemed to run in the Medici family,' McCarthy sniffed

in *The Stones of Florence*. There is no one she would not have judged,
but in her Baldwin piece she meets him again years later as a fellow
juror on a big prize committee in France and she and Spender want
to give it to poor, dying Edmund Wilson back in America (to out-
live is to forgive) and they're the only ones who do, until Baldwin
sweeps in late and seduces the committee with his cool eloquence
about Edmund Wilson. The prize went to Wilson.

'Beware the easiness of the catastrophe—the catastrophic way
out of every poem.' David Kalstone. I don't have it. This is from
Chris Benfey. In *Becoming a Poet: Elizabeth Bishop with Marianne
Moore and Robert Lowell*, Kalstone says that Lowell's use of the
letters of others began before *The Dolphin*. I knew better than to
bring up to Lizzie the raw material of poetry in its rawness. Let the
church say amen.

> In the evening there was a moon in the eastern sky out-
> classing every miracle. It hung over Lexington Avenue
> where the stores were at last closed and where many
> little shoes and blouses were enchained for the night's
> sleep.

When Lizzie talked about taking the bus across the park to see
Mary in the hospital, I thought back to this piece, 'Cross-town.'
From the autobiography issue of *Antaeus*, back in 1980. 'Ah, York
Avenue, the thoroughfare of hospitals.' She wouldn't let me draw
her into a long-distance conversation about 'a whole city built on
obstinacy.' She said she wasn't sure she'd call it a story, and at the
same time she really didn't like me calling her stories 'tone poems.' It was a frame for stray thoughts about Rousseau's paranoia
and the question of whether he was also a liar. She'd forgotten
the couples glimpsed in 'Cross-town.' The well-bred Yankee artists somewhat too backward for the city; the happy pair abruptly
transported from Kentucky, to be near the hospitals, perhaps. In-

teresting that I would make the connection. It meant everything to her to sit on the bus and to work out what she wanted to say. Lizzie is sure Mary understood everything she said, even when she could not respond. The point to me is the narrator is not from this world of couples. I did not say this to her. But she is from this place:

> Only writers have the possibility of autobiography, this singularity, this exercise of option by way of adjectives and paragraphs.

Old Campaigner.
She brought up a line from Marianne Moore:
—*After everything we have loved is lost, then we revive.*
She said she didn't think Marianne Moore was talking about recuperation, recovery. She said it felt to her as though she used 'revive' to mean wisdom.

Acknowledgments

I am grateful to Harriet Lowell for her permission to quote so generously from the works of her parents, Robert Lowell and Elizabeth Hardwick.

I am fortunate to have been able to rely on the scholarship and wise counsel of Saskia Hamilton.

I thank Alexis Adler (Alexis Adler Photography Archive), Aaron Brookner (Estate of Howard Brookner), the Estate of Henri Cartier-Bresson, Nan Goldin, Evelyn Hofer, Annie Leibovitz, Harriet Lowell, Dominique Nabokov, Lisa Shea, and the Estate of Thomas Victor for the use of the photographs reproduced in this book.

Some parts of this book have appeared, in different form, in *The New Yorker* and *The New York Review of Books*.

My gratitude also to Lynn Nesbit, of Janklow & Nesbit; to my stalwart editor at FSG, Jonathan Galassi; and to Mitzi Angel, Greg Villepique, Katharine Liptak, Songhee Kim, Na Kim, and Henry Kaufman.

I thank Jacob Epstein, Helen Epstein, Ryan Roberts, Fernanda Eberstadt, Isabel Fonseca, and Carl Ginsberg. I wish also to thank Wendy Weiss.

I treasure the honor of having had Margo Jefferson's advice.

Carol Archer convinced me to write this memoir and stood firm. I can't begin to thank her for her help.

And then there's James.